# The Cambridge Companion to Crime Fiction

*The Cambridge Companion to Crime Fiction* covers British and American crime fiction from the eighteenth century to the end of the twentieth. As well as d
Chr
play
cha
and Vic
polic   **M**
by   ...national team of established specialists, offers students invaluable reference material including a chronology and guides to further reading. The volume aims to ensure that its readers will be grounded in the history of crime fiction and its critical reception.

UNIVERSITY COLLEGE

ature, French

black detectives, crime in film and on TV,

postmodernist uses of the detective form. The collection,

# THE CAMBRIDGE
# COMPANION TO
# CRIME FICTION

MARTIN PRIESTMAN

CAMBRIDGE
UNIVERSITY PRESS

PUBLISHED BY THE PRESS SYNDICATE OF THE UNIVERSITY OF CAMBRIDGE
The Pitt Building, Trumpington Street, Cambridge, United Kingdom

CAMBRIDGE UNIVERSITY PRESS
The Edinburgh Building, Cambridge, CB2 2RU, UK
40 West 20th Street, New York, NY 10011–4211, USA
477 Williamstown Road, Port Melbourne, VIC 3207, Australia
Ruiz de Alarcón 13, 28014 Madrid, Spain
Dock House, The Waterfront, Cape Town 8001, South Africa

http://www.cambridge.org

First published 2003

Printed in the United Kingdom at the University Press, Cambridge

*Typeface* Sabon 10/13 pt.    *System* LATEX 2ε   [TB]

*A catalogue record for this book is available from the British Library*

ISBN 0 521 80399 3 hardback
ISBN 0 521 00871 9 paperback

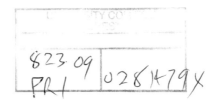

# CONTENTS

CONTENTS

# NOTES ON CONTRIBUTORS

IAN A. BELL is Professor and Head of English at the University of Wales, Swansea. His main publications include *Literature and Crime in Augustan England* (1981), *Defoe's Fiction* (1985) and *Henry Fielding: Authorship and Authority* (1994). He has written extensively on eighteenth-century literature, Scottish literature and crime fiction.

DAVID GLOVER is a Senior Lecturer in the Department of English at the University of Southampton. He is the author of *Vampires, Mummies, and Liberals: Bram Stoker and the Politics of Popular Fiction* (1996). His most recent book, co-authored with Cora Kaplan, is *Genders* (2000). He is currently working on a cultural history of the 1905 Aliens Act.

MARTIN A. KAYMAN is a Professor in the Centre for Critical and Cultural Theory at Cardiff University, where he teaches Cultural Criticism and English Literature. He is the author of *From Bow Street to Baker Street: Mystery, Detection, Narrative* (1992) and of various articles on law and literature. From 1997 to 2003 he was the editor of the *European English Messenger.*

STEPHEN KNIGHT, a Professor of English Literature at Cardiff University, is the author of *Form and Ideology in Crime Fiction* (1980) and *Continent of Mystery: A Thematic History of Australian Crime Fiction* (1997). His most recent books are *Robin Hood: A Mythic Biography* and *Crime Fiction, 1800–2000: Detection, Death, Diversity* (both 2003). He has written essays and taught courses on crime fiction for some time and was for 10 years the crime fiction reviewer of the *Sydney Morning Herald.*

LAURA MARCUS is a Reader in English at the University of Sussex. She has published widely on nineteenth- and twentieth-century literature and culture. Recent books include *Auto/biographical Discourses: Criticism, Theory, Practice* (1998) and she has edited Marie Belloc Lowndes' *The Lodger* (1996) and *Twelve Women Detective Stories* (1997). She is currently writing a book on cinema and modernism, and co-editing *The Cambridge History of Twentieth-Century English Literature*.

NICKIANNE MOODY is Head of Media and Cultural Studies at Liverpool John Moores University. She is a convenor of the Association for Research in Popular Fiction and editor of its journal *Diegesis*. She has co-edited *Medical Fictions* (1998) and *Consuming Pleasure* (2000), and published widely on film, TV, science fiction, fantasy and romance as well as crime fiction.

LEROY L. PANEK is Professor of English and Chair of the English department at McDaniel College, Maryland. He has written extensively on popular fiction: recent books include *The American Police Novel: A History* (2003) and *New Hard-boiled Writers: 1970s–1990s* (2000). His *Watteau's Shepherds: The Detective Novel in Britain* (1979) and his *Introduction to the Detective Story* (1987) both received Edgar Allan Poe Awards from the Mystery Writers of America; he has also received the George Dove Award from the Popular Culture Association of America.

ANDREW PEPPER is a Lecturer in English and American Literature at Queen's University Belfast and author of *The Contemporary American Crime Novel: Race, Ethnicity, Gender, Class* (2000). He is currently working on a critical history of crime fiction to be published by Palgrave.

DENNIS PORTER was until recently Professor of French and Comparative Literature at the University of Massachusetts, Amherst. His books include *The Pursuit of Crime: Art and Ideology in Detective Fiction* (1981), *Haunted Journeys: Desire and Transgression in European Travel Writing* (1991), and *Rousseau's Legacy: Emergence and Eclipse of the Writer in France* (1995). In recent years he has devoted most of his writing life to works for the stage, and is the recipient of a number of awards in the field.

MARTIN PRIESTMAN is a Professor of English at Roehampton University of Surrey. Books on crime fiction include *Detective Fiction and Literature: The Figure on the Carpet* (1990) and *Crime Fiction from Poe to the Present* (1998). He has also published *Cowper's Task Structure and Influence* (1983) and *Romantic Atheism: Poetry and Freethought, 1780–1830* (1999). He is currently editing the works of Charles Darwin's grandfather, Erasmus.

LYN PYKETT is a Professor of English and Pro Vice-Chancellor at the University of Wales Aberystwyth. She has written numerous books and articles on nineteenth- and early twentieth-century fiction and culture. Her books include *The Improper Feminine: The Women's Sensation Novel and the New Woman Writing* (1992), *The Sensation Novel from 'The Woman in White' to 'The Moonstone'* (1994), and *Engendering Fictions: The English Novel in the Early Twentieth Century* (1995). Her most recent work includes a book on Charles Dickens and a forthcoming edition of May Sinclair's novel *The Creators*. She is currently writing a book on Wilkie Collins.

MAUREEN T. REDDY is a Professor of English at Rhode Island College. Her books include *Sisters in Crime: Feminism and the Crime Novel* (1988), *Crossing the Color Line: Race, Parenting, and Culture* (1996) and *Traces, Codes, and Clues: Reading Race in Crime Fiction* (2003), as well as several edited collections. She is currently working on a book about constructions of race and nation in Irish popular culture.

SITA A SCHÜTT was until recently an Assistant Professor in English Language and Literature at Bilkent University, Ankara. Her doctoral research consisted of a comparative cultural study on the emergence of the detective story in France and in England. She has published articles on Ford Madox Ford and comparative popular fiction, including work on technology and early British spy fiction. She is currently writing a novel.

DAVID SEED is a Professor in American Literature at Liverpool University and is a Fellow of the English Association. He has published books on Joseph Heller, Thomas Pynchon, James Joyce, and other writers. He edits the Science Fiction Texts and Studies Series for Liverpool University Press. Among his recent books are *American Science Fiction and the Cold War* and *Imagining Apocalypse* (1999). His main research areas lie in Gothic and modern fiction.

# CRIME FICTION: A CHRONOLOGY

(No list can hope to cover this vast genre adequately. In general, this one follows the emphases of the chapters in the present book; otherwise, the texts named are their authors' earliest and/or most significant. Historical events are in bold typeface.)

1722 Daniel Defoe, *Moll Flanders* (UK)
1725 **Execution of 'Thieftaker General' Jonathan Wild (UK)**
1728 John Gay, *The Beggar's Opera* (UK)
1743 Henry Fielding, *Jonathan Wild* (UK)
1749 **Fielding becomes chief London magistrate; he and his brother John go on to form the Bow Street Runners (UK)**
1751 Fielding, *An Enquiry into the Causes of the late Increase of Robbers* (UK)
1773 First *Newgate Calendar* (UK)
1783 **US achieves Independence from Britain**
1789 **The French Revolution**
1794 William Godwin, *Caleb Williams* (UK)
1796 Ann Radcliffe, *The Mysteries of Udolpho* (UK)
1798 Mary Wollstonecraft, *The Wrongs of Woman* (UK)
1799 **Joseph Fouché heads first efficient police force (Fr)**
1809 **Eugène François Vidocq chief of police (Fr)**
1821 James Fenimore Cooper, *The Spy* (US)
1828 **Sir Robert Peel founds Metropolitan Police (UK)**
     Vidocq, *Mémoires* (Fr)
1830 Edward Bulwer Lytton, *Paul Clifford* (UK)
1832 Bulwer Lytton, *Eugene Aram* (UK)
1834 William Harrison Ainsworth, *Rookwood* (UK)
1839 Charles Dickens, *Oliver Twist* (UK)
1840 Ainsworth, *Jack Sheppard: A Romance of the Robber-Hero* (UK)
1841 Edgar Allan Poe, 'The Murders in the Rue Morgue' (US)

| | |
|---|---|
| 1842 | Detective Police established in London |
| 1843 | 'Day and Night' Police established in New York |
| 1852 | Allan Pinkerton founds National Detective Agency (US) |
| 1853 | Dickens, *Bleak House* (UK) |
| 1856 | London Police model established throughout UK |
| | 'Waters' (William Russell), *Recollections of a Detective Police Officer* (UK) |
| 1857 | Married Women's Property and Matrimonial Causes Acts enable married women to own property and seek divorce for cruelty (UK) |
| 1860 | Wilkie Collins, *The Woman in White* (UK) |
| 1861 | Ellen Wood, *East Lynne* (UK) |
| 1861–5 | American Civil War |
| | Anon., *Experiences of a Lady Detective* (UK) |
| 1862 | Mary Elizabeth Braddon, *Lady Audley's Secret* (UK) |
| 1863 | Emile Gaboriau, *L'Affaire Lerouge* (Fr.) |
| 1866 | Capital punishment abolished for most crimes except murder (UK) |
| 1868 | Collins, *The Moonstone* (UK) |
| 1869 | Gaboriau, *Monsieur Lecoq* (Fr.) |
| 1878 | Plain-clothes CID established at New Scotland Yard (UK) |
| | Anna K. Green, *The Leavenworth Case* (US) |
| 1886 | Fergus Hume, *The Mystery of a Hansom Cab* (Australia) |
| 1887 | National Union of Women's Suffrage Societies founded (UK) |
| | Arthur Conan Doyle, *A Study in Scarlet* (UK) |
| 1892 | Doyle, *The Adventures of Sherlock Holmes* (UK) |
| 1894 | Catherine Louisa Pirkis, *The Experiences of Loveday Brooke, Lady Detective* (UK) |
| 1899 | E. W. Hornung, *Raffles, the Amateur Cracksman* (UK) |
| 1900 | Matthias MacDonnell Bodkin, *Dora Myrl, The Lady Detective* (UK) |
| 1901 | Rudyard Kipling, *Kim* (UK) |
| 1903 | Erskine Childers, *The Riddle of the Sands* (UK) |
| | *The Great Train Robbery* (US film) |
| 1905–10 | Suffragette campaign of civil disobedience (UK) |
| 1905 | Edgar Wallace, *The Four Just Men* (UK) |
| | William Le Queux, *The Czar's Spy* (UK) |
| 1907 | Maurice Leblanc, *Arsène Lupin, Gentleman-Cambrioleur* (Fr.) |
| | Gaston Leroux, *Le Mystère de la Chambre Jaune* (Fr.) |
| | Joseph Conrad, *The Secret Agent* (UK) |

| | |
|---|---|
| 1908 | Richard Austin Freeman starts Dr Thorndyke stories (UK) |
| | G. K. Chesterton, *The Man Who Was Thursday* (UK) |
| | Mary Roberts Rinehart, *The Circular Staircase* (US) |
| 1910 | Baroness Orczy, *Lady Molly of Scotland Yard* (UK) |
| | A. E. W. Mason, *At the Villa Rose* (UK) |
| 1911 | **Isabella Goodwin becomes first detective policewoman in New York** |
| | Chesterton, *The Innocence of Father Brown* (UK) |
| | Pierre Souvestre and Marcel Allain, *Fantômas* (Fr) |
| 1912 | **British Board of Film Censors established (UK)** |
| 1913 | E. C. Bentley, *Trent's Last Case* (UK) |
| | Sax Rohmer, *The Insidious Fu Manchu* (UK) |
| 1914–18 | **First World War** |
| 1915 | John Buchan, *The Thirty-Nine Steps* (UK) |
| 1918 | **Women over thirty get the vote (UK)** |
| 1919 | **Prohibition of alcohol (US)** |
| | **First women police (UK)** |
| 1920 | 'Sapper' (H. C. McNeile), *Bulldog Drummond* (UK) |
| | Agatha Christie, *The Mysterious Affair at Styles* (UK) |
| | H. C. Bailey, *Call Mr Fortune* (UK) |
| | Freeman Wills Crofts, *The Cask* (UK) |
| | E. Phillips Oppenheim, *The Great Impersonation* (UK) |
| 1922 | **US film industry sets up self-censoring 'Hays code'** |
| 1923 | Dorothy L. Sayers, *Whose Body?* (UK) |
| 1925 | Wallace, *The Mind of Mr J. G. Reeder* (UK) |
| 1926 | **General Strike (UK)** |
| | Christie, *The Murder of Roger Ackroyd* (UK) |
| | Joseph T. Shaw edits *Black Mask* magazine (US) |
| 1927 | S. S. Van Dine, *The Benson Murder Case* (US) |
| 1928 | William Somerset Maugham, *Ashenden* (UK) |
| 1929 | **Wall Street Crash, leading to Great Depression (US)** |
| | Anthony Berkeley (A. B. Cox), *The Poisoned Chocolates Case* (UK) |
| | W. R. Burnett, *Little Caesar* (US) |
| | Dashiell Hammett, *Red Harvest* (US) |
| | Ellery Queen, *The Roman Hat Mystery* (US) |
| | Margery Allingham, *The Crime at Black Dudley* (UK) |
| | Josephine Tey, *The Man in the Queue* (UK) |
| 1930 | Christie, *The Murder at the Vicarage* (first Miss Marple novel) (UK) |

|  | John Dickson Carr, *It Walks by Night* (UK) |
|---|---|
|  | Hammett, *The Maltese Falcon* (US) |
| 1931 | Francis Iles (A. B. Cox), *Malice Aforethought* (UK) |
|  | Georges Simenon, *Pietr-le-Letton* (Fr) |
|  | William Faulkner, *Sanctuary* (US) |
|  | *Little Caesar* (US film) |
|  | *Public Enemy* (US film) |
| 1932 | Gladys Mitchell, *The Saltmarsh Murders* (UK) |
|  | *Scarface* (US film) |
|  | *I Am a Fugitive from a Chain Gang* (US film) |
| 1933 | **Prohibition repealed (US)** |
| 1934 | Ngaio Marsh, *A Man Lay Dead* (UK) |
|  | Rex Stout, *Fer de Lance* (US) |
|  | James M. Cain, *The Postman Always Rings Twice* (US) |
| 1935 | Sayers, *Gaudy Night* (UK) |
|  | Carr, *The Hollow Man* (UK) |
|  | Nicholas Blake, *A Question of Proof* (UK) |
|  | Michael Innes, *Death at the President's Lodging* (UK) |
|  | *The Thirty-Nine Steps* (UK film) |
| 1936 | James M. Cain, *Double Indemnity* (US) |
| 1938 | Graham Greene, *Brighton Rock* (UK) |
|  | *Angels with Dirty Faces* (US film) |
| 1939–45/6 | **Second World War** |
| 1939 | Raymond Chandler, *The Big Sleep* (US) |
|  | Geoffrey Household, *Rogue Male* (UK) |
|  | James Hadley Chase, *No Orchids for Miss Blandish* (US) |
|  | Eric Ambler, *The Mask of Demetrios* (UK) |
|  | *The Roaring Twenties* (US film) |
| 1940 | Chandler, *Farewell, My Lovely* (US) |
|  | Cornell Woolrich, *The Bride Wore Black* (US) |
| 1941 | **US enters Second World War (-1946)** |
|  | Christianna Brand, *Heads You Lose* (UK) |
|  | *The Maltese Falcon* (US film) |
| 1942 | Jorge Luis Borges, 'Death and the Compass' (Argentina) |
| 1943 | Graham Greene, *The Ministry of Fear* (UK) |
| 1944 | Edmund Crispin, *The Gilded Fly* (UK) |
|  | *Double Indemnity* (US film) |
| 1945–51 | **Labour Party establishes Welfare State (UK)** |
|  | Lawrence Treat, *V as in Victim* (US) |
| 1946 | *The Big Sleep* (US film) |
|  | *The Killers* (US film) |

| | |
|---|---|
| 1947 | Mickey Spillane, *I, The Jury* (US) |
| | Julian Symons, *A Man Called Jones* (UK) |
| 1949 | Patricia Highsmith, *Strangers on a Train* (US) |
| | Ross Macdonald, *The Moving Target* (US) |
| | *The Blue Lamp* (UK film) |
| 1950–52 | **Joseph McCarthy heads anti-Communist drive in US** |
| 1951 | *Strangers on a Train* (US film) |
| | *The Lavender Hill Mob* (UK film) |
| | Simenon, *Les mémoires de Maigret* (Fr) |
| 1952 | Allingham, *The Tiger in the Smoke* (UK) |
| | Hillary Waugh, *Last Seen Wearing* (US) |
| | Jim Thompson, *The Killer Inside Me* (US) |
| 1953 | Chandler, *The Long Goodbye* (US) |
| | Ian Fleming, *Casino Royale* (UK) |
| | Alain Robbe-Grillet, *Les Gommes* (Fr) |
| 1954–6 | *Fabian of the Yard* (UK TV series) |
| 1955 | J. J. Marric (John Creasey), *Gideon's Day* (UK) |
| 1955–68 | *Dragnet* (US TV series) |
| 1955–76 | *Dixon of Dock Green* (UK TV series) |
| 1956 | Ed McBain, *Cop Hater* (US) |
| 1958 | Colin Watson, *Coffin Scarcely Used* (UK) |
| | Greene, *Our Man in Havana* (UK) |
| 1959 | Robert Bloch, *Psycho* (US) |
| 1959–67 | *No Hiding Place* (UK TV series) |
| 1960 | *Psycho* (US film) |
| | *Perry Mason* (US TV series) |
| 1961 | **Berlin Wall marks intensification of Cold War** |
| | John le Carré, *Call for the Dead* (UK) |
| 1961–9 | *The Avengers* (UK TV series) |
| 1962 | **Cuban missile crisis** |
| | Nicolas Freeling, *Love in Amsterdam* (UK) |
| | P. D. James, *Cover her Face* (UK) |
| | Dick Francis, *Dead Cert* (UK) |
| | Len Deighton, *The Ipcress File* (UK) |
| | *Dr No* (UK film) |
| 1962–78 | *Z Cars* (UK TV series) |
| 1963 | **Assassination of President Kennedy (US)** |
| | le Carré, *The Spy Who Came in from the Cold* (UK) |
| 1964 | **Civil Rights Acts outlaw racial and sexual discrimination (US)** |
| | **Betty Friedan's *The Feminine Mystique* launches 'second wave' feminist movement (US)** |

US embroiled in Vietnam War (till 1973)
Ruth Rendell, *From Doon with Death* (UK)
H. R. F. Keating, *The Perfect Murder* (UK)
Amanda Cross, *In the Last Analysis* (US)
Chester Himes, *Cotton Comes to Harlem* (US)

1965    **Anti-police riots in Watts, Los Angeles (US)**
**Capital punishment abolished (UK)**
John Ball, *In the Heat of the Night* (US)
Truman Capote, *In Cold Blood* (US)

1966    *Miranda* v. *Arizona* **case establishes suspects' rights against**
**self-incrimination (US)**
Thomas Pynchon, *The Crying of Lot 49* (US)

1966–9    *The Untouchables* (US TV series)

1968    **Martin Luther King assassinated (US)**
**'Police riot' in Chicago, against protestors at Democratic**
**Party convention (US)**
Peter Dickinson, *Skin Deep* (UK)

1969    **Special Patrol Groups set up to tackle specific problems (UK)**

1970    Joseph Wambaugh, *The New Centurions* (US)
Peter Lovesey, *Wobble to Death* (UK)
Reginald Hill, *A Clubbable Woman* (UK)

1971    Frederick Forsyth, *The Day of the Jackal* (UK)
Ross Macdonald, *The Underground Man* (US)
James McClure, *The Steam Pig* (South Africa)
*Get Carter* (UK film)
*Dirty Harry* (US film)

1972    **Capital punishment suspended (US)**
**Knapp Report on New York police corruption (US)**
**'Bloody Sunday' escalates Northern Irish troubles (UK)**
Lillian O'Donnell, *The Phone Call* (US)
*The Godfather* (US film)
James, *An Unsuitable Job for a Woman* (UK)

1972–9    *Columbo* (US TV series)

1974    **Watergate scandal forces President Nixon's resignation (US)**
le Carré, *Tinker, Tailor, Soldier, Spy* (UK)

1975    **Sex Discrimination and Equal Pay Acts outlaw workplace**
**discrimination (UK)**
Colin Dexter, *Last Bus to Woodstock* (UK)

1975–8    *The Sweeney* (UK TV series)

1975–9    *Starsky and Hutch* (US TV series)

| | |
|---|---|
| 1976 | **Capital punishment restored in some states (US)** |
| | **Race Relations Act (UK)** |
| | Dell Shannon, *Streets of Death* (US) |
| 1977 | Rendell, *A Judgement in Stone* (UK) |
| | Marcia Muller, *Edwin of the Iron Shoes* (US) |
| | Ellis Peters, *A Morbid Taste for Bones* (UK) |
| | Elmore Leonard, *Unknown Man 89* (US) |
| 1977–82 | *Charlie's Angels* (US TV series) |
| 1978 | William Hjortsberg, *Falling Angel* (US) |
| 1979 | **Conservative victory under Margaret Thatcher (UK)** |
| 1980 | Liza Cody, *Dupe* (UK) |
| 1981 | **Republican victory under Ronald Reagan (US)** |
| | Thomas Harris, *Red Dragon* (US) |
| 1981–7 | *Magnum PI* (US TV series) |
| 1982 | Sara Paretsky, *Indemnity Only* (US) |
| 1982–8 | *Cagney and Lacey* (US TV series) |
| 1984 | Barbara Wilson, *Murder in the Collective* (US) |
| | Katherine V. Forrest, *Amateur City* (US) |
| | William Caunitz, *One Police Plaza* (US) |
| | Umberto Eco, *The Name of the Rose* (It.) |
| | James Ellroy, *Blood on the Moon* (US) |
| 1985 | Leonard, *Glitz* (US) |
| 1985–90 | *Miami Vice* (US TV series) |
| 1986 | Sue Grafton, *A is for Alibi* (US) |
| 1987 | Paul Auster, *The New York Trilogy* (US) |
| | Ian Rankin, *Knots and Crosses* (UK) |
| | Caroline Graham, *The Killings at Badger's Drift* (UK) |
| | Val McDermid, *Report for Murder* (UK) |
| 1987–2000 | *Inspector Morse* (UK TV series) |
| 1988 | Michael Dibdin, *Ratking* (UK) |
| | Eleanor Taylor Bland, *See No Evil* (US) |
| | Elizabeth George, *A Great Deliverance* (UK) |
| 1989 | **End of the Cold War** |
| | Thomas Harris, *The Silence of the Lambs* (US) |
| | James Lee Burke, *Heaven's Prisoners* (US) |
| 1990 | Patricia Cornwell, *Postmortem* (US) |
| | Walter Mosley, *Devil in a Blue Dress* (US) |
| | Valerie Wilson Wesley, *When Death Comes Stealing* (US) |
| | R. D. Wingfield, *A Touch of Frost* (UK) |
| | *Goodfellas* (US film) |

| | |
|---|---|
| 1991 | Bret Easton Ellis, *American Psycho* (US) |
| | *Reservoir Dogs* (US film) |
| | *Boyz N the Hood* (US film) |
| | *Prime Suspect* (UK TV drama) |
| 1992 | Peter Høeg, *Smilla's Sense of Snow* (Danish; trans. 1993) |
| | Barbara Neely, *Blanche on the Lam* (US) |
| | James Sallis, *The Long Legged Fly* (US) |
| 1993 | Carl Hiaasen, *Strip Tease* (US) |
| | Minette Walters, *The Sculptress* (UK) |
| | Frances Fyfield, *Shadow Play* (UK) |
| | **Murder of black teenager Stephen Lawrence, leading to charges of police negligence and institutional racism (UK)** |
| 1994 | Linda Grant, *A Woman's Place* (US) |
| | *Pulp Fiction* (US film) |
| 1994– | *The Bill* (UK TV series) |
| 1995 | Ellroy, *American Tabloid* (US) |
| | Val McDermid, *The Mermaids Singing* (UK) |
| | Susanna Moore, *In the Cut* (US) |
| | *Seven* (US film) |
| 1997 | **Labour victory under Tony Blair (UK)** |
| | Grace Edwards, *If I Should Die* (US) |
| 1999 | James Sallis, *Bluebottle* (US) |
| | Rendell, *Harm Done* (UK) |
| | Dibdin, *Blood Rain* (UK) |
| | Dexter, *The Remorseful Day* (UK) |
| | Jake Arnott, *The Long Firm* (UK) |

MARTIN PRIESTMAN

# Introduction: crime fiction and detective fiction

Until quite recently, the words 'Cambridge Companion' and 'Crime Fiction' would have seemed mutually exclusive. Crime fiction was certainly written about, but on the assumption that readers and author were already dedicated fans, happy to ponder together the exact chronology of Sherlock Holmes's life-story or the mystery of Dr Watson's Christian name. Where the authors claimed some academic credentials, their love for the genre was owned up to as a guilty pleasure – W. H. Auden called it 'an addiction like tobacco or alcohol' – or juxtaposed to the world of 'proper' culture with tongue a fair way into cheek, as in Dorothy L. Sayers's demonstration that when writing the *Poetics*, what Aristotle desired 'in his heart of hearts . . . was a good detective story'.[1]

Since the 1960s, however, the presumed barriers between 'high' and 'low' literature have been progressively dismantled. If only – at first – as indicators of a great many readers' needs and anxieties, crime texts were increasingly seen as worthy of close analysis, and by now there are thousands of carefully argued, well-researched, elegantly written studies of the crime genre available and awaiting further comment. Like any new development this emergence has a specific history, any given intersection of which is likely to reveal different terminologies as well as different critical preoccupations. Up to the early 1980s, study of the form was still focused mainly on 'detective' or 'mystery' fiction, and nodded back to the half-serious 'rules' which had been drawn up for the genre in the inter-war period and stressed the figure of the detective and the author's fair handling of clues. This tradition is well discussed in Stephen Knight's chapter on 'the Golden Age' in the present book.

It was with Julian Symons's groundbreaking *Bloody Murder* (1972; US title *Mortal Consequences*) that the need for this fence against the barbarian hordes began to be queried, as its subtitle, *From the Detective Story to the Crime Novel*, suggests. Once the continuity with such adjacent forms as the thriller, spy novel and police procedural was established, the peculiar historical specificity of the mystery detective whodunnit stood out in sharper relief – stimulating new kinds of investigation into the question of why such a rigid, in many ways thin and unsatisfying, formula should have come into being when and how it did, and remained so enduringly popular. As the crime genre itself developed – often in challenge to its own earlier assumptions, as with the women and black detectives of the 1980s and 1990s – it became increasingly relevant to consider the gender, race and class implications of its various metamorphoses, as well as its ever-growing importance as a staple of the filmic and televisual iconography underlying so much of contemporary culture.

This Companion aims to reflect the most important of these debates, at least as they stand at the start of the third millennium. But while some chapters (for instance those by Ian A. Bell, Lyn Pykett, David Seed, David Glover and Nickianne Moody) explore the depiction of crime with no necessary detective element, others do focus round the mystery whodunnit form which will still constitute the heart of the crime genre for many readers. The chapters by (for instance) Martin A. Kayman, Stephen Knight, Dennis Porter, Martin Priestman and Maureen T. Reddy take different developments of the detective form as their main focus, while Laura Marcus assumes it as the model for a certain vein of postmodern exploration.

I shall briefly summarise the traditional story of the growth of 'detective fiction' which held sole sway until recently, to serve as a point of entry to the back-history from which more recent debates and emphases have developed. According to this account, then, the detective story was invented in 1841 by Edgar Allan Poe, who acknowledged some debt to the structure as well as content of William Godwin's earlier novel *Caleb Williams* (1794). In the 1860s the form pioneered in Poe's short stories at last found its way into the novels of Emile Gaboriau in France and Wilkie Collins in England: Collins's The *Moonstone* (1868) is normally celebrated as the first great detective novel. It took another twenty-odd years for the form to reach its first pinnacle of popularity with Arthur Conan Doyle's creation of Sherlock Holmes, followed by smaller luminaries such as G. K. Chesterton's Father Brown. Once again, it took time for the newly popular form to migrate from short story to novel, but this was achieved during the inter-war 'Golden Age' dominated by Agatha Christie and a galaxy of somewhat lesser 'Queens of Crime'. Meanwhile, in the USA, a new form evolved in conscious opposition to this genteelly 'English' model: the hardboiled private eye fiction of Dashiell Hammett and Raymond Chandler. In some accounts, that is virtually the end of the story; in others, later developments are either seen as continuations of these two great 'national' traditions, or as deplorable fallings-off from them.

Presenting the agreed history in this way oversimplifies, of course. Many studies accompany it with a far wider scale of reference to other works and writers, and draw entirely sensible distinctions between crime fiction in general and the detective mystery in particular. It is, in any case, a useful and largely accurate way of describing some key moments in the latter's development. Its danger is that, in looking chiefly for the first stirrings of something recognisably like Doyle, Christie or Chandler, it imposes a model of quasi-evolutionary striving on a past which was often interested in other things entirely, and tends to overlook the pre-existing genres and ways of writing about crime from which the present canon historically emerged.

As Ian A. Bell's chapter in the present book shows, the voluminous crime writing of the eighteenth century cast a long shadow over later representations of criminality, but allowed no 'textual space' for the figure of the detective. Though such a figure has been argued to emerge in Godwin's radical novel *Caleb Williams*, Poe's praise for the novel's backwards construction so as to keep 'the *dénouement* constantly in view' is qualified by the fact that the hero's discovery of his master's crimes occurs less than halfway through, and by Godwin's own uncertainty as to what the dénouement should be.[2] There is less to quarrel with in the standard view that Poe's own 'Murders in the Rue Morgue' represented the first story structured entirely round the ingenious deductions of a charismatic detective, although Martin A. Kayman shows that Dupin's two most important cases hardly concern crime at all, and his one attempt to solve an actual murder ('The Mystery of Marie Rogêt', 1842) shows him at his least effective.

Although Emile Gaboriau's key role in creating the detective novel is widely recognised, the difficulty of obtaining English versions has frequently led to airy waves in his direction (sometimes confusing his two leading detectives) rather than the kind of focused analysis given in Sita A. Schütt's chapter, which also demonstrates the continuing importance of crime and detection in French writing from the groundbreaking 'true-life' memoirs of the bandit-turned-police-chief Vidocq to the masterly Maigret novels of Georges Simenon.

It is when we return to the British novel that the quest for purely 'detective' antecedents again produces an over-limited and somewhat distorted picture. Collins's *The Moonstone* has been discussed in luxuriant depth by critics seeking the origins of the British detective-hero or even a kind of psychological template for all other detective novels.[3] What is not always sufficiently recognised by such accounts is *The Moonstone*'s place in a more slowly evolving history of the Victorian novelistic treatment of crime. As explored by Lyn Pykett in her chapter, this history ranges from the 'Newgate novels' of the 1830s–1840s, whose empathy with the lusty criminality of the previous century soon made them politically suspect, to the 'Sensation novels' of the 1860s, which shocked readers just as much by placing more small-scale, intimate crimes at the heart of modern middle- and upper-class homes. By a relatively small re-emphasis, *The Moonstone* shifts the focus from the crime itself – which turns out barely to be one – to its investigation. However, though regularly hailed as the first great English detective hero, the able but thwarted Sergeant Cuff is dismissed from the case after wrongly accusing the heroine, and his place taken by a doctor's assistant whose detective credentials are limited to his inside knowledge of the workings of opium. The figure of the detective-hero who unravels a crime single-handed through a mixture of persistence and ingenious deduction is in fact better represented in Robert Audley, who uncovers his young aunt's near-murder of her inconvenient first husband in what is normally listed as the purest of 'Sensation novels', Mary Elizabeth Braddon's *Lady Audley's Secret* (1862).

With Doyle's creation of the Sherlock Holmes series, detective fiction became for the first time an indubitably popular and repeatable genre format. It now knows what it is and what it is trying to do, as does its public; and while there is a simultaneous burgeoning of many other popular crime-related formulae, it becomes a respectably full-time job to analyse the numerous variants of this one. Martin A. Kayman explores some of these variants, but also some of the other kinds of short narrative from which they emerge, such as the supposedly true-life memoirs of the police detective 'Waters' (1849) which, while not conforming to the later 'rules' of whodunnitry, helped to build up public identification with the still partly distrusted figure of the detective policeman, and hence with the process of detection itself.

The emergence of a new kind of slimmed-down, highly goal-directed detective novel in the so-called 'Golden Age' between the two world wars is also a demonstrable fact once a few significant antecedents are acknowledged (including some of the French ones noted in Sita A. Schütt's chapter). However, the common assumption that this form flourished only in Britain while post-Poe American detection still waited to be born is one of many oversimplifications corrected by Stephen Knight, in a chapter which also draws attention to the way in which this period's penchant for drawing up lists of 'rules' for the genre has bedevilled later attempts to discuss crime fiction in the round. As background to Dennis Porter's chapter on the American private-eye fiction of Hammett, Chandler and others from the late 1920s on, we need to note the formative importance of such 'Golden Age' American writers as S. S. Van Dine, as well as the great popularity – from at least the 1880s – of the dime novels featuring Nick Carter and other such quasi-detective heroes, and the parallel growth (as traced in David Glover's chapter on the Thriller) of crime narratives where detection is not the chief or only interest and where criminal milieux and outlooks are often explored from the inside.

From the unlikely soil of the white-male-centred private-eye form have sprung two of the most dramatic developments of the past thirty years. Though Maureen T. Reddy glances back to the occasional lady detectives of the Holmes era (also explored by Martin A. Kayman), her main emphasis is on the women private eyes who emerged in the wake of the 1970s feminist revival. By the 1990s several of these female protagonists are black; and a discussion of them also culminates Andrew Pepper's history of the black detective hero, which moves from the police-based fiction of Chester Himes through the 1980s discovery of the private eye as an effective vehicle for exploring the frustrations and aspirations of being black in a white-run world.

The traditional interest in the charismatic detective has tended to focus attention on the (British) eccentric amateur and (American) embittered private eye, to the near-exclusion of the many fictional police detectives whose strength lies in teamwork rather than solitary brilliance. In the more-than half-century since the Second World War, a growing demand for a semblance of realism has been met by giving the main detective roles to the only people actually empowered to investigate serious crime: the police. Since police fiction has developed differently in the US and the UK, LeRoy L. Panek's and Martin Priestman's chapters handle them separately; but both show how the attempt to apply rigid single-hero whodunnit rules to this genre is becoming increasingly futile. Another kind of professional – the spy – appeals in another way to the reader's desire to plug into a world of detective-like expertise although, as David Seed's chapter shows, the fortunes of spy fiction have fluctuated in tune with dramatic changes in the public perception of international relations.

It would be hard to overestimate the impact of film and, later, television on the public idea both of crime fiction and of crime itself. Yet studies of the genre's relation to the visual media have tended to focus on two main areas, both chiefly from the 1930s to 1950s: the *film noir* which includes (but is not confined to) influential screen versions of Hammett and Chandler, and the work of Alfred Hitchcock where crime – if not necessarily detection – combines in various ways with horror motifs. Nickianne Moody's chapter evinces an array of evidence that filmic representations of crime – and concomitant concerns about their visceral impact on public attitudes – began much earlier and have continued to evolve in significant new directions, particularly since the post-war arrival of television. Partly thanks to the imagery created by these media, the narrative patterns of crime and detective fiction have embedded themselves deep in contemporary consciousness, in ways which have provided a springboard for some of the most interesting experiments with fictional form by 'serious' postmodernist writers since the Second World War. As Laura Marcus's concluding chapter indicates, far from being a somewhat sleazy black-sheep cousin belatedly admitted to the house of fiction by a side door, the crime story has some claim to have driven the main structural transformations of narrative for (at least) the last half-century.

As with any book aiming to comprehend such a vast genre, some omissions have sadly been inevitable: doubtless of many well-loved individual works, as well as of any non-Anglophone fiction apart from the French or high-cultural. Less apology is due for the occasional overlaps of material – and even, at times, the disagreements – between chapters. For the reader of this book from cover to cover as well as for those using it to chase up particular interests, the aim is to provide a sense of the genre's history as multi-layered rather than unidirectional, and of its criticism as in process rather than univocal. At the same time, we hope that much of the best that has been and can be said about crime fiction in the early 2000s is represented – through direct argument or through references as comprehensive as we could make them – here.

## NOTES

1 See W. H. Auden, 'The Guilty Vicarage' (1948), and Dorothy L. Sayers, 'Aristotle on Detective Fiction' (1946), both reprinted in Robin W. Winks, ed., *Detective Fiction: A Collection of Critical Essays* (Englewood Cliffs, NJ: Prentice-Hall, 1980).
2 Edgar Allan Poe, 'The Philosophy of Composition' (1846), reprinted in David Galloway, ed., *Selected Writings* (Harmondsworth: Penguin, 1967), p. 480. For Godwin's uncertainty about the ending, see p. 15 below.
3 See Charles Rycroft, 'A Detective Story: Psychoanalytic Observations', *Psychoanalytic Quarterly*, 26 (1957), 229–45; Albert D. Hutter, 'Dreams, Transformations, and Literature: The Implications of Detective Fiction', *Victorian Studies* 19 (1975), 181–209.

# 1

IAN A. BELL

# Eighteenth-century crime writing

The literature of the eighteenth century is suffused with crime, but handles it in a wholly different way from that of the nineteenth and twentieth. Looking back across those centuries, it is easy to trace this difference to the penal realities of the time: the absence of any reliable system of policing, or of the detection of criminals on any routine basis. Furthermore, there seems to have been little ideological belief that this could or indeed needed to be done effectively. What system there was was largely privatised: the 'prosecution' of theft was the responsibility of the injured party, who might offer a reward for information or hire an agent. This situation fed straight into the hands of gangsters such as the notorious Jonathan Wild, who arranged in turn for the robberies, the receipt of the reward for returning the goods and, when it suited him, the arrest of the supposed thieves – usually members of his own gang – in his self-proclaimed role of 'Thieftaker General'.[1] Alternatively, the authorities relied on members of the public to detect crime as it happened and summon the watch – parochially-based and with few autonomous powers beyond responding to calls for arrest. The main tool of law-enforcement was the fear of horrific punishment if caught: the so-called 'Bloody Code' which penalised even minor thefts with death. The code was partly self-defeating, in that juries who felt the punishment too great for the crime might well acquit; and there were various other means – from bribery to the kind of apparent Christian repentance shown by the thief-heroine of Daniel Defoe's novel *Moll Flanders* (1722) – of escaping the death penalty or commuting it to a lesser punishment such as transportation.

For many eighteenth-century writers, the *locus classicus* for presenting and commenting on this situation was Newgate, London's main prison, from which the most celebrated condemned criminals took their last ride through excited crowds to the gallows at Tyburn. At the 'low', popular end of the market, ballads and 'true narratives' relating criminals' lives and (often fabricated) last confessions constituted a love–hate discourse between the condemned and the public (many of whose members may have felt simply lucky that they had not yet gone the same way), which found a more mass-produced expression in the various collections of such lives, known generically from 1773 on as *The Newgate Calendar*. Defoe's experience in writing up such lives – such as that of the popular house-breaker Jack Sheppard[2] – stood him in good stead when creating the Newgate-destined Moll and the criminal heroes of several other novels. For more respectable writers, too, the term 'Newgate' is used to evoke a whole complex of crime-related issues, as in John Gay's 'Newgate pastoral' *The Beggar's Opera* (1728),[3] whose massive stage success owed much to its implied comparison of Wild to the corrupt Prime Minister Robert Walpole in the figure of the gangster-businessman Peachum; a parallel repeated in Henry Fielding's satirical fantasy *Jonathan Wild* (1743), whose Preface presents 'Newgate' in almost metaphysical terms as 'human nature with its mask off'.[4] And if Newgate is central to the literary vision of London crime and its treatment, rural law enforcement is handled no less virulently, in the many depictions of local squire-magistrates passing down their ignorant prejudices as justice in novels such as Fielding's *Joseph Andrews* (1742), *Tom Jones* (1749) and *Amelia* (1751).

In the eighteenth century, then, crime writing is not confined to a single generic or conventional form, designed for a particular audience. And, though often comic, it is not reassuring in intent but intrinsically contentious, willing to confront and disquiet rather than to comfort like the predominantly recreational detective fiction of later centuries. In the nineteenth century, the role of the newly-fashioned detective as an agent of consolation or security is both commercially and ideologically central to the subsequent project of popular crime writing. As Stephen Knight puts it, writing of Sherlock Holmes:

> The captivated readers had faith in modern systems of scientific and rational enquiry to order an uncertain and troubling world, but feeling they lacked these powers themselves they, like many audiences before them, needed a suitably equipped hero to mediate psychic protection.[5]

The phrase 'psychic protection' is highly suggestive here, as is the inclusion of 'faith'. In a meticulously detailed and internally plausible textual belief-system, designed to reinforce the audience's sense of security, the detective becomes the reader's personal custodian, guaranteeing safe passage and neutralising the threat of even the most cunning criminals. Sherlock Holmes himself may be a bit weird and cranky, like Hercule Poirot and all those others, he may even have his own agenda, but he is on our side despite everything.

Looking back beyond Sherlock Holmes and his rivals to the eighteenth century, we see that the cacophonous writing about crime in that period allows its readers no such psychic protection, and arises from no such shared faith in the efficacy of any belief system. The discourse of crime writing at the time of the 'Bloody Code' mediates and articulates deep anxiety rather than consolation. Eighteenth-century commentators were describing a world they saw as replete with rogues and desperadoes of all kinds, a world without detectives, without even much of a police force, without reliable insurance companies or other mechanisms of personal protection, and with an inefficient and often flagrantly corrupt court and prison system. The law was clearly imperfect, both in its conception and in its implementation. It cannot have been comforting to see that on those relatively rare occasions when villains were apprehended and brought to a kind of justice – like the rapist Lovelace dying in a duel at the end of Richardson's *Clarissa* (1749) – it was more likely to be the result of anachronistic personal codes of honour and revenge than through the operations of any recognised civil authority.

In eighteenth-century writing, criminals are only brought to trial, if at all, by confession or by the use of paid or otherwise rewarded informants. The 'idea of a detective' is never given any textual space. At the end of Daniel Defoe's last novel *Roxana* (1724), for instance, the eponymous murderess and polygamist fears the devastating effects of her own internalised sense of guilt and the possible treachery of her creature Amy more than she fears investigation by any 'authorities'.

Roxana's sense of the potential for dishonour among thieves was borne out by contemporary accounts of just this kind of betrayal, particularly in the many accounts of the events surrounding the trial of Jonathan Wild. After all, if a figure as frightening and powerful as Wild could not command loyalty, who could? In John Gay's poem, 'Newgate's Garland' (1724), the courtroom assault on Wild by 'Blueskin' (one of his gang) is seen as both threatening and fitting:

> Ye Gallants of *Newgate*, whose Fingers are nice,
> In diving in Pockets, or cogging of Dice,
> Ye Sharpers so rich, who can buy off the Noose,
> Ye honester poor Rogues, who die in your Shoes,
>  Attend and draw near,
>  Good News ye shall hear,
>  How *Jonathan's* Throat was cut from Ear to Ear;
> How *Blueskin's* sharp Penknife hath set you at Ease,
> And every Man round me may rob, if he please.[6]

Here the potentially welcome news for the law-abiding of the fall of Jonathan Wild only seems to herald further anarchy, as though the law as it stands is

at best an ineffective restraint on the human desire to pillage and plunder –
'And every Man round me may rob, if he please'.

The paradoxical case of Jonathan Wild – both master-criminal and thief-taker – shows great instability in contemporary notions of justice. Even more striking are those examples, like Daniel Defoe's *Captain Singleton* (1721) or *Moll Flanders*, where the criminal-narrator seems to suffer almost nothing at the end of the tale. Undergoing a spiritual awakening of some kind, or at least claiming to, he/she is allowed to keep the spoils of a life of crime, and to live on more or less happily ever after. There is, in these texts, a kind of slippage between notions of 'crime' and notions of 'vice', the first to be excused by 'necessity', the second obliterated by 'repentance'. In his preface to *Moll Flanders*, posing as the editor of memorandums written by the 'famous' heroine herself, Defoe tries hard to present the tale as an exemplary life history, as illustrating and confirming the values of penitence. But, with that characteristic disarming frankness of his, he also makes us aware of the ironies in the survival of his characters:

> . . . how they came both to England again, about eight Years, in which time they were grown very Rich, and where she liv'd, it seems, to be very old; but was not so extraordinary a Penitent, as she was at first . . .[7]

Moll's combination of financial security and moral amnesia may be ironic, whether Defoe really knows it or not, but it is not untypical. She lays her hands on the convenient idea of repentance as readily as she does on any other unguarded valuable. And, after all, why not? The conceptual structure invoked may seem shaky, and the book's moral vision may end up lacking in coherence, but then few eighteenth-century texts seek to achieve full clarity or consistency.

Furthermore, when suspects were brought before a formal tribunal, rather than merely brought before the judgement of readers – as Henry Fielding portrays so forcefully in the court of Justice Thrasher at the opening of his last novel *Amelia* (1751) – it was likely to be presented as a shabby and rather sordid affair, with no real sense of justice or closure achieved. Fielding, himself a serving magistrate since 1748/9, ironically acknowledges that Thrasher 'had some few imperfections in his magistratical Capacity' and we can have little confidence in his judgements:

> Sirrah, your Tongue betrays your Guilt. You are an *Irishman*, and that is always sufficient Evidence with me.[8]

*Plus ça change* . . . Fielding is by no means alone in this perception of the inherent incompetence of the legal tribunal. The courtroom presided over by Francis Goodchild, as depicted in William Hogarth's graphic sequence

*Industry and Idleness* (1747), seems blind to its own corruptions – the feckless Tom Idle is condemned with a bribe changing hands, as Goodchild shields his eyes – and in the famous lines of Alexander Pope from 1714:

> Mean while declining from the Noon of Day,
> The Sun obliquely shoots his burning Ray;
> The hungry Judges soon the Sentence sign,
> And Wretches hang, that jurymen may dine.[9]

The contempt for judges, lawyers and attornies is widespread at this time, becoming almost conventional. In Jonathan Swift's *Gulliver's Travels* (1726), the hapless hero tries to explain the current state of the law in Britain to his Houyhnhnm master:

> I said there was a society of men among us, bred up from their youth in the art of proving by words multiplied for the purpose, that white is black, and black is white, according as they are paid. To this society all the rest of the people are slaves.[10]

As we think of the way the officers of the law are portrayed, we must not forget that the abductor and would-be rapist Mr B – in Richardson's *Pamela* (1740) is a Justice of the Peace, as is the well-intentioned but dangerously naïve Squire Allworthy in Fielding's *Tom Jones* (1749).

In some famous lines from *The Beggar's Opera*, it must be clear that the state and its operatives were seen by few with optimism. As Peachum the thieftaker and gang-boss explains,

> A Lawyer is an honest Employment, so is mine. Like me too he acts in a double Capacity, both against Rogues and for 'em; for 'tis but fitting that we should protect and encourage Cheats, since we live by them.[11]

The law may be an ass, but maybe that is the best we can hope for in the circumstances.

The comforting comradeship and playfulness which distinguishes much subsequent crime fiction is almost entirely missing from eighteenth-century writing, and in its stead we see a much more urgent and disturbing sense of crisis. The tone of measured scorn is obvious. Though they may write with controlled irony, eighteenth-century commentators are seriously perturbed by the here and now. The crimes they describe are immediate and local threats to the self and to property. In a flagrantly material discourse, the threats of murder and larceny are part of the realised conditions of contemporary life.

Defoe's *Moll Flanders* may be signed 'Written in year 1683' but her description of London street life is clearly set nearer the moment of publication in 1722, her accounts of the cells of Newgate prison and of transportation to

Virginia seeming otherwise anachronistic, making it an account of crime as contemporary as that offered by John Gay in *Trivia; or, The Art of Walking the Streets in London* (1716) and in *The Beggar's Opera*. By being made so mundane, so immediate and (if I may) so in-your-face, crime became for readers and writers alike the defining literary feature of contemporary urban life.

An example of the centrality of crime and the attendant sense of immediate crisis can be found in Samuel Johnson's poem, *London* (1738):

> A single Jail, in Alfred's golden Reign,
> Could half the Nation's Criminals contain;
> Fair Justice then, without Constraint ador'd
> Held high the steady Scale, but sheath'd the Sword;
> No Spies were paid, no *Special Juries* known,
> Blest Age! but ah! How diff'rent from our own![12]

These are not Johnson's own words, of course, but part of the embittered farewell from 'injur'd Thales', who is so horrified by the conditions of contemporary urban life that he is preparing for voluntary exile on 'Cambria's solitary shore'. Convinced that since the days of King Alfred one thousand years earlier things have been going steadily downhill all the way, Thales – like Henry Fielding's Man of the Hill in *Tom Jones* or like Alexander Pope himself in his *Epistle to Dr Arbuthnot* – sees no way out other than by turning his back on urban life and becoming a recluse.

The central point in Thales's account seems to be the flourishing condition of criminality, and the effete impotence of the law in response. In fact, the speaker seems to point to a kind of similitude between crime and the law – instead of being in opposition to each other, they are 'here' in complicity: 'Their Ambush here relentless Ruffians lay,/ And here the fell Attorney prowls for prey'.[13] By using the persona of Thales, Johnson may distance himself slightly from these sentiments, but by voicing them at all – by erasing the moral difference between ruffians and attornies – he distances himself further from the Whiggish progressivist accounts of the role of law in the development of civilisation, such as that most powerfully and publicly expressed in William Blackstone's *Commentaries on the Laws of England* (1766).

And here Johnson, otherwise a famous enthusiast for the pleasures of urban life, articulates the contradiction which lies at the heart of the discourse of eighteenth-century crime writing – the ideological conflict between the atavistic and the ameliorist.

The atavistic account of crime – expressing the sense that these 'Ruffians' are indeed 'relentless', and that they are 'here' – has already been dwelt on. For many commentators in the first half of the eighteenth century, specifically the major satirists, the proximity and visibility of criminals was only to be expected. Human nature was fundamentally dark and selfish, after all, so criminality was actually the default setting for the newly-developed styles of urban life. As Peachum puts it in *The Beggar's Opera:*

> Through all the Employments of Life
>     Each Neighbour abuses his Brother;
> Whore and Rogue they call Husband and Wife:
>     All Professions be-rogue one another.
> The Priest calls the Lawyer a Cheat,
>     The Lawyer be-knaves the Divine;
> And the Statesman because he's so great,
>     Thinks his trade as honest as mine.[14]

Such a bleak and cynical view, identifying a purely materialist Hobbesian world, represents the shadowy side of Augustan civilisation.

The atavistic view of crime was so pervasive and persuasive that it has come to be seen as hegemonic. But we must be cautious of taking deliberately ironic and oppositional writers like Gay, Swift and Pope as our cultural brokers. Although their sardonic account has survived in the best condition – irony improves with age, panegyric tarnishes – for contemporaries it existed in dialogue with more optimistic versions. By concentrating on those voices calling for reform and improvement in the law and its implementation, on those voices which saw these as necessary, possible and desirable, we can detect a more hopefully ameliorist account of crime in the second half of the eighteenth century.

As one historian has put it, 'Lord Macaulay's generalisation that the history of England is the history of progress is as true of the criminal law of this country as of any of the other social institutions of which it is a part'.[15] While we may not fully share this optimism – despite some evidence of prison reform, more consistent sentencing, the decline in public executions, and the beginnings of a new police force – there are visible points in the discourse of crime writing in the second half of the eighteenth century when writers and commentators *thought* they could effect improvements.

This can be seen in the later career of Henry Fielding. Having become a magistrate in 1748/9, the previously oppositional writer set about the task of reformation of the law with some gusto. Seeing the situation as desperate but not hopeless, he announced his new vocation in *A Charge delivered to the Grand Jury* (1749), and developed ameliorist projects in subsequent pamphlets, *An Enquiry into the Causes of the late Increase of Robbers* (1751) and *A Proposal for making an effectual Provision for the Poor* (1753). In these pamphlets, Fielding leaves behind him the voice of mordant celebration, audible in earlier satire and in his version of *Jonathan Wild* (1743), in which crime merely confirms the perception that contemporary culture has lost its way. In its place we hear the first strains of the reforming voice, in which the law is a perfectible mechanism for the improvement of social welfare. Such a note is even audible in *Amelia* (1751):

> It will probably be objected, that the small Imperfections which I am about to produce, do not lie in the Laws themselves, but in the ill Execution of them; but, with Submission, this appears to me to be no less an Absurdity, than to say of any Machine that it is excellently made, tho' incapable of performing its Functions.[16]

Set conveniently at the mid-point of the century, we may take this as the fulcrum moment when criticism of criminals switches to become criticism of the laws and of their implementation. Unlike Johnson's sombre account, or Gay's zestful cynicism, Fielding here seems half optimistic: not only ought we to improve the laws and our execution of them, but perhaps we can.

As Fielding moves away from individually venial lawyers, criminals and judges to the state of the law itself, he prepares the way for the more abstract institutional critique found in the 'Jacobin' novels of William Godwin, Robert Bage and Mary Wollstonecraft. These developed the reformist project initiated by Fielding, but added a heightened sense of injustice and an early-Romantic conviction of human possibility. Moving away from the atavistic account of crime, these writers further developed the ameliorist account towards a confrontational and revolutionary plea for justice and the rights of man.

Something of the angry urgency of these novels' project is suggested by their titles. Bage's *Hermsprong, or Man As He is Not* (1796) ironically echoes the title of his earlier *Man As He Is* (1792), which presented the hero's support for notions of equal justice as realistic. In *Hermsprong*, they are seen as achievable only by an improbably idealised outsider brought up in the American wilderness, and only after he has been brought to trial by the old-school country landowner Lord Grondale, on charges which include reading radical books and trying to ameliorate miners' working conditions. Furthermore, his escape from the clutches of the law is only achieved by a surprise revelation of noble birth more appropriate to the fantastic genre of romance than to any realistic exploration of 'man as he is'. Though unfinished at her death, Wollstonecraft's *The Wrongs of Woman, or Maria* (1798) similarly ironises the more hopeful vision of her earlier treatise *A Vindication of the Rights of Woman* (1792). For leaving her sexually abusive husband, the heroine is arrested and brought to a trial which robs her of her daughter and property and condemns her to a madhouse. Here she joins forces with a female warder who has been similarly victimised lower down the social scale – reinforcing the overall impression that for women the whole world is one 'vast prison'.[17]

Both these novels were preceded by William Godwin's *Caleb Williams* (1794), whose original title – *Things As They Are* – may well be another reaction to Bage's 1792 title. Since it has sometimes been held up as an early version of the detective novel, it is worth considering at somewhat greater length. Caleb, servant and secretary to the noble Falkland, slowly unearths the fact that his master has murdered Tyrell, a brutal fellow-squire, and laid a false trail of evidence leading to the execution of two innocent men. However, this discovery occurs less than half-way through the book, the rest of which is devoted to Falkland's efforts to silence him, and Godwin was radically undecided as to whether to end the novel with Falkland's final broken confession in open court, or with Caleb's descent into self-doubting madness. The latter's discovery of the truth is thus only the start of the process of legal, political and mental persecution Godwin is chiefly interested in, as a way of demonstrating the critique of present-day injustices analysed more philosophically in his *Enquiry into Political Justice* of the previous year (1793). Further belying the 'ur-detective' model, the concrete 'evidence' of Falkland's guilt is tantalisingly concealed from us in a trunk whose contents clearly obsess him but are never revealed: rather than through any complex deductions *à la* detective fiction, it is entirely through Falkland's own overwrought reactions to his initially innocent probings that Caleb guesses the truth.

Seeing *Caleb* as centrally concerned with the workings of conscience on a once-noble mind relates it far more strongly to one of the late eighteenth century's most prevalent fictional genres: the gothic. From the first gothic novel – Horace Walpole's *The Castle of Otranto* (1764) – onwards, powerful men with guilty secrets had been forced to confess their crimes by a variety of pressures ranging from hauntings (by a huge suit of armour in *Otranto*) to more internalised torments, as well as the actual amassing of evidence by the more innocent characters. As Maureen T. Reddy points out in her chapter, the gothic novels of Ann Radcliffe – some of which predate *Caleb* – focus largely on such investigations by the tyrant's female victims. The most striking difference between *Caleb* and other gothic novels and plays is that it is set in the context of contemporary British power relations. It is significant that its own popular success was far outstripped by that of George Colman the Younger's dramatisation *The Iron Chest* (1796) which, while making much more detective-fictional, climactic use of the evidence in the eponymous chest, also sets the action safely back in the seventeenth century. The play's success owed much to the fact that, thus distanced, the

Falkland character becomes a wholly recognisable gothic hero-villain, and the Caleb character simply the somewhat lightweight *ingénu* who stumbles on the truth. It is, then, in its modernising of a familiar theme that *Caleb* really breaks new ground, but – and it is here that the narrow quest for purely 'detective' antecedents has introduced an unnecessary distortion – it is the ground of the paranoid political thriller rather than that of the detective mystery.

While the message of the Jacobin novels hardly constitutes a demand for more policing (the spies and agents of justice are generally the most unpleasant characters), the earlier nineteenth century saw a slow dismantling of the Bloody Code, and of the squirearchy's grip on all aspects of local justice, whose corollary was and needed to be the slow building-up of confidence in the proactive, professional police force founded (for London at least) in 1829. As the severity of punishment lessened somewhat, trust in the efficiency of administering it needed to grow. It was in this ideological context, arguably, that the detective hero was born.

## NOTES

1 The complex career of Wild is explored in Gerald Howson's *It Takes a Thief: The Life and Times of Jonathan Wild* (London: Cresset Library, 1987).

2 See Daniel Defoe, *The History of the Remarkable Life of John Sheppard, etc.* (1724) in George A. Aitken, ed., *Romances and Narratives by Daniel Defoe*, vol. 16 (London: Dent, 1895).

3 The term 'Newgate pastoral' was actually Swift's; see Harold Williams, ed., *The Correspondence of Jonathan Swift*, 5 vols. (Oxford: Clarendon, 1963–5), vol. 2, p. 215 (30 August 1716).

4 Henry Fielding, *Jonathan Wild* (1743), ed. David Nokes (London: Penguin, 1986), p. 30.

5 Stephen Knight, *Form and Ideology in Crime Fiction* (London and Basingstoke: Macmillan, 1980), p. 67.

6 John Gay, 'Newgate's Garland' (1724), in Vinton A. Dearing, with Charles E. Beckwith, eds., *John Gay: Poetry and Prose*, vol. 1 (Oxford: Clarendon, 1974), p. 28. The poem's authorship is sometimes contested.

7 Daniel Defoe, *Moll Flanders* (1722; Oxford: Shakespeare's Head, 1927), p. xi.

8 Henry Fielding, *Amelia*, ed. M. C. Battestin (Oxford: Clarendon, 1983), pp. 21, 22. *Amelia* was published in 1751, but internal evidence suggests that the courtroom and Newgate scenes take place in 1733.

9 Alexander Pope, *The Rape of the Lock* (1714), in Herbert Davis, ed., *Pope: Poetical works*, vol. 3 (Oxford: Oxford University Press, 1996), pp. 19–23.

10 Jonathan Swift, *Gulliver's Travels* (1726), in Louis A. Landa, ed., *Gulliver's Travels and Other Writings*, vol. 4 (Oxford: Oxford University Press, 1976), Bk. 4, Chap. 5, pp. 200–1.

11 John Gay, *The Beggar's Opera* (1728), eds. Brian Loughrey and T. O. Treadwell (London: Penguin, 1986), Act 1, Scene 1, p. 43.

12 Samuel Johnson, *London* (1738), in J. D. Fleeman ed., *The Complete English Poems* (Harmondsworth: Penguin, 1971), p. 68.

13 Johnson, *London*, ll. 15–16.

14 *The Beggar's Opera*, Act 1, Scene 1, p. 43.

15 Sir Leon Radzinowicz, *A History of English Criminal Law and its Administration from 1750: Volume 1, The Movement for Reform* (London: Stevens & Sons, 1948), p. ix.

16 Fielding, *Amelia*, p. 19.

17 Mary Wollstonecraft, *The Wrongs of Woman, or Maria* (1798), in *Mary and The Wrongs of Woman*, ed. Gary Kelly (Oxford University Press, 1980), p. 79.

# 2

LYN PYKETT

# The Newgate novel and sensation fiction, 1830–1868

Has not the delineation of crime, in every age, been the more especial and chosen thesis of the greatest masters of art . . . ? . . . In *all* the classic tragic prose fictions preceding our own age, criminals have afforded the prominent characters and crime the essential material. . . . The criminal along with the supernatural is one of the two main agencies of moral terror in literature.[1]

The Newgate[2] novel and the sensation novel were sub-genres of the literature of crime, which enjoyed a relatively brief but quite extraordinary popular success in the 1830s and 1840s and the 1860s respectively. The Newgate novel was associated exclusively with male authors. The sensation novelists, on the other hand, included a number of best-selling female authors, and this fact made for important differences of emphasis in the two sub-genres, and also for significant differences in the critical response to them. Both generated debates whose terms extended beyond the literary, and which overlapped in interesting ways. Thus, as well as being entertaining and often absorbing narratives in their own right, these novels and the controversies they engendered tell us a great deal about cultural anxieties and social and literary change at two key points in the Victorian period. Newgate novels enjoyed enormous popularity and some notoriety in the early 1830s, and generated great debate and controversy in the late 1830s and the 1840s. They looked back to the eighteenth-century literature of crime and also to the radical indictments of oppressive legal and penal systems at the turn of the eighteenth and nineteenth centuries; for example to William Godwin's *Caleb Williams* (1794) and Thomas Holcroft's *Memoirs of Bryan Perdue* (1805). Newgate fiction also exerted considerable influence on the representation of crime in the nineteenth-century novel in general, and on the development of such later genres or sub-genres as the sensation novel and the detective novel. Newgate novels were crime novels, and, in some cases historical novels, which chronicled the 'adventures and escapes of independent, courageous criminals, often legendary eighteenth-century robbers and highwaymen'.[3] Their settings ranged from castles to 'flash kens' (drinking dens frequented by thieves and other *habitués* of the criminal underworld), and they often mingled lower- and upper-class characters. According to their critics, they romanticised and glamorised crime and low life, and invited sympathy with criminals rather than with the victims of crime by making their criminal subjects the hunted object of a chase, by focusing on their motivation or psychology, and by representing them as the victims of circumstance or society. Newgate novels took their name, as they took some of their leading characters and plots, from the various versions of the *Newgate Calendar*, which, from its first appearance in 1773, satisfied the popular fascination with crime and criminals by gathering together accounts of the lives, trials, confessions, punishments and/or escapes from, or evasions of the law of celebrated criminals. Andrew Knapp and William Baldwin, the editors of the best-known nineteenth-century edition of these chronicles of crime (published in parts in the early years of the century, and then in volume form between 1824 and 1828), offered them to the public as works of moral improvement, whose purpose was to provide a 'necessary example of punishment to offenders', and 'to record examples' in order that those who are 'unhappily moved with the passion of acquiring wealth by violence, or stimulated by the heinous sin of revenge to shed the blood of a fellow creature, may have before them a picture of the torment of mind and bodily sufferings of such offenders'. This double purpose was deemed to make the *Newgate Calendar*:

> highly acceptable to all ranks and conditions of men; for we shall find, in the course of these volumes, that crime has always been followed by punishment; and that, in many circumstances, the most artful secrecy could not screen the offenders from detection, nor the utmost ingenuity shield them from the strong arm of impartial justice.[4]

It is clear, however, that much of the appeal of the various versions of the *Newgate Calendar* to their first readers derived from the way in which they made a spectacle of 'deviant' or socially transgressive behaviour, and also of the violent and public manner of the punishment of such behaviour.

If the sound and fury generated by Newgate fiction – especially in the late 1830s and 1840s – was out of all proportion to the number of novels to which the Newgate label was attached, this is partly a consequence of the literary clout (and access to the pages of the periodical press) of the main protagonists, and partly because of the cultural pervasiveness of the Newgate phenomenon through the numerous stage adaptations of the novels, and the taking up of Newgate themes in the rapidly growing penny press. The controversy about Newgate fiction was both literary and social. It was a debate about the nature and future of the novel as a literary form, and it was also a response to social upheaval and unrest at home and on the continent of Europe. As R. D. Altick points out, by 'a sweeping association of robbers and murderers with rioters and strikers, influential critics . . . found . . . the Newgate novel's romanticizing of criminals . . . inimical to public safety.'[5]

Who were the Newgate novelists and which of their works were Newgate novels? Both the Newgate novel and the Newgate novelist were to a large extent journalistic constructs. As Keith Hollingsworth observes in his authoritative history of the genre, 'we are dealing with a school defined by its contemporary critics',[6] rather than by the novelists to whose works the Newgate label was attached. Edward Bulwer (after 1843 Edward Bulwer Lytton) was the first of the Newgate novelists, and his novel *Paul Clifford*, published in 1830, the first of the Newgate novels – although the earlier *Pelham, or Adventures of a Gentleman* (1828) also has the 'Newgate' preoccupation with dissoluteness, seduction and betrayal and murder, and is partly set in the criminal underworld. Bulwer's *Eugene Aram* (1832) confirmed the Newgate trend, with its criminal hero, based on a real murderer. A couple of years later William Harrison Ainsworth entered the lists with *Rookwood* (1834), his romance about the highwayman Dick Turpin, published in the same year as Charles Whitehead's fictional *Autobiography of Jack Ketch* and his *Lives of the Highwaymen*. Charles Dickens's *Oliver Twist* (serialised in *Bentley's Miscellany* from 1837–9) was seen by contemporaries as a Newgate novel and was drawn into the centre of a new phase of the Newgate controversy in 1839–41. However, the most sensational and most popular Newgate novel was Ainsworth's tale of the housebreaker *Jack Sheppard*, also serialised in *Bentleys*. Like sensation fiction in the 1860s, Newgate fiction was subjected to satirical comment and imitation by *Punch*, and it also spawned full-length parodies, most notably Thackeray's *Catherine: A Story*, serialised in 1839–40 in *Fraser's Magazine*, a periodical which played a leading role in both naming and attacking the Newgate novel.

Given the long association of crime with the novel noted by Bulwer in the quotation at the head of this essay, and confirmed by modern historians of the origins and development of the novel,[7] and by other contributors to the present volume, what, if anything, was different about the Newgate novel and why did it generate such a controversy? I shall try to answer this question by looking briefly at the main examples of the sub-genre, before going on to explore the Newgate phenomenon in relation to some of the social and literary conditions of its production.

*Paul Clifford*, the first novel to attract the Newgate label, is an historical novel which recounts the story of a man of mysterious parentage whose apparently well-born mother dies early in his infancy leaving him in the charge of 'Mother' Lobkins, the landlady of the Mug, a 'flash ken' frequented by

London criminals and dashing highwaymen. Observing Paul's avid consumption of Newgate chronicles of highwaymen such as Dick Turpin, Mrs Lobkins diverts his literary interests by putting him to work with Peter McGrawler, editor of the 'Asinaeum', who teaches him to write 'tickling', 'slashing' or 'plastering' (i.e. flattering) reviews.[8] (This attack on the *Athenaeum* which had been critical of Bulwer's earlier attempts at fiction is the beginning of the literary wrangling and in-fighting which marked the construction and reception of the Newgate novel.) At the age of sixteen Paul is sent to the 'house of correction' for pick-pocketing, despite his innocence of the offence. Alienated from society by this injustice, and schooled in crime by his prison experience, Paul escapes, joins a band of highwaymen and becomes their leader. Subsequently, as 'Captain Clifford', Paul enters society (ostensibly to make his fortune through a calculated marriage) and falls in love with the heiress Lucy Brandon. At this point the plot becomes complicated in a manner typical of the eighteenth- and nineteenth-century novel. Lucy is also being pursued by Lord Mauleverer, assisted by her uncle – the ambitious lawyer William Brandon – whom Mauleverer helps to a judgeship. Paul joins his highwayman companions on one last exploit – to rob Mauleverer – is apprehended (after helping them to escape), and tried before Judge Brandon. Meanwhile numerous twists and turns of the plot reveal that the mysteries of Paul's parentage are connected with the murky pasts of Judge Brandon and Mauleverer and, in a thrilling climax to the trial scene, Judge Brandon learns that he is Paul's father. He is obliged to pronounce the death sentence on his newly discovered son, but subsequently commutes it to one of transportation to Australia. The novel ends with a brief account of Paul and Lucy's happy life in America where they have lived as good citizens for many years since Paul's escape from the penal colony.

Paul's career as a highwayman and his speech at his trial owe something to the *Newgate Calendars* which Bulwer read in preparation for his novel, but Paul's eloquence, his education, daring and honour make him (paradoxically perhaps) both the stuff of legend and boys' own adventures, and the vehicle of a reforming message. For this prototypical Newgate novel is also, as Louis Cazamian noted, a prototype of the Victorian 'social novel with a purpose', which addressed 'the grave problems which concerned the whole of society, discussed them in their entirety, and proposed formulas or vague aspirations for the total reform of human relations'.[9] *Paul Clifford* is, among other things, an investigation of crime and punishment, and an attack on the unreformed legal and penal code. It seeks to challenge its readers' assumptions about the nature and causes of crime and their prescriptions for punishment by demonstrating that the legal and penal systems of Clifford's day were oppressive, corrupt, inhumane and ineffective. In a Preface added in 1840, at the height of the Newgate controversy (and thus possibly a *post hoc* rationalisation and sanitisation of his aims in the light of the moral furore directed at Newgate fiction), Bulwer claimed that one of his objects in *Paul Clifford* had been 'to draw attention to two errors in our penal institutions, viz., a vicious Prison-discipline and a sanguinary Criminal Code'. It should be remembered that *Paul Clifford* looks back to a time when there were over 200 capital offences on the statute book, for crimes ranging from murder and highway robbery to sheep-stealing and impersonating a Chelsea Pensioner (an inmate of the Chelsea Royal Hospital for old or infirm soldiers), and when policing was haphazard and corrupt and prisons brutal and insanitary. It was published at a time when there had already been a twenty-year campaign for the reform of the criminal code and the prison system, and when Peel's campaigns for police reform had begun to bear fruit with the establishment of the Metropolitan Police Office in 1829. Prison reform took rather longer: it was only in 1835 that the Prison Act established inspectors of prisons on the model of the factory inspectorate.

*Paul Clifford* encourages its readers to ask, as Paul Clifford does of Lucy Brandon, 'What is Crime?' Paul's answer suggests that crime is both a social construct and the product of inequitable social conditions:

> Men embody their worst prejudices, their most evil passions, in a heterogeneous and contradictory code; and whatever breaks this code they term a crime. When they make no distinction in the penalty – that is to say, in the estimation – awarded both to murder and to a petty theft imposed on the weak will by famine, we ask nothing else to convince us that they are ignorant of the very nature of guilt, and that they make up in ferocity for the want of wisdom.[10]

If Paul is the criminal-as-victim, he is also an eloquent spokesman for social and legal reform. Thus in the speech which he makes in his own defence (felons did not have the right to a defence counsel before 1836), he attacks the system that has made him and which is about to condemn him.

> Your laws are but of two classes; the one makes criminals, the other punishes them. I have suffered by the one – I am about to perish by the other. . . . Seven years ago I was sent to the house of correction for an offence which I did not commit; I went thither, a boy who had never infringed a single law – I came forth, in a few weeks, a man who was prepared to break all laws! . . . your legislation made me what I am! and it now *destroys me, as it destroys thousands, for being what it made me*! . . . Let those whom the law protects consider it a protector; when did it ever protect *me*? When did it ever protect the poor man? The government of a state, the institutions of law, profess to provide for all those who 'obey.' Mark! A man hungers – do you feed him? He

is naked – do you clothe him? If not, you break your covenant, you drive him back to the first law of nature, and you hang him, not because he is guilty, but because you have left him naked and starving![11]

Bulwer's philosophy of circumstance and his reforming agenda owe a great deal to the utilitarian philosophy of Jeremy Bentham (who believed that if laws and institutions failed the test of efficiency and usefulness they should be abolished or changed) and to William Godwin's *Caleb Williams*, a novel of crime, pursuit and detection designed to demonstrate how the powerful tyrannise their less privileged fellows. As Patrick Brantlinger has pointed out, the novel's tendency to trivialise its reforming subject-matter may also be attributed to its Benthamite agenda, with its implication that the serious social wrongs which it represents can easily be righted.[12] However, the problem is also one of fictional form and treatment, notably Bulwer's glamorisation of his highwaymen by treating them as noble rogues, borrowing from eighteenth-century fiction and from the *Beggar's Opera*. The unevenness of tone also derives from the way in which he satirises actual public figures by portraying them as highwaymen, and from his use of his novel to wage a highly personalised form of warfare on contemporary literary figures and institutions.

When it first appeared *Paul Clifford* raised some critical eyebrows with its tendency to linger 'too long in the haunts of vice',[13] and its supposedly misguided attempt to put the blame for crime on society rather than the criminal,[14] but much of the critical fury was retrospective, gaining in force as the Newgate controversy developed. The initial critical response to Bulwer's next novel, *Eugene Aram* (1832) was more divided, but in the 1840s this book became 'a storm-center of the Newgate controversy'.[15] *Eugene Aram*, whose hero was an actual murderer who had been hanged in 1759, 'took Europe by storm'.[16] Unlike its predecessor, however, it could not justify its focus on crime and a criminal in terms of a reforming agenda. Instead *Eugene Aram* is a kind of case study of a criminal psychology, an example of that 'aesthetic rewriting of crime' which, according to Michel Foucault, occurred in the nineteenth century to produce a literature in which 'crime is glorified, because it is one of the fine arts, because it can be the work only of exceptional natures, because it reveals the monstrousness of the strong and powerful, because villainy is yet another mode of privilege . . . The great murders are not for the pedlars of petty crime.'[17]

The historical Aram was a self-taught village school-teacher who deserted his wife and seven children after conspiring with an acquaintance to kill Daniel Clarke, but was subsequently traced and tried for murder when Clarke's bones were discovered in a cave fourteen years later. Bulwer's Aram is not the humble schoolmaster of history but the more Byronic figure of the lonely scholar and enthusiast for knowledge who engages in metaphysical speculations in (sometimes) gothic landscapes. The deserted wife and children are not mentioned in Bulwer's version, and the murdered man is made to seem more deserving of his fate (he is a serial philanderer rather than the young married man of the original). Bulwer also adds a plot complication by having Aram brought to justice by a man who is not only the son of the murdered Clarke, but also the jilted lover of Madeline Lester, who is in love with the scholar. The novel ends with Aram's long, self-justificatory testament, his attempted suicide and his death.

Aram's testament as published in the original version of the novel is symptomatic of what early reviewers saw as the novel's moral ambiguity. Aram's *apologia* justifies his involvement in Clarke's murder as a rational choice undertaken to alleviate his poverty, and by 'one bold wrong' to 'purchase the power of good' (the good being the intellectual discovery he is on the brink of making). The murder is further justified on the grounds that it offers society a benefit by removing an immoral man from its midst. Unlike official social morality, Aram does not deal in moral absolutes, but in specific instances:

> In the individual instance it was easy for me to deem that I had committed no crime. I had destroyed a man, noxious to the world; with the wealth by which *he* afflicted society *I* had been the means of blessing many; in the individual consequences mankind had really gained by my deed.[18]

Such guilt as Aram displays also relates to individual consequences, notably the anguish his crime (or, more specifically, its discovery) has inflicted on Madeline and her family.

The fictional Aram's reasoning may be specious, but his calculations of the greatest happiness of the greatest number had a respectable philosophical pedigree in the early nineteenth century. Aram may fall short of the tragic grandeur with which Bulwer sought to invest him, but he clearly had the sympathy of his creator. This latter point was underlined in the Preface to the 1840 edition of the novel, in which Bulwer set his character apart from the common herd of criminals.

> The guilt of Eugene Aram is not that of a vulgar ruffian; it leads to views and considerations vitally and wholly distinct from those with which profligate knavery and brutal cruelty revolt and displease us in the literature of Newgate and the Hulks.

So great became Bulwer's desire to distance his hero from the literature of Newgate that in 1849 he made significant changes to Aram's confession and to other passages which had been interpreted as presenting a criminal in an admirable light, and added a preface which made Aram a more acceptable hero for the times. In short, from 1849 onwards, Aram was no longer guilty of premeditated murder, but was merely an accomplice in a robbery.

If *Eugene Aram* contained some gothic effects, the next of the Newgate novels, William Harrison Ainsworth's *Rookwood* (1834) was a more thoroughgoing reworking of gothic, which self-consciously sought to substitute an 'old English highwayman' for the more exotic Italian brigands favoured by Ann Radcliffe, the influential eighteenth-century writer of gothic romances,[19] in an otherwise Radcliffian mix of a family curse, a secret marriage, an inheritance plot, and a struggle between half-brothers, in such gothic settings as an old manor house and a ghastly burial ground. The old English highwayman whom Ainsworth resurrected for his romance was Dick Turpin (also horse-thief, sheep-stealer, house-breaker and occasional smuggler) who was hanged in 1739. Turpin was one of the boyhood heroes of the fictional Paul Clifford, as well as of countless actual boys, including the young Ainsworth. Turpin has little plot function in *Rookwood*, but he adds considerably to its colourfulness and raciness, not to mention its romanticisation of the criminal. Ainsworth's Turpin is a staunch advocate of the gentlemanly calling of the highwayman, and celebrates some of his illustrious predecessors in song, just as Ainsworth eulogises his hero in prose. Ainsworth's Turpin is the last of the 'knights of the road', the final flowering of that 'passionate love of enterprise' before the modern 'degeneration from the grand tobyman to the cracksman and the sneak, about whom there are no redeeming features'.[20] *Rookwood* was an enormous success with readers, going through five editions in just three years. Although several reviewers responded well to its fast-moving narrative, others disliked its representation of 'the highwayman and his slang . . . as if in themselves they had some claim to admiration'.[21] Others were unsure how to categorise it: the *Edinburgh*, which reviewed the fourth edition in 1837, was puzzled as to whether it was a romance or 'a melodrama compounded of the *Castle Spectre* and the *Newgate Calendar*'.[22]

The relatively low-key debate about the Newgate novels' moral ambivalence and unwholesome fascination with crime and low life that had been conducted in the pages of the middle-class periodical press in the early 1830s, was considerably amplified at the end of the decade by the response to two serialised novels (both illustrated by George Cruikshank), which, for part of their run, appeared side by side in the monthly magazine, *Bentley's Miscellany*. The first of these novels was Dickens's *Oliver Twist* (February 1837–April 1839), and the other was Ainsworth's *Jack Sheppard* (January 1839–February 1840), one of the most successful of all the Newgate novels. Chief among those orchestrating the campaign against these novels was William Makepeace Thackerary, who was closely associated with *Fraser's*, the monthly whose objections to the Newgate novel in the early 1830s had been, at times, indistinguishable from its personalised attacks on Bulwer. *Fraser's Magazine* serialised Thackeray's anti-Newgate novel, *Catherine: A Story* between May 1839 and February 1840, and also published essays in which he and others attacked the contemporary fascination with crime and the contemporary literature of crime.

Now that Dickens has secured a place (as far as these things are ever secure) in the English literary canon as the Shakespeare of the novel, it is salutary to recall that his novels were first written in response to, and reviewed (and sometimes dismissed) in terms of, the literary fashions of their day. Thus *Great Expectations* was first reviewed alongside Wilkie Collins's *The Woman in White* as a rather less successful example than Collins's of a sensation novel.[23] Similarly, *Oliver Twist* was read as a Newgate novel, and became caught up in (indeed was one of provocations of) the renewed Newgate controversy in the early 1840s. Dickens's writing career is, of course, a prime example of the novel's close association with crime. All of his writing, from the newspaper sketches of the 1830s (later collected as *Sketches by Boz*) to the unfinished *The Mystery of Edwin Drood* (1870), reveals a fascination with crime, criminals and prisons. The two series of *Sketches by Boz*, which appeared in 1836, repeatedly focus on criminals and low life, with curiously mixed effects: on the one hand they make a spectacle of criminality for the consumer of the tapestry of urban life, and on the other hand they serve to shock the middle-class readers into seeing aspects of city life which they would normally not encounter, or would pass by with averted gaze. 'The Prisoners' Van' and 'Criminal Courts', for example, depict young people already hardened by poverty and on the brink of a life of prostitution and thievery, while 'Seven Dials', 'Gin-Shops' and 'The Pawnbroker's Shop' all focus the reader's gaze on poor neighbourhoods often associated with crime. 'A Visit to Newgate' (especially written for inclusion in the first series of the collected *Sketches*) requires the reader to engage with what goes on inside the walls of 'this gloomy depository of the guilt and misery of London' by describing the prison's architecture and geography and providing a series of sketches of its inmates, including the Newgate tale which Boz invents for the imaginary occupant of the condemned cell.

*Oliver Twist's* Newgate credentials are evident in its re-working of elements of *Paul Clifford*. It too is the tale of an orphan of mysterious parentage, brought up in low company, and of his training as a criminal, his youthful arrest, and the struggle between the respectable and the criminal worlds for possession of him. Dickens took his criminal types and criminal scenes partly from the Newgate literature, partly from his own observation, and partly from contemporary newspaper police reports and articles on juvenile crime. Fagin also has his origins in newspaper reports of the exploits of Ikey Solomon the notorious fence and trainer of pick-pockets. Other Newgate elements include the depiction of the habitats and inhabitants of the criminal underworld. Like the other Newgate novelists Dickens was accused of representing criminals too sympathetically. Certainly, as Edmund Wilson pointed out, Dickens had a peculiar identification with the social outsider, and especially with the dark obsessions of the murderer and thief.[24] In *Oliver Twist* this can be seen in the attempt to get inside the mind of the criminal in the scenes following Sikes's brutal killing of Nancy, and in the impressionistic (almost stream of consciousness) chapter on Fagin's last night in the condemned cell in Chapter 52.

Another of Dickens's novels with Newgate connections is his historical novel *Barnaby Rudge* (1841). Among other things this is a tale of the 'No Popery!' Gordon riots of 1780, in which Newgate Prison was stormed and burned. It also spoke to and from the social unrest and disillusion of the post-reform era of the 1830s, indicating its author's ambivalent attitude to radical protest: he mocks or demonises the rioters, but there is an extraordinary energy in the writing about the attacks on the symbols of power and authority and the emptying of the condemned cells which seems to tell a different story. *Barnaby Rudge's* Newgate affinities can also be seen in its tale of the murderer, Old Rudge, who after escaping justice for many years is eventually incarcerated in Newgate, liberated by the rioters, recaptured and subsequently hanged. Another victim of the hangman (and of upper-class corruption and social inequality) is the malcontent Hugh, the bastard son of Sir John Chester and a gypsy mother who was hanged, when Hugh was in his infancy, for the crime of passing forged notes. Also hanged is Dennis the Hangman, whom Dickens represents as the corrupt instrument of an oppressive system, who cannot believe that the system he upholds can destroy him.

> When . . . [Dennis] bethought himself, how the Statute Book regarded him as a kind of Universal Medicine applicable to men, women and children, of every age and variety of criminal constitution; . . . when he recollected that whatever Ministry was in or out, he remained their peculiar pet and panacea, and that for his sake England stood single and conspicuous among the civilized nations . . . he felt certain that the national gratitude *must* relieve him from the consequences of his late proceedings, and would certainly restore him to his old place in the happy social system.[25]

In short, in *Barnaby Rudge* Dickens takes up *Paul Clifford's* theme of oppressive laws as instruments of an oppressive system.

Although *Barnaby Rudge* appeared shortly after the high point of the Newgate controversy it did not attract the Newgate label. It was *Oliver Twist* that took the full force of the attack that was unleashed on the Newgate novel following the publication of *Jack Sheppard*, one of the great popular successes of 1839. Ainsworth's romance sold 300 copies a week when it was first issued in volume form, and was immediately adapted for the stage; by the end of 1839 there were eight versions showing at various London theatres. The historical Jack Sheppard was a carpenter's apprentice who, after a brief life of petty crime, arrests (once by the notorious thieftaker Jonathan Wild), and daring escapes, was hanged in 1724 at the age of twenty-one. Sheppard was one of the legendary criminals of his day, and Ainsworth renewed that legend for the nineteenth century. *Jack Sheppard*, which is divided into three 'epochs' (1703, 1715, and 1724), is 'a sort of Hogarthian novel',[26] the tale of one idle and one industrious apprentice – Jack Sheppard and Thames Darrell – both apprenticed to a London carpenter. The extremely complicated plot involves a true heir (Thames) being kept from his inheritance by a scheming relative and his accomplice Jonathan Wild. After various adventures in which Thames never strays from the path of righteousness, he is revealed to be a marquis and marries the carpenter's daughter. Jack, on the other hand, embarks on his criminal career, and the climax of the narrative is his progress from Newgate to his public execution (amidst riotous scenes) at Tyburn. Throughout the novel Jack is presented very sympathetically. He remains loyal to Darrell and risks his life in assisting him against Wild's machinations. His crimes are skipped over whereas his daring escapes are dwelled on in exciting detail. The criminality of Jack's behaviour is acquired, but his nobility of character is innate: it derives from his mother – to whom he is admirably devoted – and who is discovered to have been well-born. Several explanations have been offered for *Jack Sheppard*'s success. Perhaps it offered its readers a safe (and historically distanced) opportunity to identify with a social outsider in the era of Chartism. Alternatively it might be seen as a post-reform tale of an unreformed legal and penal system, which allowed readers to identify with a boys' own adventurer seeking to outwit a corrupt and oppressive *ancien régime*.

Whatever the reasons for its popularity, this novel certainly re-ignited the Newgate controversy. Even before it had completed its serial run *Jack Sheppard* was attacked by the *Athenaeum* as 'a bad book, and what is worse . . . one of a class of bad books, got up for a bad public'. It is 'a history of vulgar and disgusting atrocities'; 'a melodramatic story of motiveless crime and impossible folly, connected with personages of high degree'; and, perhaps worse still, 'an attempt is made to invest Sheppard with good qualities, which are incompatible with his character and position'.[27] Essentially the *Athenaeum* objected to what it (and other critics) saw as the Newgate novels' inappropriate hybridity, or mixing together of what would be better kept separate. Thus, critics of Newgate fiction deplored its mixing of high- and low-life characters, and the combining of high- and low-class characteristics in a single character. They objected to mixed motives and mixed morality, preferring the security of a moral universe in which the good and bad, the criminal and the law abiding are readily identifiable as such. Mixed genres and modes of representation were also deemed suspect. By 1841 *Punch* was turning the notion of the Newgate novel as an unwholesome mixture into a joke with which to beat both *Jack Sheppard* and *Oliver Twist*, in its 'Literary Recipe' for 'A STARTLING ROMANCE'.

> Take a small boy, charity, factory, carpenter's apprentice, or otherwise, as occasion may serve – stew him down in vice – garnish largely with oaths and flash songs – Boil him in a cauldron of crime and improbabilities. Season equally with good and bad qualities . . . petty larceny, affection, benevolence, and burglary, honour and housebreaking, amiability and arson . . . Stew down a mad mother – a gang of robbers – several pistols – a bloody knife. Serve up with a couple of murders – and season with a hanging-match.
>
> N.B. alter the ingredients to a beadle and a workhouse – the scenes may be the same, but the whole flavour of vice will be lost, and the boy will turn out a perfect pattern. – Strongly recommended for weak stomachs.[28]

As already noted, one of the most concerted attacks in this phase of the Newgate controversy came from Thackeray, whose *Catherine: A Story* was written specifically – according to the advertisement that accompanied volume publication – 'to counteract the injurious influence of some popular fictions of that day, which made heroes of highwaymen and burglars, and created a false sympathy for the vicious and criminal'. Like many Newgate novels, this anti-Newgate work takes the form of an historical novel: it is set in the 'the glorious reign of Queen Anne' when 'there existed certain characters, and befell a series of adventures' which merit fictional treatment, 'since they are strictly in accordance with the present fashionable style and taste . . . have been already partly described in the "Newgate Calendar"' and are *'agreeably low, delightfully disgusting, and at the same time eminently pleasing and pathetic'*.[29] Thackeray's story of Catherine Hayes, who conspired with others to murder her husband (and was burned alive at Tyburn in 1726), is indeed taken from the *Newgate Calendar*. However, notwithstanding his conviction that since the 'public will hear of nothing but rogues . . . poor authors, who must live, . . . [should] paint such thieves as they are: not dandy, poetical, rosewater thieves; but real downright scoundrels, leading scoundrelly lives, drunken, profligate, dissolute, low; as scoundrels will be',[30] Thackeray's depiction of his villainess is rather sympathetic. It would appear that even the anti-Newgate novel cannot avoid the mixed feelings of the genre which it seeks to parody.

The Newgate controversy as it developed in the 1840s was in part a debate about what could and could not (or *should* and *should not*) be represented in the novel, and about what *forms* or *modes* of representation were appropriate to the novel. It was a debate about the changing nature and status of the novel, and its relationship with what Thackeray called the 'middling classes' and to other cultural forms, and it was also a contest about fictional *realism*. In *Catherine* and in other *Fraser's* pieces, Thackeray attacked the Newgate writers for misleading the 'middling classes' because 'they are not writing from knowledge and experience', and also because they 'dare not tell the *whole* truth' about their low-life characters: 'ruffians whose occupations are thievery, murder, and prostitution.'[31]

> What figments these novelists tell us! Boz, who knows life well, knows that his Miss Nancy is the most unreal fantastical personage possible; no more like a thief's mistress than one of Gessner's shepherdesses resembles a real country wench. He dare not tell the truth concerning such young ladies . . . Not being able to paint the whole portrait, he has no right to present one or two favourable points as characterizing the whole; and therefore, in fact, had better leave the picture alone altogether.'[32]

In the Preface to the 1841 edition of *Oliver Twist*, written in response to Thackeray's attack, Dickens defended his practice in terms of both verisimilitude and social utility. First, he asserted that Nancy was '[s]uggested to my mind long ago – long before I dealt in fiction – by what I often saw and read of, in actual life around me, I have for years, tracked it through many profligate and noisome ways'. Quite simply the representation of 'the conduct and character of the girl . . . IS TRUE.' Secondly, he claimed that his painting of 'such associates in crime as really do exist . . . in all their deformity . . . as they really are' was something 'which would be of service to society'.

As the last remark indicates, the Newgate debate was also a debate about the influence of fiction. From *Paul Clifford* onwards, reviewers had been concerned about the effects on middle-class readers (and on the lower-class audiences of stage adaptations) of becoming sympathetically involved with the doings of noble highwaymen, sentimental burglars, and whores with hearts of gold. Bulwer, for example, wrote dismissively of journalistic talk about the 'weak minds of circulating library readers' and 'the young and impressionable'.[33] This aspect of the debate was fuelled by the case of Benjamin Courvoisier, a twenty-three-year-old valet who was hanged for cutting his master's throat, and who claimed (or so it was reported) that he was prompted to do so by his reading of *Jack Sheppard*. (Courvoisier was the man whom Thackeray was going to see hanged in the essay quoted earlier.)

The Newgate debate was also a debate about hierarchies, both social and literary. It was about keeping the different classes of society separate both in fiction and as readers of fiction. One of the objections to the Newgate novel was that it imported the literature of the streets (popular ballads, and broadsheets gallows confessions) to the drawing room, and it is worth noting that the intensification of the Newgate controversy in the 1840s coincided with the extraordinary success of cheap publications such as W. G. Reynolds's long-running novel series *The Mysteries of London*, which combined romanticised criminals and a carnivalised low life with contemporary political debates and radical sentiment. Like the sensation debate twenty years later, the Newgate controversy was a contest over the nature of the novel and its position in the hierarchy of cultural production in an age of increasing literacy and proliferation of print forms. This is evident in 'A Word to the Public', the polemic Bulwer attached in 1847 to *Lucretia* (1846), his 'arsenical' novel based on the story of Thomas Griffiths Wainewright (1794–1847), artist, forger and poisoner, which continued the Newgate controversy. Bulwer's stance was partly that of the professional writer competing in the cultural marketplace with the popular theatre and the newspaper press, and partly that of the novelist claiming a place for his chosen form in the literary hierarchy. Bulwer was particularly anxious about the competition from newspapers, asserting the superior moral and psychological complexity of fiction, and deriding the hypocrisy that deplored in the novel what was freely represented in the pages of the daily and weekly press.

> The essential characteristic of this age and land is *publicity*. There exists a press which bares at once to the universal eye every example of guilt that comes before a legal tribunal. In these very newspapers which would forbid a romance writer to depict crime with all that he can suggest to demonstrate its causes, portray its hideousness, insist on its inevitable doom . . . the meanest secrets of the prison-house are explored. To find the true literature of Newgate and Tyburn, you have only to open the newspaper on your table.[34]

In the 1860s the sensation novel and the sensation debate were also closely intertwined with developments in the newspaper press. The growth of cheap newspapers following the abolition of the stamp tax on newspapers in 1855, and the tendency of both the expanding penny press and the middle-class newspapers to include more crime reporting was one factor in the creation of the market for sensation novels. Real life crime, as reported in contemporary newspapers rather than the *Newgate Calendars* also provided the plots for sensation novels.[35] These ranged from notorious murder trials such as the Road Murder (1860), in which the sixteen-year-old Constance Kent was acquitted of the bloody murder of her four-year-old brother, and the 1857 trial of Madeline Smith, who was accused of killing her lover by putting arsenic in his cocoa, to the Yelverton bigamy-divorce trial which drew attention to marital irregularities and the chaotic state of the marriage laws. The changing state of upper and middle-class marriage was also highlighted by the reporting of the proceedings of the new Divorce Court, created after the passing of the Matrimonial Causes Act of 1857. In the late 1850s the newspapers were also full of sensational stories of the great social evil of prostitution, and scandals of wrongful imprisonment in lunatic asylums. All of these things found their way into the plots of sensation novels.

Most twentieth-century commentators have claimed Wilkie Collins's *The Woman in White* (which began its serialisation in Dickens's magazine *All the Year Round* in November 1859) as the first true sensation novel. However, Margaret Oliphant uses the term 'sensation' in a review in *Blackwoods* in May 1855, when, writing of *Antonina* (1850), *Basil* (1852), and *Hide and Seek* (1854), she notes that the '"sensation," which it is the design of Mr. Wilkie Collins to raise in our monotonous bosom, is – horror'.[36] Ellen (Mrs Henry) Wood's *East Lynne*, serialised in the *New Monthly Magazine* (January 1860 to September 1861) was labelled 'sensational' in the *Sixpenny Magazine* in September 1861. Dickens's *Great Expectations*, published in *All The Year Round* from December 1860 to August 1861, was also reviewed as a sensation novel, but its stories of Molly the murderess and Magwitch, the transported convict who is eventually hanged, have more in common with the Newgate novel. One of the most successful of all sensation novels was Mary Elizabeth Braddon's *Lady Audley's Secret* (1861–2),[37] a tale of a scheming bigamist, and arsonist. Braddon went on to produce numerous sensation novels throughout the 1860s, alternating them with what she saw as more serious attempts at the art of fiction. Rhoda Broughton, 'Ouida' (Marie Louise de la Ramée) and Charles Reade all wrote novels which received the 'sensational' tag, and George Eliot, Anthony Trollope and Thomas Hardy also imitated aspects of sensationalism, as did countless other writers who have totally disappeared from critical view.[38]

Like the Newgate novel, the sensation genre was a journalistic construct, a label attached by reviewers to novels whose plots centred on criminal deeds, or social transgressions and illicit passions, and which 'preached to the nerves'.[39] Sensation novels were tales of modern life that dealt in nervous, psychological, sexual and social shocks, and had complicated plots involving bigamy, adultery, seduction, fraud, forgery, blackmail, kidnapping and, sometimes, murder. It will be evident from this description that many of the novels of the 1840s and 1850s (including *Jane Eyre, The Tenant of Wildfell*

*Hall*, *Dombey and Son*, and *Bleak House*) would have been labelled sensation novels if they had appeared in the 1860s. It is also clear that sensation plots and methods to some extent overlap with those of the Newgate novel. One of the main differences between them was that sensation fiction dealt with upper- and middle-class crime and transgression in a modern (rather than an historical) setting. In the sensation novel the scene of the crime was more likely to be the home than the road, the drawing room rather than the drinking den. The sensation novel did not depict the criminal underworld, but rather it explored the dark underside of respectable society: the family is the locus of crime, and the secrets of the family are responsible for most of the plot complications, and in most cases crime and punishment circulates entirely within the family. Although the law court was the source of many sensation plots, sensation novels do not end in the courtroom or the prison. Crime is dealt with in and by the family. For example, in *The Woman in White* Walter Hartright and his sister-in-law, Marian Halcombe have to become detectives in order to right various wrongs without the formal assistance of the law, which is 'still . . . the pre-engaged servant of the long purse'.[40] Braddon's bigamous and murderous Lady Audley is never formally accused of any crime, and is sentenced to death-by-boredom in a Belgian *maison de santé* by her nephew Robert, who detects her crimes and acts as both jury and judge in determining her guilt and fixing her punishment. Although a famous detective policeman is involved in *The Moonstone*, Cuff, the professional detective, fails to solve the case of the theft of the diamond; the solution of the crime is effected by the members of the family in which it occurred, and the criminal is punished by the original owners of this twice-stolen stone.

One of the more important differences between sensation fiction and the Newgate novel is the shift of focus from crime to detection. This change of emphasis may be linked to changes in policing such as the formation of the new Detective Police in 1842, and the development, in the wake of the new divorce laws, of an army of private detectives, those confidential spies of modern times (referred to in Collins's *Armadale*), who were charged with rooting out the secrets of the family. It may also be the result of a change in the cultural meaning of crime and the criminal, and a movement from a society controlled by the spectacle of punishment to one morally managed by discipline. By the 1860s crime was no longer perceived as constituting a world of its own, 'one that invertedly mirrored the respectable world'.[41] Rather crime was now seen as an integral part of the respectable world, and it was often represented in sensation novels as a particularly individualistic form of the Victorian doctrine of self-help. A world in which everyone was potentially a criminal was a world of universal suspicion in which everyone became a detective or a suspect, hence the 'detective fever' of *The Moonstone*. As D. A. Miller has argued (following Foucault), such a society was a surveillance society, one in which citizens learned to police each other and themselves.[42] The sensation novel's preaching to the nerves, what Ann Cvetkovich denotes as an 'economy of sensation', is part of this 'hermeneutics of suspicion', in which 'every fact that excites a sensation merits investigation'.[43] The sensation novel was thus a means of both articulating and managing the universal suspicion on which modern urban society was founded.

If one particularly striking difference between the sensation novel and its Newgate predecessors was the greater prominence given to female criminals, another was the sensation novel's development of the female (amateur) detective. Marian Halcombe in Collins's *The Woman in White* is the first of several female protagonists in sensation novels who escape the restrictions of what Marian describes as 'petticoat existence' to hunt out male wrongdoings and seek to right both private and social wrongs. Magdalen Vanstone, the heroine of *No Name* (1862), becomes a kind of detective in order to hunt out the secrets of her family and to strike back against the 'cruel law' which renders her and her sister illegitimate, and deprives them of their right to their father's property. Mary Elizabeth Braddon's Eleanor Vane (*Eleanor's Victory*, 1863) and Jenny Milsom (*Run To Earth*, 1868) both turn detective in order to solve and avenge the mysterious deaths of their respective fathers.

The sensation novel and the sensation debate, like the Newgate phenomenon before them, were also part of a contest about literary and social hierarchies, about the cultural status of the novel, the influence of fiction, and about realism. Opponents of the sensation novel objected to its mixed characters, moral ambiguity, and mixed feelings – in short, to the ways in which the plots and narrative methods of sensation novels repeatedly put their readers in the position of having to suspend or revise moral judgements. Reviewers were also concerned about mixed readerships. W. Fraser Rae, for example, was less perturbed by the content of Mary Elizabeth Braddon's novels than by their promiscuous readership:

> Others before her have written stories of blood and lust, of atrocious crimes and hardened criminals, and these have excited the interest of a very wide circle of readers. But the class that welcomed them was the lowest in the social scale, as well as in mental capacity. To Miss Braddon belongs the credit of having . . . *temporarily succeeded in making the literature of the Kitchen the favourite reading of the Drawing room*.[44]

The sensation novel's relationship with the newspaper press was also a source of critical anxiety. Sensation novels were often described as 'newspaper novels', in which 'the England of today's newspapers crops up at every step'.[45]

Critics of sensation fiction, like the Newgate critics, were also concerned about the injurious effects on the young and on women of reading these 'thrilling' novels. However, their main fear seems not to have been that sensation novels would lead their readers into a life of crime, but that their excitements would produce moral and social disorder by 'willingly and designedly draw[ing] a picture of life which . . . make[s] reality insipid and the routine of ordinary existence intolerable to the imagination'.[46] As far as reality and realism were concerned, the objection to the sensation novel was not that its authors did not know enough about their 'unpleasant' subjects, nor that they were afraid to represent them in their entirety (as Thackeray claimed of the Newgate writers), rather they were accused of knowing too much (especially if they were women), and of failing to draw the veil over what would be better left unrepresented in fiction. Thus Henry James remarked that Mary Elizabeth Braddon knows 'much that ladies are not accustomed to know',[47] and Margaret Oliphant objected to the 'openness' with which women novelists represent the feelings and physical desires of their female characters.[48] However, despite their supposedly greater explicitness, sensation novelists were, like the Newgate novelists, accused of being unrealistic. This time the charge was not that they glamorised villainy, but rather that they presented an exaggerated version of the modern world. Thus Oliphant observed that while modern life 'no doubt . . . has great crimes, calamities, and mysteries hidden in its bosom', anyone judging modern life by Collins's fiction 'will form a very inadequate opinion' of it.[49] Like Bulwer before them, however, the sensation novelists only had to turn to the newspapers in order to validate their own claims to reality of presentation. Indeed, as a recent critic has argued, sensation fiction could claim to be '*more* "real" than realism', not only because of its 'connection to actual events', but also because it could 'undercut realist fiction's claim to superior truthfulness by exposing the very artificiality of its conventions'[50] – through its self-conscious plotting, its use of the conventions of romance and melodrama, its fragmented narrative with multiple narrators (Collins), or its direct addresses to the reader (Braddon and Wood).

Like Newgate novels, sensation fiction was seen by many contemporary critics as both a symptom and cause of social corruption. The products of a depraved public taste, they corrupted the public appetite by feeding it. They were both seen, to use the phrase Thackeray applied to Newgate novels, as 'absolute drugs on the literary market'.[51] Critical fulminations about the corruption of public taste masked more fundamental concerns about the ways in which these two examples of the nineteenth-century literature of crime appeared to challenge the ideological, aesthetic, and moral orthodoxies of their day. Newgate and sensation fiction, and the furore that they provoked, provide interesting examples of cultural appropriation and the blurring of the boundaries between high and low culture during the extended process of the birth of a modern mass media. Moreover, it is not entirely coincidental that each emerged in a decade of reform debate and agitation. Both Newgate and sensation novels were preoccupied with the changing relations between classes and changing legal and social structures, and often (though by no means uniformly) pointed to the need for further change.

## NOTES

1 Edward Bulwer Lytton, 'A Word to the Public', in *Lucretia* (1846), reprinted in Juliet John, ed., *Cult Criminals: The Newgate Novels, 1830–47*, 6 vols. (London: Routledge, Thoemmes, 1998), vol. 3, p. 305. All references to Bulwer's novels are to this reprint series.

2 So named after the main prison for condemned criminals in eighteenth- and early nineteenth-century London. See Chap. 1, pp. 7–8, for a fuller discussion of the term.

3 Beth Kalikoff, *Murder and Moral Decay in Victorian Popular Literature* (Ann Arbor: UMI Research Press, 1987), p.35.

4 Andrew Knapp and William Baldwin, eds., *The Newgate Calendar; comprising interesting memoirs of the most notorious characters who have been convicted of outrages on the laws of England, etc.*, 4 vols. (London: J. Robins & Co., 1824–8), vol. 1, p. iv.

5 R. D. Altick, *Victorian Studies in Scarlet: Murders and Manners in the Age of Victoria* (London: Dent, 1972), p. 73.

6 Keith Hollingsworth, *The Newgate Novel, 1830–1847: Bulwer, Ainsworth, Dickens and Thackeray* (Detroit: Wayne State University Press, 1963), p. 14.

7 See, for example, Lennard Davis, *Factual Fictions: The Origins of the English Novel*, (New York: Columbia University Press, 1983).

8 Edward Bulwer, *Paul Clifford* (1830), Chap. 5, in John, ed., *Cult Criminals*.

9 Louis Cazamian, *The Social Novel in England, 1830–1850: Dickens, Disraeli, Mrs Gaskell, Kingsley* (1904), translated, with a foreword, by Martin Fido (London: Routledge & Kegan Paul, 1973), p. 4.

10 Bulwer, *Paul Clifford*, Bk. 2, Chap. 6, reprinted in John ed., *Cult Criminals*, vol. i, p. 226.

11 *Ibid.*, Bk. 3, Chap. 3 reprinted in John, ed., *Cult Criminals*, vol. 1, pp. 443–4.

12 Patrick Brantlinger, *The Spirit of Reform: British Literature and Politics, 1832–67* (Cambridge, MA: Harvard University Press, 1977), 35–8.

13 'Mr Bulwer's Novels – *Eugene Aram*', *Edinburgh Review*, 55 (1832), 208–19, at 212.

14 'Mr Edward Lytton Bulwer's Novels; and Remarks on Novel-writing', *Fraser's Magazine*, 1 (1830), 509–32, at 530.

15 Hollingsworth, *The Newgate Novel*, p. 82.

16 Michael Sadleir, *Bulwer and his Wife: A Panorama, 1803–1836* (London: Constable, 1933), p. 245.

17 Michel Foucault, *Discipline and Punish: The Birth of the Prison* translated from the French by Alan Sheridan (Harmondsworth: Penguin, 1979), pp. 67–8.

18 Edward Bulwer Lytton, *Eugene Aram* (1832), Bk. 5, Chap. 7, reprinted in John, ed., *Cult Criminals*, vol. 2, p. 416.

19 William Harrison Ainsworth, 'Preface' to the 1849 edition of *Rookwood*.

20 William Harrison Ainsworth, *Rookwood*, Author's Copyright Edition (London: George Routledge, n.d.), Bk. 3, Chap. 5, p. 184. The 'tobyman' or highwayman was a bolder and more dashing criminal than the 'cracksman' (house-breaker) or sneak thief.

21 *Examiner*, 18 May 1834, p. 308.

22 'Recent English Romances', *Edinburgh Review*, 65 (1837), 195.

23 Margaret Oliphant, 'Sensation Novels', *Blackwood's*, 91 (1862), 564–84.

24 Edmund Wilson, 'Dickens: the Two Scrooges', in *The Wound and the Bow: Seven Studies in Literature* (1941; London: Methuen, 1961), pp. 1–93.

25 Charles Dickens, *Barnaby Rudge* (1841; London: Chapman & Hall undated), Chap. 74, pp. 698–9.

26 William Harrison Ainsworth, letter in S. M. Ellis, *William Harrison Ainsworth and His Friends* (London: John Lane, 1911), p. 328.

27 *The Athenaeum*, 26 October 1839, p. 803.

28 *Punch*, 7 August 1841, p. 39.

29 William Thackeray, *Catherine: A Story*, Chap. 1 (emphasis added).

30 *Ibid.*, Chap. 3.

31 'Horae Catnachianae: a Dissertation upon Ballads', *Fraser's* 19 (1839), 407–24, and 'Another Last Chapter', in the serial version of *Catherine*, *Fraser's* 21 (1840), 202–12. James Catnach was a publisher whose 'Seven Bards of Seven Dials' kept the penny-public well supplied with chapbooks, ballads and broadsides on murders, executions and other interesting matters in the 1840s. See R. D. Altick, *The English Common Reader: A Social History of the Mass Reading Public, 1800–1900* (1957; Ohio State University Press, 1998), p. 287.

32 'Going to See a Man Hanged' *Fraser's* 22 (1840), 150–8.

33 Bulwer, 'A Word to the Public', p. 308.

34 *Ibid.*, p. 314.

35 Wilkie Collins's *The Moonstone* is an exception to this general rule, as its plot seems to have been inspired by Collins's reading of the account of a late-eighteenth century case in Maurice Mejan's *Recueil des causes célèbres* (1808), which he discovered on a Paris bookstall in 1856.

36 Margaret Oliphant, 'Modern Novelists – Great and Small', *Blackwood's*, 77 (1855), 554–68, at 566.

37 *Lady Audley's Secret* began life as a weekly serial in *Robin Goodfellow*, which closed thirteen weeks into the novel's run in September 1861. It re-ran in the *Sixpenny Magazine* from January to December 1862, and was published in volume form by Tinsley in 1862. From March to August 1863 it was re-serialised in twenty-two weekly parts in the *London Journal*.

38 Margot McCarthy has recently identified 180 works of fiction which were reviewed as sensation novels in just two periodicals, *The Athenaeum* and the *Saturday Review*, in the 1860s and 1870s. See M. McCarthy, 'The Construction of Identity in Victorian Sensation Fiction' (DPhil. thesis, University of Oxford, 2000).

39 Quoted in H. L. Mansel, 'Sensation novels', *Quarterly Review* 133 (1863), 481–514, at 482.

40 Wilkie Collins, *The Woman in White* (Harmondsworth: Penguin, 1974), Preamble, p. 33.
41 Martin Wiener, *Reconstructing the Criminal: Culture, Law and Policy in England, 1830–1914* (Cambridge University Press, 1990), p. 20.
42 D. A. Miller, *The Novel and the Police* (Berkeley: University of California Press, 1988).
43 Ann Cvetkovich, *Mixed Feelings: Feminism, Mass Culture and Victorian Sensationalism* (New Brunswick, NJ: Rutgers University Press), p. 74.
44 W. Fraser Rae, 'Sensation Novelists: Miss Braddon', *North British Review* 43 (1865), 180–204, at 204, emphasis added.
45 Henry James, 'Miss Braddon', *The Nation*, 9 November 1864, pp. 593–5, p. 594.
46 'Our Female Sensation Novelists', *Christian Remembrancer* 46 (1863), 209–36, at 212.
47 James, 'Miss Braddon', p. 594.
48 Margaret Oliphant, 'Novels', *Blackwood's*, 102 (1867), 257–80, at 209.
49 Oliphant, 'Modern Novelists – Great and Small', p. 567.
50 Mary Elizabeth Braddon, *Aurora Floyd* (1868), ed. and intro. Richard Nemesvari and Lisa Surridge (Peterborough, Ontario: Broadview Press, 1998), p. 15.
51 Quoted in Hollingsworth, *The Newgate Novel* p. 149.

# 3

MARTIN A. KAYMAN

# The short story from Poe to Chesterton

Just as it is possible to expand the idea of detective fiction back to episodes in the Bible, oriental tales, and folk riddles,[1] so too the short story can be dissolved into any form of brief tale. But, as Walter Allen suggests, the emergence of the nineteenth-century short story is, precisely, a *modern* phenomenon.[2] By the same token, the appearance of a new and modern kind of protagonist from the mid-nineteenth century, who has come to be called 'the detective', marks a distinction from earlier mysteries. In both cases, Edgar Allan Poe plays a crucial innovative role.

While the form initiated by Nathaniel Hawthorne's *Twice-Told Tales* (1837) and Poe's *Tales of the Grotesque and Arabesque* (1840) flourished in America, the short story failed to make as great an impression in Britain until the end of the century, held back by the success of the three-decker or serialised novel. However, when it did take off, this was in no small part due to the success of Arthur Conan Doyle's detective stories in George Newnes's *Strand Magazine* (founded in 1891).

The destinies of both the short story and the detective story were, then, closely related to the history of magazine publication in each country. These followed different rhythms, but, in the magazines aimed at the general public, works of fiction, literary or popular, were to be found, in varying proportions, alongside texts dealing with history and biography, travel and adventure, and information on contemporary society and public affairs. In Britain it was particularly the latter, as in George Newnes's first successful enterprise, *Tit-bits* (1881), which dominated the popular market, juxtaposing fragmented selections of events from the contemporary world as a form of amusement for the mass public.

The British literary short story of the end of the century shared this interest in contemporary social reality. The naturalist work of authors like Arnold Bennett and H. G. Wells was close in style and concerns to the new journalism.[3] Likewise, Arthur Morrison, author of literary naturalist works like *A Child of the Jago* (1896), was also responsible for the Martin Hewitt detective stories (1894–6). By the same token, many detectives, like Hewitt himself, have journalists as their chroniclers and/or assistants and, throughout the genre, newspaper reports provide vital sources of information about crimes. So the relation between the detective story and journalism is not simply one of contiguity on the pages of the new popular magazines. As Clive Bloom has pointed out, the detective story is 'the only fiction that *insists* it is dealing with facts'.[4]

To begin with, the first 'detective stories' to style themselves as such consisted in purportedly real accounts or memoirs. The earliest literary application of the epithet occurs in 1850 with Charles Dickens's 'Three "Detective" Anecdotes', one of a series of articles reporting the activities of real London detectives as observed by the journalist himself for *Household Words*.[5] More importantly, the 1850s also initiated what Ellery Queen calls a 'flood of detective "reminiscences"', written by supposedly real officers, such as Thomas Waters, James McGovan and James McLevy.[6]

Although authors like 'Waters' (ghosted by the journalist William Russell) lay claim to the title of 'detective', and may pretend to peculiar Dupin-like acumen, these are generally stories of the chase. Nonetheless, Waters combats contemporary prejudices against detectives as vulgar spies who threatened privacy and liberty, by making police detection a gentlemanly profession. He joined the force after being robbed of his independence by a gambling fraud, which becomes his first case, thereby turning personal revenge into public service. He enjoys considerable autonomy and respect from his chief. However, despite his superior class and intelligence, he actually catches criminals through the traditional means of following, spying on and deceiving his prey, backed by an uncanny accuracy of suspicion and the invaluable aid of Providence. In the context of popular anxieties about the force, a significant contribution of these tales is, then, to align the detective as an agent of Providence as much in the vindication of the falsely accused as in the punishment of villains.

The insistence that the story is dealing with facts also constitutes, in a narratological sense, the fundamental structure of the more classic puzzle-solving 'detective' genre, in that the test the story sets itself is that the tale the detective eventually tells does correspond to the fragmentary 'facts' which the narrator has displayed objectively before us as the brute material of the world.

Curiously, a similar insistence extends to the internal history of the genre, and is key to Doyle's resurrection of Poe as his precursor when, in *A Study in Scarlet* (1887), Holmes compares himself to Dupin and Lecoq, treating them as really existing historical figures.[7] Doyle's success in presenting fiction as fact is apparent both in the remarkable status of Sherlock Holmes himself in the popular imagination and the extent to which Holmes's London has established itself as a stereotypical vision of Victorian London.

This, again, is not incidental. Nineteenth-century detection's concern with the city is another significant aspect of its modernity. Indeed, G. K. Chesterton claimed that 'The first essential value of the detective story lies in this, that it is the earliest and only form of popular literature in which is expressed some sense of the poetry of modern life', by which he means 'the poetry of London', an urban text of histories and meanings waiting to be read.[8] Chesterton exemplifies this theory in the very first Father Brown story, 'The Blue Cross' (*The Innocence of Father Brown*, 1911), but rarely elsewhere, and while most detectives have offices in the city, a great many of their cases do seem to occur in country houses; what is important here, as, no doubt, for the suburban commuters who formed a large part of the magazine readership, is the sense of connection to contemporary urban reality.

With the growing urban centres linked by rail and telegraph, the popular magazines operated as a medium for advertising designed to build a national market for consumer goods (albeit with different intensities in the USA and Britain).[9] The connection between the magazine as a medium for the detective story and for the modern culture of consumption is often thematised both in the crucial role played by the railway and telegraph systems themselves and in the presence of (usually false or entrapping) adverts, fraudulent commercial or financial schemes, and retail theft. That is not always the case, and detective stories are divided between those, most frequently American, set in the world of industry and finance, and those which dwell on the family and the home. With British stories in particular, the public dimension is often provided by the trace of Empire – the precious stone brought back from India, the missing brother or wife who returns from Australia, or the crime committed in the past in America.

The fact that the detective story is a product of the emergent magazine culture and the economy it promoted supports Martin Priestman's emphasis on the Holmesian detective story as a *series*.[10] In contrast to the serial publication of long novels, here each tale is self-contained, the detective's solution providing full narrative satisfaction, but so managed as to stimulate an appetite for another, similar story – so much so that, notoriously, popular demand and apparently irresistible commercial pressures made it impossible for Doyle to kill Holmes off as he wished in 1893. As Priestman also argues, the structure of the series is reproduced in the epistemology of the stories themselves, where (bearing in mind the experience of *Tit-bits*) all singular fragments and events are finally shown to be connected in a coherent linear series and to add up to a meaningful and reassuring picture of social order – or, as Jacques Futrelle's 'Thinking Machine' detective, Professor S. F. X. Van

Dusen (1906–7), repeatedly declares: 'Two and two make four, not *some* times but *all* the time.'[11]

Considering the detective short story in terms of series highlights its principal agent of coherence: the figure of the protagonist. This is what 'brands' the particular commodity on offer. Yet, although most of the heroes of detective fiction are distinguished by some personal eccentricity, they are not exactly 'characters' in the customary literary-realist sense. Rather, they are identified by their methodologies or approaches. This brings us to another definitively modern urban phenomenon: the police.

Because the appearance of Poe's short stories coincides with the creation of the 'Detective Department' of the Metropolitan Police (1842), detective fiction is seen by many critics as a literary reflection of, if not propaganda for, a new form of social administration and control based on state surveillance. As I suggested in relation to Waters, making the detective a sympathetic and respectable hero can be seen as assuaging concerns about growing state power, a fear represented by the French system – a presence from the Prefect in Poe's Dupin tales through to Robert Barr's ironic treatment of the theme in *The Triumphs of Eugène Valmont* (1906).[12] In this sense, detective stories are open to the charge of being fictional promotions of the values of the modern police discipline, defending bourgeois property values, sexual morality and bureaucratic rationalities. However, the simultaneous creation of 'the detective story' and 'the Detective Department' does not necessarily condemn Poe's fiction to being an ideological counterpart.

Likewise, viewing Poe, as Dorothy Sayers typically does, primarily as a repository of situations and devices exploited by later writers narrows the way in which the tales are read.[13] If one looks at the Dupin series without such retrospective preconceptions, one might wonder to what extent they really are about crime and detection (a word Poe does not use, preferring 'analysis'). 'The Murders in the Rue Morgue' (1841), so often cited as the first 'detective story', does not, strictly speaking, concern a murder at all: the entire mistake of the police (and the reader) was to look for a human agent for an act of violence that, as Dupin reveals, could only have been committed by a ferocious animal. The question of crime is moot in a different way in 'The Purloined Letter' (1845), where Dupin steals back a letter the Minister, an old personal enemy, had taken from the Queen. The existence of this letter is, apparently, evidence of her disloyalty to her husband, which the Minister had been using to blackmail her politically. We only really find what looks like an unambiguous crime in the least cited of Dupin's cases, 'The Mystery of Marie Rogêt' (1842), where Poe tries to solve the mystery of the actual disappearance of Mary Rogers, transposed from New York to Paris. But even here the likelihood is that the young woman was not murdered as Dupin and the authorities had originally suspected, but died undergoing an abortion.[14] In other words, the closest we get to straightforward crime is the case Dupin fails to solve and which contributes least to the genre.

Similarly, Dupin has no particular concern with upholding justice or the social order. Rather, he is a recluse of obscure, nocturnal and bookish habits. Although not averse to receiving rewards (or pursuing personal debt or revenge), he is motivated by the specific intellectual problem, rather than by social or ethical values. It is not just that the narrator informs us that he recounts the story of the Rue Morgue primarily to illustrate the intellectual characteristics of the Chevalier, but that much of the tale is taken up by lengthy discussions of his psychological, analytic and linguistic theories. Thus, although the three stories do allow us to refer to a 'series', Dupin does not suggest the potential for an infinite continuation. He is written, appears, intervenes, to make a number of philosophical and literary points, not to become a social myth.

Central to Dupin's methodology is the need for an imaginative symmetry between the investigator and the object of his inquiry. The point is repeatedly made that, for ordinary affairs, the institutions of the newspapers, the police and the law courts, which mimic the 'mass' by reasoning on the average, are generally adequate. Dupin is concerned with another sort of problem, precisely those where the sort of positivist values celebrated later by Holmes and others do not apply. Here, Dupin suggests, a new epistemological synthesis is needed, combining the exactness of mathematical science with the speculative potential of philosophy and poetry: what he calls 'calculating upon the unforeseen'.[15]

In this context, due importance should be given to the fact that Dupin's very first startling intervention is his ability to 'read the mind' of his colleague. The episode is recounted so that Dupin can expound the 'method – if method there is – by which you have been enabled to fathom my soul in this matter'.[16] By claiming a secular method for seeing into the psyche ('soul'), he is seeking to occupy a territory that G. K. Chesterton's Father Brown will try to claim back for the priesthood at the end of the century.

The mind-reading episode serves, furthermore, as a prelude to a description of the culprit which puts the narrator in mind of a lunatic. Thus Dupin the 'analyst' of both ordinary mental processes and pathological behaviour may also be linked to J. Sheridan LeFanu's Dr Martin Hesselius, a 'medical philosopher' and expert on 'Metaphysical Medicine' whose 'case studies' are reported to us by his medical secretary.[17] Hesselius applies his imaginary synthesis of modern material science and spiritualist philosophy to 'uncanny' mysteries which are recognisable to us as metaphorical explorations of the sexual unconscious. His subjects include a priest haunted to suicide by the hallucination of a monkey ('Green Tea', 1869) and a murderous lesbian vampire ('Carmilla', 1871–2). In short, Dupin should be considered not only in relation to the development of the criminal detective, but also to the psychological 'analyst' – what, in the title story of *The Dream Doctor* (1913), Arthur B. Reeve refers to as 'what the Freudists call the psychanalysis, the soul analysis' of the patient.[18]

The vogue for scientific detectives around the time of Holmes's success reflects yet another characteristic of modernity: the emergence of the intellectual professions as new repositories of social power. In *The Silent Bullet* (1912), Reeve's Craig Kennedy argues that 'To-day it is the college professor who is the arbitrator in labour disputes, who reforms our currency, who heads our tariff commissions, and conserves our farms and forests. We have professors of everything – why not professors of crime?'[19] More perhaps than making heroes out of policemen, the short story of the period explores the heroism of the intellectual, the class of academics, professionals, civil servants and white-collar workers whose mental labour was to be so important to the twentieth century.

The power of the intellect in its purest form is explored by the 'armchair detectives' like Futrelle's 'The Thinking Machine'. Although distinguished with various academic titles, Professor August S. F. X. Van Dusen makes little use of specialised knowledge. Indeed, he earned his sobriquet by beating the world chess champion without any knowledge of the game beyond the rules. The physical appearance of this anti-social and sedentary hero is an unpleasant caricature of pure intellect: he has a puny body, with squinting, watery eyes and a very broad brow set in an enormous head with straw-yellow hair. His cleverness makes him arrogant and impatient, and his explanations impress largely because few of the elements in the account have been placed before the reader in advance. By insisting that masterminds are committing crimes invisibly all around us, he plays on the fear of the power of intellectuals against whom only a greater intellectual, however unlikeable, can protect us. On the other hand, as in his most celebrated case, 'The Problem of Cell 13' (1907), his success often relies as much on good fortune and the legwork of his journalist friend, Hutchinson Hatch, as on his own mental powers.[20]

Although also pale, thin and impolite, Baroness Orzcy's Old Man in the Corner (1901–4) presents a different sort of intellectual. Rather than inhabiting the masculine chambers of other cerebral detectives, he pops up at the journalist Polly Burton's table at the local ABC café unbidden, and proceeds to clear up unsolved mysteries. He shows her photographs of the protagonists and resumes the proceedings of inquests or trials, and subsequently, as he nervously knots and unknots a piece of string, he ties the details together into a solution. Since what the intellectual most values is intelligence, the Old Man rarely wishes to see the perpetrators of these brilliant deceptions punished. Rather, perhaps like the reader of detective stories, he admires the criminal's artistic or strategic skill – to the point where, in the final story, he himself becomes both the narrator and the perpetrator.

The principal alternative to the intellectual as pure thinker is the trained scientist, employing not only the power of rational thought but that of specialised knowledge and, most of all, of scientific instruments.

In many cases, the particular expertise of the intellectual hero remains of little relevance. L. T. Meade and Robert Eustace's *The Brotherhood of the Seven Kings* (1899) recounts the struggles of Norman Head, an independently wealthy research biologist, against the Queen of an ancient secret society based in Naples, who has gained access to London society through her miraculous cures in order to further its greedy purposes. The science here is largely as sensationalist as the plot and even in L. T. Meade and Clifford Halifax MD's 'medical mysteries', *Stories from the Diary of a Doctor* (1894), the medicine is little more than a topical pretext for more sensationalism.

The scientific detective *par excellence* is Richard Austin Freeman's Dr John Evelyn Thorndyke (first series 1908–9), a specialist in medical jurisprudence, reputedly modelled on Dr Alfred Swaine Taylor, the founder of the new discipline. Thorndyke's expertise lies in things rather than people; his power comes not from a superhuman intellect, but from specialised knowledge, technology and method. He carries a miniaturised 'portable laboratory' to the crime scene and collects material samples for microscopic analysis. Thorndyke represents the scientific principle 'that all facts, in any way relating to a case, should be collected impartially and without reference to any theory, and each fact, no matter how trivial or apparently irrelevant, carefully studied'.[21] The problem is that this process may prove somewhat tedious to the reader. Not so, certainly, to the author, who believed that detective fiction was essentially an 'intellectual satisfaction' whose 'real connoisseurs . . . are to be found among men of the definitely intellectual class: theologians, scholars, lawyers, and to a less extent, perhaps, doctors and men of science'.[22] With a view to their delight, beginning with 'The Case of Oscar Brodski' (1912), he initiated a series of 'inverted detective stories', which, having shown the reader the crime and the culprit, made the process of detection the centre of narrative interest.

Where Dr Thorndyke is accurate and somewhat dry in his science and consequently in his narrative, Arthur B. Reeve's stories stretch the limits of contemporary science and technology. Professor Craig Kennedy, assisted by his friend, the journalist Walter Jennings, usually concludes his cases by assembling the interested parties in his teaching room and giving them a lecture and demonstration in science which is, at the same time, the solution to the crime.

Kennedy's use of science and technology is both sensationalist and based in fact (it is also, like many others of the time, frequently racist). Many of the devices he relies on for his solutions may sound made-up, but instruments like the 'sphymomanometer', the 'plethysmograph', the 'detectaphone' and the 'optophone' were all contemporary medical or electrical technologies, as actual as other early twentieth-century inventions like blood typing, the silencer, the microphone and the oxyacetylene torch, all of which Kennedy uses – along, as we have seen, with Freudian dream analysis. Most discoveries and inventions are credited to their originators, although Reeve does sometimes push contemporary technology beyond its real capacities at the time (including a fancifully simple lie-detector, electrico-cardiac resuscitation, and X-ray movies). On the other hand, the milieu in which the crimes take place, featuring financiers and industrialists, society ladies undergoing scientific beauty treatments, inventors (of synthetic rubber, airplanes that can hover or remote-controlled torpedoes), and Latin American revolutionary gun-runners, connect this fascinating new technology to the contemporary industrial and political world.

Why, then, was Sherlock Holmes so much more successful than other scientific detectives? There are certainly literary reasons. Conventional literary history, which views earlier detective fiction as a series of anticipations of Doyle, can be turned on its head to argue that the elements of the Sherlock Holmes character and stories are skilfully selected from tried and tested elements in earlier sensational novelists and story writers. But that is far from accounting for the verve of Doyle's writing, the ingenuity of the stories and the skill and economy of their construction. The problem-setting and solving structure provides fundamental narrative satisfactions, but, as Stephen Knight has shown, at least in the two principal collections, *The Adventures of Sherlock Holmes* (1892) and *Memoirs of Sherlock Holmes* (1894), Doyle plays enough variation on the pattern to keep it constantly fresh.[23]

Doyle expertly achieved the right balance of elements to provide the male middle-classes with relaxing reading which flattered them by providing an intellectual adventure, while assuaging their anxieties about the modern world. The stories celebrate the materialism of the age, showing that the ordinary small objects of everyday existence, if observed properly, have stories, create atmospheres, point directions.[24] At the same time, they celebrate the capacity of rationalism to organise the material of existence meaningfully, and the power of the rational individual to protect us from semiotic and moral chaos. Yet the crimes are rarely excessively troubling (and, although we do find murders, on the other hand in many stories there is no crime at all).

Holmes deals largely with family irregularities and the consequences of selfishness, rather than dangers endemic to the system.[25]

It is generally agreed that, for all the talk of detecting, it is not the plotting or the intellectual work which are the key to the success of these stories, but the very special 'character' of Sherlock Holmes.[26] In this sense, notwithstanding his remarkable abilities, Holmes is a considerably more reassuring figure than his competitors or imitators. In relation to any Dupin-like 'decadence', the anti-social Bohemianism and cocaine-taking of the first two novellas are rapidly attenuated. Although an intellectual, he has no cultural pretensions, and is always eager for action. He remains intimidating, frequently brusque, arrogant and aloof, but he is never morally repulsive. Furthermore, Holmes frequently displays a sympathetic concern about the outcome, particularly in family matters, and lets his own mask slip often enough to persuade us of the, albeit eccentric, humanity within.

But most importantly, we are cushioned from potentially alienating characteristics by Watson, who mediates our attitudes to the hero. It is reassuring to find, for example, that, although we may not be as bright as Holmes, we are at least smarter than his colleague. Himself a professional man, Watson lets us know that we are not supposed to feel challenged by Holmes's intelligence, but to trust it. Embodying the sturdy middle-class virtues that Holmes affects to despise just as he protects them, the good doctor strikes us as an eminently reliable narrator – a matter of equal importance to our belief in the detective's genius (no cheating) as it is in our identification with the narrator's moral assessment of his friend. Mind you, Holmes himself is critical of his friend's reliability as a writer, complaining that 'You have degraded what should have been a course of lectures into a series of tales'.[27] But for the reader it is of course a blessing to have the rigour of logic and the demands of science filtered through the informed admiration of our friendly intermediary.

This is just as well in another sense: as Knight again points out, Doyle's misnaming of Holmes's methodology as 'deduction' is far from incidental.[28] Ousby likewise recognises that 'The stories' relation to the details of contemporary science is tenuous', while Michael Shepherd calls Holmes's method 'a counterfeit, a simulacrum of the real thing'.[29] This is not to deny the obvious: that Holmes convinces and amuses with his identification and articulation of clues and his felicitous erudition; the reader accedes with the same satisfied wonder as Watson to his claims for his powers of observation and reasoning. However, unlike Thorndyke's scrupulous detail or Reeve's technology, this is not concerned with scientific accuracy or actuality but, as Knight puts it, with 'the aura of science'.[30] The reader is impressed, made to feel part of a modern scientific world which, although he can never master it, neither bores nor alienates – most of all, which protects him while demanding nothing of him.

According to Holmes, the 'ideal detective' requires not only 'the power of observation and that of deduction' but also 'knowledge',[31] and the pieces of obscure information with which he is constantly surprising us are often as decisive as any supposedly deductive rigour. As well as types of tobacco, poisons, reagents and so on, he has an encyclopaedic knowledge of criminal cases and the fact that 'I am able to guide myself by the thousands of other similar cases which occur to my memory'[32] is a further reassurance that crime generally fits into established patterns.

Holmes's powerful knowledge is the result of systematic study and well-organised filing. He studies scientifically, conducts experiments, and accumulates knowledge, but, in contrast to Watson, the trained military surgeon (or any other professional), he obeys his own curriculum. He is not following 'any course of reading which might fit him for a degree in science or any other recognized portal which would give him an entrance into the learned world'.[33] In other words, though a specialist, neither he nor his specialism seek institutional validation; his expertise consists in what he decides he needs to know in order to do what he wants to do – and, while he continues to improve his knowledge, he is famously unperturbed by his own areas of ignorance.

Holmes then is a self-styled expert (no doubt as many of his well-informed, observant and rational white-collar readers would like to see themselves), requiring no formal qualification to provide him with his professional authority. Interestingly, his famous trick (comparable to Dupin's mind-reading) and the subject of his article on 'The Book of Life', is his ability 'on meeting a fellow-mortal . . . at a glance to distinguish the history of the man, and the trade or profession to which he belongs'.[34] On the other hand, he does not expect people to understand what it is he does for a living: 'I'm a consulting detective, if you can understand what that is'.[35] Well, how could you? The profession for which his idiosyncratic training qualifies him is unique to the bundle of methods and knowledge that his character embodies: 'That is why I have chosen my own particular profession, or rather created it, for I am the only one in the world.'[36] In short, Holmes's profession is simply who he is, what he knows, how he thinks. It is no wonder then that he is regarded by most critics and the general public as the personification of 'the Great Detective': he is a unique creation, whose professional standing is validated by no other institutions than himself – and his readers.

Rather than challenge Holmes in the scientific department, some authors reacted by creating detectives who were intended to be remarkable by their reassuring ordinariness and who celebrate the power of common sense and perseverance. Arthur Morrison's Martin Hewitt, for example, 'had always as little of the aspect of the conventional detective as may be imagined' and claims to have 'no system beyond a judicious use of ordinary faculties' – what he elsewhere refers to as 'common sense and a sharp pair of eyes'.[37] He is independent and demand for his services allows him to work for a high fee, refusing cases on the speculative basis of reward. Hewitt retains much of his origins as a solicitor's clerk: he is your reliable non-specialist professional person.

Matthias McDonnell Bodkin's Paul Beck likewise relies on common sense, a hound-like pursuit of the suspect and good luck to show up the pretentious 'new school' of 'scientific' policemen: 'I just go by rule of thumb, and muddle and puzzle out my cases as best I can.'[38] For Beck 'There is not any science in detective work.'[39] There is a certain inventiveness and topicality about some of Beck's cases, but his main claim to fame is his marriage to Dora Myrl, the 'Lady Detective' who features in Bodkin's next series of stories. The two meet in *The Capture of Paul Beck* (1909), and their son goes on to solve a crime at university in *Young Beck, a Chip off the Old Block* (1911).

Women have been a constant as victims of crime since the three Dupin cases and, as Catherine Belsey has shown, as a phenomenon Holmes can neither explain nor ignore, they are the great unspoken threat to his 'project of explicitness'.[40] Through popular sensation and crime fiction, actresses and dancers appear frequently, married to, or seeking to marry, wealthy aristocrats – alternatively, American wives bring them fresh capital. Governesses, sometimes with secret children of their own, turn out to be blackmailers or poisoners. And, in some cases, exotic women play the part of international criminal mastermind. Such literary representations have to be read in relation to another feature of the late nineteenth century: the growing demand by women for access to productive employment and the professions, not to mention the right to political representation.

So, a woman detective? The difficulty is apparent in Fergus Hume's *Hagar of the Pawn-Shop: The Gypsy Detective* (1898). Apart from the fact that Hume goes to a romantic outlaw community for his heroine, her career merely fills the space between her falling in love with Eustace Lorn, and their marriage on his return with the rightful heir of the shop she has been minding. The very different career of Baroness Orczy's *Lady Molly of Scotland Yard* (1910) is framed by a secret marriage, only revealed in the last story, when she proves the innocence of her falsely imprisoned husband, after which she retires as head of the 'Female Department'. Although temporarily alone in the world, both women are morally protected by being 'spoken for'.

Dora Myrl is in a quite different position: the orphaned daughter of a Cambridge don, she has a Cambridge degree and has qualified as a doctor.

But, failing to obtain a practice and having no taste for teaching, she has worked as 'a telegraph girl, a telephone girl, a lady journalist' before becoming a lady's companion.[41] In the course of her domestic duties, where she discovers her ability to combine 'womanly sympathy' with the timely capacity to 'surprise her secret',[42] she finds her vocation as a detective. Capable of wielding a revolver and deciphering (simple) codes, she treats her early cases as a game in which she pits her wits, sometimes flirtatiously, against the villain, and it is in this tone that she finds herself on the other side to Paul Beck in the novel *The Capture of Paul Beck* (1909), which, when she recognises that he was right, results in their joining forces and getting engaged.

In many ways, policing represented a particularly problematic area for female access, since it put into question both the place of women in the public sphere, and the gender basis of the service itself: to what extent could women be allowed to come into contact with the realities of the streets, and to what extent was force or protection at the heart of policing?

Police matrons, frequently wives or widows of police officers, existed in a number of US cities by the 1890s, and, exceptionally, one of them, Isabella Goodwin, was actually appointed a detective in New York in 1912. In Britain, it was only during the First World War that women patrols were set up, largely to control prostitution.[43] In policing, as in nursing and teaching, women were initially employed for their supposed skills in gaining the confidence of and caring for the young and vulnerable and were frequently detached for these purposes to places of popular amusement, like parks, dance-halls and cinemas.

Rather than the intellectual, it is, then, the actress whose presence one most feels in stories of 'lady detectives' during the period: the figure who, with her capacity for disguise, pretence and deceit, embodies both the cultural stereotype of the promiscuous, mendacious and hysterical woman and the troubling spy-like activities of traditional detectives as they infiltrate private spaces and gain people's confidence. The 'lady detective' can only operate if her 'acting' is made respectable – at the same time re-validating both the stereotype of the woman and the practices of undercover police.

The earliest example, Mrs Paschal, the protagonist of the anonymously authored *Experiences of a Lady Detective* (1861), is well-born and educated, and enters the 'new profession' armed with the moral strength of respectable middle-aged widowhood. Working under the orders of the intellectually superior Colonel Warner, her explicitly 'feminine' skills are unashamedly those of the spy and the disguised gainer of confidences. But from the start, Mrs Paschal's real-life play-acting in the cause of the law is contrasted with that of actresses with unexplained sources of income, like 'The Mysterious Countess' who is the object of her first case. Between the stock mysteries of jewel theft and the more melodramatic activities of Italian secret societies, Paschal is able to apply her remarkable intuition by adopting disguise and infiltrating domestic space as an agent for modern sexual discipline and proper filial and marital behaviour.

George Sims's Dorcas Dene (1897) avoids any scandalous associations of play-acting by retiring from the profession almost as soon as she starts in order to marry an artist friend of her father's. But her husband's blindness obliges her to go back to work. Rather than return to the stage, she accepts the offer of her neighbour, a retired police officer, to become a detective, on the grounds that 'You have plenty of shrewd common sense, you are a keen observer, and you have been an actress.'[44] Dorcas stipulates that she will give up if she finds that the job 'involved any sacrifice of my womanly instincts', but her first case, which involves tracking down a man who had abandoned his wife and children, overcomes any reluctance. Besides the defence offered by her common sense, Dorcas's exposure to the world of crime is protected by the fact that the cases are introduced, discussed, and often solved in her suburban living room, in the company of her husband, her mother, her pet dog, and Saxon, the narrator.

As befits an aristocrat, the histrionic tendencies of Orczy's Lady Molly are disciplined by inheritance and class: as the daughter of the Earl of Flintshire and a French actress, from whom she inherited 'all her beauty and none of her faults',[45] she is able both to disguise herself (even as a maid) and to move at ease in high society. With disguise made thus respectable, room is created for the heroine's other professional qualifications: her feminine tact and her woman's specialised knowledge, particularly of the servant class, of fashion, and of the psychology of women in relation to their children and lovers. But she is mainly valued for her unfailing womanly intuition.

The ability to suspect the right person while all about you are suspecting the wrong one is a staple of detection; with lady detectives it is turned from an unpleasant suspiciousness verging on cynicism to a moral intuition. To this and the talent for acting, female detectives, especially bourgeois heroines (as we have just seen with Dorcas Dene), add another quality of the 'ordinary', anti-scientific detective: common sense.

This is the quality most prized in his employee by the owner of the private agency where the most independent of the lady detectives, Catherine Louisa Pirkis's Loveday Brooke (1894), takes up work after finding herself penniless and without, as she sees it, any 'marketable accomplishments'.[46] This is not true, for, according to her boss, she is shrewd, practical and clear-headed, as well as having 'so much common sense that it amounts to genius'. But Brooke has one further important quality for the professional employability of the 'New Woman': 'the faculty – so rare among women – of carrying out orders to the very letter'. This view is not contradicted by any disobedience on the part of the employee but, through her cases, Brooke not only demonstrates a superior intelligence to everyone else, including her employer, but also adds to her capacities for disguise and conversation a rare fund of esoteric knowledge of such things as millinery, domestic organisation and Wesleyanism, but also Genoese guild rings, heraldry and cabman's slang.

I suggested that an important gesture early in this history was Dupin's claim to have a method for seeing into the soul of others. While Poe's eccentric investigator is one who identifies intellectually and imaginatively with his opponent, G. K. Chesterton's hero, Father Brown, claims that his methodology is based on a moral identification with the criminal, an encounter with one's own capacity for evil that he calls 'a religious exercise'.[47] With his invention of the priest-detective, Chesterton seeks to claim back the territory of modern mystery from the rationalist intellectuals who were the masculine backbone of the genre.

Even in terms of the narrative, Father Brown is self-effacing to the point of virtual invisibility, underrated by everyone, including the unadvised reader. However, in the first stories of *The Innocence of Father Brown* (1911), he defeats both Flambeau, the great French crook, the master of disguise and ingenious deceits, whom he brings to repentance and makes his partner, and the great French detective, Valentin, driven by his rationalist anti-clericalism to murder an American millionaire who he believes is about to commit his capital resources to the Catholic Church. Placing himself outside both these traditions, Brown also challenges the notion of a 'thinking-machine', on the grounds that machines are precisely incapable of thought[48] and the lie-detector, on the basis that responses always require interpretation[49] while one story is dedicated to ridiculing the science of criminology ('The Absence of Mr Glass').

Father Brown agrees with Dupin on the need to 'reckon on the unforeseen',[50] but this comes in a discourse justifying miracles, not method. His case – and the stories do constitute a serial argument – is that simplicity, a quality of the miraculous, is the test of truth, while complexity is a property of the tyranny of mysticism and superstition. Through the five collections (*The Wisdom of Father Brown*, 1913; *The Incredulity of Father Brown*, 1923; *The Secret of Father Brown*, 1927; and *The Scandal of Father Brown*, 1935), Father Brown proves his point against oriental mystics and their followers, promoters of new sects and religions, of philanthropic optimism, phrenology and spiritualism, and, more generally, against people (particularly socially and economically powerful men) who fail to understand events because of their credulity. With characteristic (if laboured) intelligence and irony, in 'The Resurrection of Father Brown' (1923), he places himself, the reluctant hero of short stories published in American magazines, at the centre of a Doyle-like attempt to exploit that credulity by killing him off and resurrecting him.

One of Brown's trademarks is the paradox, and the central one is that credulity in the mystical is a consequence of contemporary materialism and lack of belief in God, while Roman Catholicism is on the side of common sense. He only makes the latter assertion explicitly in a parenthesis,[51] but the claim is substantiated in his detective activities, as he repeatedly, in a late and sudden realisation of how stupid he had been, demystifies the apparently impossible or monstrous events with down-to-earth explanations. This process of detection depends not on scientific rationality but precisely on a common sense which is allied to an intuitive insight into the culprit, most particularly into their corruption. Father Brown's ultimate claim to expertise is that, as a priest and a Catholic, he has a greater sense of evil than non-believers.

The paradox, which characterises Father Brown's conversational style, is a good figure for this attempt to raise the genre into something that is simultaneously entertaining and ideologically influential. His studiously unsettling interventions are intended, like the stories it would seem, to amuse by their outrageousness, while pungently containing a fundamental truth. But Father Brown's relative lack of popularity suggests that the detective story was not capable of taking that weight, especially when it involves the atmospheric, frequently Gothic, descriptive writing that Chesterton engages in to generate the appearance of complexity that his hero will simplify, or to conjure the necessary aura of the mysterious, mystical and evil. Likewise many readers are likely to find that the 'clever' remarks of the Holmesian detective become here sententious and his overworked humility as tiresome as Van Dusen's arrogance. Chesterton believed that detection in the modern city was a form of 'knight-errantry'[52]; twentieth-century readers were to prefer the tougher chivalry and terser style of Dashiell Hammett's and Raymond Chandler's streetwise private eyes.

## NOTES

1 See Dorothy L. Sayers, ed., *Great Short Stories of Detection, Mystery and Horror* (London: Victor Gollancz, 1928).
2 Walter Allen, *The Short Story in English* (Oxford: Clarendon Press, 1981), pp. 3–5, 24–9.
3 *Ibid.*, pp. 21–3.
4 Clive Bloom, 'Capitalising on Poe's Detective: the Dollars and Sense of Nineteenth-Century Detective Fiction', in *Nineteenth-Century Suspense: From Poe to Conan Doyle*, ed. Clive Bloom *et al.* (London: Macmillan, 1988), p. 14.

5 Charles Dickens, 'Three "Detective" Anecdotes' (1850), in *The Uncommercial Traveller and Reprinted Pieces* (London: Oxford University Press, 1958), pp. 504–12. This volume also reprints Dickens's 'The Detective Police' (1850) and 'On Duty with Inspector Field' (1851).

6 See Ellery Queen, *Queen's Quorum: A History of the Detective-Crime Short Story as Revealed by the 106 Most Important Books Published in This Field since 1845* (Boston: Little, Brown & Co., 1951), pp. 13–14. Waters's 1849 articles from *Chambers's Edinburgh Review* were published in New York as *Recollections of a Policeman* (1853) and in London as *Recollections of a Detective Police-Officer* (1856).

7 Arthur Conan Doyle, *The Penguin Complete Sherlock Holmes* (Harmondsworth: Penguin, 1981), pp. 24–5.

8 G. K. Chesterton, 'A Defence of Detective Stories' (1902), reprinted in Howard Haycraft, ed., *The Art of the Mystery Story: A Collection of Critical Essays* (1946; New York: Carroll & Graf, 1983), p. 4.

9 See David Reed, *The Popular Magazine in Britain and the United States 1880–1960* (London: The British Library, 1997).

10 See Martin Priestman, *Detective Fiction and Literature: The Figure on the Carpet* (Basingstoke: Macmillan, 1990), Chap. 5.

11 Jacques Futrelle, *Great Cases of the Thinking Machine*, ed. E. F. Bleiler (New York: Dover, 1976), p. 37.

12 See Robert Barr, *The Triumphs of Eugène Valmont* (1906), ed. Stephen Knight (Oxford: Oxford University Press, 1997).

13 Sayers, *Great Short Stories*, p. 17.

14 In preparing the story for book publication in 1845, Poe altered the ending to take account of this evidence. See the version and notes published in Edgar Allan Poe, *The Collected Works of Edgar Allan Poe*, ed. T. Mabbott, 3 vols. (Cambridge, MA: Harvard University Press, 1978), vol. 3, pp. 715–88.

15 Poe, *The Collected Works*, vol. 3, p. 752.

16 *Ibid.*, vol. 2, p. 533.

17 See J. Sheridan LeFanu, *Best Ghost Stories of J. S. LeFanu*, ed. E. F. Bleiler (New York: Dover, 1964).

18 Arthur B. Reeve, *The Dream Doctor: The New Adventures of Craig Kennedy, Scientific Detective* (1913; London: Hodder & Stoughton, 1916), p. 30.

19 Arthur B. Reeve, *The Silent Bullet: The Early Exploits of Craig Kennedy, Scientific Detective* (1912; London: Hodder & Stoughton, 1916), p. 8.

20 See Jacques Futrelle, 'The Problem of Cell 13' (1907), in Hugh Greene, ed., *More Rivals of Sherlock Holmes* (Harmondsworth: Penguin, 1973), pp. 128–68.

21 R. Austin Freeman, 'Ship of the Desert', in *The Famous Cases of Dr Thorndyke* (London: Hodder & Stoughton, 1929), p. 253.

22 R. Austin Freeman, 'The Art of the Detective Story' (1924), in H. Haycraft, ed., *The Art of the Mystery Story*, pp. 11–12. However, we should note that in 1902–3, with John James Pitcairn, Freeman wrote a series of short stories under the pseudonym of Clifford Ashdown about a gentleman-crook (collected as *The Adventures of Romney Pringle*, 1902). Doyle's brother-in-law, E. W. Hornung, also wrote stories about a more famous gentleman rogue, A. J. Raffles, the first volume being collected under the title, *The Amateur Cracksman* (1899).

23 Stephen Knight, *Form and Ideology in Crime Fiction* (London: Macmillan Press, 1980), pp. 75–8. Holmes first appeared in the novellas *A Study in Scarlet* (1887) and *The Sign of Four* (1890). The twenty-three stories collected in the next two volumes are commonly regarded as his best. Despite Doyle's feeling that his literary talents were worthy of finer things, he was persuaded by popular demand to resurrect Holmes, producing the stories collected as *The Return of Sherlock Holmes* (1905), *His Last Bow* (1917) and *The Case Book of Sherlock Holmes* (1927), and two more novellas: *The Hound of the Baskervilles* (1902) and *The Valley of Fear* (1915).

24 See Ian Ousby, *Bloodhounds of Heaven: The Detective in English Fiction from Godwin to Doyle* (Cambridge, MA: Harvard University Press, 1976), p. 155 and Knight, *Form and Ideology*, p. 74.

25 See Knight's analysis of the crimes in the *Adventures* in *Form and Ideology*, pp. 87–91. The invention of a 'master criminal', Moriarty, is basically a device to enable Doyle to do away with Holmes – a crime more successfully achieved by Doyle himself, accompanied by Newnes, in Robert Barr's parody, 'The Adventure of the Second Swag', appended to *The Triumphs of Eugène Valmont*, pp. 212–20.

26 See, for example, Howard Haycraft, *Murder for Pleasure: The Life and Times of the Detective Story* (London: Davies, 1942), p. 54.

27 Doyle, *The Penguin Complete Sherlock Holmes*, p. 317.

28 Knight, *Form and Ideology*, p. 86.

29 Ousby, *Bloodhounds of Heaven*, p. 153; Michael Shepherd, *Sherlock Holmes and the Case of Dr Freud* (London: Tavistock, 1985), p. 20.

30 Knight, *Form and Ideology*, p. 79.

31 Doyle, *The Penguin Complete Sherlock Holmes*, p. 91.

32 *Ibid.*, p. 176.

33 *Ibid.*, p. 20.

34 *Ibid.*, p. 23.

35 *Ibid.*, p. 24.

36 *Ibid.*, p. 90.

37 Arthur Morrison, *Martin Hewitt, Investigator* (New York: Harper & Brothers, 1907), pp. 4–5, p. 28. Morrison also wrote stories about a crooked detective called Dorrington – see 'The Affair of the "Avalanche Bicycle and Tyre Co., Limited"', in Hugh Greene, ed., *The Rivals of Sherlock Holmes: Early Detective Stories* (Harmondsworth: Penguin, 1971), pp. 98–123.

38 Matthias MacDonnell Bodkin, *Paul Beck, the Rule of Thumb Detective* (London: C. A. Pearson, 1898), p. 30.

39 *Ibid.*, p. 83.

40 Catherine Belsey, *Critical Practice*, 2nd edn (London: Routledge, 2002), p. 106.

41 Matthias MacDonnell Bodkin, *Dora Myrl, the Lady Detective* (London: Chatto & Windus, 1900), p. 6.

42 Bodkin, *Dora Myrl*, p. 8.

43 See Kerry Seagrave, *Policewomen: A History* (Jefferson, NC McFarland & Co., 1995).

44 George R. Sims, *Dorcas Dene, Detective: Her Life and Adventures* (1919 ed.; London: Greenhill, 1986), p. 11. Originally published in 1897.

45 Baroness Orczy, *Lady Molly of Scotland Yard* (1910; London: Cassell & Co., 1912), p. 294.
46 Catherine Louisa Pirkis, *The Experiences of Loveday Brooke, Lady Detective* (1894), ed. Michele Slung (New York: Dover, 1986), pp. 2–3.
47 See G. K. Chesterton, *The Secret Of Father Brown* (1927) in *The Penguin Complete Father Brown* (Harmondsworth: Penguin, 1981), pp. 464–6.
48 G. K. Chesterton, *The Innocence of Father Brown* (1911), in *The Penguin Complete Father Brown*, p. 11.
49 *Ibid.*, p. 221.
50 *Ibid.*, p. 11.
51 *Ibid.*, p. 44.
52 Chesterton, 'A Defence of Detective Stories', p. 6.

# 4

SITA A. SCHÜTT

# French crime fiction

'The detection of crime is evidently not an art that has been cultivated in England.' 'Our Detective Police', *Chambers Journal*, 1884.

It is not for nothing that Moriarty was otherwise known as the Napoleon of crime, that Poe's Chevalier Dupin invented ratiocination from a comfortable armchair in a darkened room in Paris, or, for that matter, that Sherlock Holmes takes such pains to scoff at the French police, notably a certain detective named Lecoq, who, he claims, 'was a miserable bungler'.[1] French contributions to the development of crime fiction, in particular the detective story, are significant in the sense that one cannot conceive of the developments in nineteenth-century English detective fiction without them. Holmes's arrogance towards the continental police, notably the French, nevertheless bespeaks a certain amount of insecurity with regard to the fearsome reputation of the French police established during Fouché's reign of terror under Napoleon, a reputation further consolidated throughout the nineteenth century.

The need to assert British supremacy in a matter so relatively trite as detective fiction has its roots in a tradition of political and cultural Anglo-French rivalry. For the English, in the wake of the Napoleonic wars, veritable Gallophobia reigned, with posters depicting John Bull quashing various manifestations of the French.[2] 'France was the national enemy. Behaviourally, it was represented as a moral pit, a place of sexual adventure and infidelity, the paradise of atheists, a place of refuge for the bankrupt and the disgraced'.[3]

The English were also wary of French institutions such as the police system, making the first bobbies 'a subject of almost universal obloquy, both as harbinger of French depotism and as a burden on rates'.[4] The English Detective Police Department, created in 1842, was made up of poorly trained detectives whose failure to solve crime was much criticised by the press, anxious about soaring crime rates. Journalistic accounts of the efficient French police provocatively called for the department's reform, along the lines of the French model. However, French methods, though successful, were seen as despotic. A liberal democracy could not be seen to endorse a system of surveillance, trickery and disguise.

Hostility towards French policing methods was matched by anxiety about French culture generally, as it was represented in French literature. Condemnation of certain French novels was unrelenting: in the late nineteenth century Zola's novels were considered 'poisonous stuff',[5] with translator and publisher Henry Vizetelly put on trial and imprisoned for their translation. But even earlier than this, the Parisian press and French writers were considered a contagious influence, as an 1836 review of contemporary French novelists sternly points out:

> 'It was not without considerable hesitation that we undertook to bring that mass of profligacy before the eyes of the British public. We feared that the very names now transcribed might seem to sully our paper. [. . .]
> The habit of labelling *vials* or packets of POISON with that cautionary description may, though very rarely, have prompted or facilitated a murder or suicide – but how many ignorant and heedless persons has it not saved from destruction?'[6]

Needless to say, this kind of review – with its detailed plot summaries – could only succeed in whetting the British appetite for more.

### Policing, surveillance and Memoirs

France, then, whose revolutions, coups and insurrections were bred by a dizzying succession of political regimes, was a country notorious for its policing, implementing the first police organisation in 1667. Rigorous police surveillance was considered indispensible and was both a means of keeping a check on citizens and a powerful tool in controlling political opposition. By the early nineteenth century a publishing trend whose success lay in the 'unveiling' of the secret machinations of the police created a context in which a criminal-turned-detective could earn fame and wealth through the publication of his life-story.

Eugène François Vidocq, a French brigand turned head of the Sûreté (the French criminal investigation department) published the story of his conversion in a series of best-selling memoirs in 1828. Caught one too many times, Vidocq was recruited as an informer, or *mouton*. His information proved to be so good that he was put to work for the detective police. He centralised the detective department, created a record system and remained Chief of Police from 1809 to 1827. The memoirs, full of accounts of his criminal days, followed by equally lurid adventures detailing his activities as a policeman, where detective methods are limited to various acts of provocation, disguise, and incitement to betrayal, were instant best-sellers in France and in England. Vidocq's 'police methods' had little if any of the famous Cartesian spirit of rational inquiry that were epitomised in Poe's Chevalier Dupin less than two decades later. Vidocq succeeded in capturing the contemporary imagination primarily through his vigour, his adventures and, importantly, his early accounts of 'brigandage' which fed off an extant tradition of criminal memoirs,[7] part of a popular publishing trend in which the exploits of pre-revolutionary French brigands were continuously re-issued, and where the outlaw's heroic status was often an index of popular discontent with the existing regime.

His is the first success story, injecting glamour, romance and adventure into the secret corridors of the *préfecture de police*, and Balzac, Hugo and others were much inspired by the 'French Police Hero'. Balzac, for instance, famously bases the character of Vautrin on Vidocq, in *Le Père Goriot* (1834), *Illusions Perdues* (1843) and *Splendeurs et Misères des Courtisanes* (1847). For the first time, a representative of the police was heroic and a source of literary inspiration. *The Westminister Review* declared him 'the most famous thief taker the world has ever known' and the *Literary Gazette* declared him 'the perfect hero'.[8]

The authenticity of Vidocq's memoirs, however, is to some extent debatable. The editor who bought the rights to the manuscript was doing so with the intention of serving the interests of the political opposition to Charles X. Vidocq's memoirs were supposed to reveal the extent of the tyranny and abuse exerted by the political police and in order to 'spice' up Vidocq's autobiography, the editor, Tenon, slyly suggested a 'reviseur'. The product was a manuscript which Vidocq claimed was far more 'immoral' than anything he had written, although he blamed this on the style of the writing rather than the content.[9] His outrage, however, only served to reinforce the credibility of his conversion. Thereafter, various other ghostwritten volumes were published, the fourth of which Vidocq refused to sign. Many journalists exploited this opportunity, and Vidocq endlessly tried to rectify things, issuing his own accounts and persuading others to publish them as '*Les Vrais Mémoires . . .*',[10] thereby ensuring the endless production and reproduction of the narrative of his life-story for an increasingly hooked readership.

The political ambiguity which characterises future fictional detectives derives in part from the fascination generated by accounts of Vidocq's careers on both sides of the law. Institutions that represent justice and the law are inevitably prone to error. Detectives who have experienced the 'criminal underworld', understand the criminal mind better and are able to catch 'criminals' more successfully although, as a consequence of their previous experience, they remain, to a certain degree, isolated from the institutions they represent. Yet conversion can lead to a firmer belief in justice, thus detectives with either a criminal past or a developed sense of criminal complicity can be trusted to remedy any 'mistakes' made by the law. This takes the form of the detective ignoring a request that they cease their investigation, when they intuit that an innocent person has been accused. Such detectives thus seem on the one hand to uphold 'justice' outside or despite the system but, on the other, manage to convince the system that they are right, thereby ultimately consolidating its power.

Vidocq's memoirs are symptomatic of the public fascination with crime and the police, to which the numerous literary publications – both around his life-story, but also on other aspects of crime – testify. Part of this fascination derived from the increasing incidence of crime and its reporting. By the early nineteenth century, the population of Paris had doubled since the seventeenth century. The overcrowding of the city resulted in an increase not only in crime, but disease, against the spreading of which the Paris sewers were first constructed. Cemeteries, too, were overflowing, and the construction of the catacombs was devised as a means of dealing with extra corpses. The sewers and the catacombs became a literal and technological 'underground' by which means the city became in some senses, more accessible but also more vulnerable. The sewers, also used for the fast transport of letters in pneumatic tubes,[11] provided a network of circulation not just for waste or documents, but also for fugitives from the heavily policed streets. The catacombs, opened to the public since 1809, provided citizens with a spectacle of death beneath the city's surface which had its correspondence in the detailed crime-reporting that was going on in the city's newspapers, notably, in the *Gazette des Tribunaux*, founded in 1825, whose detailed descriptions of crimes and trials provided material for many a novelist.

Crime-reporting, already in some sense episodic – when covering the stages of a trial, for instance – was complemented by the increased demand for serialised fiction. Often solicited by editors anxious to increase circulation, works such as Balzac's *Une Ténébreuse Affaire* (serialised from 1843), based on Fouché's reign of terror, Eugène Sue's *Les Mystères de Paris* (1843) and Dumas's *Le Comte de Monte Cristo* (1844) – to name just a few – came to the public as series. Authors were highly paid and newspapers relied on their contribution as a guarantee of profitable circulation. It is in this publishing context that the author who invented the first novel-length detective protagonist came into his own.

## Emile Gaboriau (1832–1873)

Emile Gaboriau, the first writer to dramatise full-scale police investigations and to make heroes of the detectives who lead them, provided the prototypes for three different kinds of fictional detectives: the eccentric amateur, Le Père Tabaret; the zealous and brilliant professional, Monsieur Lecoq; and the genius outsider, unnamed hero of Gaboriau's posthumously published work *Le Petit Vieux des Batignolles* (*The Little Old Man of Batignolles*) (1876).

Born in 1832, Gaboriau grew up in the Provinces, where he worked briefly as a notary whilst avidly reading the works of Fenimore Cooper, Ann Radcliffe and Edgar Allan Poe (who inspired him to write a series of imitations), before moving to Paris to become a writer. There he met and worked for Paul Féval, the sensation novelist, dramatist and publisher, as secretary and editor. During this period, he became well-versed in factual crime, attended numerous trials and studied French criminal law. In 1865, he wrote his first so-called 'roman judiciaire' (a name he devised with his editors), *L'Affaire Lerouge* (*The Lerouge Case*) (1865), serialised in the newspaper, *Le Soleil*, which brought him instant success. Gaboriau's work succeeded in revitalising the circulation of *Le Soleil*, and his name was consequently famous throughout France. In *The Lerouge Case* he implements an entirely original departure in French fiction: a detective, Le Père Tabaret, as protagonist. His subsequent novels, all equally successful and serialised, celebrate the acumen of a second detective, Monsieur Lecoq, a disciple of Le Père Tabaret. They include *Le Crime d'Orcival* (1866), *Le Dossier No. 113* (1867), *Les Esclaves de Paris* (1868), *Monsieur Lecoq* (1869), *La Vie Infernale* (1870), *La Corde au Cou* (1873) and *L'Argent des Autres* (1874). He also wrote plays and comic and ironic novels such as *Les Marriages d'Aventures* (1862) and *Les Gens du Bureau* (1862).

Gaboriau was quickly translated and widely read in England. The first official translation appeared in Boston in 1870 and in England in 1881, although pirated translations found their way across the Atlantic and thence to England before then. Gaboriau was evidently extremely popular, judging by the number of editions issued, and was also recommended reading for lawyers wishing for an overview of French judicial procedures.[12]

However, his fame was short-lived in the history of detective novels; nowadays he is referred to but only four of his works are still published. Many of his techniques were adopted and adapted, not least by Conan Doyle, who borrowed Gaboriau's method of inserting a long, detailed historical romance explicating characters' motives and histories in the middle of the investigation. Many of Holmes's techniques and characteristics can also be traced directly to Gaboriau's detectives.

In *The Lerouge Case*, Gaboriau's first detective, Le Père Tabaret, comes to a realisation of his 'vocation' towards the end of his life when he begins reading police memoirs:

> '. . . I too can read; and I read all the books I bought, and I collected all I could find which related, no matter how little, to the police. Memoirs, reports, pamphlets, speeches, letters, novels – all were suited to me'.

He becomes fascinated by the 'mysterious power' emanating from the Rue Jérusalem, admires the 'artful' and 'penetrating detectives . . . who follow crime on the trail, armed with the law, through the brushwood of legality, as relentlessly as the savages of Cooper pursue their enemies in the depth of the American forest', and is 'seized' by the desire to 'become a wheel of this admirable machine, – a small assistance in the punishment of crime and the triumph of innocence'.[13]

Tabaret's confession is a bookish one. His fascination with police memoirs mirrors the newly acquired tastes of the French reading public and yet it is a fascination which bizarrely combines the 'romance' of detection, and the heroic aspects of the chase, with a humble desire to serve 'this admirable machine'.

In *The Lerouge Case*, Tabaret uncovers a 'baby swap' plot that has gone awry and resulted in the murder of the nursemaid Claudine Lerouge. In this novel, Tabaret astounds the local police with his abilities and establishes himself as a detective proper. Nevertheless he is not infallible and allows his feelings to interfere with his judgement. He discovers that the young man he considers almost as a son, is, in fact, the murderer. His error is not fatal – though it provides an excuse for the inserted historical section – the wicked are punished and the good rewarded, whilst allowing the newly created fictional detective-hero to remain comfortingly human. If *The Lerouge Case* is still tentative about its hero and his investigation, its success enabled Gaboriau to provide his readers with a second more forceful (because official) detective, Monsieur Lecoq.

Monsieur Lecoq, whose name echoes that of Vidocq (and foreshadows Sherlock), makes a marginal appearance in *The Lerouge Case*, where he is presented as an 'old offender', but is re-presented in *Monsieur Lecoq* as a poor but brilliant mathematician. In the novel bearing his name, and in *Le Crime D'Orcival*, he has become the detective in charge: the eccentric but terrifyingly efficient member of the police force. He proves himself a brilliant detective through his recognition that the common man believed to be the perpetrator of a gory crime in a seedy tavern in Paris is actually a duke goaded to the act through a long and dark history of passion, betrayal and blackmail. All the evidence, however, points against him, and the tale is predominantly that of Lecoq's quest for proof of what he, and he alone, is certain of. Using inductive reasoning, subtle tracking techniques, outrageous disguises and original forensic methods, Lecoq combines Vidocq's sportsmanship and knowledge of the criminal world with Dupin's ratiocination. Although a part of the system, and ambitious for promotion, he works according to his instincts with all the passion and pride of an artist. Showing an awareness of the new technological aids that help the work of the criminal, Gaboriau endows his detective with foresight, creativity and open-mindedness with regard to new scientific methods for criminal investigation. However, his detectives have their foibles, amongst which is their tendency to fall in love.

In *Le Dossier No. 113* (*File No. 113*), Lecoq is hardly present at all, but it transpires that he has only taken on this case, in heaviest disguise, to revenge himself on a lover (Nina) who jilted him for another man. His pseudonym throughout the affair has been Caldas, and it is in the person of Verduret, an elderly bespectacled gentleman, that he helps to save Nina's lover, who is accused of stealing a large sum of money from the bank in which he works. In so doing, he uncovers an intricate history of love, fratricide, illegitimacy and blackmail. The novel ends with the revelation of Verduret/Caldas's true identity, and his motives:

> 'Then Caldas avenged himself in his own way. He made the woman who deserted him recognize his immense superiority over his rival. Weak, timid, and helpless, the rival was disgraced, and falling over the verge of a precipice, when the powerful hand of Caldas reached forth and saved him.
>
> 'You understand now, do you not? The woman is Nina, the rival is yourself; and Caldas is' – With a quick, dexterous movement, he threw off his wig and whiskers, and stood before them the real, intelligent, proud Lecoq.
>
> 'Caldas', cried Nina.
>
> 'No, not Caldas, not Verduret any longer: but Lecoq, the detective!'[14]

Lecoq emerges as 'the detective' from a veritable vaudeville show of personalities – the elderly avuncular figure, the jilted lover. The characters that have populated countless historical, sensational and romantic plots are replaced, in some sense, by the all-powerful detective who, without necessarily being the central character, authenticates the story. Yet in giving his true identity, Lecoq also thereby renounces the character of lover. In Gaboriau's last work, a new detective emerges, untrammelled by personal feelings, incited by the pure flame of the investigation itself.

Published posthumously in 1876, *The Little Old Man of Batignolles, A Chapter of a Detective's Memoirs* was probably written in the 1860s and is in many respects untypical of Gaboriau's works. For a start, it is a short narrative. It also introduces an anonymous detective, a poor medical student who spends his time observing the mysterious comings and goings of his neighbour, Méchenet. This latter befriends him and takes him to a scene of crime thereby revealing his profession. He is a detective. The crime in question is murder. The body of an old man has been found, with the incriminating inscription of the letters '*MONIS* . . .' in blood at his side, apparently written as he lay dying. The police claim that this is the clue that definitely identifies the murderer, as 'Monis' is the beginning of the name Monistique, the old man's nephew and heir. The young medical student, however, finds himself quickly noting all kinds of details around the scene of the crime, in particular the fact that the bloody inscription has been written with the victim's *left* hand, which strikes him as suspicious. This amongst other observations leads him to question the conclusions drawn by the police. As such, the practice of detection in this story is shown to require talent and inspiration: the plodding fact-gathering methods of the police need the injection of imaginative genius for justice to be dealt. The 'newcomer' detective himself leads the isolated life of an artist, and the criminal, in the last instance, is revealed as an *artiste manqué*.

Masquerading as an early memoir of a great detective, *The Little Old Man of Batignolles* thus demystifies the work of the professional police, whilst endowing the 'real' detective with genius of a kind. Although the status of professional detective is shown as marginal, that of the genius detective is even more so. He lacks experience and knowledge of the system and wishes to go straight after the culprit. In this episode he learns that this is impossible: the 'system' cannot function through idiosyncratic proofs, and must therefore be learned and mastered as efficiently as possible. This creates a further degree of difficulty, rendering the ultimate success of the detective more laudable still. The story itself, however, is slightly less straightforward than it first appears to be, and its resolution is remarkably tongue-in-cheek, giving the criminal some credit for his hitherto unapplauded ingenuity. The 'genius' newcomer initially noticed that the index finger of the *left* hand of the victim was stained with blood, proving that the murderer and not the victim had written the name with the intention of casting blame on Monistique. It is this observation that sets the two investigators on what turns out to be the right trail. However, when they do finally capture the culprit and explain their evidence to him, he is furious:

> 'God! What it is like to be an artist!' he shouted.
> And looking at us with pity, he added: 'Didn't you know? M. Pigoreau was left-handed! And so an error in the investigation led to the discovery of the murderer.'[15]

The criminal, in this case, has proved to be too clever for his own good: the very detail with which he has planned the falsification of the evidence was the clue to his presence on the scene of the crime. 'To be an artist' in this case, is to have taken too much pride in a mediocre work. The killing of an old defenceless man is hardly a work of art, although the very fact that 'error' led to truth is a double-edged sword: it is the way crime ought to be solved and yet, in this case, reveals that the very process that enables its resolution is (pleasantly) fallible.

The 'error' in the investigation is about 'left-handedness' and writing. The story itself uses writing, the 'memoirs', as antidote to criminality, but the idea of not knowing which hand has been used lends a greater ambiguity to both the act of writing itself and the victim. To have been left-handed in the nineteenth century was also to have been backward, if not downright deviant.[16] That the criminal alone shows knowledge of this, speaks of a kind of fraternity between himself and the victim. That is, in some senses, the victim himself is thereby encrypted in the codes of underworld, his death is not a cause for special grief and the murderer emerges as less wicked with his cleverness enhanced. He is angry that his brilliance has been overlooked and expresses no regret for his action. This lack of repentance is evident at the beginning of the narrative, where the narrator, in a preamble that introduces and justifies the writing of his memoirs, quotes the criminal's reaction upon his arrest:

> 'Ah! If I had only known the methods used by the police, and how impossible it is to escape from them, I would have remained an honest man!
> It was these words which inspired me to write my memoirs.
> 'If I had only known . . .!'[17]

The criminal has no regret whatsoever for the criminal acts he has committed. The fictional inspiration for the memoirs is to scare off future law-breakers by letting them know how much more their adversaries know – know about them, that is, know about tracking them down, know about seeing them and catching them as they carry out 'war on society'. The phrase 'how impossible it is to escape from them' is ambivalent, as its sequel 'I would have remained an honest man' is a conditional, not a moral, preference.

The narrator then continues with the justification for his memoirs:

> And I publish my recollections today in the hope, no I will go further, in the firm conviction that I have accomplished a highly moral task and one of exceptional value.
> Is it not desirable to strip crime of her sinister poetry, to show her as she really is: cowardly, ignoble, abject and repulsive!

Is it not desirable to prove that the most wretched beings in the world are those madmen who have declared war on society?

That is what I claim to do.

There is an implicit problem, evidently, in crime's 'sinister poetry'. The phrase 'to strip crime of her sinister poetry' relates to one of the themes of this short narrative: the transferral of 'artistry' from the criminal to the detective. It also emphasises the ambiguous status of the criminal: the detective necessarily inherits or partakes of (if only in the unravelling) this 'sinister poetry'.

Gaboriau's remaining fragment, published after his early death at the age of forty-one, lost, found and re-issued, nicely brings together both the genres' origins and its future development. As a fictional detective memoir, masquerading as a kind of crime-prevention document, and as a narrative that has the power to outlive its author, it heralds a breed of super-detectives, Sherlock Holmes in particular, and of accompanying crimes and criminals that equally outlive their creators.

Although an amalgam of Poe and Gaboriau provided Conan Doyle with the basic recipe for his new detective, Sherlock Holmes's success goes beyond the mere combination of these influences. Conan Doyle's stories were rapidly translated and Holmes became an international by-word for the act of detection. The French too, took Holmes seriously, going so far as to implement his methods of identifying tobacco ash in their police laboratories in Lyons. Conan Doyle was also highly esteemed by Edmond Locard, one of France's top criminologists. He is nonetheless light- heartedly taken to task in subsequent French crime fiction, a friendly reminder that French detectives, and indeed their criminals, have lost none of their brilliance or flair.

## Gaston Leroux (1868–1927)

First published in the newspaper L'Illustration, Gaston Leroux's novel, Le Mystère de La Chambre Jaune (Mystery of the Yellow Chamber) (1907), is a 'closed-room mystery' solved by the acumen of the Descartes-inspired investigative journalist Rouletabille. Leroux claimed that he wished to create 'something better' than both Poe and Conan Doyle.[18]

The perpetrator of the attempted murder of Mlle Strangerson, daughter of the famous scientist Professor Strangerson, turns out to be none other than one of France's most renowned detectives, Frederic Larson, who, in reality, is none other than the notorious criminal 'Ballmeyer'. The latter, secretly married to Mlle Strangerson in her youth, and still madly in love with her, seeks to prevent her marriage to Robert Darzac.

Narrated by Rouletabille's friend, Sinclair, a law student, who though not as obtuse as Watson, remains in the dark throughout the investigation, the 'mystery' is centred principally around how the assassin was able to leave the yellow chamber when it was locked from the inside and surrounded on the outside. As the plot unfolds, the highly competitive Rouletabille desires nothing more than to outdo the Parisian detective. His methodology is overtly Cartesian, and he claims that he will resolve the apparently inexplicable using pure reason. He disparages Larson's techniques, which, he claims, are entirely based on Conan Doyle.

A strong influence on Agatha Christie's country-house mysteries, the novel relies heavily on detailed reasoning that leads step-by-step from room to rooftop and is complete with floor-plans, diagrams and lists. Frequent references to Poe are made, yet the novel combines the latter's ratiocination with plenty of action: the killer strikes more than once, and is known to have access to the chateau's grounds, if not to actually inhabit them.

Professor Strangerson's scientific research, accomplished with the help of his daughter, concerns an investigation into 'the dissociation of matter'. The research, though never central to the narrative, nonetheless informs it. The assassin manages to escape twice, in a way that suggests either supernatural intervention, or the very subject-matter of the Professor's work. However, the Strangersons – as their name suggests – remain estranged from the novel's actual plot, which foregrounds the investigation led by the young, curiously infantile journalist, who, unlike other members of his profession, is bent on really finding out the truth of the affair. The truth of the 'affair' turns out to be more than he bargains for as it transpires that Larson and Mlle Strangerson are in fact Rouletabille's own parents. An Oedipal show-down with his father takes place in a following novel, *Le Parfum de la Dame en Noir* (*Perfume of the Lady in Black*) (1909).

The journalist, then, as fictional protagonist, is not only in some way the generator of crime in terms of reportage, that is, seeking out crime stories and embellishing them for newspapers to sell, but significantly its literary product: the scientist and the detective-bandit in the shape of Rouletabille's actual parents, as well as literary predecessors, produce a new breed of criminal investigator.

## Maurice Leblanc (1864–1941)

The reversibility of the criminal element in Leroux's novel is well within the boundaries already established by the series written by his contemporary Maurice Leblanc, whose '*gentleman-cambrioleur*', Arsène Lupin, first appeared in 1904. Solicited by the publisher Pierre Laffite for his new journal '*Je Sais Tout*', Arsène Lupin fulfilled the request for a thoroughly French hero'.[19]

Created in the same light-hearted vein as Conan Doyle's brother-in-law E. W. Hornung's gentleman-thief, Raffles (in *The Amateur Cracksman*, 1899), Lupin is not, however, simply the French riposte to Sherlock Holmes, although he takes on and defeats a certain 'Herlock Sholmès'. Leblanc was apparently inspired by the real-life character Alexandre Jacob, an anarchist who financially supported his cause by robbery and who was arrested in 1903. The need for a new French hero was created not simply by a national competitiveness awoken by the international success of the new English super-detective, but also a desire to re-establish national pride: in ridiculing Kaiser Wilhelm II in one of his escapades, Lupin takes revenge for the French defeat in the 1870–1 Franco-Prussian war.[20] Lupin's charismatic exploits on the 'wrong' side of the law are necessarily informed by contemporary detective fiction, and though often creating puzzles for the indulgent but exasperated French police, Lupin sometimes finds himself – to his own amusement – helping them out. This occurs most notably in the novel *813* (1910), where a ruthless assassin ascribes a series of cold-blooded murders to Lupin, who is then honour-bound to clear his own name. Whereas Lupin might rob the rich, he would never kill, and the public adore him accordingly.

Elegant, refined, and brilliant, Lupin is the master of disguise and a formidable escape artist. Powerfully supported by his band of faithful followers, he effortlessly eludes the arm of the law, whilst occasionally suffering minor setbacks, notably, of course, in the realm of love. Unlike Robin Hood, he robs to make himself richer, although he occasionally helps those who have been made to suffer unjustly and provides a system of anonymous reparation when necessary. Prefiguring the far more sinister Fantômas, yet imitating the detectives who pursue him, Lupin appears and reappears in various guises. In 'Arsène Lupin Escapes' (1910), he succeeds in altering his physical appearance to the extent that the trusty Inspector Ganimard, described as 'almost as good' as Sherlock Holmes, claims that the man on trial is not actually Arsène Lupin, and thereby ensures his release.

Creating a super-criminal who is also a hero makes him less of a 'criminal'. In the wake of so much rigorous French policing, Lupin is a flamboyant reminder of flair, freedom and exquisite good taste, recalling his middle-class French readers to the possibilities of a more spirited sense of the Cartesian, and also, what might be called an inspired sense of free-market economy. Lupin increases his wealth through his intelligence, often thereby uncovering layers of hypocrisy and falseness. The rich that he robs are sometimes rich in appearance only and are discovered to have been themselves cheating society – using fake bonds or replacing genuine gems with artificial stones, yet using these as guarantees in obtaining securities and loans. Thus, although he is a 'gentleman-thief', he fittingly represents the class he robs from.

Yet his gallantry, chivalry and, most importantly, his expertise in painting, antiques and jewellery, make him superior to most of his victims. If those he steals from are also revealed as criminals, and worse, hypocrites, then he also represents an equalising force, who, rather like Sherlock Holmes, doesn't work to change the established order, but merely to remind its citizens of the old-fashioned prerequisites for belonging. 'Real' criminals are ruffians, and thus Arsène Lupin remains a bizarre contradiction: an aristocratic robber who nonetheless serves to remind readers of society's fundamental inequalities.

If Arsène Lupin is a larger-than-life bandit hero, who gaily leaves his signature at the scene of the crime and constantly writes letters to the press, his successor on the criminal-as-protagonist front is chillingly recognisable precisely because he never leaves a calling card.

### *Pierre Souvestre* (1874–1914) *and Marcel Allain* (1885–1970)

'Fantômas.'
'What did you say?'
'I said: Fantômas.'
'And what does that mean?'
'Nothing. . . . . Everything?'
'But what is it?'
'Nobody. . . . And yet, yes, it is somebody!'
'And what does that somebody do?'
'Spreads terror!'[21]

Product of a frenetic literary collaboration between Pierre Souvestre and Marcel Allain, Fantômas, the amorphous criminal who is nobody, somebody and to some extent, everybody, came into being in February 1911, and appeared in thirty-two novels, a series which only came to an end with Souvestre's death.

After the 'charming' adventures of Lupin, Fantômas comes to the public as a sinister and shocking incarnation of wickedness. The steady increase in unsolved crime is partly accounted for by his ubitiquous presence. He is obsessively pursued by the famous Inspector Juve, who has made him his personal enemy and has sworn to uncover his real identity and arrest him. Fantômas exists primarily because Juve believes in him, although in a final episode, the metaphoric interdependency of the criminal and the detective is made literal when the two are revealed to be brothers.

Fantômas, although regarded as a lawyer's joke, a figment of the detective's over-wrought imagination, a too simple device and scapegoat for any un-explained crime, embodies society's worst enemy. His presence everywhere remains, however, throughout the series, an absence. Since anyone is a po-tential suspect, no-one is entirely innocent; even Juve, at one point, becomes a likely candidate. However, it is Juve's quest for him and his methods of investigation that bind together the otherwise fragmentary episodes.

Fantômas is ruthless and kills mercilessly: decapitating aristocrats, dump-ing sleeping bodies on railway lines, blowing up entire ocean liners. Yet he would do anything for his lover, the beautiful Lady Beltham – he does ac-tually murder her husband and stuff him in a trunk. As fitting mate to the Emperor of Crime she appears in several, mostly aristocratic, incarnations and would do, and does, anything for him. Appropriately, the lover of the most French of criminals is (or pretends to be) an English aristocrat.

If Lecoq, Lupin and Larson were masters of disguise, Fantômas is the genius of dissimulation, able to appear as the young and vigorous lover of Lady Beltham, the elderly father of Charles Rampert, an anonymous small-time employee and an eminent Professor of Psychology, Professor Swelding. At the end of the first series of adventures, Fantômas, in the guise of one Gurn, is arrested, tried and condemned to death. Lady Beltham arranges for a swap to take place between her lover and an actor who has gained fame impersonating him. Fantômas/Gurn's death is finally performed 'for real' by this actor, in front of a huge crowd of spectators. As such, the fake execution mirrors the insubstantiality and interchangeability that makes of Fantômas such an enduring character. As readers we suspect the actor of being Fantômas, until he is executed. And in fact, there is no reason that he couldn't have been, apart from our knowledge that 'Fantômas' always escapes. Only Juve, who notices that the man who is guillotined is not 'pale' from fear, but wearing a white mask of make-up, realises that Fantômas is still at large, thus enabling the continuation of the series. Fantômas exists primarily as 'mask' but one that cannot ever be removed, for indeed, there is no-one behind it.

Created on the eve of the First World War, Fantômas is a superlative criminal, a monster whose crimes perhaps, and their consumption by avid readers, are symptomatic of how in its representation, imagined evil defuses concern with real social and political problems, yet simultaneously foreshad-ows greater monstrosities to come.

In post-war crime fiction, that of the Belgian writer Simenon in particular, the criminal element is internalised, as it is in the 'hardboiled' school of American crime-writing. If Fantômas showed that he could be 'anyone', Simenon's novels reveal how anyone can be 'Fantômas'. The criminal is no longer a hulking silhouette on the balcony, but is present in each individual to a greater or lesser degree.

## Georges Simenon (1903–1989)

The Belgian writer who was one of the most prolific novelists of his time, who, it is claimed, made love to over 10,000 women and became a multi-millionaire, is most famous as the creator of the detective, Jules Maigret.

A powerful detective in the Parisian *Préfecture*, Maigret's origins are humble and his private pleasures are those of the *petit bourgeois*. Nonetheless, he dresses a tad more elegantly than his '*confrères*' and has his picture constantly in the press. Although he occupies a high position as *Commissaire de la Police*, he is often to be found investigating cases on the side, by accident, or against the wishes of highly-placed officials in the judicial system. He is recognisable for his physical corpulence (ironically 'maigre' means thin'), his patience, his penchant for his pipe and his beer, and his paternal interest in and sympathy with 'his' criminals.

Simenon wrote seventy-five Maigret novels, although, like Conan Doyle, he tried to place his inspector into early retirement, in order to write 'serious' novels. The Maigret series derives its interest and popularity not so much from the process of logical induction or the complexities of plot, as from the psychological portraits of 'criminal' characters and the depiction of landscapes and settings which are often as bleak as the crimes they provide a backdrop for.

Simenon, like his Inspector, did not attend University, due to his father's financial situation – although he attended a series of lectures on forensic science at the University of Lieges whilst working as a reporter. His career as full-time journalist, commencing at the age of sixteen and providing the basis of economic and efficient writing techniques, ended shortly afterwards when he moved to Paris and began to earn a living writing pulp fiction and articles. Maigret came to him famously during an extended boat trip with his wife Tigy.

> Had I drunk one, two or even three little glasses of schnapps and bitters? In any case after an hour, feeling rather sleepy, I began to see the powerful and imposing bulk of a gentleman emerging, who it seemed to me would make an acceptable detective inspector. During the course of the day I gave this character a number of accessories; a pipe, a bowler hat, a heavy overcoat with a velvet collar. And as my deserted barge was cold and damp, I furnished his office with an old cast-iron stove. . . . By noon the next day the first chapter of Pietr-le-Letton had been written.[22]

Written in 1929 and published in 1931, *Pietr-le-Letton* (*The Strange Case of Peter the Lett*) is considered the first complete Maigret novel and in it are established many of the features which characterise the series. Maigret's need for warmth and 'fire' supersedes even the desire for drink as he unrelentingly tracks down a famous international criminal and avenges the death of his friend and colleague through a haze of rain and physical pain.

In contrast to his fictional predecessors, Maigret is far from flamboyant, deeply appreciative of his wife, whose fragrant stews are ever bubbling, and disparaging of 'logical' methods, preferring to use his intuition and instinct. He champions the underdog, uncovers hypocrisy, and is concerned above all to understand human motives.

For all the bourgeois values Maigret seems so comfortable with, he nonetheless, as Francis Lacassin points out, remains an anti-hero with something of the artist in him. His investigations are creative processes in which he subverts the traditional pattern of the criminal as father, where the criminal instigates the narrative act of investigation, and the detective as son is created in reaction to the criminal. He is or becomes, 'father' to his criminals and the act of understanding them reflects their creation as characters, mirroring Simenon's own authorial process.[23]

Simenon, like Souvestre and Allain, Gaboriau and Leblanc, wrote at great speed, spewing forth novels at an astonishing rate and earning a great deal of money from them. His style, in contrast, is sparse and the scientific details of the investigation remain marginal to the plot. Where previous heroes leapt around either in pursuit or in escape, Maigret plants himself somewhere – usually visibly – and waits until his prey decides to make a move. Unlike Lecoq or Lupin and Rouletabille, Maigret is not ambitious (apart from having once wished to be a Doctor) and doesn't seek to impress or astound. He is grimly aware of social reality and refuses to vilify those who have 'wronged' society. Yet he uses severe interrogation techniques and psychological tricks on his suspects in order to obtain confessions, and this is something that has its antecedents in Lecoq's investigative methods, stemming from French judicial procedure where criminals are sometimes kept in solitary confinement and observed. Although with Maigret, the criminal-detective complicity reaches a finely-tuned peak, Maigret's sympathy never threatens his integrity.

Simenon kept writing the Maigret series throughout his literary career: the dogged pipe-smoking detective attracted a readership as devoted to his investigations as himself and Maigret's international popularity finally gave the Francophone world a detective (and not a criminal) whose fame is as enduring as that of Sherlock Holmes. Although his methods are deliberately non-scientific, his relation to the criminal world is a function of the French context in which crime-writing first emerged and developed.

From its origins in Vidocq's memoirs, French crime fiction both demarcates and blurs the distinctions between those fleeing the law and those representing it. If, in nineteenth-century English detective stories, criminals are often foreign, the French, on the whole, proudly produce criminals from their own ranks, either converting these into super-star police heroes or allowing them to remain maverick characters in their own right. Celebrated outlaws, when created by a society that experienced revolution, embody a fight for freedom and for social justice. The ability to produce detectives who not only equal them, but who have to deal with complex bureaucratic procedures in order to arrest them, assures readers that whilst the reminder of heroic deeds beyond the pale of the law might occasionally benefit the nation, the nation is firmly if flexibly equipped to deal justice.

Although the English were wary of the repercussions not only of revolution, or French policing systems, but of the dangerous perusal of 'French novels', the widespread popularity of these series, in which criminals as well as detectives took centre-stage, are proof not only of their irresistibility – labels of 'POISON' notwithstanding – but also of a significant contribution towards the evolution of the genre.

## NOTES

1 Arthur Conan Doyle, *A Study in Scarlet, The Complete Longer Stories* (London: John Murray, 1929), p. 23.
2 Jeannine Surel, 'John Bull', trans. Kathy Hodgkins, in Raphael Samuel, ed., *John Bull, The Making and Unmaking of British National Identity*, (London: Routledge, 1989), p. 10.
3 Samuel, ed., *John Bull*, pp. xxiv–xxv.
4 *Ibid.*, p. xx. Policemen were nicknamed 'bobbies' after the founder of Britain's police system, Sir Robert Peel.
5 Patrick Brantlinger, 'The Case of the Poisonous Book: Mass Literacy as Threat in Nineteenth-Century British Fiction', *Victorian Review* 20 (Winter 1994), 119.
6 Anon., 'French Novels', *Quarterly Review*, 56 (1836), 65–6.
7 See Régis Messac, *Le Detective-Novel et l'Influence de la Pensée Scientifique* (Paris: Slatkine Reprints, 1975), p. 102.
8 Ian Ousby, *Bloodhounds of Heaven: The Detective in English Fiction From Godwin to Doyle* (Cambridge, MA: Harvard University Press, 1976), p. 55.
9 Eugène François Vidocq, *Mémoires de Vidocq, Chef de la Police de Sûreté, jusqu'en 1827, aujourd'hui propriétaire et fabricant de papiers à Saint-Marché* (Paris: Tenon, 1828), pp. i–ii.
10 For full details see Eugène François Vidocq, *Les Vrais Mémoires de Vidocq presentés, annotés et commentés par Jean Savant* (Paris: Editions Corra, 1950).

11 Christopher Prendergast, 'Paris and the Nineteenth Century', *Writing the City* (Oxford: Blackwell, 1992), p. 10.
12 Alfred E. Gathorne-Hardy, 'The Examination of Prisoners: Emile Gaboriau', *The National Review*, 3 July 1884, p. 593.
13 Emile Gaboriau, *The Lerouge Case* (1865; London: Vizetelly & Co., 1884), p. 24.
14 Emile Gaboriau, *File No. 113* (1867; London: George Routledge and Sons, 1887), pp. 189–90.
15 Emile Gaboriau, *The Little Old Man of Batignolles, A Chapter of a Detective's Memoirs*, (1876), in T. J. Hale, ed., *Great French Detective Stories* (London: The Bodley Head, 1983), p. 87.
16 Havelock Ellis, *The Criminal* (London: Walter Scott, 1890), p. 108.
17 Gaboriau, *Little Old Man of Batignolles*, p. 41.
18 Daniel Fondanèché, *Le Roman Policier, thèmes et études* (Paris: Ellipses, 2000), p. 31.
19 *Ibid.*, p. 29. '*Cambrioleur*' means thief.
20 See *ibid.*, p. 29.
21 Marcel Allain, Pierre Souvestre, *Fantômas*, trans. Cranstoun Metcalfe (London, Stanley Paul & Co., 1915), p. 9.
22 Patrick Marnham, *The Man who wasn't Maigret, A Portrait of Georges Simenon* (London: Penguin, 1992), pp. 130–1.
23 Francis Lacassin, *Mythologie du Roman Policier* (Paris: Union Général d'Editions, 1974), p. 173.

# 5

STEPHEN KNIGHT

# The golden age

The golden age of crime fiction is usually taken as the period between the two world wars,[1] though some start it earlier, with the publication of E. C. Bentley's *Trent's Last Case* in 1913,[2] and the first critic to use the term dated it from 1918 to 1930, followed by 'the Moderns'[3]; major texts in 'golden age' style were also produced after 1940, both by new writers and by figures from the earlier period. The term 'golden age' has been criticised as being unduly homogenous[4] and seen as inappropriately 'replete with romantic associations'[5]: in fact the types of crime fiction produced in this period were far from uniform – the psychothriller and the procedural began, there was a wide range of practice in the mystery and the stories do regularly represent types of social and personal unease which would contradict a notion of an idyllic 'golden' period.

However, while recognising variety in the period, as well as the relative uncertainty of its borders, it is still possible to identify a coherent set of practices which were shared, to a greater or lesser extent, by most of the writers then at work. Elements that were randomly present in earlier crime fiction suddenly become a norm, like multiple suspects, and some earlier tendencies largely disappear, notably the use of coincidence and historical explanations. A genre of crime fiction, best named for its central mechanism as the clue-puzzle and epitomised by Agatha Christie and 'S. S. Van Dine', clearly forms a recognisable entity by the mid-1920s.

Murder is now essential as the central crime, as is confirmed in titles: by the 1920s the words 'murder' 'death' and 'blood', rarely seen before, seem compulsory, especially in the USA where euphemistic English titles often became more sanguinary.

The setting of the crime is enclosed in some way. G. K. Chesterton's concept from 1902 that the detective story is the romance of the modern city[6] does not prove true; though more stories were set in the city than is often realised, it would still be in a sequestered area, an apartment or at most a few streets, and the archetypal setting of the English novels (unlike most of the American ones) was a more or less secluded country house – indeed Raymond Williams sees the detective novel as an evolution of the country-house literary tradition, though a house based on capital riches, not landed wealth.[7]

The story is also socially enclosed: lower classes, especially professional criminals, play very minor roles. The criminal comes from among the social circle of the victim, and servants are very rarely guilty – and if so will usually be in some form of social disguise. The master-villains who were so popular in the early twentieth century[8] and who survive to the present in thrillers are not found in the clue-puzzle.

The wider politics of the context are ignored: as Julian Symons observed for Christie's characters 1926 was not the year of the General Strike.[9] The elements of capitalist malpractice that dominate the first chapter of *Trent's Last Case* and provide the motive for murder in Mary Roberts Rinehart's *The Circular Staircase* (1908) are rarely represented in the classic clue-puzzle.

The victim will be a man or (quite often) a woman of some importance and wealth, though that position is rarely of long-standing or antique respectability: instability is constant. The victim is also a person of little emotive value; he or she is not mourned, nor is the real pain and degradation of violent death represented.

Detection is rational rather than active or intuitional, a method which fits with the unemotional presentation of the crime. It will be undertaken by someone, usually a man, who is either an amateur or, especially later in the period, a police official who is distinguished (usually on a class basis) from the run-of-the-mill police. But even the amateur often has a friend or relative who is himself a high-ranking police official, such as Ellery Queen's father or Peter Wimsey's eventual brother-in-law.

The rational and at most semi-official detection will focus strongly on circumstantial evidence and will eventually ratify it, properly interpreted, as a means of identifying the criminal. Sometimes there will be a gesture towards 'psychology' – as in Christie and Van Dine – but this is almost always merely a matter of human types and likely motives, not depth analysis.

The writing style will usually match the rational circumstantial detection in being decidedly plain, expressing what Dennis Porter calls a sense of 'social conformity, circumspection, and sobriety',[10] with neither authorial voice nor characters given any elaboration. Even when there is more detail in the detective's persona it will tend to be two-dimensional as with learning (Philo Vance, Peter Wimsey), eccentricity (Nero Wolfe, Hercule Poirot), or apparent folly (Reggie Fortune, Peter Wimsey again). More elaborate writing and depth characterisation appear in writers who move towards the psychothriller like Dorothy L. Sayers or A. B. Cox.

There will be a range of suspects, all of whom appear capable of the crime and are equipped with motives; this is a development from the earlier period, and may be stimulated by the need for a fuller plot in the novel: largely absent in the nineteenth-century short stories, it is a marked feature of Wilkie Collins's *The Moonstone* (1868), A. K. Green's *The Leavenworth Case* (1878) and Gaston Leroux's *The Mystery of the Yellow Room* (1908).

Romance is rare – though it can occur, both between two suspects and between the detective and a possible suspect. Contemporary commentators were largely against romance in the clue-puzzle, some implying it is hostile to the rational tone, others pointing out that this feature tends to remove people from the suspect list.

The identification of the criminal is usually the end of the story. It is very rare for execution to be included, though suicide or an appropriate accident can intervene; if the police arrest the murderer this is represented without melodrama: as with the victim's death, the tone is cerebral and contained.

The most striking of the clue-puzzle features, setting it clearly apart from its predecessors, are the multiple suspects and the rational analysis of determinedly circumstantial evidence. These standard features mesh strongly with the most widely known and most unusual element of the clue-puzzle form, the fact that the reader is challenged to match the detective's process of identifying the murderer and there should therefore be 'fair play': the reader must be informed of each clue that the detective sees. Some earlier stories, such as Doyle's 'The Golden Pince Nez' (1905) and Chesterton's 'The Blue Cross' (1911) did present clues, but this was not a central or genre-defining practice until the clue-puzzle formed.

Whether readers actually were so closely involved in detection or not, the form insists this is a possibility, and there was widespread critical recognition that the modern crime fiction story had been reshaped along the lines outlined above. An early book on the form appeared in 1913 by Carolyn Wells who, like Mary Roberts Rinehart, wrote early woman-focused mysteries in America. She proposed a classical origin for crime fiction, including Voltaire, outlined many of the clue-puzzle features, especially its 'stirring mental exercise',[11] deprecated servants as murderers as well as elaborate writing, pity for the victim and a range of plot clichés; she recommended a psychological approach and even suggested the murderer might be wrongly exonerated early in the story. The book was not published in Britain (nor were most of her novels), but it is tempting to think Christie read a copy, perhaps through her American relatives.

In the mid-to-late 1920s a whole series of accounts of the form appeared. R. Austin Freeman in 1924 praised its 'mental gymnastics' and 'intellectual satisfaction',[12] while E. M. Wrong, an Oxford historian, insisted in 1926 on 'a code of fair play to the reader',[13] gave a full account of possible classical sources and more probable nineteenth-century ones, recognised Christie as a major figure and disliked psychological sympathy for the criminal.[14] This recognition of the clue-puzzle was shared by Willard Huntington Wright, the real name of S. S. Van Dine, who wrote an introduction to a Scribner's anthology in 1927, the year after his *The Benson Murder Case* appeared with great success. He emphasised 'the category of riddles'[15] and frowned on anything which detracted from the puzzle; he criticised Christie for being artificial (which comes oddly from him) and gave a list of clichés much like that found in Wells. The best-known of these critiques was Dorothy L. Sayers's 1928 anthology introduction: she fully recognised the clue-puzzle and gave it the now familiar ancient genealogy, but also set out a programme for 'a new and less rigid formula . . . linking it more closely to the novel of manners'.[16] While her own practice would later pursue this aim, the pure clue-puzzle was at the time widely recognised and codified: both Van Dine and Ronald Knox (himself the author of some intelligent and entertaining puzzles) produced lists of rules and Knox's formed the basis for the oath of the Detection Club that he set up with Sayers, Chesterton, E. C. Bentley and A. B. Cox among others. Van Dine's list,[17] which was published first, emphasises clarity and unity of technique, as well as fair play, matters which Knox repeats in condensed form,[18] adding advice against plagiarism: individual rights and duties are always central to the form.

In a short period, the clue-puzzle had emerged as a dominant form, a fact charted by A. E. W. Mason's two most successful mysteries. *At the Villa Rose* (1910) has a clever, vain detective, Inspecteur Hanaud, and he solves a murder in a large house. But the murder is done by a gang assisted by a servant, with few clues and no other suspects, and the mystery is resolved two-thirds of the way through: the rest is explanation. In 1924 Mason produced *The House of the Arrow* with the same detective and a similar setting, but this time there are multiple suspects, many fair clues (not quite all of them though), an investigation leading to a dramatically revealing climax, and the illusions – a pen doubling as a poisoned arrow, a clock seen in a mirror – beloved of the clue-puzzle form.

The triumph of the form is so clear and sudden that some contextual forces must be suspected as causing this remarkable development. One cause was that these books were novels. The basic late nineteenth-century mystery was the short story, with a single puzzling event and a single villain, deftly exposed by a detective who reveals few clues before the end. Mystery might well play a role in the longer form of the three-decker novel but only rarely was it elaborated to the length required and then the method was usually a slow development of a single enigma with elaborate setting and characterisation, as in Mary Braddon's *Lady Audley's Secret* (1862). But when in the 1890s the three-decker novel collapsed, a sensational mystery plot was one of the viable forms for the newly popular one-volume novels – in George Gissing's *New Grub Street* (1891), producing one is recommended to a novelist blocked on his new three-decker. The short story does not die – most of the between-the-wars writers produced stories along with their novels, and there are even curious hybrids, books presented as novels which are really a collection of stories, such as H. C. Bailey's popular *Call Mr Fortune* (1920) – but the novel is the classic form of the clue-puzzle and the multiple suspect plot fills it well, though there may also be other thematic causes for its popularity, as will be discussed later.

Another crucial element in the development of the new form was the gender of its audience. The magazines that carried short stories, *The Strand*, *Pearson's*, *Windsor* and so on, were designed for men, though they often had sections for the family. But lending libraries which, as Colin Watson has outlined,[19] were the basic medium for dissemination of the new clue-puzzle novels had a 75 percent female audience. The tendency towards intellect and observation, rather than heroic action, and the marked limitation of strong masculinity in the detective heroes shape a form which is increasingly read, and written, by women. In 1913 Carolyn Wells listed eight other women crime writers,[20] and the role of major women writers in the classic form is well known.

It was a man, though, who took a major step in de-heroising the detective. In his autobiography E. C. Bentley said that, in turning to crime fiction in *Trent's Last Case* (1913), he was keen to present a detective who was 'recognizable as a human being'[21]: he made his hero Philip Trent fall in (reciprocated) love with the widow of the dead Sigsbee Manderson, and give a basically false interpretation of the evidence. But Bentley did not create the classical clue-puzzle mode of multiple suspects, and most of the final section – before the last twist – is about Trent's love-life. The belated sequel of 1935, *Trent's Own Case* (co-written with H. Warner Allen), follows the clue-puzzle formulae fully: he may have made a crucial step with the detective, but the development of the new form was in other hands.

Christie is the crucial figure: as Symons comments, her work is 'original in the sense that it is a puzzle story which is solely that'[22] and Martin Priestman identifies her as the originator of 'a pattern of extraordinary resilience'.[23] Agatha Christie was a well-bred young woman with almost no formal education – though, revealingly, she would have chosen mathematics, according to Jessica Mann[24] – when in 1916 her elder sister challenged her to write a novel. She later (through Poirot in *The Clocks*, 1963) acknowledged the power of Leroux's *The Mystery of the Yellow Room* and must have read

Doyle and Bentley, probably Rinehart as well, who was widely published in Britain. *The Mysterious Affair at Styles* appeared in 1920 and it gathers together the archetypal features of the clue-puzzle.

From the start Christie's less than heroic detective Hercule Poirot relies on his 'little grey cells', but in fact his method and focus are primarily domestic: a central question is why the spills on the mantelpiece were re-arranged. Because the crucial information comes through knowledge associated with a female sphere,[25] the detective model is significantly feminised, though it was not until 1930 in *Murder at the Vicarage* that Christie created her own woman investigator, Miss Marple. The intricate plotting of the early Christie novels could rise to spectacular conclusions: in *The Murder of Roger Ackroyd* (1926), in *And Then There Were None* (1939, originally one of her nursery-rhyme titles, *Ten Little Niggers*) and *Murder on the Orient Express* (1934) she staggered the reader with her solutions. Both *The Mystery of the Yellow Room* and Israel Zangwill's *The Big Bow Mystery* (1892) had ended with outrageous surprises, but Christie had the art of making the reader acknowledge, in admiring bafflement, that the final coup was the only possible outcome of her cunning plotting.

Not all her novels were so operatically elaborate, but her energy and variety were consistent. Priestman's account of ten major novels shows a wide range of concerns: the 'central motives are . . . money, fear of exposure and sexual jealousy'[26] and he shows that her focus on women characters included victims, murderers and sympathetic characters.[27] Christie invoked a world of unnerving uncertainty, in which only the fiction of detection brought security.

Some commentators, mostly American, have found the novels little more than meaningless riddles, as in Raymond Chandler's celebrated dismissal of events at 'Cheesecake Manor' as ludicrously artificial.[28] It is certainly true that the novels are restricted in setting, class and behaviour, realising in a mandarin way the patterns of a southern English high bourgeois world (not, as many Americans think, an upper-class world) and insistently euphemising death, passion and politics. Yet as Robert Barnard has shown,[29] there is recurrent conflict in this world, and Alison Light sees uncertainty as a basic pattern.[30] Styles is a nest of jealousy and unease; Roger Ackroyd's house is full of impostures and anxiety. Christie's criminals are traitors to the class and world which is so calmly described, and their identification, through the systems of limited knowledge and essentially domestic inquiry, is a process of exorcising the threats that this society nervously anticipates within its own membership: the multiple suspect structure has special meaning in a competitive individualist world.

The perfected clue-puzzle was the form adopted by the scholarly American art-historian and intellectual journalist Willard Huntington Wright when he entered crime fiction as S. S. Van Dine. *The Benson Murder Case* sold rapidly in 1926 and his intricate, learning-heavy New York puzzles dominated the US market, with twelve novels and eleven films, until the irresistible rise of the private eye thriller in the mid and late 1930s. His detective Philo Vance is an archetypal East Coast American Europhile; Ogden Nash said famously that 'Philo Vance needs a kick in the pance', but it is hard to read the early novels, especially the footnotes, without feeling that Wright was, as Bentley had done with Trent and Christie would with Mrs Oliver, to some extent guying both himself and the form.

His plots locate murder in the social and financial life of New York. With an intricate timetable of visitors and telephone calls Van Dine moves steadily – sometimes turgidly – through a range of suspects and their movements before finding a key physical clue. As in Christie, events are euphemised, even to the point of improbability: in a review of *The Benson Murder Case*, Dashiell Hammett noted that in reality the gun would have knocked the victim halfway across the room, and he thought the major clue was that someone had lifted him back into the chair.[31] But such mundane actuality is not the business of a Van Dine text: it is in part an intricate puzzle, in part an assertion of the conflicted energy of New York social and financial circles, and also a characteristic statement – like those then being made by Hollywood – that whatever Europe might develop, America can do better.

Just as the early American women crime writers have been overlooked, the strength of the American clue-puzzle tends to be disregarded by British commentators and deprecated by the tough-guy preferences of most American academics. S. S. Van Dine was followed by the Ellery Queen novels: T. J. Binyon calls them 'the most artificial of all detective stories' but he also identifies their 'impeccable fairness'.[32] Frederic Dannay and Manfred B. Lee, the two cousins who wrote as 'Ellery Queen' about a detective with the same name, won a publisher's competition with *The Roman Hat Mystery* (1929) and remained both creators and critics of the form: their *Queen's Quorum*[33] is a scholarly and enthusiastic account of the best short crime stories and from 1941 they edited the influential *Ellery Queen's Mystery Magazine*.

Ellery Queen produced the purest clue-puzzles; their early novels include a formal 'Challenge to the Reader', advising that all clues have now been fairly given. The plots are highly intricate, turning on the possibilities of physical data – locked rooms, wrong corpses in the coffin, how many cups of coffee are in a pot. They can feel mechanical – Symons speaks of the 'relentlessly analytical treatment of every possible clue'[34] – but they can also use melodramatic and improbable detail: *The American Gun Mystery* (1933) depends on a horse keeping a spare gun in its mouth during a New York rodeo event, and in *The Chinese Orange Mystery* (1934) the corpse has all his clothes turned round to conceal the fact that he was a clergyman. Ellery Queen combines the grotesque with the mundane, but not only for excitement: like Van Dine, Queen clearly had a sense of the possible violence of the city, that these luxurious, secure-seeming residences can be penetrated by some yet unidentified force.

Rex Stout, starting with *Fer de Lance* (1934), is another writer who descends from S. S. Van Dine; his detective is also enormously learned, but he is not active like Philo Vance, and solves his cases from his desk, with lengthy periods of relaxation among his orchids. Nero Wolfe is based on Mycroft rather than Sherlock Holmes and his inactivity calls up an unusually energetic Watson figure in Archie Goodwin. Stout writes in a less arch way than Van Dine or Queen and his plotting is not as intense as theirs: he dilutes the mandarin New York mode, which developed an American romance of the city quite different from that of the contemporary and ultimately more influential West Coast thriller.

It was in Britain that the clue-puzzle had its richest development, and not everybody followed Christie. 1920, her first year, saw two other major writers newly at work who had their own patterns and their own influence. Freeman Wills Crofts's *The Cask* was the first of thirty-two novels which combined the rigorous detail of R. Austin Freeman with a down-to-earth detecting method much like the plodding, prolific and popular J. S. Fletcher. Crofts's well-known Inspector French did not emerge until 1925 in what was for Crofts an unusually dramatic title, *Inspector French's Greatest Case*, but all his novels share a meticulous, sometimes mechanical, attention to detail in a world less secluded than Christie's, with an emphasis on public transport, especially railway trains and timetables. Both W. H. Wright and Raymond Chandler admired Croft's craftsmanship,[35] as did W. H. Auden (see below), and his work shows that ordinary lives and plain investigation could be part of 'golden age' crime fiction. He had followers in this demotic mode such as John Rhode and Henry Wade: Symons uses the term 'humdrum' for Crofts and his school, implying a negative judgement, both aesthetic and social, which was not apparent in the bookshops and libraries of the period.

Also in 1920 H. C. Bailey, regarded in the period as a major author, produced the sequential story-collection *Call Mr Fortune*. As skilful as Freeman's Dr Thorndyke, Fortune is plump, talkative and as humane as Trent. He affects the disarming foolish manner that would soon be found in Peter Wimsey and Albert Campion, and not unlike Sayers and Allingham, Bailey has a distinctive style, frequently writing with a seemingly casual subtlety that validates the judgements Fortune makes about people, which can lead to a decision to set them free as Holmes sometimes did or even, in a more radical instance, also in the first book, to throw a villain out of a window to his death.

Bailey seems to have influenced Sayers in the nature of her detective and also the sense that crime stories could have a social and moral edge. Her first novel, *Whose Body?* (1923), is a closely plotted puzzle combining circumstantial detail and sometimes strained events; she gives Peter Wimsey a personality milder than Fortune's and a very wide cultural expertise: many people have found both charming. *Strong Poison* (1930) has a more credible mystery plot with good but not over-stressed characterisation, notably in the women who surround Lord Peter – Miss Climpson, a Marple avatar, Miss Murchison, a young professional woman, and the somewhat ironic self-representation of Harriet Vane, arrested innocent and beloved of Wimsey.

In her quest for 'the novel of manners' Sayers turned towards, as she later said,[36] a more literary mode in the spirit of Collins and Sheridan Lefanu. The balance of mystery and manners was difficult: *The Nine Tailors* (1934) offers a criminal plot both banal and improbable and a wealth of colour – campanology, fen weather and Christian symbolism. John G. Cawelti found the religious subtleties of the book impressive enough to override its criminographical deficiencies, but Edmund Wilson thought it 'one of the dullest books I have ever encountered'.[37] The logic of Sayers's literary approach took her, in *Gaudy Night* (1935), to write a book without a murder, interweaving issues of gender, independence, learning and romance, and responses have ranged from the adulation of fans to rejection, even from an enthusiast like Janet Hitchman, who feels it 'definitely her worst'.[38]

Sayers was not alone in her search for human colour in the crime novel. In 1929 Margery Allingham produced her first Albert Campion mystery, *The Crime at Black Dudley*, and she has remained a major name. Most of her early novels are, as Jessica Mann notes (pp. 189–93), in keeping with her family's literary habits, crime-focused fantasies with nobility, country houses, international gangs and a detective of noble, possibly royal birth. The liveliest of these is *Sweet Danger* (1933) but Allingham's more serious side appeared in *Police at the Funeral* (1931), a dark story of murder and mania outside Cambridge and in the more satirical but also sharp-edged *The Fashion in Shrouds* (1938) which deals with London theatre and the fashion industry and includes Campion's sister, a talented, passionate and troubled woman like Sayers's Vane. Both the Cambridge family and the London set are riven with anxiety and conflict – including a snobbishness shared by the characters and, sometimes, as Symons notes,[39] the author – and Campion is as much confessor to a troubled period as decoder of contradictory evidence.

Another of Sayers's near contemporaries remodelled the clue-puzzle in a more influential way. Anthony Berkeley Cox, a journalist and all-round writer, was early involved in the activities of the Detection Club, and in *The Poisoned Chocolates Case* (1929), he used and mocked the detectives and techniques of his contemporaries (Christie did much the same in the less feted *Partners in Crime*, also in 1929). Starting with *The Layton Court Mystery* (1925) he created an anti-heroic detective in Roger Sheringham, languid and rude as well as percipient, but Cox's main claim to historical standing is in taking more seriously than most the interest in psychology in crime fiction. This had been explored by Americans – Wells and Rinehart, Arthur B. Reeve and C. Daly King (a psychologist who wrote the quite complex 'Obelists' series), mentioned by Christie and Van Dine and explored more fully by Sayers in her troubled characters. But Cox is the first to make psychological use of the 'inverted' story, where the murderer is revealed from the start. Freeman had pioneered this variation to emphasise Dr Thorndyke's explanatory genius, but Cox felt, like Sayers, that 'the detective story is in the process of developing into the novel' and sought to write 'the story of a murder rather than the story of the detection of a murder'.[40]

For this project he chose the name Francis Iles (from his own smuggler ancestor[41]) in *Malice Aforethought* (1931) and *Before the Fact* (1932). *Malice Aforethought* focuses inwardly on the neurotic fantasies of a murder with disturbing credibility, while the more complex narrative of *Before the Fact* uses the unreliable viewpoint of the fated woman, to construct, like a clue-puzzle in reverse, an account of her husband's developing criminality. But Cox's view is social as well as personal: the final sequence, and the title, suggest that many people's behaviour may make them accomplices to murder, including their own. Cox's modern standing is partly due to Julian Symons, who made him the climax of his chapter on the 1930s in *Bloody Murder* and apparently saw him as a prior validation of his own fiction in the 1950s and 1960s, but Cox was acknowledged in his time as a major figure and might well have been an influence on Margaret Millar, the powerful American creator of psychothrillers in the 1940s and 1950s.

A major technician of the form, John Dickson Carr, was born in America but long resident in Britain (because of his prolific production he also wrote as Carter Dickson). He started with a French detective, Henri Bencolin, but although *It Walks by Night* (1930) is rich in colour and melodrama, its plot is not particularly ingenious or convincing, nor is that of the hectic action of the American-set, detective-free *Poison in Jest* (1932). But in his later work Carr combines real ingenuity (Symons speaks of his 'astonishing skill'[42]) and rich context with the disbelief-suspending force of a larger-than-life detective. Gideon Fell, modelled on G. K. Chesterton, dominates the talk, action and detection, though by being fat, sedentary and literary he is still a variant on the heroic model; Sir Henry Merivale, the detective in the Carter Dickson series, is an equally large-scale figure. Carr can be detailed and meticulous, as in Fell's famous 'locked room lecture' in Chapter 17 of *The Hollow Man* (1935; in the USA *The Three Coffins*), but equally impressive is the rich texture of his novels. Fell also says in his lecture that he likes his murders 'frequent, gory and grotesque' and, as S. T. Joshi explains, Carr saw gruesomeness, suggestions of the supernatural and broad caricature as a proper part of the inherently fantastic puzzle form.[43] In the same inherently unrealistic way the crimes and motivations in his story tend towards a readily dismissed derangement rather than the social and financial anxieties which underlie the crime in many of the 'golden age' writers.

Ngaio Marsh followed Sayers and Allingham with a gentleman police detective named Alleyn, after the Elizabethan actor who founded the high-class London school that Chandler attended. Marsh, born in New Zealand and living in 1930s London, produced mysteries with often banal outcomes – in *The Nursing Home Murder* (1935) a well-constructed puzzle is resolved through accident and blamed on madness. Her contextual material, whether to do with theatre, art, or sometimes New Zealand is often interesting and this has for many readers redeemed her limitations in puzzle-construction. Fully located overseas were Arthur Upfield's Australian outback mysteries with the exotic half-Aboriginal detective, bizarrely named Napoleon Bonaparte. But the aura of difference is misleading: Upfield's settings, though geographically enormous, are effectively enclosed, and he offers a standard clue-puzzle pattern of detailed observation, many suspects and red herrings, but his detective now seems a racially patronising fiction, as fits a thoroughly colonial clue-puzzle.

'Michael Innes', actually the Oxford don J. I. M. Stewart, established himself by the late 1930s as a specialist in witty and literary mysteries, with another well-born policeman, Appleby, who eventually inherits a title. As far-fetched and literary as Sayers but without her continuing interest in social and religious forces – Symons calls him a 'farceur'[44] – Stewart was an exotic but popular taste. Nicholas Blake was also highly placed – the pseudonym conceals Cecil Day Lewis, one of the major 1930s poets. Starting with *A Question of Proof* (1935), his detective hero Nigel Strangeways is physically modelled on W. H. Auden. A sense of unease with wealth and leisure comes through the texts, especially the later pre-war ones, and Blake, briefly a member of the Communist Party, can be linked to the small group of leftist crime writers of the period. The better-known, Montagu Slater and Eric Ambler, wrote spy stories, but there were some in mainstream crime fiction, as Andy Croft has noted, like Maurice Richardson.[45]

Other writers were admired in the period and still command respect: Patricia Wentworth with her spinster detective Miss Silver in *The Grey Mask* (1928), pre-dating Miss Marple; Josephine Tey with her uneasily veridical novels, starting with *The Man in the Queue* (1929); Georgette Heyer, better known for romances, with clever and socially aware stories like *Death in the Stocks* (1935); Gladys Mitchell, whose formidable detective Mrs (later Dame) Adela Lestrange Bradley was both a psychiatrist and a conscious feminist – *The Saltmarsh Murders* (1932) was a considerable success; Mignon Eberhart who continued the Wells-Rinehart tradition of female evaluative analysis (slightingly called, by Odgen Nash again, the 'Had I But Known' approach), starting with *The Patient in Room 18* (1929); Cyril Hare whose lucid legal mysteries started with *Tenant for Death* (1937); Josephine Bell, whose sequence of realistic, detective-free crime stories, especially *The Port of London Murders* (1938) still seem up to date; even Edgar Wallace, the best-selling thriller writer who started with a puzzle in *The Four Just Men* (1906) and produced crisp detective short stories in *The Mind of Mr J. G. Reeder* (1925).

World-wide in range, intensely popular in Britain and America, having a clear structure and variations, the classic clue-puzzle was a major literary formation. The causes for its development and success have been widely discussed, though not agreed upon. Most analysts recognise one aspect of the form as a puzzle or even, like Jacques Barzun, a riddle,[46] facilitating what Freeman in 1924 called 'mental gymnastics' or what H. R. F. Keating has recently described as 'simple and uncomplicated mental comfort'.[47] Some commentators point to the almost exactly contemporary development of the crossword puzzle, also requiring literary skills, close attention to detail and providing a sense of a problem neatly solved: 'Torquemada', the famous *Observer* crossword creator, reviewed crime fiction in the same pages and E. B. Punshon published *Crossword Mystery* (1934) where a crossword solution was a crucial clue.

Solving the puzzle, however, often has a wider meaning, as the revealed criminal is also exposed as without moral sense and rejecting the practices of normal society. E. M. Wrong made this claim for crime fiction and so, according to Malcolm J. Turnbull, did Cox[48]; Christie herself consistently saw 'evil' as the motivating force in a criminal.[49] George Grella's view that crime fiction is a 'comedy'[50] sees the resolution as restoring order to a threatened social calm, while others saw this function as para-religious: C. Day Lewis, writing under his criminographical pseudonym Nicholas Blake, linked 'the rise of crime fiction with the decline of religion at the end of the Victorian era'[51] and Erik Routley sees the whole motive of the detective story as essentially 'Puritan', rejecting excess in any form, murderous, sexual, even convivial.[52]

W. H. Auden felt the structure of the 'golden age' story was concerned with the individual and religion, not with social conflict. In his essay 'The Guilty Vicarage' (1948) he sees the conflict of 'innocence and guilt' as central, the reader's sense of personal guilt being consolingly displaced on to the criminal by the 'exceptional individual who is himself in a state of grace'.[53] Although Auden takes Father Brown as an example he also sees this quasi-priestly role at work in plainer mysteries – Freeman Wills Crofts, with Doyle and Chesterton, is one of the only three authors he finds 'completely satisfactory'.[54] Even the inherently hostile Edmund Wilson thought the form drew on 'an all-pervasive feeling of guilt and . . . the fear of impending disaster'.[55]

Another way of decoding the texts in terms of personal guilt is Freudian: Geraldine Pederson-Krag and Charles Rycroft are the best-known interpreters of crime fiction to suggest that the murder stands for the family drama of parental sex, and that the detective's investigations mirror the gaze of the anxious child.[56] This reading of the inner power of the clue-puzzle has not appealed to many – though it is curiously congruent with Auden's sense of the ideal victim being like a father or mother,[57] and this kind of analysis might well deserve reviving in the light of Slavoj Žižek's recent linking of the detective and the psychoanalyst.[58]

Barzun's opinion that crime fiction is essentially a 'tale' connects it implicitly with the ages-long tradition of folk-tale and popular narratives.[59] He stresses a formal element, insisting that the well-shaped quality of the tale is everything. Tsvetan Todorov finds structural power deep in the clue-puzzle through its being two overlapping stories, in which the detective's narrative exposes the true story concealed by the criminal.[60] Grella pursues Barzun's implications in thinking, in the light of Northrop Frye, of the form as a version of 'folk-tale', with implied functions for the folk who create and consume the tales,[61] and this reading is taken further by LeRoy L. Panek in *Watteau's Shepherds*,[62] where he sees the role of the tale as being ludic, that is playful both for relaxation and also to exercise and confirm a whole range of social values, in terms of Johan Huizinga's well-known concept of play as a central human and social mechanism.

All of these separate explanations, from simple puzzle to deep play, through various sorts of anxiety and its displacement, are summarised in an essay by Richard Raskin which groups social and psychological functions into four areas: 'Ludic Functions' including riddle, tale and play; 'Wish-fulfilment Functions' which can involve identification with murderer, detective and even victim; 'Tension Reduction Functions' which deal with displacements of anxiety (including some that may arise from uncontrolled wish-fulfilment) and 'Orienting Functions' which deal with 'social myths' or ideologies.[63] The major clue-puzzles provide rich material in all categories, and Raskin shows in detail how variously potent can be the meanings of the classic clue-puzzle fiction – and other crime fiction genres as well.

Relating to Raskin's third and fourth categories are explanations of the causes and successes of crime fiction which understand it in terms of its period. Some think that in the post-war period, people basically wanted relaxation: Light calls it 'a literature of convalescence'[64] and Priestman names the form 'A Version of Pastoral'.[65] Maxwell Perkins, S. S. Van Dine's editor, felt that behind the success of the form lay 'the anxieties and afflictions of a tragic decade',[66] and the reading of Christie offered by Robert Barnard and Stephen Knight would see the texts as both confronting and also resolving a range of contemporary anxieties: David Trotter sums up his account of English detective fiction by saying that 'it can encompass some fairly major phobias and disruptions'.[67] David I. Grossvogel sees the form as an inherently conservative assertion that 'law, order and property are secure',[68] while Ernest Mandel argues that the detective story is a classic piece of bourgeois culture, shaped to conceal the exploitative reality of class society.[69]

The date of the clue-puzzle must raise the question to what extent it is a version of modernism. Some have thought it was in fact a refuge from modernism: Barzun because of its narrative integrity, and Marjorie Nicolson, an American professor of English writing in 1929, because it established 'a re-belief in a universe governed by cause and effect' and because she was 'weary unto death of introspective and psychological literature'.[70] But it could be argued that the plain flat style, so clear in Christie but common elsewhere, the formal concerns which Barzun applauds, the anonymity of the authorial voice which is so common, and especially the way in which the texts continuously expose identity to be a constructed illusion, are all aspects of modernism. Alison Light sees 'golden age' crime fiction as offering a 'conservative modernism' in much this way,[71] while Priestman sees aspects of 'pre-post-modernism' in the form[72]; it may well be that Sayers and Cox sought a more humanist and character-based form because of the mechanistic modernist structure at the core of the clue-puzzle.

But, like much modernism itself, the texts cannot be seen as fully opposed to humanist individualism. One explanation of the power of the novel as a genre is that it constructs a place for the reader to share the author's intelligence and omniscience: the classic statement of this view is by Catherine Belsey.[73] The clue-puzzle does this directly in inviting the reader to participate, and many of its compulsive features emphasise this function: the need for 'fair play', the reader-testing obsession with red herrings, the dropping of the intermediary Watson, the flat style and the two-dimensional characterisation all create a space for the reader to encounter the author and construct a writerly self.

Escapist but also displacing real anxieties; enclosed in setting but suggesting that the enclosure in itself contains deep personal threats; clever but always implying that you the reader could be as clever; modernist to some degree but also inherently humanist: the 'golden age' clue-puzzle is a highly complex form combining both consolation and anxiety, tests and treats, for those readers who found the form so compulsive in the period – and may still do today.

## NOTES

1 This is the period indicated in Chaps. 7 and 8 of Julian Symons's influential *Bloody Murder: From the Detective Story to the Crime Novel: A History*, 2nd edn (Harmondsworth: Penguin, 1985); in Rosemary Herbert, ed., *The Oxford Companion to Crime and Mystery* the period is given as 1918–39 (New York: Oxford University Press, 1999), p. 186.

2 LeRoy L. Panek, *Watteau's Shepherds: The Detective Novel in Britain 1914–40* (Bowling Green, OH: Popular Press, 1979).

3 Howard Haycraft, *Murder for Pleasure: The Life and Times of the Detective Story* (London: Davies, 1942).

4 Marion Shaw and Sabine Vanacker, *Reflecting on Miss Marple* (London: Routledge, 1991), p. 10.

5 Sally R. Munt, *Murder by the Book? Feminism and the Crime Novel* (London: Routledge, 1994), p. 8.

6 G. K. Chesterton, 'A Defence of Detective Stories' (1902), reprinted in Howard Haycraft, ed., *The Art of the Mystery Story: A Collection of Critical Essays*, 2nd edn (1946; New York: Caroll and Graf, 1983), pp. 4–5.

7 Raymond Williams, *The Country and the City* (London: Chatto, 1973), pp. 298–9.

8 T. J. Binyon, *'Murder Will Out': The Detective in Fiction* (Oxford: Oxford University Press, 1989), pp. 127–8.

9 Symons, *Bloody Murder*, p. 96.

10 Dennis Porter, *The Pursuit of Crime: Art and Ideology in Crime Fiction* (New Haven: Yale University Press, 1980), p. 135.

11 Carolyn Wells, *The Technique of the Mystery Story* (Springfield: The Home Correspondence School, 1913), p. 63.

12 R. Austin Freeman, 'The Art of the Detective Story' (1924), reprinted in Haycraft, ed., *The Art of the Mystery Story*, p. 11.

13 E. M. Wrong, 'Introduction' to *Crime and Detection* (1926), reprinted in Haycraft, ed., *The Art of the Mystery Story*, p. 23.

14 *Ibid.*, pp. 22 and 26.

15 Willard Huntington Wright, 'Introduction' to *The Great Detective Stories* (1927), reprinted in Haycraft, ed., *The Art of the Mystery Story*, p. 35.

16 Dorothy L. Sayers, 'Introduction' to *The Omnibus of Crime* (1928), reprinted in Haycraft, ed., *The Art of the Mystery Story*, pp. 108–9.

17 S. S. Van Dine, 'Twenty Rules for Writing Detective Stories' (1928), reprinted in Haycraft, ed., *The Art of the Mystery Story*, pp. 189–93.

18 Ronald A. Knox, 'A Detective Story Decalogue', from his 'Introduction' to *The Best Detective Stories of 1928* (1929), reprinted in Haycraft, ed., *The Art of the Mystery Story*, pp. 194–6.

19 Colin Watson, *Snobbery with Violence: English Crime Stories and Their Audience* (London: Eyre and Spottiswoode, 1971), Chap. 2, 'Mr Smith, Mr Boot and others'.

20 Wells, *Technique of the Mystery Story*, p. 313.

21 E. C. Bentley, *Those Days* (London: Constable, 1940), p. 252.

22 Symons, *Bloody Murder*, p. 92.

23 Martin Priestman, *Crime Fiction from Poe to the Present* (Plymouth: Northcote House, 1998), p. 19.

24 Jessica Mann, *Deadlier than the Male: An Investigation into Feminine Crime Writing* (Newton Abbot: David and Charles, 1981), pp. 124–5.

25 This issue is discussed in Stephen Knight, *Form and Ideology in Crime Fiction* (London: Macmillan, 1980), pp. 109–10.

26 Martin Priestman, *Detective Fiction and Literature: The Figure on the Carpet* (Basingstoke: Macmillan, 1990), pp. 154–60.

27 *Ibid.*, p. 155.

28 Raymond Chandler, 'The Simple Art of Murder', (1944), reprinted in Haycraft, ed., *The Art of the Mystery Story*, p. 231.

29 Robert Barnard, *A Talent to Deceive: An Appreciation of Agatha Christie* (London: Collins, 1980), Chap. 6, 'Strategies of Deception'.

30 Alison Light, *Forever England: Femininity, Literature and Conservatism between the Wars* (London: Routledge, 1991), pp. 57–9.

31 Dashiell Hammett, review of *The Benson Murder Case*, *Saturday Review of Literature*, New York, 15 January 1927, reprinted in Haycraft, ed., *The Art of the Mystery Story*, p. 382.

32 Binyon, '*Murder Will Out*', p. 62.

33 Ellery Queen, *Queen's Quorum: A History of the Detective Crime Short Story as Revealed by the 106 Most Important Books Published in this Field since 1845* (Boston: Little, Brown & Co., 1951).

34 Symons, *Bloody Murder*, p. 111.

35 See Wright, 'Introduction', p. 61 and Chandler, 'The Simple Art of Murder', p. 229.

36 Dorothy L. Sayers, 'Gaudy Night' (1937), reprinted in Haycraft, ed., *The Art of the Mystery Story*, p. 209.

37 John G. Cawelti, 'The Art of the Classical Detective Story: Artistic Failures and Successes: Christie and Sayers', part of Chap. 5 of his *Adventure, Mystery, and Romance: Formula Stories as Art and Popular Culture* (Chicago: University of Chicago Press, 1976), reprinted in Robin Winks, ed., *Detective Fiction: A Collection of Critical Essays* (Englewood Cliffs, NJ: Prentice-Hall, 1980), pp. 193–9; Edmund Wilson, 'Who Cares Who Killed Roger Ackroyd?' (1945), reprinted in Haycraft, ed., *The Art of the Mystery Story*, p. 392.

38 Janet Hitchman, *Such a Strange Lady: An Introduction to Dorothy L. Sayers* (London: New English Library, 1975), p. 108.

39 Julian Symons, 'Margery Allingham', in his *Criminal Practices* (London: Macmillan, 1994), pp. 63–4.

40 Anthony Berkeley, 'Preface' to *The Second Shot* (London: Hodder and Stoughton, 1930), pp. 5 and 7.

41 Malcolm J. Turnbull, *Elusion Aforethought: The Life and Writing of Anthony Berkeley Cox* (Bowling Green, OH: Popular Press, 1996), p. 5.

42 Symons, *Bloody Murder*, p. 110.

43 S. T. Joshi, *John Dickson Carr: A Critical Study* (Bowling Green, OH: Popular Press, 1990), pp. 98–101.

44 Symons, *Bloody Murder*, p. 115.

45 Andy Croft, 'Worlds Without End Foisted Upon the Future – Some Antecedents of *Nineteen Eighty Four*,' in C. Norris, ed., *Inside the Myth* (London: Lawrence and Wishart, 1984), pp. 183–216.

46 Jacques Barzun, 'Detection and the Literary Art' (1961), reprinted in Winks, ed., *Detective Fiction*, p. 145.

47 See H. R. F. Keating, in Herbert, ed., *Oxford Companion to Crime and Mystery*, p. 186.

48 Wrong, 'Introduction', p. 31 and Turnbull, *Elusion Aforethought*, p. 115.

49 See also Christie's comment to this effect in her *An Autobiography* (London: Collins, 1977), p. 527; this is also discussed by Light, *Forever England*, pp. 100–1.

50 George Grella, 'The Formal Detective Novel' (1976), reprinted in Winks, *Detective Fiction*, p. 88.

51 Nicholas Blake, 'Introduction' to Haycraft, *Murder for Pleasure*, p. xx.

52 Erik Routley, 'The Case Against the Detective Story', (1972), reprinted in Winks, ed., *Detective Fiction*, pp. 176–8.

53 W. H. Auden, 'The Guilty Vicarage', (1948), reprinted in Winks, ed., *Detective Fiction*, pp. 16 and 21.

54 *Ibid.*, p. 20.

55 Edmund Wilson, 'Why Do People Read Detective Stories' (1944), reprinted in his *Classics and Commercials: A Literary Chronicle of the Forties* (London: Allen, 1951), p. 236.

56 Charles Rycroft, 'Analysis of a Detective Story', in his *Imagination and Reality* (London: Hogarth, 1968); Geraldine Pederson-Krag, 'Detective Stories and the Primal Scene', *Psychoanalytic Quarterly* 18 (1949), 207–14, reprinted in Glenn W. Most and William W. Stowe, *The Poetics of Murder* (New York: Harcourt, Brace and Jovanovich, 1983), pp. 14–20.

57 Auden, 'The Guilty Vicarage', p. 19.

58 Slavoj Žižek, 'The Detective and the Analyst', *Literature and Psychology*, 36 (1990), 27–46; see also his 'Two Ways to Avoid the Real of Desire', in his *Looking Awry: An Introduction to Jacques Lacan through Popular Culture* (Cambridge, MA: Massachusetts Institute of Technology Press, 1992).

59 Barzun, 'Detection and the Literary Art', pp. 144–53.

60 Tzvetan Todorov, 'The Typology of Detective Fiction', in his *The Poetics of Prose*, trans. R. Howard (Oxford: Oxford University Press, 1977).

61 Grella, 'The Formal Detective Novel', p. 93.
62 Panek, *Watteau's Shepherds*, pp. 18–19.
63 Richard Raskin, 'The Pleasures and Politics of Detective Fiction', *Clues*, 13 (1992), 71–113.
64 Light, *Forever England*, p. 69.
65 This is the title of Chap. 9 of *Detective Fiction and Literature: The Figure on the Carpet*.
66 Jon Tuska, *Philo Vance: The Life and Times of S. S. Van Dine* (Bowling Green, OH: Popular Press, 1971), p. 20.
67 David Trotter, *The English Novel in History* (London: Routledge, 1993), p. 228.
68 David I. Grossvogel, *Mystery and its Fictions: From Oedipus to Agatha Christie* (Baltimore: Johns Hopkins University Press, 1979), p. 52.
69 Ernest Mandel, 'A Marxist Interpretation of the Crime Story' (1984), reprinted in Winks, ed., *Detective Fiction*, pp. 211 and 215.
70 Marjorie Nicolson, 'The Professor and the Detective' (1929), reprinted in Haycraft, ed., *The Art of the Mystery Story*, pp. 112 and 114.
71 Light, *Forever England*, pp. 65–75.
72 Priestman, *Detective Fiction and Literature*, p. 152.
73 Catherine Belsey, *Critical Practice* (London: Methuen, 1980), especially Chap. 3, 'Addressing the Subject'.

# 6

DENNIS PORTER

# The private eye

Given that it contains a potent and provocative pun, 'private eye' is as good a title as any for a chapter on the emergence of a home-grown, American sub-genre of crime fiction. The obvious alternative, 'hardboiled', is appropriately folksy in its reference to a tough-minded behavioural code but covers more territory and is less resonant. In association with 'private', the eye/I(nvestigator) in question already conjures up some of the defining characteristics of what was to become a popular heroic type in the American grain. A private eye suggests among other things: a solitary eye, and the (forbidden) pleasures associated with Freud's scopic drive[1]; a non-organisation man's eye, like the frontier scout's or the cowboy's; an eye that trusts no other; an eye that's licensed to look; and even, by extrapolation, an eye for hire. To propose further that private eye also connotes those specifically American concepts of 'orneriness' and 'libertarianism' is a stretch, but to anyone familiar with the fictional type, the connection is soon apparent.

That the first appearance of this new ideal type in mass popular fiction occurs at a specific time and place is by now a familiar fact of literary history. The time is, of course, the 1920s and 1930s, and the place at issue is not simply America, but the American far west with a particular emphasis on the state where the advancing frontier finally ran out of land, and where the American dream may be said to have come to an end in more than one sense, California, north and south.

The emergence of private eye crime fiction and the heroic type associated with it depended on a particular historical, socio-economic and cultural conjuncture. On the level of history, it was the decades following the civil war or the so-called Gilded Age that laid the foundations of the modern American industrial capitalist system which was more or less fully formed by the 1920s. The economic take-off associated with the first industrial revolution of iron, steel, steam power, a nation-wide network of railroads, and rapid urbanisation had by then metamorphosed into the age of electricity, the wireless, the telephone, the automobile, the skyscraper and, of course, the moving pictures. Old agrarian America had given way to a new, fast evolving social and material environment characterised by monopoly capitalism, unprecedented wealth especially for the few, the struggle between capital and labour, heightened class conflict, and the progressive massification of everyday life.

In the cultural sphere, the first chroniclers of the new urban reality were, on the one hand, literary naturalists such as Stephen Crane and Theodore Dreiser, and, on the other, the muckraking journalists, of whom Lincoln Steffens is the best known. The theme suggested by the title of the latter's *The Shame of the Cities* (1904) was for the earliest major authors of private eye fictions, Dashiell Hammett (1894–1961) and Raymond Chandler (1888–1959) a familiar one. Urban blight, corrupt political machines, and de facto disenfranchisement of significant sections of the population through graft and influence-peddling were part of the background in which crime of a new and organised kind was to become endemic. It is thus not altogether a coincidence if H. L. Mencken and George Jean Nathan's *Black Mask* magazine, in which both Hammett and Chandler got their start, first appeared in the year after the 18th Amendment to the Constitution was finally ratified, 1919, and the era of Prohibition began. Probably the most deeply misguided piece of legislation of the American twentieth century, its effect was to turn hundreds of thousands of ordinary working and middle-class Americans into criminals, and to create a society in which crime syndicates flourished in the effort to cater to an appetite that could not be contained. With Prohibition the stage was set for an unprecedented wave of crime associated in the popular mind with speed and fire power, fast cars and machine guns. The new frontier the fictional private eyes were to confront was the lapsed, anything-goes world of a jazz age America as it was already mutating into the era of the Great Depression. The time was ripe for the emergence in a popular literary genre of a disabused, anti-authoritarian, muckraking hero, who, instead of fleeing to Europe, like the sophisticates of lost generation fiction, stayed at home to confront crime and corruption on the increasingly unlovely streets of modern urban America.

Raymond Chandler (who else?) expressed most memorably the originality of Hammett's contribution – from the latter's early *Black Mask* stories and his first novel, *Red Harvest* (1929) on – in a celebrated essay that, after Thomas De Quincey in the early nineteenth century ('On Murder Considered as One of the Fine Arts'), he called 'The Simple Art of Murder' (1944): 'Hammett gave murder back to the kind of people who commit it for reasons, not just to provide a corpse; and with the means at hand, not hand-wrought dueling pistols, curare and tropical fish. He put these people down on paper as they were, and he made them talk and think in the language customarily used for these purposes.'[2]

It is characteristic of Chandler that, even more than the weaponry and the motivation of modern American crime, he highlights the importance of language. If classic golden age British crime fiction derives, on one level, from comedy of manners, and chooses a narrative style appropriate to that genre, private eye stories share much of their material with American literary realism – an American realism, moreover, that since Mark Twain involved 'telling it like it is' by means of the spoken language ordinary people themselves used to communicate their experience of the world.

In honorific terms that might have surprised Hammett, Chandler goes on in the same essay to celebrate the character of the latter's private eye – who made his first appearance in the form of the so-called Continental Op in early stories and *Red Harvest* and, even more memorably, as Sam Spade in *The Maltese Falcon* (1930): 'Down these mean streets a man must go who is not himself mean, who is neither tarnished nor afraid. The detective in this kind of story must be such a man. He is the hero, he is everything. He must be a complete man and a common man and yet an unusual man. He must be, to use a rather weathered phrase, a man of honor . . .'[3]

The surprise in the first sentence is in the modal, 'must.' The second makes clear that an updated secular humanist ethic is supposedly at work, one that embodies an idea of duty and of a professional code of conduct. The new and specifically American note sounded is not in the invocation of honour or of a kind of chivalry – Sherlock Holmes had long been the familiar embodiment of that tradition for late Victorian society – but in the emphasis on the commonness of the uncommon man required for the job in the contemporary US. In brief, the private eye is held up to be the stubbornly democratic hero of a post-heroic age, righting wrongs in a fallen urban world in which the traditional institutions and guardians of the law, whether out of incompetence, cynicism or corruption, are no longer up to the task – from the lawmakers themselves and the middle-class citizens who vote them into power to those who execute the law, including the cop on the beat, the local sheriff in his office, and the judge in his courtroom. Fortunately, however, the world-weary, disabused private eyes of the novels themselves are at their best less priggish, more fallibly human, and, intermittently at least, more susceptible to temptation than Chandler suggests here.

There are, of course, literary precedents and foreshadowings of Hammett's creations. Bret Harte's and Jack London's action fiction had opened up the material of American frontier life, and familiarised readers with recognisably American heroic types. Mark Twain had long before adapted the American vernacular for serious literary purposes, and given a new satiric edge to tall tales and Western humour. There had also been a significant shift from dime novel to pulp magazine, from stories of the wild west – scouts, cowboys, and outlaws – into more modern narratives of city life. As James D. Hart pointed out, before the nineteenth century ended there was even a precedent for the urban investigator as popular hero: 'Dime novels of shootings in the Wild West had led to the subject of banditry, and tales of frontier lawlessness in turn led to ones about the more sophisticated crimes of Broadway and the Bowery. In 1886 Russell Coryell created the first of the Nick Cartér stories and the dime novel plunged into a world of detectives and cardsharps, of opium dens and abductions.'[4] Yet none of the material Hart refers to approaches the literary sophistication or the tough-minded authenticity Hammett was to bring to a mass popular genre.

His preparation for the writer's role that he only took up when tuberculosis rendered him unfit for a regular job was itself very much in the American grain. Hammett had first been one of the legendary 'men of action' apparently preferred as writers by J. T. Shaw, the editor of *Black Mask* magazine after 1926. Before he became a *poète maudit* of the urban frontier, Sam Hammett (Dashiell was originally his pen name) had knocked about the country and had held jobs as freight clerk, stevedore, timekeeper, yardman, labourer, and nail-machine operator as well as Pinkerton agent and ambulance corps man. And in Hammett's telling at least even his own mother's proverbial admonitions took a hardboiled form: 'Never go out in a boat without oars – and don't waste your time on a woman who can't cook.'[5]

The change of register Hammett's writing represents is apparent from the opening paragraph of the work that is generally taken to be the first full-length novel of the new, hardboiled type, *Red Harvest* (1929). The strength and vibrancy of the use of the vernacular here is a reminder of what Chandler had in mind. First published in instalments in *Black Mask*, the novel appeared in volume form (another resonant coincidence?) in the year of the stock-market crash, when America was suddenly forced to rethink its dominant socioeconomic ideology in a wholly unprecedented way: 'I first heard Personville called Poisonville by a red-haired mucker named Hickey Dewey in the Big Ship at Butte. He also called a shirt a shoit. I didn't think anything of what he had done to the city's name. Later I heard men who could manage their r's give it the same pronunciation. I still didn't see anything in it but the meaningless sort of humor that used to make richardsnary the thieves' word for dictionary. A few years later I went to Personville and learned better.'[6]

It is fitting if Hammett's first full-length novel in the genre opens with an evocation of the landscape of modern American industrial capitalism and uses the 'eye/I' in question to observe it and report on it. The setting of *Red Harvest* is the kind of company town that, long before he ever thought of becoming a writer, Hammett had experienced first-hand in the Western mining town of Butte, Montana, where, as a Pinkerton agent, he had been hired by the Anaconda Copper Company in the role of strike-breaker. As in that plot staple of so many Westerns, the Continental Op is brought in from out-side (San Francisco in this case) to clean up a corrupt town. However, there is a complexity to Hammett's plot that not only gives rise to the sustained suspense and frequent reversals associated with crime fiction in general, it is also structured so as to allow for significant character development in the narrator/hero himself. As its title implies, there is a heightened level of vi-olence in *Red Harvest*, involving multiple bloody murders, shootouts, and, by the standards of politer crime fiction, a massive application of fire power. It is moreover a violence that the Continental Op is self-conscious enough to realise threatens to taint his own moral being. And a similarly disturbing moral ambiguity prevails at the dénouement as far as the community as a whole is concerned. Although the Op has accomplished his mission of cleans-ing the town of the goons and hoodlums who had originally been brought in as strike-breakers, the corrosive political power of the mine-owner himself has not been broken.

One of the most widely imitated features of *Red Harvest* is Hammett's use of the first person as narrative voice and as point of view, since together they embody a whole way of observing and representing the world. Not only is what is said important but how it is said and the voice that says it. Like his contemporary, Ernest Hemingway, who was conducting similar experiments in a pared-down language for fiction (Hemingway's earliest story collection, *In Our Time,* appeared in 1925), from the opening paragraph of his first novel, Hammett showed how the apparently ordinary, spoken American language could be made to transcend itself in the direction of a new urban poetry. With its staccato rhythm, its echoing vowels, its alliterative energy, its no-nonsense American names, its use of period slang (mucker), and its laconic wit, the evocation of Personville is a sophisticated verbal exercise in the anti-picturesque. At the same time, the voice establishes itself as a distinctly male voice, the voice of a man who has knocked about a bit, and knows how to handle himself on a tough urban street or in an unfashionable neighbourhood dive. The reader in any case is immediately alerted to the fact that, for good reason, he is worlds away from the polite speech of S. S. Van Dine's contemporary American detective fictions, not to speak of those of such British golden age writers as Dorothy L. Sayers and Agatha Christie.

Hammett's most polished work in the genre is *The Maltese Falcon* (1930). Not only does this novel offer the most developed and memorable embodi-ment of the private eye type in Hammett's *oeuvre*, Sam Spade, it also presents a range of other mysterious and richly drawn, eccentric characters, whose names, like those of Dickens, have a larger than life, allegorical resonance, including the Middle Eastern dandy, Joel Cairo, the oratorically puffed-up fat man, Caspar Gutman, and the pouting little hit-man, Wilmer. The hero's own name in a sense says it all, especially when contrasted with that, for example, of the oh, so continental and very New York Philo Vance of Van Dine. In an unmistakable act of auto-identification, Hammett gives Spade his own first name. The choice of Spade itself, on the other hand, clearly signals that a character who shares a name with a common tool, and with a proverbially honest tool at that, is a man of the people destined to speak the truth as he sees it, plainly and clearly. Yet in spite of the suggestively evoked setting of the fog-shrouded city of San Francisco, *The Maltese Falcon* does distance itself in a number of ways from the gritty, socioeconomic realism of *Red Harvest* and points ahead at least as much to *The Thin Man* (1934) and the urbane Nick Charles. In his 1930 work, Hammett draws on situations from some of his earlier stories in order to create a suspense-filled plot in which the abrupt twists and reversals also have the function of underpinning a hardboiled philosophy of life. Spade is a more self-contained, sophisticated, and physically attractive version of the Continental Op, who is not above having an affair with his partner's wife; and, after the murder of that partner in the opening pages, he becomes the quintessential lone operator. The search he is initially hired to undertake by the enigmatic Miss Wonderly (alias Miss Leblanc, alias Brigid O'Shaugnessy) rapidly metamorphoses into the kind of quest associated with adventure novels, namely, that of the supposedly jewel-encrusted, gold bird referred to in the title. But like almost everything else, including most of the characters, nothing in Sam Spade's San Francisco is what it seems to be. People appear and disappear or turn up inconveniently dead. Deceit and the double-cross in the obsessive pursuit of wealth, or even occasionally of sex, are a way of life. Thus it is characteristic finally of Hammett's sardonic wit that what Alfred Hitchcock called 'the Macguffin' – the pretext, insignificant in itself, that is the trigger of the narrative quest – is in this case invested for once with symbolic significance. The bird when it is finally recovered proves, like almost everyone involved, to be a fake. Thus the dénouement takes the satisfactory form of the culmination of a cruel and protracted, practical joke, perpetrated by no one in particular on what turns out to be a freakish gang of comic bunglers who thoroughly deserve what they get, including the seductive Miss O'Shaugnessy herself. It is, therefore, only logical that in the end Spade, who may have fallen for her, happily turns her over to the police for the murder of his partner. In what was to become an iconic gesture in the genre, he declares: 'I won't play the sap for you.'[7] In private eye crime fiction, chivalry, toward a certain kind of woman at least, clearly has its limits. Needless to say, although the murders are solved, the real bird, if it ever existed, is never found. If there is any literary realism in *The Maltese Falcon* then, apart from a few evocations of settings, it is to be found in a kind of witty, laconic, hard-bitten philosophy of life that insists on the absurdity and randomness of events, and the individual's existential loneliness, as the anecdote Spade tells about a certain Flitcraft is designed to suggest. The falling beam that is said to have nearly killed the man, as he was walking by a building site on his way to work, ends up changing his life, but not exactly as he had intended, and not exactly for the better. Hammett was in many ways a writer who was always doubting himself and always striving to reinvent himself; and with *The Maltese Falcon* he produced what is in some respects also the first comic thriller – something that John Huston exploited brilliantly in his 1941 film version with the formidable Humphrey Bogart as Sam Spade and as memorable a cast of character actors as has ever been assembled. The trick in Hammett's novel was in skillfully dosing the indispensable menace and suspense of the thriller genre with a corrosive, wise-guy wit.

The paradox of Hammett is how slim yet influential his *oeuvre* is. Of the total of five novels he published over the course of little more than half a dozen years, only two stand out along with a few early stories. His second novel, *The Dain Curse* (1929), also features the Continental Op in an unsatisfactory confection set in San Francisco again that reads like a convoluted melodrama and turns the tough private eye into a talky and rather sentimental character – he commits himself to rescuing the leading lady from her supposed familial curse and her morphine addiction. *The Glass Key* (1931) is a more complex novel that returns again to the politically radical theme of corruption in American public life. But the task of investigation is undertaken by an amateur detective, who shares relatively few of the traits of the private eye type; and the authorial cynicism projected ends up being both programmatic and predictable. Finally, *The Thin Man* (1934) was written when Hammett had left California for New York. Already a binge drinker with a self-destructive streak and a developing writer's block, he was by then involved in his long and tormented love affair with the playwright, Lillian Hellman. In many ways his last novel is a potboiler, albeit one that has an occasional brittle charm, and seems to have been designed to cash in on his substantial reputation at the time. Cynicism in *The Thin Man* has given way to a kind of world-weary flippancy as a result of which Nick Charles, the retired San Francisco detective hero, is only occasionally diverted from his drinking and his party-going in luxury New York hotel rooms by the admonitions of his rich and sophisticated heiress of a wife. It is difficult not to recognise in Nick Charles in a caricatural, self-mocking form a self-portrait of Hammett himself and the downhill path his own life was taking during his long relationship with the formidable Hellman – whose own capacity for edgy repartee and heavy drinking are clearly reflected in the portrait of Nora.

All traces of Hammett's politically radical sympathies have disappeared from his last novel that along with the madcap bonhomie is pervaded by a sense of futility.

If Hammett largely invented a new language, a new investigator, and a new (symbolic) landscape for American crime fiction, Chandler, who a decade later got his own start publishing stories in *Black Mask* magazine, took that material and gave it a highly polished form in twenty-seven stories, seven novels and five screenplays on which he collaborated. Together they constitute the most important corpus of works in the private eye genre. Given that Chandler was forty-five when he published his first story in *Black Mask*, it is even harder to understand Chandler's ambitions and the significance of his achievement than it is Hammett's without some reference to his life.

It was the accidents of familial history – a divorce and the lack of visible means of support – that led Chandler's Irish Quaker mother to leave Chicago and return to her birthplace in Ireland with her seven-year-old son. From there they soon moved to London. And it was in or near that city that the young Chandler spent the greater part of his formative years. Obviously influential was the time he spent at Dulwich College, a distinguished British public school in Greater London's south eastern suburbs, where among other things he was exposed to a range of classic literature and learned to write. Dulwich College is after all the same institution that fostered the talents of the young P. G. Wodehouse and C. S. Forester. Part of the consequence of that education in Chandler's case was that on leaving school at seventeen, after a few false starts he attempted to live the writer's life, and for a time even settled in Bloomsbury. He struggled to combine work as a reporter with the writing of poetry in a late romantic vein, did pieces for a literary magazine, and even published an unmemorable first short story, 'The Rose-Leaf Romance'. By 1912, however, after having spent some sixteen years in Europe, for financial reasons he felt obliged to give up his dream of the life of a man of letters in Edwardian England and return to the United States. He eventually settled in Southern California and with some reluctance fell into the life of a successful businessman in the oil industry. It was not, in fact, until some twenty years after his earlier literary efforts that the Californian oilman lost his job and decided to try seriously once again to earn his living by the pen – less, it seems, as a consequence of the economic depression than because the heavy drinking in which he indulged left him unfit for normal office work for days at a stretch. This time round after exploring the possibilities and with an older wife to support, he decided to try his hand at the decidedly down-market material published by the pulps.

What Chandler seems to have retained from his earlier brief incarnation as a late romantic, English poet is a taste for the writer's craft and a literary self-consciousness that surpassed even Hammett's – a taste that was fortunately later honed on the works of such major American twentieth-century writers as Theodore Dreiser, Sherwood Anderson, Ernest Hemingway, Ring Lardner and T. S. Eliot as well as on Hammett and Erle Stanley Gardner. Yet the theme of failed romantic quest and the cult of fine writing suggest that the writer with whom Chandler had the greatest affinity was Scott Fitzgerald. Writing in the 1940s, Chandler noted tartly that the art of detective stories was yet to be acknowledged by the critical establishment: 'Neither in this country nor in England has there been any critical recognition that far more art goes into these books at their best than into any number of goosed history or social-significance rubbish. The psychological foundation for the immense popularity with all sorts of people of the novel about murder or crime or mystery hasn't been scratched.'[8] The tribute subsequently paid his work, in particular by such major writers as W. H. Auden, Evelyn Waugh and J. D. Salinger among others, must have gone a long way to assuage the sense of neglect expressed here.

Chandler himself was fully aware of the irony of his situation as a writer of detective stories, and occasionally refers to it with some bitterness. Writing about a work by the quintessentially Edwardian man of letters, Max Beerbohm, he commented: 'I found it sad reading. It belongs to the age of taste, to which I once belonged. It is possible that like Beerbohm I was born half a century too late, and that I, too, belong to an age of grace. I could so easily have become something that our world has no use for'[9] – including, one is tempted to add, another of those effete, early twentieth-century romantics whose work failed to survive the cataclysmic changes wrought by the First World War and the demands of the mass publishing industry. Yet in spite of such melancholy reflections, it is the creative tension between his high-brow literary ambition and the low-brow fictional material in which he worked that goes a long way to explain Chandler's singular achievement. For a combination of reasons, Hammett never lived to exploit fully the potential of the private eye genre. It took a rare talent like Chandler to ensure that it would make possible much of the best and most influential crime writing through the middle decades of the twentieth century and beyond; and that it would also have a major impact on world cinema. It is precisely the ironic disjunction between Chandler's urge to write scenes and sentences as artfully and flawlessly as he possibly could and the mass popular material on which he exercised his talent that explains such masterpieces as *The Big Sleep* (1939), *Farewell, my Lovely* (1940), and *The Long Goodbye* (1953). In the course of his career, he came to appreciate more fully, like Gustave Flaubert 100 years earlier, that great literary art could rise above genre limits, and the realist's material of average and less than average life: 'My whole career is based on the idea that the formula doesn't matter, the thing that counts is what you do with the formula; that is to say, it is a matter of style.'[10]

*The Big Sleep* is as stunning a first novel as one could hope for. This is true on a number of levels. The work is typically episodic in structure, and unified by an investigator and an investigative purpose in which the dramatisation of scene and dialogue generates the suspenseful immediacy that characterises private eye fiction at its best. At the same time – in spite of a few bloopers caused by material cobbled together from earlier stories – the complex plot itself is characterised by a kind of aesthetic wit, since it takes the form of an unnecessary journey. It opens and closes with a scene on the Sternwood estate that implies Philip Marlowe, Chandler's Private Eye, need have looked no further for his first murderer than the first character he meets after the butler, Colonel Sternwood's disturbed younger daughter, Carmen – she even pretends to faint into his arms. The difference between the end and the beginning is that by then not only have a series of violent crimes been solved but the story told has also revealed satisfying truths about life only hinted at in the hidden metaphor of the title. 'The Big Sleep', we learn, is death itself. In terms of the creation of character, Marlowe himself was Chandler's thoughtfully stylish recasting of the model furnished in particular by Sam Spade. And many of the other characters in the novel, starting with the thin-blooded, post-alcoholic Colonel Sternwood in his hothouse, are drawn with an arresting vividness. A similar richly precise attention is also paid to locale. In this as in other respects, *The Big Sleep* furnishes the prototype of what was to become a recognisable Chandler crime novel. He exploits his mystery plot in order to evoke in turn, with the kind of suggestive realist detail that transcends realism, the Sternwood family's multi-millionaire estate, a blackmailing gay man's pad done up in 1930s *chinoiserie*, the hall of justice, a petty hoodlum's apartment, a gangster's upscale casino, a sinister garage by night, and assorted hotels and offices. Although private eye fiction has always had the reputation of offering fast-paced action writing – art and ratiocination were supposed to be the preserve of detective fiction out of the Poe and Doyle tradition – Chandler takes pleasure in lingering over descriptions of decor and atmosphere by means of consciously worked up tableaux that run the gamut from the exotically opulent to the seedy and downright sordid.

Above all, *The Big Sleep* is narrated in the inimitable voice of Chandler's narrator. If Philip Marlowe speaks in an American vernacular, it is the vernacular with a difference, the vernacular heightened and burnished to the level of street-wise poetry – poetry, that is, not so much in the high-brow literary tradition as in the sense Roman Jakobson gave to the word when he described the poetic function of language as that in which the medium knowingly and suggestively reflects back on its own materiality as patterned sound.[11]

If, as Billy Wilder famously said, with Chandler 'a kind of lightning struck on every page,' it is no accident.[12] Such for Chandler were the writerly effects that made literary creation worthwhile: 'But a writer who hates the actual writing, who gets no joy out of the creation of magic by words, to me is simply not a writer at all. The actual writing is what you live for.'[13] It is instructive to compare this view with that of Agatha Christie for whom the pleasure was chiefly in the elaboration of plot, and the writing itself something of a chore. The most characteristic mark of a Chandler novel is, in fact, a quality of stylish extravagance that is to be found in the evocation of place or decor (Colonel Sternwood's hothouse in *The Big Sleep* – 'The plants filled the place, a forest of them, with nasty meaty leaves and stalks like the newly washed fingers of dead men . . . ,'[14]); in the description of memorable characters; in the crisp, throw-away lines of dialogue to be found in almost any chapter of his best works; and in the moments of hard-bitten philosophising about life in which Marlowe occasionally engages especially in his solitary dénouements: 'What did it matter where you lay once you were dead? In a dirty sump or in a marble tower on top of a high hill? . . . You just slept the big sleep, not caring about the nastiness of how you died or where you fell. Me, I was part of the nastiness.'[15]

The quintessence of Chandler's style is what came to be known as a 'Chandlerism'. That is, in the finality of his one- or two-liners that elevates the wise-crack of an American, urban folk tradition to the level of a hardboiled conceit. The thrill of reading him is often less in the pleasurable fear associated with suspense or the unravelling of mystery than in discovering through his imagery what a face has in common with a collapsed lung or a mouth with a wilted lettuce. He put his personal cachet on the genre by combining the epigrammatic flourish of Oscar Wilde with the moral environment of Hemingway's 'The Killers'.

As for Chandler's Philip Marlowe, the very anglophone name suggests right away that he will at the very least be a more stylish version of the Hammett prototype, who enjoys using the language not simply to 'tell it like it is', but to tell it vividly and with wit. In the popular idiom of the time, he is a wise-cracking wise guy. Like Hammett's private eyes before him, Marlowe combines the roles of muck-raker and racket-buster. In behavioural terms, this means he is first of all a pragmatic man of action but one with a work ethic that requires him to take all the punishment low-life hitmen or venal cops can hand out and come back for more. And in spite of the good looks and the aura of romantic longing with which Chandler endows him, there is a sense in which Marlowe, like other fictional Private Eyes, is the small business man as hero. Unlike the upper-class swells with their private incomes of Golden Age British detective fiction, Marlowe works in a service industry where he does what it takes to make an honest living. His hourly fee plus expenses are the means by which he supports his loner's marginal but honourable life. Ideologically then, he is an anti-elitist and even populist hero. Formed by the new, Californian West, he expresses little respect for the Eastern Seaboard and its establishment values. In many ways he shares the attitudes and values of ordinary working Americans toward the rich and the powerful in business or government, who seemed to have failed them so badly during the inter-war years. Thus if modest circumstances are not always a sign of moral rectitude, to be rich in Chandler's fiction takes a lot of explaining. As Marlowe comments in his first incarnation: 'To hell with the rich. They make me sick'[16] – a sentiment that was calculated to go over well in a nation still seared by the memory of the recent Great Depression. The contemporary populist attitudes Marlowe embodies in spite of his stylish wit also extend to a kind of casual period racism that colours the otherwise memorable vignettes of minority types he encounters in the course of his investigations. The irony is, of course, that even when he is expressing his distaste of, say, the living room of a Harvard-educated aesthete like Lindsay Marriott, he does so with stunning verbal aplomb: 'It was the kind of room where people sit with their feet in their laps and sip absinthe through lumps of sugar and talk with high affected voices and sometimes just squeak. It was a room where everything could happen except work.'[17] The most stylish of the fictional private eyes sometimes cohabits awkwardly with the voice of the rugged populist.

His second novel, and Chandler's own favourite, *Farewell, my Lovely*, has a lot in common with *The Big Sleep*. It features once again Philip Marlowe, and is narrated by him, if anything, in an even more stylishly stylised vernacular. Its convoluted plot, too, was derived from the cannibalisation of a number of Chandler's earlier stories. It has a number of exotic motifs, including a rare jade necklace more typically to be found in a work of the polite British tradition. It has a wide range of vividly drawn characters, including the love-struck hoodlum, Moose Molloy – 'a big man but not more than six feet five inches tall and not wider than a beer truck' – and the Indian – 'He had a big flat face and a high-bridged fleshy nose that looked as hard as the prow of a cruiser. He had lidless eyes, drooping jowls, the shoulders of a blacksmith and the short apparently awkward legs of a chimpanzee.'[18] Chandler also elaborates more fully on the way Marlowe is both drawn to and distances himself from women. Worldly and experienced, he may have an eye for a beautiful woman – especially in his period taste for sultry sexy blondes – but the ambivalence is such that his relationships in the end go nowhere. When offered the chance of marriage to the attractive and apparently virtuous Anne Riordan, he walks away from the opportunity. That this is a peculiarly Chandler novel without precedent in the crime fiction genre is above all evident in its central themes. At the heart of all the mystery and intrigue, the disguises, the mistaken identities, the murders, the thefts and the blackmail of typical crime fiction, one finds a tale of old-fashioned romance. Moreover, the dénouement does for once communicate a genuine revelation. The two murderers are in the end the work's unlikely heroes. The first, Moose Molloy, is animated by romantic love for his long lost Velma, who has metamorphosed into Helen Grayle. The second, Velma/Helen herself, is moved by a sentimental loyalty to the rich, older man who rescued her from her marginal life as lounge singer. Never has Chandler sounded more like Fitzgerald, in fact, or Philip Marlowe like Nick Carraway, than in Marlowe's lament for lost loveliness, this time on the Pacific coast: 'After a while there was a faint smell of ocean. Not very much, but as if they had kept this much to remind people this had once been a clean open beach where the waves came in and creamed and the wind blew and you could smell something besides hot fat and cold sweat.'[19]

Chandler completed five other novels after *The Big Sleep* and *Farewell, my Lovely* but by general consent, only one of them is considered to have reached the level of his first two. Apart from the effect on his self-esteem, it did not matter financially at least, since by then a number of his works had been optioned by film studios and made into films – starting with versions of *Farewell, my Lovely* (*Murder, my Sweet,* 1944) and probably his least successful novel, *The High Window* (1942) (*Time to Kill,* 1942). The best adaptation of all Chandler's novels, however, was Howard Hawks's tough and polished version of *The Big Sleep* (1946). Like Hammett before him, Chandler had also embarked on a lucrative, if sometimes frustrating career as a screen writer, beginning with his collaboration with Billy Wilder on adapting James M. Cain's *Double Indemnity* into a *film noir* classic that became a model for the genre, and including work on Alfred Hitchcock's equally memorable adaptation of Patricia Highsmith's *Strangers on a Train* (1951).

In this connection, it is worth noting in passing the important general impact of private eye fiction on American film. Some of the most memorable productions of the Hollywood studios of the 1940s and 1950s, in particular, were *films noirs* in which even where the works of Hammett, Chandler and others were not adapted outright, the cynical *Weltanschauung*, formats, milieux, character types and language their work projected were frequently conflated, on the one hand, with a new, self-consciously urban film aesthetic and, on the other, with the genre of the dark crime thriller, that was popularised above all by the novels of James M. Cain himself.

Chandler's sixth and longest novel, *The Long Goodbye*, is his most complex and ambitious, and the one in which he comes closest to transcending the limits of the genre. Philip Marlowe returns, but now in his early forties he is maturer and more emotionally vulnerable than before. Moreover, the search he undertakes turns out to be less on behalf of a client than into himself. As much as anything, *The Long Goodbye* is, in fact, a character study. It goes a long way to breaking the unwritten rules of the genre by making the private eye himself the focus of the psychological investigation, and includes the story of Marlowe's most rewarding relationship with a woman. The work has the plot of a typical Chandler crime novel with two notable murders, but the first mystery Marlowe finds himself caught up in concerns a friend and drinking companion, Terry Lennox, who with Marlowe's help flees to Mexico when his wife is found murdered. When Marlowe is later hired to do a real job, it is by Eileen, the beautiful blonde wife of a novelist, Roger Wade, who combines a drinking problem with a writer's block, like his author, but who, unlike his author, winds up dead. Once again people turn out to be more or less than they at first appear, including Eileen, the sister of Lennox's murdered wife; and the same is true of Lennox himself, who returns incognito, only to be rejected by Marlowe in the end. *The Long Goodbye* is more personal than Chandler's other works in the genre, even if its main theme of the loss of innocence is in some sense a Chandler staple. The difference here is that it is Marlowe who finds himself the victim of a kind of love, that takes the outward form of stubborn loyalty. Unfortunately, the man involved proves unworthy of his trust.

The most direct successor of the tradition of Hammett and Chandler was Ross Macdonald (1915–83). He is deservedly the best-known figure among the second generation of authors of private eye fiction, and with two dozen novels to his credit the author of the largest number of significant works in the genre. If on the whole his contribution now seems less original than either Hammett's or Chandler's, in a number of respects his work does represent an interesting new departure. Macdonald's first novel, *Dark Tunnel*, was published in 1943 but it took him some time to find his niche; and it was not until the 1960s that he began to achieve substantial popular and critical success. His most important contributions to the private eye genre are the series of Lew Archer novels, the first of which, *The Moving Target*, appeared in 1949. But it is with *The Goodbye Look* (1969) and *The Underground Man* (1971) that he finally came to be widely acknowledged as a worthy heir of his great predecessors. Many of the familiar private eye behavioural patterns and themes are there. The setting of the Lew Archer novels is Southern California, only this time it is not so much the sprawling, multi-racial Los Angeles area, with its highly diverse neighbourhoods and ethnicities, as the affluent, upper-middle-class and largely white city of Santa Barbara (the Santa Teresa of the novels). The figure of Lew Archer is noticeably less of a tough guy than Sam Spade or Philip Marlowe. He is not so fast with fists or mouth, although he, too, knows how to strong-arm a hoodlum when necessary and can take the occasional beating that is the ritualised proof of a private eye's power to survive in a tough world. Like his predecessors, too, he is a rueful loner who is occasionally drawn to but suspicious of attachments to women and all they imply: 'I began to remember that I had no son either. A man got lonely in the stucco wilderness, pushing forty with no chick, no child.'[20] Also, Macdonald's private eye projects the genre's and his personal sense of the corrupting power of wealth that seems to have derived from the poverty of his early Canadian years. California's blue-bloods, like its recently rich, typically evince a ruthless will to survive at the top of the heap in a world where social mobility means the potential to sink vertiginously as well as rise. At the same time the novels express a relatively unsentimental view of the poor, who tend to be marginal types and petty crooks, struggling against the odds to grab some of that Californian wealth and glamour that seems to have unjustly eluded them. There is also in the Lew Archer novels a lower middle class of domestic servants and hired hands, who cater to the rich but whose relationship with their employers is often characterised by a form of class *ressentiment* that ends up taking a violent form.

What chiefly sets Macdonald's Lew Archer novels apart from those of his peers, however, is, first, the updating of the setting and, second, the character of the plots that issue in the bloody crimes. If the setting remains California, it is no longer the state of the late Depression era or the immediate post-Second World War years, so familiar from Chandler. *The Barbarous Coast* (1956) suggests in its punningly ironic title (connoting, on the one hand, the swashbuckling adventures of an older "Barbary coast" and, on the other, the deceptively manicured beauty of sunny Santa Barbara itself) a certain continuity with his predecessors' view of a state where a rapacious humanity had gone a long way to besmirch the original natural beauty. By the time of *The Underground Man*, the theme of the exhaustion of the American dream is given much more contemporary substance. In that work Macdonald foregrounds the moods and attitudes of a state that had grown fearful and self-doubting as a consequence of the sociopolitical turmoil of the 1960s and a new sense of the finite character of even that state's abundant natural resources – Macdonald himself took up the environmentalist cause in campaigning to save the Californian condor and to prevent drilling for oil off the coast of Santa Barbara. It is significant in this connection that, in *The Underground Man,* the private eye's investigative task is played out against the background of a wild fire, stoked by the hot Santa Ana winds, that threatens to go roaring down the wooded canyons toward the ocean, leaving behind the black skeletons of millionaire-dollar homes. And the familiar threat of subsequent mudslides is also evoked, following as they do the impact of the rainy season on bare hill sides. If the elemental threat of fire and flood suggests mythic devastation as well as the folly of contemporary real estate development, the other side of the sixties, the political side also plays a role. The generation gap that so frequently divides parents and children in Macdonald's fiction is given a new hard-edged, ideologically grounded form in the light of the emergence of a politicised counter-culture and the cult of mind-expanding drugs associated with it.

As with the apocalyptic imagery of destruction just referred to, however, the generation gap in the later Lew Archer novels has a mythic as well as a sociopolitical dimension. Macdonald's complex plots frequently turn on the search for dead, lost or estranged parents or children. The violent dénouements of such searches are typically revealed by Archer to be the result of long unresolved familial passions. The author's own experience of psychoanalysis led him to explore much more than his predecessors the psychic as opposed to the sociological motivation of violent crime. As a result, Lew Archer sometimes sounds more like a therapist than an investigator as he patiently elicits information on the traumas that lie buried in the psyches of clients, victims and assorted suspects. The ambiguity of his situation is neatly sized up in a comment from a fearful young mother whose secrets he is trying to probe: 'I've always known about voyeurs. But you're an auditeur, aren't you?'[21] The comment also alludes indirectly to the guilty pleasures of the reader of crime fiction as well as of the investigator. The suggestive power of Macdonald's multi-faceted fictions can be observed in two final examples. First, in *The Goodbye Look* the stolen gold box that Lew Archer is originally brought in to recover is, on the one hand, a Hitchcockian 'Macguffin' and, on the other, a kind of mythic or Pandora's box that once opened wreaks unsuspected havoc in the lives of all those who at one time or another have been connected with it. Secondly, the title of *The Underground Man* literalises what in Dostoievski's use of the same title had been metaphoric. Macdonald's 'underground man' turns out to be the long-buried corpse of a murdered father in whose grave his son is subsequently laid. The grim dénouement of the son's search for a long lost father is a repetition of the original murder and an ironic cohabitation in death that had never occurred in life.

Macdonald's contemporary, Mickey Spillane (1918–) is probably the writer in the genre whose reputation has suffered most with the passage of time. Starting in the late 1940s with *I, the Jury* (1947), Spillane published a considerable body of work over some forty years but his early originality soon degenerated into formula. The high point of his popularity was the 1950s and 1960s, which not coincidentally was also the height of the Cold War. The name Spillane chose for his private eye, Mike Hammer, has a brutal allegorical simplicity to it. And there is, in fact, a distinct unidimensionality to the character, especially when he is compared to Hammett's or Chandler's detective heroes. Moral ambiguity or self-doubt are not intended to be Hammer's forte. Spillane, in fact, pushes far beyond the limits of his predecessors in the graphic representation of scenes of mayhem that are reported by his narrator hero with a provocatively disturbing tough-guy nonchalance. He is given carte blanche by his author not only to see that a certain idea of justice is done, but that it is done with an undisguised pleasure in inflicting pain, especially if those who committed the crimes are set up as somehow psychologically warped or the ideological enemies of right-thinking Americans. Moreover, all vestige of the chivalric attitude towards women intermittently displayed by a Marlowe has disappeared from Hammer. What are defined in context as evil women meet the same brutal fate as men. Spillane then clearly has a talent for fast-paced action writing. But the blood-churning climaxes of his private eye novels, in which a ritual beating typically precedes an execution, take the form of a lynching party of one.

Other authors of private eye crime thrillers who in recent decades have made memorable contributions to updating the genre include Robert B. Parker (1932–) and Walter Mosley (1952–). James Ellroy (1948–), who in some of the most stylistically self-conscious writing in the field since Chandler may be said to have put the 'hard' back into 'hardboiled', works, strictly speaking, in the sub-genre of the (corrupt, i.e., LAPD) police procedural. The interest and originality of Mosley is in the way he weaves pointed sociopolitical commentary into his hard-driving narratives. A couple of generations after Chester Himes he created a black detective hero, Easy Rawlins, who, unlike Himes's Harlem police detectives, is a private investigator, albeit something of an underground one who moonlights as a janitor and does not even have an office to call his own. Through a series of five novels, starting with *Devil in a Blue Dress* (1990) through *A Little Yellow Dog* (1996), Easy is represented as living in the black Watts section of Los Angeles. He typically takes up his investigative task under pressure from white authority figures or so as to help victims of violent crime in the community. In that sense, like Chandler's Philip Marlowe, he recognises that a rough and ready ethical imperative goes with the job. Unlike Marlowe he lives in a relationship of solidarity with the community he calls home. As a result, Easy stays behind once the crime has been solved, has ongoing relationships with mostly black women, even fathers children, and occasionally works with his disturbingly psychopathic alter ego, Mouse. Like Himes before him, Mosley consciously updates the motifs and structures of the genre he inherited from his white predecessors in order to represent some of the harsher truths about what it meant to be black in America in the American century. To this end, he has adopted the ambitious scheme of locating each of his five Easy Rawlins novels in a different year over three decades, starting in the 1940s. There is thus an important dimension of historical and social realist critique in Mosley's work that harks back to the political radicalism of Hammett's *Red Harvest*. Finally, not only does he resort to the black vernacular to get his narratives told right, he also sketches in with telling realist detail the different milieux of contemporary black urban life, including such representative locales of social interaction as the often mean streets themselves along with mainly black apartment buildings, churches, clubs and bars.

It long seemed that the private eye was a self-consciously and aggressively male genre. Not only did the representation of women characters seem frequently limited and even misogynistic, in the light of period attitudes it was impossible to imagine a woman in the private eye's role. The classic stance of the latter towards the women he encounters was expressed early by Hammett's Continental Op: 'You think I'm a man and you're woman. That's wrong. I'm a manhunter and you're something that has been running in front of me.'[21] As for the heroic private eye's role itself, as I point out in *The Pursuit of Crime*: 'To be hardboiled and to have retained a heroic integrity was to be a man. The culture had generated no precedent for a tough-talking, worldly-wise woman, capable of defending herself in the roughest company, who also possessed the indispensable heroic qualities of physical attractiveness and virtue. A woman in the private eye's role would have been conceivable only as fallen or comic, as Belle Watling (*Gone with the Wind*) or Annie Oakley (*Annie Get Your Gun*).'[22] Verisimilitude would also seem to require that a lone female investigator who submitted to being slugged, drugged, or otherwise assaulted like her hardboiled male counterparts would also suffer forms of sexual aggression that come up against the boundaries conventionally tolerated in the genre.

Nevertheless, it was a sign of the times and of the extension of feminist thinking into popular mass culture that by the early 1970s female private eyes did begin to appear – even if they can hardly be said to conform fully to the hardboiled male prototype. Surprisingly, it was a British author, P. D. James, who first produced a model for the genre in the figure of Cordelia Gray in *An Unsuitable Job for a Woman* (1972). Although the work is too subtle to be simply programmatic, there is clear feminist purpose in the way the actual narrative sets out to prove the title wrong. Further, James does an imaginative job of creating an appealingly modern young woman in her intelligent, tough-minded, sexually knowing, and resourceful young heroine, Cordelia Gray. On the American side of the Atlantic it is Marcia Muller who is usually credited with having created the first female private detective in *Edwin of the Iron Shoes* (1977). By the 1980s she was joined by Sara Paretsky and Sue Grafton, both of whom have produced important bodies of work in the genre with astute, articulate, and thoroughly autonomous female detectives who embody a recognisable range of contemporary behaviours, attitudes and feelings.

## NOTES

1  The eroticised pleasure of looking as an end in itself.
2  Raymond Chandler, in James Nelson, ed., *The Simple Art of Murder* (New York: Norton, 1968), p. 530.
3  *Ibid.*, p. 533.
4  James D. Hart, *The Popular Book: A History of America's Literary Taste* (Berkeley: University of California Press, 1950), p. 156.
5  William F. Nolan, *Dashiell Hammett: A Casebook* (Santa Barbara: McNally and Loftin, 1969), pp. 11–12.
6  Dashiell Hammett, *Red Harvest* (1929), in *The Novels of Dashiell Hammett* (New York: Knopf, 1965), p. 3.
7  Hammett, *The Maltese Falcon* (1930), in *Novels of Dashiell Hammett*, p. 195.
8  Frank MacShane, *The Life of Raymond Chandler* (London: Jonathan Cape, 1976), p. 138.
9  *Ibid.*, p. 76.
10  *Ibid.*, p. 64.
11  See, e.g., Roman Jakobson, 'Linguistics and Poetics', in Thomas A. Sebeok, ed., *Style in Language* (Cambridge, MA: MIT Press, 1960).
12  Miriam Gross, ed., *The World of Raymond Chandler* (New York: A & W, 1978), p. 47.
13  MacShane, *Life of Raymond Chandler*, p. 209.
14  Raymond Chandler, *The Big Sleep* (1989; New York: Ballantine, 1971), p. 5.
15  *Ibid.*, pp. 215–16.
16  *Ibid.*, p. 59.
17  Raymond Chandler, *Farewell, my Lovely* (1940; London: Penguin, 1949), p. 46.
18  *Ibid.*, pp. 7, 124.
19  *Ibid.*, p. 39.
20  Ross Macdonald, *The Barbarous Coast* (1956; New York: Bantam, 1957), pp. 46–7.
21  Ross Macdonald, *The Underground Man* (1971; New York: Bantam, 1974), p. 139.
22  Nolan, *Dashiell Hammett*, p. 23.
23  Dennis Porter, *The Pursuit of Crime* (New Haven: Yale University Press, 1981), p. 183.

# 7

DAVID SEED

# Spy fiction

The spy story is a close but distinct variation on the tale of detection with the difference that there is no discrete crime involved but rather a covert action which, as John Cawelti and Bruce Rosenberg argue, transgresses conventional, moral, or legal boundaries.[1] The action is self-evidently political since it involves national rivalries and constantly veers towards a paranoid vision of 'violation by *outside* agencies' and 'violation of individual autonomy by *internal* agencies'.[2] A further distinction from the detection genre is that the investigator is often himself an agent and therefore, unlike Todorov's ideally detached detective, is implicated in the very processes he is investigating.[3] And since the genre is defined by its international subject, the novels can only be partly explained through formalist analyses like that of Bruce Merry.[4] Espionage fiction became popular in two periods – the turn of the century and the 1960s – when popular anxieties were growing over the credibility of government processes. Its narratives therefore manifest what Michael Denning calls 'cover stories' where the surface action screens a complex play of ideology. Initially spying contrasted unfavourably with an ethic of open courage. Reviewing Somerset Maugham's *Ashenden* in 1928, D. H. Lawrence declared: 'Spying is a dirty business, and Secret Service altogether is a world of under-dogs, a world in which the meanest passions are given play'.[5] However, by 1966 this distaste had become replaced by a perception of centrality. A character in Kingsley Amis's *The Anti-Death League* (1966) can plausibly claim that the spy is a 'uniquely characteristic and significant figure of our time'.[6] The history of spy fiction is one of a gradual shift from the margins to the sixties when espionage novels flooded the market and serious critical attention began to be paid to the genre.[7] Even Jacques Barzun, in the course of a lofty and largely negative meditation on spy fiction, admits that 'the soul of the spy is somehow the model of our own; his actions and his trappings fulfil our unsatisfied desires'.[8]

Although spies are depicted as early as Homer's *Odyssey*, the first novel to deal centrally with espionage was Fenimore Cooper's *The Spy* (1821) which is set in the war between Britain and the newly independent United States. Because this war was played out on American soil 'great numbers', we are told, 'wore masks which even to this day have not been thrown aside'.[9] The action takes place in Westchester County, a border territory between the two sides. Cooper's eponymous spy is one Harvey Birch who 'dresses and acts as though he is not a part of ordered, structured society'.[10] Birch exploits the mask of a pedlar to travel through the battle lines covertly acting for the new country. Cooper dramatises a conflict between two forms of heroism in this novel, that of bold military confrontation and the covert actions of Birch. The latter are rarely confined just to collecting information, but also involve daring rescues. In that respect Cooper set a pattern followed later by Baroness Orczy whose *Scarlet Pimpernel* (1905, constantly reprinted up to the end of the 1930s) similarly dramatises a disparity between Sir Percy Blakeney's overt languid mask and his secret assistance of aristocratic refugees from the French Revolution. Cooper has real difficulty in confirming Birch's courage, as if in opposition to the negative connotations of the term 'spy', and has to resort in his conclusion to depicting a secret meeting between Birch and Washington where the latter confers a national recognition which might otherwise be missed.

In an outstanding study of the origins of British spy fiction, David Stafford attributes the rise of these novels to an underlying feeling of national insecurity in the face of changing international relations: 'The world presented by these novels is a dangerous and treacherous one in which Britain is the target of the envy, hostility, of the other European powers, singly or collectively according to context'.[11] In order to keep the distinction clear between them and us, spying was what other countries did, whereas the unsung national heroes of this new fiction were typically young, male, athletic, and gentlemen, usually only making amateur excursions into the field of espionage.

By the 1890s the paranoid fear of the 'enemies within' had become established in fiction which was closely linked to the new-found power of the popular press. William Le Queux exploited his links with the press baron Lord Northcliffe to serialise works like *The Invasion of 1910* (1906) and *The Spies of the Kaiser* (1909). Indeed Nicholas Hiley has shown that Le Queux enjoyed a uniquely close relation to the British secret service, being fed information and constructing narratives which helped sustain fears of German spies in Britain.[12] Le Queux developed a calculatedly sensational style which drew the maximum effect from cliff-hanging chapter-endings, heavily signalled climaxes, and a rapid momentum to events. Even when the ostensible subject lay abroad, he brought his narratives to bear on the predicament of Britain. Thus, in *The Czar's Spy* (1905) the jockeying between Russia and Finland over the latter's independence spills over into a series of assassinations within Britain. Although Le Queux makes the rather smug point that the spy cultures of St Petersburg and Finland are alien to the British, he simultaneously dramatises the fact that London is no longer safe, thanks in part to its émigré population. Such xenophobia surfaces in Walter Wood's *The Enemy in our Midst* (1906) which describes a conspiracy by bogus German immigrants to take over London. This invasion has already subdued whole sections of the capital: 'Soho was riddled with them. There, as in Stepney, entire streets were held by aliens'.[13]

Undoubtedly one of the main appeals of early spy fiction was that it promised the reader access to processes taking place behind official history, to what Conan Doyle describes in one of his stories as 'that secret history of a nation which is so much more intimate and interesting than its public chronicles'.[14] The term 'secret' recurs in turn-of-the-century titles with increasing frequency and a semantic shift takes place in the usage of the phrase 'secret service' away from spontaneous amateur patriotism. As intelligence services are consolidated in Britain and elsewhere, secret service becomes institutionalised into *the* Secret Service and we shall see how this sets up tensions in narratives which attempt to contrast plucky and essentially individualistic Britons against the professional espionage supposedly only practised by other countries.

Apart from Le Queux, the novelist usually credited with shaping the spy genre is E. Phillips Oppenheim whose frankly conservative novels combined narrative with social sophistication. *The Great Impersonation* (1920) weaves an unusually benign variation on the theme of German aggression. It is based on the unlikely premise that the British-educated Baron Leopold von Ragastein could substitute for his British counterpart Sir Everard Dominey in German East Africa and then take up the latter's home life convincingly. The main narrative question is therefore whether anyone will see through his disguise which is skilfully presented as acting out a whole social role rather than simply donning different clothes. The action of the novel plays itself out mostly in Dominey's country house where Ragastein's contacts with the British ruling elite enable him to act as a 'confidential correspondent who can day by day reflect the changing psychology of the British mind in all its phases'.[15] Ragastein's German identity becomes almost completely submerged in his new guise which assumes a set of social codes common to both cultures. This fact in itself excludes any demonic presentation of the Germans and one of the most interesting developments to take place in the novel is the gradual revelation of a power struggle taking place within Germany just before the First World War. Ultimately Oppenheim is using his protagonist to personify the best qualities of Germany in order to dramatise their collapse in the world war.

The one 'invasion scare' novel to have remained in print right up to the present is Erskine Childers's *The Riddle of the Sands* (1903) which has survived because it totally avoids the sensationalism and xenophobia of Le Queux and other contemporaries. Childers skilfully integrates a narrative of a yachting cruise on the Frisian coast with a tale of detection where the land itself becomes the source of mystery. The novel includes within the text a number of maps and charts so that we can follow the latter's logic in its discussions of the strategic importance of the north-west coast of Germany for launching an invasion fleet towards England. Although Childers claimed he had invented the whole thing, such a plan was considered by Germany in the 1890s and the novel was taken so seriously that it was assessed by the Director of Naval Intelligence.[16]

The novel is 'edited' by Childers and narrated by a Foreign Office employee called Carruthers. He responds to a call from his friend Davies to join him on his yacht, ostensibly for a holiday. Once Carruthers arrives, Davies describes how he has met a Captain Dollmann whom he suspects of being a spy partly because he has tried to run him aground when he realises that Davies is exploring the coast. Carruthers possesses linguistic competence in German; Davies is the seaman. Together they make up the two sides of a single investigating consciousness. When Davies asks Carruthers if he looks like a spy, his friend refers ironically to 'those romantic gentlemen that one reads of in sixpenny magazines', each 'with a Kodak in his tie-pin, a sketch-book in the lining of his coat, and a selection of disguises in his hand luggage'.[17] Because the spy genre has been concerned from the very beginning with issues of representation and plausibility such self-conscious gestures are common. Here Carruthers anticipates and deflects the implied reader's scepticism towards the subject.

Of course the image does not fit at all. Childers establishes the credentials of his protagonists as investigators through their common rejection of the old-fashioned glamorous image of the spy and cues in his own narrative method which rejects melodrama in favour of a slow and patient examination of characters, events, and terrain. Childers's management of suspense through small details drew particular praise from John Buchan who saw *The Riddle of the Sands* as one of the best examples of the modern adventure story. 'It is a tale of the puzzling out of a mystery', he declared, 'which only gradually reveals itself, and not till the very end reaches its true magnificence'.[18] The culminating realisation comes when Carruthers senses that he is witnessing history in the making: 'I was assisting at an experimental rehearsal of a greater scene, to be enacted, perhaps, in the near future', of a sea-borne invasion of England.[19] In a rare instance of political action following fiction, two officers of Naval Intelligence were arrested in 1910 and charged with spying. They had been using *The Riddle of the Sands* as a guide to their investigations of German fortifications and the novel was subsequently produced as evidence in their trial.[20]

Kipling's *Kim* (1901) helped to establish the metaphor of spying as the Great Game, although the phrase originally denoted Anglo-Russian rivalry for the Central Asian sphere of imperial influence. *Kim* narrates an idealised process of discovery through the wide-eyed perspective of its boy protagonist. For Kim the Indian sub-continent exists as a vast inexhaustible spectacle which he can relish as he travels across country with his companion, a Tibetan holy man from the north. There is a smooth continuity in the novel from Kim's education on the road to his tuition at the hands of the mysterious Lurgan, from whom Kim learns memory games which gradually initiate him into the larger enterprise of imperial surveillance. This initiation is only partial as Kim is told: 'the Game is so large that one sees but a little at a time'.[21] Social behaviour becomes transformed into theatre. At one point a saddhu or holy man, whose disguise Kim has helped to construct, engages in a slanging match with a British policeman where covert messages are encoded as curses.

Kipling conflates the figure of a spiritual quest with Kim's travelling and with his participation in the survey of India. As Martin Green points out, 'the activity for which Kim is being trained is surveying, which brings together the activities of climbing, observing, native disguise, etc., under the aegis of imperialism'.[22] Surveying offers a means of imperial control through measurement and simply extends Kim's appropriating gaze. When he encounters a Russian and a Frenchman, who emerge from the northern mountains and claim to be heading for Simla (one of the British administrative centres), the Great Game of imperial rivalry between Russia and Britain is played out in miniature as a drama of cultural response. The Russian shows himself to be a purist who detests the 'monstrous hybridism of East and West', whereas Kim personifies a receptivity to all the cultures of India.[23] Kipling presents espionage here as a form of cultural invasion based on ignorance and made all the more blatant by the threadbare nature of the invaders' disguise.

By the early 1900s many of the conventions of the spy story had become well enough established for mainstream writers to use them in farce and black comedy. Joseph Conrad's *The Secret Agent* (1907) centres on Verloc, a former secret agent who has since become the very image of bourgeois prosperity. So it is with incredulity that it is remembered that once Verloc's 'warnings had the power to change the schemes and the date of royal, imperial grand-ducal journeys, and sometimes cause them to be put off altogether!'.[24] In the present Verloc's 'cover' is as thin as the wrappings on the shady goods he sells from his shop and the imagery of conspiracy has been transposed on to his furtive customers for pornography. As Avrom Fleishman shows, the term 'secret' is used within the novel to cover a far broader range of qualities than espionage, typically characterising 'human states of being, emotions, conditions, and moral qualities'.[25] Secrecy is repeatedly identified with ignorance and obscurity, as represented in the fog where Stevie accidentally blows himself up. Appearances constantly skew from inner substance. When the Assistant Commissioner changes clothes to investigate the bombing he is surprised at his 'foreign appearance'; and when the Verlocs' estrangement from each other is approaching its culmination Winnie's face becomes a mask and her husband's that of a painted automaton.

G. K. Chesterton's *The Man Who Was Thursday* (1908) similarly uses the conventions of covert action to burlesque a view of reality. The novel describes the efforts of a detective, Gabriel Syme, to penetrate the Central Anarchist Council. He does this by pretending to be an Anarchist himself but experiences a whole sequence of ludicrous revelations where supposed subversives prove to be members of the same detective force. Chesterton captures the farcical tempo of events by showing his characters constantly in pursuit of each other. For instance, Syme is dogged round London by the 'Professor' whose sheer speed of movement contrasts grotesquely with his aged appearance. And this is the main point of the novel. Chesterton dramatises Syme's search as an unexpected process of alienation from reality where landscapes become destabilised. The more revelations he witnesses, the more society seems engaged in a huge collective masquerade. At one point he wonders: 'Was there anything that was apart from what it seemed?'[26] The clichés of disguise and the irony that the detectives themselves become spies all build up to a comic climax at the end of the novel where conflict and masquerade have become established as states of being.

Neither Conrad nor Chesterton take seriously the idea of the nation under threat which is central to John Buchan's Richard Hannay novels, one of the earliest sequences of espionage novels to be linked by a recurrent hero. In *Mr Standfast* (1919) Hannay experiences a moment of revelation of an idealised rural England, a place of 'peace, deep and holy and ancient'.[27] The numerous parallels with *Pilgrim's Progress* in this novel invest the home country with a special spiritual value usually left implicit by Buchan, but which functions as a motivation for the hero's actions. Cawelti and Rosenberg have found a quality of connectedness in Buchan's plots which relates to his characteristic blend of nationalism and spiritual destiny: 'In Buchan's world, there is really no coincidence or accident. What appears to be chance is actually the mysterious and enigmatic working of providence'.[28] This means that the novels symbolically re-enact the establishment of a desired order threatened by malign forces. Even here, however, there is an ambivalence within Buchan's narratives. At the beginning of *The Thirty-Nine Steps* (1915) Hannay is totally bored with his present life and more or less waiting for his adventures to begin. The ordered national life which his efforts are directed towards protecting is too static to allow the existence of adventure which forms the very basis of Hannay's identity. There is thus a tension between the desire for the exotic and the exciting on the one hand, and the ritual confirmation of national and imperial order towards which the novels move.

Many critics have noted that Hannay is a classic clubland hero who exists within but is not quite defined by the British establishment.[29] He is a former engineer from South Africa, a skilled amateur at codes, an athlete, and above all a gentleman. His political connections are all personal so that, without ever having an official position, Hannay is bonded into the ruling elite. There is very little discussion of the ethics of secret service in Buchan. Instead, Hannay enacts an ideology of patriotic commitment by improvising his way through sequences of danger. Characteristically he receives his commission at the beginning of the novels. He then undergoes a series of trials where he demonstrates a skill at disguise. Hannay's mentor Pieter Pienaar gives him the following crucial advice which differentiates his kind of acting from false beards or similar paraphernalia: 'the secret of playing a part was to think yourself into it. You could never keep it up, he said, unless you could manage to convince yourself you were *it*.'[30] Accordingly much of the suspense of *The Thirty-Nine Steps* centres on Hannay's capacity to adopt convincing disguises at very short notice and to penetrate those of his enemies. In *The Thirty-Nine Steps* and *Mr Standfast* the mystery is located within Britain and suspense is generated as the most familiar scenes are demonstrated to be the sources of internal subversion. Buchan manages a superb slow-motion climax to *The Thirty-Nine Steps* when Hannay and the reader with him wait to see what possible discrepancy there could be in 'three ordinary, game-playing, suburban Englishmen' at a coastal holiday resort.[31] A chance gesture by one of the conspirators triggers Hannay's recognition and forces the dénouement.

In general the forces which Buchan lines up in opposition fit a manichaean polarity between good and evil which culminates in the apocalyptic battle for Erzurum at the end of *Greenmantle* (1916). However, *The Three Hostages* (1924) reflects a post-war loss of certainties by Buchan in its narrative of Hannay's struggle with the master criminal Medina. Among his many talents Medina numbers hypnotism which he even uses successfully on Hannay who 'seemed to be repeating a lesson at someone's dictation'.[32] Just as the barrier between the conscious and unconscious is blurring, so the ambivalence over the villain becomes even more striking than in earlier novels since Medina is a suave, engaging, and obviously civilised man who could pass muster effortlessly in the upper echelons of British society.

The period after the First World War saw a number of shifts in the style and structure of spy fiction. Distinctions between 'sides' blur. The apocalyptic expectation of the 'big show' or ultimate confrontation between opposing forces which informs Buchan and Le Queux gives way to less clear narrative sequences. Somerset Maugham's *Ashenden* (1928), which was based on that author's experiences of a posting in Switzerland for British Intelligence, opens with an introduction which draws the reader's attention to the differences between fact and fiction.[33] In *Ashenden* the narrator argues that typically he was confronted with isolated incidents and images: 'The material it [the Intelligence Service] offers for stories is scrappy and pointless'.[34] Although Maugham claims to have reshaped his material to make it more coherent, he stayed true to his perception of never having 'had the advantage of seeing a completed action'.[35] His life is summarised as if he had the most ordinary job in the world: 'Ashenden's official existence was as orderly and monotonous as a city clerk's. He saw his spies at stated intervals and paid them their wages; when he could get hold of a new one he engaged him, gave him his instructions and sent him off to Germany'.[36] This deglamorising of espionage was quite new and made a big impression on John le Carré who praised Maugham for being the first to 'write about espionage in a mood of disenchantment and almost prosaic reality'.[37]

The struggle by the protagonist to understand his situation becomes even more severe in Eric Ambler's *The Mask of Demetrios* (1939). Here Charles Latimer, a lecturer turned author of detective stories, is offered a subject by the head of the Turkish secret police who is, conveniently, a fellow enthusiast. This subject is the eponymous Demetrios, a Greek from Asia Minor who has become involved in an endless sequence of rackets and who has repeatedly changed his identity to evade capture. Unlike Ashenden, Latimer has no official connection with the intelligence agencies but he also has to travel – in his case from Istanbul, through Eastern Europe to Paris – in pursuit of his subject. In one of the best discussions of Ambler to date, Michael Denning argues that the narrator of this novel constantly ridicules Latimer's ambition of bringing together all of the facts about Demetrios into a single coherent 'biography'.[38] One reason why this should happen is that Demetrios is less a character and more a personification of the scheming which is taking place in the post-war Balkans. The different places Latimer visits become the sites for Latimer to discover more information about Demetrios and at the same time to be warned against fitting that information into patterns taken from popular fiction. Just as Demetrios appears larger than any of the masks he adopts, so national boundaries blur into a collective façade screening the machinations which cut across such limits. The drug smuggling he runs is symptomatic in being covertly financed by the Eurasian Credit Trust, an international banking organisation. Demetrios acts like an opportunistic shadow of post-war history and Ambler both puts his own inflection on the notion of secret history we have already encountered in Le Queux and anticipates later writers like Thomas Pynchon who present history as a mask for covert economic and political processes.

In Maugham and Ambler the narrative expands outwards from the protagonist whereas in Graham Greene's spy fiction the drama focuses tightly on the faith of the latter. In 1979 Greene took issue with John le Carré when the latter took him to task for perpetuating a thirties perspective on political commitment. Greene rejected le Carré's ironic view of the intelligence service, retorting: 'the confrontation between Communism and Catholicism is still very powerful'.[39] Greene himself served in Kim Philby's section of British Intelligence during the Second World War, while the latter was an undercover Soviet agent, and remained well disposed towards him even after Philby's defection to the USSR.

Greene does not separate espionage from other human activity but rather weaves that issue into dramas of commitment.[40] The protagonist 'D' of *The Confidential Agent* (1939) is carrying out a mission in wartime Britain of delivering documents about coal supplies and becomes alienated more and more from his surroundings as he is attacked, robbed and abused for being a foreigner. *The Ministry of Fear* (1943) more radically displaces its protagonist from familiar life in England when he stumbles across a spy network operating in London. Arthur Rowe starts from a position of estrangement (he was like an 'exile who has returned home after many years') and goes through a total reconstruction of his identity when wounded by a bomb.[41] The recurrent metaphor of this novel is the dream, as if the common-sense relation of life to fantasy had been inverted. Rowe tells his mother: 'You used to laugh at the books Miss Savage read – about spies, and murders, and violence, and wild motor-car chases, but, dear, that's real life [. . .] The world has been remade by William Le Queux.'[42]

What is given a paranoid edge in *The Ministry of Fear* is turned into situational comedy in *Our Man in Havana* (1958). Here Wormold, an expatriate vacuum salesman in Cuba, is manoeuvred into the British secret service by the promise of generous payments for his reports. Wormold needs the money but has no access to political secrets, so he invents some. Greene comically exploits the analogy between such secrets and consumer goods by elaborating on the name of the latest vacuum: the 'Atomic Pile Cleaner'. Just as that name superficially applies the progressive aspect of nuclear technology, so Wormold capitalises on the fear of atomic war by reporting on 'constructions' in Cuba which uncannily resemble the magnified parts of a vacuum cleaner. Initiated into a service where the 'drill' is everything, Wormold finds himself losing control of his situation. His reports might be fictions but they cause real deaths. Again and again situations collapse into black farce, as at a trade dinner where an unfortunate dog dies from the poisoned food that was intended for Wormold. The crowning irony to the novel comes when Wormold's exposure leads to him being offered an intelligence training post.

The Human Factor (1978) could be read as a reworking of Our Man in Havana, this time dramatising the issue of commitment. The protagonist Castle seems in every way a typical commuter, catching the same train to town from the suburbs every day and making a positive fetish out of the organised detail of his daily life. But Castle's life with his South African wife is built on a fear: 'They were secure – or as secure as they would ever be'.[43] They internalise security as a constant state of domestic and psychological surveillance so severe that Castle hardly notices a check being run on his section of the British intelligence service. Greene uses the metaphor of compartmentalisation – one of Castle's colleagues tells him: 'We all live in boxes' – to dramatise the pathological consequences of secrecy and the resulting need for confession.

Against this institutional ideology of containment Greene deploys a narrative method which invites the reader to recognise analogies and connections, for example between the ailments suffered by Castle's son and the dis-ease of his profession. In one of the most powerful sections of the novel Castle meets the true intimate of his life: 'The blue eyes seemed to offer complete friendship, the smile encouraged him to lay down for a short time the burden of secrecy'.[44] The blue eyes belong to Boris, Castle's Soviet handler, and a series of discrepancies in Castle's life are now explained by the revelation that he is a double agent. Greene's masterly control of information up to this point has presented to the reader essentially the public image Castle wanted to project and the trigger for him breaking cover is his dealing with a South African BOSS officer as part of a covert scheme named 'Uncle Remus' which Greene explains as a 'kind of Final Solution to the race problem. In the event of revolt by the blacks, tactical atom bombs would be used with the secret connivance of the Americans, the English and the Germans'.[45] Although Castle slightly resembles Philby in his flight to Moscow, Greene maintains a sympathetic perspective on him as a victim of multiple ironies, not least his sacrifice for a more valuable Moscow 'mole'.

Post-war spy fiction has been dominated by the James Bond novels. Ian Fleming had a senior position in Naval Intelligence during the Second World War and drew on his first-hand experiences of gadgetry, agents, and procedures for the Bond novels. Fleming was quite frank about the fantastic dimension to his series, admitting that 'James Bond is the author's pillow fantasy' of available sex and rapid glamorous action.[46] In his review of the film of *Our Man in Havana* he even pointed out that the secret agent had become an anachronism: 'as long as war is a threat, the spy is a ticking seismograph on top of the Jungfrau measuring distant atomic explosions on the other side of the world, or instruments carried in aircraft that measure the uranium or plutonium contents of the atmosphere'. Stories of the secret service therefore now had to be either incredible or farcical. Fleming's own chosen option was to 'write basically incredible stories with a straight face' using a style which partly derives from American hard-boiled crime fiction.[47] Indeed he became friends with Raymond Chandler who wrote appreciative reviews of *Diamonds Are Forever* and *Doctor No*. Fleming's career as a writer really falls into two phases. During the fifties the first Bond novels sold respectably but the turning point came with the release of the first Bond movies (*Doctor No* in 1962, *From Russia with Love* in 1963) and the revelation that President Kennedy numbered Fleming among his favourite authors. From then on, as Tony Bennett has shown, James Bond became a cultural sign expanding outwards from fiction into film, advertising, and music.[48] Bond has been parodied, accused of racism and sexism, but also continued after Fleming's death with novels by writers such as Kingsley Amis.[49]

In one of the shrewdest analyses of the Bond novels Umberto Eco has demonstrated that they function according to traditional formulaic oppositions between hero and villain, or knight (Bond) against king (his boss M).[50] It goes without saying that Bond will win through, so each narrative contains unexpected twists and reversals within a broadly reassuring plot where the forces of good will triumph. Eco's structuralist reading risks blanking out aspects of the Bond novels which must have played a major part in their popularity, namely the cultural specifics of his adventures. It is a characteristic of these novels that they constantly slow down or suspend their urgency in order to explore the worlds of wine-tasting, West End clubs, or gambling. Kingsley Amis has explained such violations of suspense and realism by seeing the Bond series as a kind of science fiction based on the premise that 'this (perhaps) couldn't happen, but let's agree that it could and accept the consequences'.[51]

Fleming himself has stated that he regularly used two narrative devices: speed and the inclusion of 'familiar household names and objects' to locate his action. This rather contradicts his other claim that he was aiming for a 'certain disciplined exoticism' since the 'equipment' of the Bond novels typically stands out as the evidence of his range of discriminating tastes. For Bond is a consumer as well as an agent and Michael Denning also demonstrates how travel and tourism are central to the novels' action.[52] Consumables, tourism, and games are the central ingredients to any Bond novel and the detail devoted to the last of these gives a new permutation of a metaphor central to spy fiction. Whether the game is cards, golf or marksmanship, in every case its performance enables Bond to demonstrate his capacity to anticipate his opponent's strategy. By minimising Bond's subjectivity, Fleming makes it all the easier for the reader, especially the male reader, to indulge fantasies of exotic travel and sexual success.

The Bond adventures have been seen as compensatory fantasies where 'Bond embodied the imaginary power that England might once again be placed at the centre of world affairs during a period when its world power status was visibly and rapidly declining'.[53] In *Live and Let Die* (1954) every phase of the action is shadowed by the wealth and facilities of the CIA. The first Bond novel, *Casino Royale* (1953), made this evident through allegory. Bond is commissioned to out-gamble le Chiffre, a criminal working for SMERSH (Fleming's anachronistic acronym for the Soviet secret service). The task is thus to break the 'cypher', one meaning of the villain's name. London bankrolls Bond but he loses and at this point CIA operative Felix Leiter makes his entry into the action, bringing 'Marshall Aid' in the form of a second, American stake. Although the primary action is played out as a struggle between Bond and le Chiffre, this action is supported by American financial aid and timely intervention by an agent who kills le Chiffre, saving Bond's life. Although the Bond novels heavily emphasise the British identity of their hero, his activities are constantly supported by American agencies, financing and know-how.

The Bond novels set a keynote of adventure and glamorous action which was slavishly imitated by some writers and against which the realist fiction of John le Carré and Len Deighton were to define themselves.[54] Le Carré recognised the popularity of Bond as a recoil from stories of 'seduced housewives, corrupted diplomats, and treacherous service officers' but chose to pursue a more austere line of enquiry in his own novels.[55] His education at public school, experience in the Intelligence Corps during the war, his teaching at Eton, and his posting in the German section of the British intelligence service all help to explain a steady focus throughout his fiction on institutions and on the relation between espionage and his national culture. Le Carré has stressed that the secret services were 'microcosms of the British condition, of our social attitudes and vanities'.[56] Secondly le Carré has explained the popularity of espionage fiction as growing out of a deep public distrust of political life which in the 1960s and 1970s was producing conspiracy narratives: 'I think that the spy novel', he told an interviewer in

1978, 'encapsulates this public wariness about political behaviour and about the set-up, the fix of society'.[57]

Le Carré's first two novels, *Call for the Dead* (1961) and *A Murder of Quality* (1962) followed the pattern of a murder mystery with an element of espionage grafted on to the action. It was not until *The Spy Who Came In From The Cold* (1963) that le Carré achieved the success that enabled him to turn to full-time writing. Set against the background of the Berlin Wall, which le Carré later described as 'perfect theatre as well as the perfect symbol of the monstrosity of ideology gone mad', this novel dramatises an intelligence mission by Alec Leamas into East Germany to dispose of his opposite number who appears to be efficiently uncovering Western agents.[58] He has to act out a role of disillusionment but the action turns into a process of estrangement where Leamas is progressively moved farther and farther from certainty over his role. Le Carré glosses this process as a psychological one. Unlike a professional actor, the secret agent experiences no relief: 'For him, deception is first a matter of self-defence. He must protect himself not only from without but from within, and against the most natural of impulses'.[59] While he thinks his role is to falsely 'finger' the brutal Neo-Nazi Mundt as a mole, Leamas emerges as the victim of deception by his own agency when it is revealed that Mundt has actually been planted by them in East German security. Secondly, Leamas falls in love with Liz, an idealistic young Communist who is used as a pawn in this deception. Leamas acts on his now total disillusionment at the end of the novel when he suicidally refuses to escape over the Wall.

Le Carré's next two novels turn a satirical spotlight on the secret service (*The Looking-Glass War*, 1965) and the Bonn diplomatic community (*A Small Town in Germany*, 1968) respectively. *The Looking-Glass War* dramatises a nostalgia for power in the British secret service which produces a dangerous loss of contact with the contemporary world. Once again, a mission is planned into East Germany but at every stage it is shown to be a self-deluding attempt to replay the commando raids of the Second World War. Le Carré peppers his text with references to Buchan, Kipling and other writers to bring out this loss of reality to which he returns in *The Tailor of Panama* (1996).

Le Carré's bleak ironies in these early novels are replaced in his Karla Trilogy by greater psychological and narrative complexity and a further development of his character George Smiley. In his plump owlish appearance and studied ordinariness Smiley combines the roles of organisation man, scholar, and man of conscience. Le Carré has explained that he wanted Smiley to represent the outmoded generation of Philby in his sense of commitment.[60] In the trilogy Smiley is an outsider and even an anachronism being superseded by a new breed of operatives.[61] Each volume of the trilogy shows the secret service malfunctioning. In the first, *Tinker, Tailor, Soldier, Spy* (1974), Smiley is commissioned with investigating the possible presence of a Soviet mole at the heart of the espionage establishment. Bill Haydon, 'our latter-day Lawrence of Arabia', plays Philby in this novel which traces out Smiley's investigation in careful detail.[62] The exposure of Philby was taken to demonstrate a difference of philosophy between two branches of the intelligence service: that of trust and personal loyalty within Philby's branch and a more bureaucratic use of files and records by MI5. The latter is the method followed by Smiley and his closest associates. As tiny discrepancies mount up, the presence of the double agent begins to show itself and Haydon is finally tricked into self-exposure. This exposure shows Haydon to be a 'romantic and a snob' addicted to deception, virtually the same terms le Carré used for Philby.[63] Graham Greene, by contrast saw him as a craftsman, a figure of belief, and what did it matter if he had betrayed his country? 'Who among us has not committed treason to something or someone more important than a country?'[64]

The second and third parts of the trilogy describe exercises in damage limitation following this exposure. *The Honourable Schoolboy* (1977) is the least unified of the three as le Carré awkwardly attempts to dovetail two subjects together: Smiley's reform of the Circus (as the secret service is known) and a project to uncover a Soviet money-laundering network in Asia, the action adventure parts of the novel. *Smiley's People* (1979) relocates the central focus on the protracted struggle between Smiley and his Soviet alter ego, Karla, his 'black Grail'. This figure suggests a quixotic quest by Smiley which he is warned against by a colleague: 'It's not a *shooting* war any more, George . . . It's grey. Half-angels fighting half-devils'.[65] Smiley discovers Karla's Achilles heel, a schizophrenic daughter who is receiving treatment in a Swiss clinic, and uses this discovery to pressurise him into defection. The conclusion to the trilogy reverses the opening scene of *The Spy Who Came In From The Cold* by transforming Karla from a disembodied name or function into a diminutive figure crossing from East Berlin and bringing with him countless Soviet intelligence secrets.

In his later novels le Carré has explored the psychological dimensions to espionage, with the result that the original polarities of his early Cold War works became replaced by more complex notions of identity. *The Little Drummer Girl* (1983) describes the increasing difficulties of a professional actress in separating theatre from reality when she is groomed in a romantic role by Israeli intelligence to trap a Palestinian bomb-maker. In *A Perfect Spy* (1986) le Carré investigates the pathology of secrecy in the figure of Magnus Pym who, like le Carré himself, has inherited a tradition of deception from his father. The novel gradually burrows through Pym's layers of disguise until we reach Axel, his Communist opposite number who accuses him of self-betrayal. With the end of the Cold War these later novels deliver critical autopsies on a situation which has disappeared, or explore post-Cold War racketeering and adventurism. *The Secret Pilgrim* (1991) makes a late coda to the Smiley series, assembling a series of reminiscences on the way in which the West fell victim to its own propaganda. Smiley rephrases a criticism which has echoed through the fiction since the Karla trilogy, that 'we concealed the very things that made us right. Our respect for the individual, our love of variety and argument'.[66]

Where le Carré set a keynote of complex ironic structures in his fiction, Len Deighton made an initial impact through his narrators' tone of voice and through documentary techniques. In his early fiction from *The Ipcress File* (1962) onwards his anonymous intelligence operative (Harry Palmer in the movie adaptations) demonstrates an ironic awareness of the class dimension to the British intelligence establishment and a familiarity with London (Deighton himself is a Londoner).[67] Drawing on the idiom of Chandleresque hardboiled fiction, Deighton consistently deglamorises the figure of the spy who is described in *Spy Line* 'like being a down-at-heel Private Eye'.[68] From the very beginning Deighton foregrounded strategy in his fiction, drawing the reader's attention to this dimension in *Funeral in Berlin* (1964) and *Spy Story* (1974) through epigraphs on chess and war games. Deighton's use of appendices to explain arcana-like D-notices gradually dropped out of his fiction in the 1970s and during the 1980s he published two trilogies: *Game, Set and Match* (1983) and *Hook, Line and Sinker* (1988–90). Each focuses on a named operative, Bernard Sampson, whose wife has defected to the Soviets. In the concluding volume of the latter sequence, Deighton breaks his pattern by changing into the third person in order to instate Sampson's wife as a character in her own right.

Spy fiction has tended to stay close to the patterns of the detective mystery in foregrounding the search for information which will confirm suspected conspiracy. However, the political thriller can also overlap with espionage narratives in some respects. To take two famous examples by Frederick Forsyth, *The Day of the Jackal* (1971) and *The Fourth Protocol* (1984) describe symbolic invasions of France and Britain by a professional assassin and a Soviet agent commissioned by a neo-Stalinist General Secretary. Each narrative describes the defensive strategies pursued by representatives of the French police and British Intelligence whose individual shrewdness sets them apart from their agencies. Once again information is central, but, as in spy fiction, it is a special kind of information which needs decoding, here the mysteries of bogus identities and the tantalising glimpses of a nuclear device being smuggled into Britain. Forsyth alternates episodes centring on the

aggressor with sequences showing the government agents' attempts to anticipate the latter's actions in a cross-cutting similar to cinematic montage where
the two narrative strands gradually converge on a climax where the aggressor is shot. These endings, as we saw in Buchan and others, symbolically
reassert the national status quo in both cases.[69]

Espionage has entered post-war American fiction as an increasingly important subject. One of Thomas Pynchon's earliest pieces, 'Under the Rose'
(1961), is a Conradian pastiche of an attempted assassination in Egypt set
against the impending Fashoda crisis of 1898 between France and Britain.
The story is situated on a historical cusp with the imminent end of a 'tradition
in espionage where everything was tacitly on a gentlemanly basis'.[70] The
transition Pynchon traces out recapitulates the shift in spy fiction away from
individual action to that of groups or institutions. *Gravity's Rainbow* (1973),
for example, dramatises the vulnerability of the investigating subject when
Tyrone Slothrop, a G.I. embroiled in the intelligence agencies at the end of
the Second World War, discovers that as a child he was sold for scientific experimentation. It is here that the main focus falls in American spy fiction: on
the threat to the self posed by the domestic workings of the secret services.[71]
William S. Burroughs packs his novels with references to secret agents who
participate in surreal conspiracies before which no area of the self remains
intact.[72] Richard Condon's famous depiction of the brainwashed assassin in
*The Manchurian Candidate* (1959) combines parental and national betrayal
of the trainee-victim and this theme recurs in later novels like James Grady's
*Six Days of the Condor* (1974) where virtually an entire research section of
the CIA is wiped out in order to protect that agency's covert drug running.

In these novels, the nature and limits of intelligence agencies are largely a
domestic problem. William F. Buckley, Jr's Blackford Oakes series from the
1970s and 1980s is something of a throwback to Bond in investing so much
priority in an exaggeratedly capable CIA troubleshooter. More typically, the
CIA itself becomes a source of mystery and threat. John Barth's *Sabbatical*
(1982) describes a yachting tour of the Chesapeake Bay made by an ex-CIA
agent who has published an exposé of covert operations. The title raises a
question: will he in fact be able to take a sabbatical or will the agency dispose
of him? That grim possibility is made explicit by a framed 'news report' on a
colleague's mysterious death. The most famous mystery in post-war America
is the assassination of Kennedy which makes up the subject of Don DeLillo's
*Libra* (1988), or rather it is the *investigation* of this mystery by an ex-CIA
data analyst. As Nicholas Branch probes into the conspiracy behind the
assassination he locates a 'theology' of secrecy built into the CIA. The cultic
aspects of intelligence agencies also concern Norman Mailer, whose massive
1991 novel *Harlot's Ghost* manages to combine a historical survey of the

CIA, an examination of the erotics of power, and a diagnosis of the dark underside of the US government, interspersed with fictional documentation like letters and telephone transcripts.

Whatever their ostensible subjects, spy novels both in Britain and the USA investigate perceptions of their authors' nations: the latter's international standing, cultural values, governmental system, and so on. Although there has been a steady increase in published criticism on this fiction, American spy novels remain relatively under-discussed and a considerable number of writers such as Robert Littell, Clifford Stoll, and Donald Freed still await sustained analysis.[73] The end of the Cold War by no means resulted in the demise of the spy novel, but it did necessitate re-alignments of agents and a re-definition of national enemies. In the wake of the events of 11 September 2001, it remains to be seen what new directions the genre will take.

## NOTES

1 John G. Cawelti and Bruce A. Rosenberg, *The Spy Story* (Chicago: University of Chicago Press, 1987), p. 13. The proximity between spy and detective fiction is proposed by Julian Symons in *Bloody Murder: From the Detective Story to the Crime Novel: A History*, 2nd edn (Harmondsworth: Penguin, 1985).

2 'Introduction' to Clive Bloom, ed., *Spy Thrillers: From Buchan to le Carre*, (London: Macmillan, 1990), p. 2.

3 Tzvetan Todorov, 'The Typology of Detective Fiction', in *The Poetics of Prose*, trans. Richard Howard (Oxford: Blackwell, 1977), pp. 44–5.

4 Bruce Merry, *Anatomy of the Spy Thriller* (Dublin: Gill and Macmillan, 1977).

5 Anthony Curtis and John Whitehead, eds., *W. Somerset Maugham: The Critical Heritage* (London: Routledge & Kegan Paul, 1987), p. 177.

6 Kingsley Amis, *The Anti-Death League* (Harmondsworth: Penguin, 1966), p. 117.

7 Andy East's 'The Spy in the Dark: A History of Espionage Fiction', *Armchair Detective* 19.i (1986), 23–40, remains a useful account. For a survey of criticism, see Lars Ole Sauerberg, 'Secret-Agent Fiction: A Survey of its Critical Literature with a Bibliography', *Clues: A Journal of Detection* 7.ii (1986), 1–31.

8 Jacques Barzun, 'Meditations on the Literature of Spying', *The American Scholar* 34 (1965), 168.

9 J. Fenimore Cooper, *The Spy* (1821; Oxford: Oxford University Press, 1968), p. 12.

10 Cawelti and Rosenberg, *The Spy Story*, p. 35.

11 David A. T. Stafford, 'Spies and Gentlemen: The Birth of the British Spy Novel, 1883–1914', *Victorian Studies* 24.iv (Summer 1981), 497–8.

12 Nicholas Hiley, 'Introduction' to William Le Queux, *Spies of the Kaiser* (London and Portland: Frank Cass, 1996), pp. vii–xxxii.

13 I. F. Clarke, ed., *The Great War with Germany, 1890–1914: Fictions and Fantasies of the War-to-come* (Liverpool: Liverpool University Press, 1997), p. 112.

14 Sir Arthur Conan Doyle, *Sherlock Holmes: The Complete Illustrated Short Stories* (London: Chancellor Press, 1985), p. 728.

15 E. Phillips Oppenheim, *The Great Impersonation* (1920; New York: Dover, 1978), p. 162. A number of Oppenheim's novels are available on the web as e-texts. LeRoy L. Panek sees Oppenheim's heroes as late embodiments of 'nineteenth-century concepts of style': *The Special Branch: The British Spy Novel, 1890–1980* (Bowling Green, OH: Popular Press, 1981), p. 24.

16 Maldwin Drummond, *The Riddle* (London: Nautical Books, 1985), p. 153.

17 Erskine Childers, *The Riddle of the Sands* (1903; St Albans: Granada, 1978), pp. 81–2.

18 John Buchan, 'Adventure Stories', *John O'London's Weekly*, 4 December 1924, p. 276.

19 Childers, *The Riddle of the Sands*, p. 258.

20 Case discussed in David Seed, 'Erskine Childers and the German Peril', *German Life and Letters* n.s. 45.i (1992), 66–73, and in Richard Deacon, *A History of the British Secret Service* (St Albans: Granada, 1980), pp. 189–90.

21 Rudyard Kipling, *Kim* (1901; Harmondsworth: Penguin, 1987), p. 217.

22 Martin Green, *Dreams of Adventure, Deeds of Empire* (London: Routledge & Kegan Paul, 1980), p. 270.

23 Kipling, *Kim*, p. 288.

24 Joseph Conrad, *The Secret Agent* (1907; Harmondsworth: Penguin, 1990), p. 63.

25 Avrom Fleishman, *Conrad's Politics* (Baltimore: Johns Hopkins Press, 1967), p. 190.

26 G. K. Chesterton, *The Man Who Was Thursday* (1908; Harmondsworth: Penguin, 1962), p. 128. Chesterton explained in a 1936 article that the novel was 'intended to describe the world of wild doubt and despair which the pessimists were generally describing at that date' (*ibid.*, p. 188).

27 John Buchan, *Mr Standfast* (1919; Oxford: Oxford University Press, 1993), p. 15.

28 Cawelti and Rosenberg, *The Spy Story*, pp. 87–8.

29 Richard Usborne's *Clubland Heroes* (1953, revised 1974) brought into currency a phrase describing the social characteristic common to the heroes of Dornford Yates, John Buchan and Sapper.

30 John Buchan, *The Thirty-Nine Steps* (1915; Oxford: Oxford University Press, 1993), p. 52.

31 *Ibid.*, p. 102.

32 John Buchan, *The Three Hostages* (1924; Oxford: Oxford University Press, 1995), p. 71.

33 For commentary on the historical importance of Maugham, see Jeanne F. Bedell, 'Somerset Maugham's *Ashenden* and the Modernization of Espionage Fiction', *Studies in Popular Culture* 7 (1984), 40–6. For information on the relation between the British intelligence service and Maugham among other writers, see Anthony Masters, *Literary Agents: The Novelist as Spy* (Oxford: Blackwell, 1987).

34 W. Somerset Maugham, *Ashenden; Or, The British Agent* (1928; London: Heinemann, 1948), p. viii.

35 *Ibid.*, p. 7.

36 *Ibid.*, p. 101.

37 Ted Morgan, *Somerset Maugham* (London: Jonathan Cape, 1980), p. 313.

38 Michael Denning, *Cover Stories: Narrative and Ideology in the British Spy Thriller* (London and New York: Routledge & Kegan Paul, 1987), p. 83.

39 Marie-Francoise Allain, *The Other Man: Conversations with Graham Greene* (London: Bodley Head, 1983), p. 99.

40 See William M. Chase, 'Spies and God's Spies: Greene's Espionage Fiction', in Jeffrey Meyers, ed., *Graham Greene: A Revaluation* (London: Macmillan, 1990), pp. 156–80.

41 Graham Greene, *The Ministry of Fear* (1943; London: Heinemann, 1962), p. 2.

42 *Ibid.*, pp. 71–2.

43 Graham Greene, *The Human Factor* (London: Vintage, 1999), p. 19.

44 *Ibid.*, p. 119.

45 Allain, *The Other Man*, p. 102.

46 Andrew Lycett, *Ian Fleming: The Man Behind James Bond* (Atlanta: Turner Publishing, 1995), p. 220.

47 *Ibid.*, p. 362.

48 Tony Bennett, 'The Bond Phenomenon', *Southern Review* 16.ii (1983), 195–225.

49 Cyril Connolly parodies Fleming in *Bond Strikes Camp* (London: Shenval Press, 1963); among other attacks on Bond, see Mordecai Richler, 'James Bond Unmasked', in Bernard Rosenberg and David Manning White eds., *Mass Culture Revisited* (New York: Van Nostrand Reinhold, 1971), pp. 341–55.

50 Umberto Eco, 'Narrative Structures in Fleming', in *The Role of the Reader: Explorations in the Semiotics of Texts* (London: Hutchinson, 1987), pp. 144–72.

51 Kingsley Amis, *The James Bond Dossier* (London: Jonathan Cape, 1965), p. 147.

52 Ian Fleming, 'How to Write a Thriller', *Weekend Telegraph*, 6 December 1997, p. 11; Denning, *Cover Stories*, p. 102.

53 Tony Bennett and Janet Woolacott, *Bond and Beyond: The Political Career of a Popular Hero* (London: Macmillan, 1987), p. 28.

54 For examples of the Bond chic where style is all see Adam Diment's Philip McAlpine series, James Mayo's Charles Hood novels, and James Leasor's *Passport To Oblivion* (1964, later retitled *Where the Spies Are*). The last of these centred on Jason Love, a country doctor turned secret agent.

55 John le Carré, 'To Russia, with Greetings', *Encounter*, May 1966, p. 4.

56 John le Carré, 'Foreword' to Bruce Page, David Leitch and Phillip Knightley, *Philby: The Spy Who Betrayed a Generation* (London: Sphere, 1977), p. 33.

57 Michael Barber, 'Hong Kong was a "Halfway House"', *Newsagent and Bookshop*, 30 November 1978, p. 22.

58 John le Carré, 'My Secret World', *Sunday Times News Review*, 17 June 1990 Section 3, p. 1.

59 John le Carré, *The Spy Who Came In From The Cold* (London: Victor Gollancz, 1963), p. 103.

60 Miriam Gross, 'The Secret World of John le Carré', *Observer Review* (3 February 1980) Section 3, p. 1.

61 Richard Bradbury, 'Reading John le Carré', in Clive Bloom, ed., *Spy Thrillers: From Buchan to le Carré* (London: Macmillan, 1990), p. 132.

62 John le Carré, *Quest for Karla* (London: Hodder & Stoughton, 1982), p. 20, repeated on p. 92.

63 *Ibid.*, p. 250.
64 Graham Greene, 'Kim Philby', in Kim Philby, *My Silent War* (St Albans: Granada, 1981), p. 7.
65 Le Carré, *Quest for Karla*, p. 828.
66 John le Carré, *The Secret Pilgrim* (London: Hodder & Stoughton, 1991), p. 116.
67 The circumstantial detail of Deighton's run-down urban settings rather under- mines Fred Erisman's claim that his heroes are romantic questers after an inward reality; 'Romantic Reality in the Spy Stories of Len Deighton', *Proceedings of 6th National Convention of Popular Culture Association* (Bowling Green, OH: Popular Press, 1976), pp. 233–50.
68 Len Deighton, *Spy Line* (London: Grafton, 1990), p. 33.
69 For excellent commentary on the thriller genre, see Jerry Palmer, *Thrillers: Genesis and Structure of a Popular Genre* (London: Arnold, 1978).
70 Thomas Pynchon, 'Under the Rose', *The Noble Savage* 3 (1961), 224.
71 Hence Bruce Merry's contrast between US agents as small figures in big organi- sations and UK agents as big figures in small organisations (Merry, *Anatomy of the Spy Thriller*, p. 36).
72 Burroughs comments on the workings of such agencies in 'The Limits of Con- trol' and 'In the Interests of National Security', both collected in his *The Adding Machine: Collected Essays* (London: Calder, 1985).
73 The studies by Cawelti and Rosenberg, Merry, Panek, and Stafford have all made important progress in extending critical attention to writers like Helen Macinnes, Donald Hamilton, and A. E. W. Mason.

# 8

DAVID GLOVER

# The thriller

When the thriller writer Robert Ludlum died in March 2001, several of his obituarists tellingly recalled the reaction of a *Washington Post* reviewer to one of the author's many, phenomenally popular novels: 'It's a lousy book. So I stayed up until 3 am to finish it.'[1] This anecdotal, tongue-in-cheek confession neatly captures the ambivalence associated with a hugely successful mode of crime writing, a guilty sense that its lack of literary merit has always somehow been inseparable from the compulsiveness with which its narrative pleasures are greedily gobbled up, relegating the thriller to the most undeserving of genres. To describe a thriller as 'deeply satisfying and sophisticated' (to pluck a blurb at random from the bookshelves) is already to beg the insidious question: *how satisfying and sophisticated can it be?*

It might be thought that this kind of sceptical response is likely to be encouraged by any type of popular literature that could be considered formulaic, or that relies upon stock characters or highly conventionalised narrative structures, or whose enjoyment comes from the repetition of certain well-worn themes or devices. But the thriller is unusual in its reliance upon, or subordination to, the single-minded drive to deliver a starkly intense literary effect. Thus, in the words of *The New York Times Book Review*'s suitably lurid verdict on the novel that famously first unleashed Dr Hannibal Lecter upon an unsuspecting public, Thomas Harris's *Red Dragon* (1981) 'is an engine designed for one purpose – to make the pulse pound, the heart palpitate, the fear glands secrete'.[2] Judgements like these, carefully filleted and recycled as paperback blurbs, make a virtual contract with potential purchasers, offering an irresistible reading experience that will stretch them to the limit. To be reckoned 'as good as the crime thriller gets', to quote from the cover of Lawrence Block's *A Walk Among The Tombstones* (1992), 'the suspense' will be 'relentless'; indeed it 'will hold readers gaga with suspense'.[3]

Of course, such overblown appeals to a hyperventilated state of pleasurably anxious unknowing can easily be dismissed as little more than a sign of the extent to which popular criticism has been debased by the inflated currency of contemporary marketing. But they do offer some important clues to the thriller's provenance and distinctiveness. The OED's earliest example of the term dates from 1889 but its broadbrush definition – 'a sensational play . . . or story' – hints at a slightly earlier literary context: the controversy surrounding the 'sensation fiction' of Wilkie Collins, Mrs Henry Wood, and M. E. Braddon in the 1860s and 1870s, novels in which the disturbing treatment of crime, mystery and betrayal brought to mind the immediacy and theatricality of Victorian stage melodrama. For good or ill, the success of these novels was thought to be both a consequence of their direct impact upon the nervous systems of their readers and a symptom of the shocks and upheavals so characteristic of the modern era. Indeed, the OED's 1889 example highlights the misgivings associated with the pursuit of the sensational in its condemnation of 'a worthless play' as nothing more than an 'invertebrate "thriller" ', a production whose emptiness and incoherence is 'theatrical' in the very worst sense. And four decades later one finds the detective writer Dorothy L. Sayers making essentially the same connection and the same critique when she complains that the 'purely Sensational thriller' piles:

> thrill . . . on thrill and mystification on mystification; the reader is led on from bewilderment to bewilderment, till everything is explained in a lump in the last chapter. This school is strong in dramatic incident and atmosphere; its weakness is a tendency to confusion and a dropping of links – its explanations do not always explain; it is never dull, but it is sometimes nonsense.[4]

By the late 1920s when Sayers wrote these words, detective fiction had become a serious business and it was becoming customary to distinguish those stories based upon 'the power of logical analysis and subtle and acute reasoning' from the 'crude and pungent sensationalism' of the vulgar thriller in which 'the writer's object is to make the reader's flesh creep'.[5] On the one hand, this distinction reflected the emergence of the modern grid of genre labels in which the mystery or classic detective story had gained a special, almost canonical status as a strict, rule-governed puzzle according to whose exacting standards of gamesmanship and fair play even the 'adventures' of Sherlock Holmes (to use Conan Doyle's preferred term) could be found wanting. Yet, at the same time, the emphasis upon cerebration as a form of self-discipline, what Sayers called 'that quiet enjoyment of the logical which we look for in our detective reading' and which marked off 'the uncritical' from 'the modern educated public', clearly carried overtones of an improving or civilising mission, calming the feverish excesses produced by the modern world and endemic to the thriller.[6]

Like all polemical contrasts, the comparison between the detective story and the thriller made by Sayers and others contained elements of caricature.

It downplayed the jokiness and artificiality of many mysteries, while failing to recognise that thrillers could work perfectly well on their own terms. The thriller was not necessarily as far-fetched or as illogical as these critics implied. Erskine Childers's bestseller *The Riddle of the Sands* (1903), a founding text of the genre, displays a meticulous eye for detail and a high moral and political seriousness, as befits a seafaring spy novel whose major concern is with national regeneration in the face of Germany's growing naval power. But, as the spy novelist Valentine Williams argued in one of the rare defences of the thriller, what ultimately matters in thriller-writing is 'plausibility' or verisimilitude, a quality that is largely genre-specific. It is not what the reader believes that counts: 'the important aim is to make him believe it', to carry the reader along by using pace and surprise to 'outweigh any inherent improbabilities of plot'.[7] This maxim is as relevant to a latter-day 'superthriller' like Thomas Harris's *Black Sunday* (1975), which takes us inside the technicalities of a terrorist plan to bomb the American Super Bowl by airship, as it was when Williams wrote his apologia forty years earlier.

Despite his insistence that the thriller's prime focus is upon action, Williams tended to blur the boundaries between it and the detective story in a way that would undoubtedly have troubled Sayers or purists like R. Austin Freeman. In fact, there are good reasons for this confusion. For one thing, writers were often capable of working in either genre. This was evidently true of Williams himself, and it was no less true of major figures like Edgar Wallace and, perhaps more surprisingly, Agatha Christie, some of whose early novels like *The Secret Adversary* (1922) or *The Seven Dials Mystery* (1929) were concocted from such thrillerish ingredients as master criminals, secret societies, and special agents. The picture is further complicated by the protean nature of the thriller, which has always been capacious enough to incorporate devices from the detective story tradition. This was particularly noticeable during the Edwardian period, in the years before the classic detective novel was perfected. Thrillers as various as Edgar Wallace's *The Four Just Men* (1905) and Sax Rohmer's novel introducing his celebrated Oriental master criminal, *The Insidious Fu Manchu* (1913), made extensive use of the locked-room murder mystery first devised by Edgar Allan Poe, for example, but combined such baffling crimes with cliffhanger techniques.

Where the thriller differs from the detective story is not in any disinclination to resort to deductive methods in solving crimes – though, to be sure, when present they necessarily occupy only a secondary role. Rather, the thriller was and still is to a large extent marked by the way in which it persistently seeks to raise the stakes of the narrative, heightening or exaggerating the experience of events by transforming them into a rising curve of danger, violence or shock. The world that the thriller attempts to realise is one that is radically uncertain in at least two major senses. On the one hand, the *scale* of the threat may appear to be vast, its ramifications immeasurable and boundless. Thus, the thriller trades in international conspiracies, invasions, wholesale corruption, serial killers who threaten entire cities or even nations and this remains the case even where the tone is relatively light-hearted or facetious, as in Leslie Charteris's 'The Saint' stories or Agatha Christie's youthful thrillers. On the other, the thriller unsettles the reader less by the magnitude of the terrors it imagines than by the *intensity* of the experience it delivers: assaults upon the fictional body, a constant awareness of the physicality of danger, sado-masochistic scenarios of torture or persecution, a descent into pathological extremes of consciousness, the inner world of the psychopath or monster. In the gruesome Belfast prologue to Chris Petit's *The Psalm Killer* (1996), for example, it is not simply the horrific description of the paramilitary execution that disturbs but its sexualisation by the murderer's female partner, shifting the scene from assassination to intercourse 'that had felt like a fuck in eternity'.[8]

Set against this kind of psychic and epistemological turbulence, any investigative impulse tends to fall short or to seem woefully inadequate, as if the deductive model cannot contain the implications of its own findings. Often the thriller is preoccupied with the enormity of what is known but cannot be proved and this leads to an urgent desire for rough justice, an impatience with official procedures, a feeling that 'details don't make much difference'.[9] Indeed, as Gilles Deleuze has perceptively noted, the question of exact truth may become sidelined, producing a hero who is identified by his recklessness, his cavalier willingness to take risks, even to allow mistakes or errors to multiply at random in the belief that they will move events forward, a procedure memorably described by Dashiell Hammett's 'Continental Op' as 'stirring things up'.[10] It has become a critical commonplace to describe the basic fantasy-structure of the thriller as that of a hero 'overcoming obstacles and dangers and accomplishing some important and moral mission'; but it is less often recognised that the thriller is equally, and in some instances, *more* concerned with creating obstacles, proliferating setbacks, traps, inconveniences, dead-ends and discomposure.[11] And in extreme cases, such as *Night Moves* (1975), Alan Sharp's remarkable swan-song to the private eye novel or William Hjortsberg's occult thriller *Falling Angel* (1978), the 'hero' may be vanquished or the narrative voice snuffed out.

The term 'thriller' emerged as a loose descriptor that could be applied to a wide range of narratives, some of which – like the spy-thriller from Childers to John le Carré – can be considered as distinct sub-genres in their own right, while others are much harder to place and seem deliberately to defy classification – James Ellroy's *American Tabloid* (1995) being a prime candidate, with its dazzling collage of espionage, paramilitarism, police work, and generalised mayhem. There is a diffuseness about the thriller, an extraordinary promiscuity of reference that produces an over-abundance of possibilities: racing thrillers (Dick Francis), legal thrillers (John Grisham), psychological thrillers (Dennis Lehane), political thrillers (Jack Higgins), futuristic thrillers (Philip Kerr), and on and on. But this condition of superfluity is not new: it was present at source and is rooted in a fluid and disordered world of popular writing where genre categories were far from fixed and where terms like 'mystery', 'thriller', 'detective story' and 'adventure' were used freely and interchangeably, the world of the dime novels, 'shilling shockers', 'yellowbacks', penny illustrated papers, and (after 1896, when the American publisher Frank Munsey changed the paper, format and target readership of his all-story magazine *The Argosy*), pulp fiction.[12]

A vivid sense of the restless, unconfined inventiveness of the early twentieth-century thriller can be gleaned from the career of the figure that dominated the field until his death in 1932, the staggeringly prolific Edgar Wallace, promoted by his publishers as the 'King of Thrillers'. His first novel *The Four Just Men* took its title from a mysterious band of foreign anarchists who have sworn to fight injustice wherever it is to be found and who are so outraged by a new Aliens Extradition Bill that they threaten to kill Britain's Foreign Secretary if he does not withdraw this attack on the right to political asylum. Too clever for the blundering forces of law and order, the anarchists turn the minister's death into the spectacular climax of the novel, awaited by hordes of expectant sightseers crowding the streets around Parliament. From the outset we know who the murderers are, but not how their crime was committed and Wallace's neat twist was to make this the basis of a competition in which readers were invited to send in their own solutions as to how the minister could have been killed while securely installed inside a sealed room and guarded by a small army of policemen. The correct answers would receive cash prizes: a foolhardy scheme which, together with the decision to take on the costs of publishing the novel himself, temporarily bankrupted the luckless author.

Wallace subsequently redeemed this failure by achieving fresh popularity with a series of imperial adventure stories set in West Africa, initially released as *Sanders of the River* in 1911, in which vigilante justice was transmuted into harsh reprisals and summary executions visited by an implacable District Commissioner upon 'a people who had neither power to reason, nor will to excuse, nor any large charity'.[13] Ezra Pound once described the author as 'Mr. Kipling's star disciple' and, whatever the validity of this view, his claim serves as a reminder that in Wallace's work the colonial context is never very far away.[14] There are imaginative continuities between the West African 'River

People' and the inhabitants of 'that section of the British Empire which lies between the northern end of Victoria Dock Road and the smelly drabness of Silvertown',[15] just as it is no accident that Tiger Tim Jordan, hero of *The Man at the Carlton* (1931), is the chief of the Rhodesian CID or that Jack Tarling in *The Daffodil Mystery* (1920) is a former member of the Shanghai police. But Wallace's re-vamping of imperial adventure motifs was also tempered by a growing fascination with the United States, both as a market for his work and as a weathervane for modernity's future. He contributed to leading American pulps like *Detective Story Magazine* before ending his career unhappily as a Hollywood scriptwriter. There are two sides to Wallace's ill-starred romance with America. At the close of *The Hand of Power* (1927), having survived the hijacking of an ocean liner carrying $50 million, the heroine Betty Carew is entranced by the sight of New York, 'the most wonderful skyline in the world', and prepares for American citizenship as she takes the hand of plucky Bill Holbrook, the young American reporter and advertising copywriter who has just saved her life.[16] In stark contrast to these Pollyannaish prospects, Wallace's brutal Prohibition saga *On the Spot* (1931) and the wholly self-explanatory *When the Gangs Came to London* (1932) sound a much darker tone. Wallace is important as an English vernacular writer, albeit an imperfect one, and he sometimes employed police, underworld and racing slang to mock the intellectual preciousness of the classic detective novel. But in his tale of the rise and fall of the Chicago gangster Tony Perelli, a narrative that echoes the trajectory of Rico Bandello in W. R. Burnett's earlier success *Little Caesar* (1929), Wallace initiated the long-running tradition of mimicking American hardboiled writing subsequently followed by Peter Cheyney and James Hadley Chase.

Wallace's heroines and female characters in general were fairly uninspired, though no more slight than Prudence Cowley in Christie's Tommy and Tuppence thrillers. Yet, despite this weakness, he managed to maintain a substantial female readership. Not only would he occasionally give women the central role, as in the female Robin Hood figures in *Kate Plus Ten* (1917) or *Four Square Jane* (1929) – criminals who are somehow not wholeheartedly criminal – but, more significantly, a typical Wallace narrative would build suspense by contriving to separate the heroine from the hero and making each the focal point of rapidly alternating episodes. In this respect Wallace's practice as a writer was very different to those found in many of the American pulp magazines which tended to employ more obviously gender-specific forms of address, visible in titles like *Action Stories*, *Battle Aces*, or even *Man Stories*. Here manliness was equated with action, speed, combat, confrontation and pursuit, and intelligence was conceived as essentially practical, mental alertness and quick thinking rather than intellectualism.

If these qualities are clearly those valorised by the thriller, pulp masculinity was available in a blur of genres and locales, ranging from the Western to South Seas adventure tales. Thus *Black Mask*, which quickly became the most inventive of crime fiction pulps, often featured Westerns or sported a Western action scene on its cover, and when it serialized Hammett's *The Maltese Falcon* between 1929 and 1930 the magazine's subtitle described its contents as 'Western, Detective and Adventure Stories'.[17] In some cases the stories could claim to straddle all three categories. Horace McCoy's adventures of Jerry Frost, a crack pilot who leads the Texas Rangers' Air Border Patrol and appeared at the same time as Hammett's Continental Op, come close enough.

The revolution in thriller writing associated with such *Black Mask* authors as Hammett, McCoy, Raoul Whitfield and Carroll John Daly was in part a refurbishing of already existing masculine cultural forms such as Allan Pinkerton's fictionalised detective memoirs and the white Anglo-Saxon muscularity of boy-sleuth Nick Carter. But it was not simply their uncompromising toughness and explicit violence that distinguished them from their predecessors – after all, even within the gentlemanly British tradition of thrillers like H. C. McNeile's Bulldog Drummond books there are scenes of unashamed brutality. In *Bulldog Drummond* (1919), for example, the eponymous ex-officer hero forces one of its villains into a bath of acid. The real difference lay in their renewed attention to demotic modes of writing, creating a style that captured the imaginations of working-class readers on both sides of the Atlantic. Indeed, in the personae created by some writers, toughness could be conflated with semi-literacy. Carroll John Daly's detectives Three-Gun Terry Mack and Race Williams, widely regarded as the first incarnations of the modern private eye, both liked to brag about their rough-and-ready language and it is significant that their tone of voice and aggressive stance were prefigured by an anonymous transitional figure from a *Black Mask* story called 'The False Burton Combs' (1922) who describes himself as 'a gentleman adventurer' or 'a soldier of fortune', as if he were some distant American cousin of Bulldog Drummond or 'The Saint' – though he is insistent that he is 'no knight errant, either'.[18]

That said, the appeal of the *Black Mask* school of crime fiction was a complex phenomenon and, as Erin A. Smith has argued, the work of Hammett, Daly, McCoy and others was susceptible to a multiplicity of readings.[19] In the first place, it was important that their protagonists all displayed a real measure of independence from the constraints of their social milieu. In *The Snarl of the Beast* (1927), Carroll John Daly's first Race Williams novel, Williams tells us that he is 'a halfway house between the law and crime; sort of working both ends against the middle', and his 'code of morals' has similarly equivocal status.[20] To be sure, Williams's credo contains echoes of earlier pulp vigilantes like Frank L. Packard's 'the Gray Seal', who is hunted by the police and the underworld alike. But in the pages of *Black Mask* the new breed of heroes eschewed the highly theatrical mastery of disguise, the near-magical shuttling between identities, so characteristic of dime novel favourites like 'Old Cap Collier' and 'Young Sleuth.' Instead, there was a strong tendency for independence to become a functional or operational value, a virtue that is only realised 'out on a job'.[21] Once again, Dashiell Hammett's Continental Op is the purest embodiment of this development, remorselessly reducing the agent's courage to a species of occupational pragmatism, producing a heroism drained of all emotional vitality except for a grim pleasure in its own destructive powers. The Op's alter ego and possible future is therefore 'the Old Man', the desk-bound line manager and latter-day patriarch 'with his gentle eyes behind gold spectacles and his mild smile, hiding the fact that fifty years of sleuthing had left him without any feelings at all on any subject'.[22]

A full treatment of Hammett's writing properly belongs to a history of the private eye, but his contribution to the thriller has been so decisive that his achievement deserves a little more discussion here. Slavoj Žižek has astutely noted the extent to which each of Hammett's five novels is unique, endlessly copied by others but never by Hammett himself.[23] Thus, the image of the corrupt, gang-ridden city in *Red Harvest* (1929) serves as the archetype of the debased public sphere of power politics and ruthless economic finagling, a city that is ripe for purging and whose portraits are legion: Chicago in W. R. Burnett's *Little Caesar*, Los Angeles in Paul Cain's *Fast One* (1932), 'Colton' in Horace McCoy's *No Pockets in a Shroud* (1937) – with a more recent variation in Ross Thomas's *The Fools in Town are on Our Side* (1970), where the city must first be corrupted *before* it can be cleansed. Words are seldom wasted upon description: 'Poisonville' is 'an ugly city of forty thousand people, set in an ugly notch between two ugly mountains that had been all dirtied up by mining'.[24] And elsewhere the bright lights and mean streets are conveyed with a sparseness of detail that virtually occludes any definite sense of place, a sudden glimpse of 'the jam of traffic: taxis, Hispano-Suizas, Fords, huge double-decked buses, leaning as they turned corners', and little more.[25] They are, in any case, mere surfaces. For behind the glitzy, tawdry, depersonalised exteriors lies a network of private offices, backrooms, hotel suites, and rear booths in restaurants or bars, secured spaces where meetings can be arranged between men seeking to make a deal, hammer out a compromise, or stage a confrontation: the true loci of power.

This ecology of male camaraderie and competition is, in Sean McCann's apt phrase, 'a vernacular terrain', an urban landscape that becomes intelligible through word of mouth.[26] But it is talk that opens out into an economy of violence, requiring exceptional forms of masculinity that are in turn inseparable from the normal practice of business and politics, however unstable those practices may ultimately prove to be. Novels like *Red Harvest* were therefore easily read – perhaps a little too easily – as a kind of social critique in which the forcefulness and cynicism of their language penetrated through to the sordid realities behind everyday life, while retaining a residual place for the tough, if world-weary, male labourer – men like the union organiser Bill Quint whose 'eyes were grey as his clothes, but not so soft'[27] and, in a more heterodox fashion, the Op too. Yet these were not the only pleasures available to *Black Mask* readers. At the opposite pole to the solid dependable greyness of the trade unionist was the style and panache of the gamblers, racketeers, reporters, and fixers who populated the hardboiled universe. Some of the harshest, most elliptical writing – best exemplified by Paul Cain's unremittingly bleak *Black Mask* stories from the early 1930s – could be illuminated by occasional flashes of dandyism. The 'tall and slim and angular' 'St. Nick' Green in Cain's collection *Seven Slayers* (1946) has 'the smooth tanned skin, bright China-blue eyes of twenty, the snowy white hair of sixty . . . and his more or less severe taste in clothes was violently relieved by a predilection for flaming-red neckties'.[28]

Women, of course, were a problem. Where they are not wholly venal like Dinah Brand in *Red Harvest*, or a murderous *femme fatale* like Brigid O'Shaughnessy in *The Maltese Falcon* (1930), their companionability is more often than not a function of their being honorary men. Gerry Kells's alcoholic lover Grandquist in Paul Cain's *Fast One* gets drunk 'in a masculine way' (to labour the point she is known only by her surname) and it is worth adding that the big and disorderly Dinah Brand comes across as the manliest of women.[29] But, curiously enough, the pulps were strikingly circumspect in their treatment of sexuality. The odd suggestive or coarse remark, usually a sexist jibe, and the occasional, discreetly muted allusion to homosexuality were as far as it was safe to go, though the fear of effeminacy or loss of virility could frequently be quite palpable. It was left to more upscale and more ambitious writers to knit the theme of sexual obsession into the hardboiled thriller narrative. Two novels stand out: William Faulkner's *Sanctuary* (1931) and James M. Cain's *The Postman Always Rings Twice* (1934) – the first, something of an anomaly for an author not normally associated with crime fiction, at least in the generic sense; the second, the opening shot in a long and influential career.

Faulkner's *Sanctuary* has many of the ingredients that belong in the thriller: murder, kidnapping, bootlegging, a sensational trial. However, Faulkner's southern Gothic sensibility pushes them in eerie, disquieting directions, creating a highly charged racialised *frisson* whose effect is sometimes sharpened and sometimes muffled by his determinedly modernist mannerisms. The judge's daughter Temple Drake is abandoned, raped, abducted and finally confined in a Memphis brothel, where she is effectively the property of her assailant, the impotent gunman Popeye. We are left in no doubt that Popeye's pistol is, like the corn-cob he employs to rape Temple, a phallic substitute, a bloody prosthesis, for we see him use it to kill a man who is a potential witness, before attacking her. Faulkner brings home the reality of Temple's rape and its after-effects by describing it in oblique, yet graphic language and dwelling on her continual bleeding while she is being driven away and when she arrives at the brothel. And he also has Temple mentally re-live her attack, intercut with her fantasies of being able to penetrate and injure Popeye in self-defence, of making him into 'a little black thing like a nigger boy' that she can control, and of transforming herself into a man.[30] This jarring exploration of fantasy was quite new, as was the degree of sexual brutality that was invoked. But Faulkner also provided a model of dispersed narration that went beyond the juxtaposition of the perspectives of hero, heroine and possibly a few minor characters, as had, for example, been characteristic of Edgar Wallace's thrillers. Instead, Faulkner showed how it was possible to begin to explicitly integrate *the agency of the criminal* into the storyline and to tack between it and the standpoints of the victim, the detective, and other, less important figures without any loss of suspense.[31] This model has practically become standard issue within the modern thriller, from Thomas Harris to Elmore Leonard. So, when James Hadley Chase took the hint and wrote *No Orchids for Miss Blandish* (1939) in un-modernist emulation of Faulkner, what mattered was not the appearance of yet another impotent psychopath who had spent his childhood cutting up live kittens with rusty scissors, but the indeterminate alternation between villain, victim and private detective, combined with the refusal to fall back on a reassuring ending that was becoming the hallmark of the bleaker hardboiled stories like Paul Cain's *Fast One*. For it was this narrative structure that brought victims and villains face to face, creating new opportunities for representing and exploring psychological tension and sexual violence.

In *The Postman Always Rings Twice*, James M. Cain (no relation) made the criminal the novel's narrator, involving the reader directly in the planning and commission of a murder. Cain did not deliberately try to adopt a tough or hardboiled style. As a professional journalist, he had always published in upmarket publications like *American Mercury*, *Atlantic Monthly*, or the *Saturday Evening Post* rather than the pulps, and he liked to claim (whether reliably or not) that he had never really been able to read Hammett or McCoy. Yet he did strive for 'a vividness of speech' that he heard all around him in the bars and streets of California, that of 'the Western roughneck . . . who has been to high school [and] completes his sentences'.[32] In short, the voice of the drifter Frank Chambers telling his story, so it finally emerges, from the condemned man's cell. The novel moves from Frank's adulterous affair with Cora to their attempts to murder her husband Nick Papadakis, the Greek owner of a roadside diner where Frank has picked up work, and then to its stormy aftermath once the murder has occurred. The brief, peculiarly intense descriptions of their lovemaking, whose violence comes close to rape, were profoundly shocking when the novel first appeared, nowhere more so than at the scene of the murder where Frank has to rough Cora up in order to make it look as if she has been in an automobile accident that has killed her husband. No sooner has Frank begun to rip her clothes than 'the breath was roaring in the back of my throat like I was some kind of an animal' and the couple are 'locked in each other's arms, and straining to get closer', alongside the car containing Nick's dead body.[33] In the end, however, the couple are barred from profiting from their crimes: Cora dies in a car crash, as Frank wildly tries to race her to a hospital, and he is charged with her murder. But the final chapter lacks the full force of true confession and Frank's final words are unrepentant, a plea that he and Cora can be together again, no matter where.

Cain's best work, as he once said of his second novella *Double Indemnity* (first serialised in *Liberty* in 1936), belongs in spirit to the Depression. Its sense of recklessness, of wrecked opportunities, of the blind contingencies of everyday life in which sex too becomes a kind of last desperate gamble, struck a tremendous chord in the thirties and forties and changed the face of crime fiction forever. In the post-Cain world there is no escape from the corrosive effects of crime: violence is compulsively re-enacted, multiplied, compounded. At the close of *Sanctuary*, Temple Drake sits beside her father in the Luxembourg Gardens looking 'sullen and discontented and sad'[34]; in James Hadley Chase's simulacrum eight years later, Miss Blandish, unable to rid her mind of the man who has raped her, throws herself to her death. And it is this strain of fatalism, licensed by Cain, that is uppermost in the work of so many of his successors. His influence not only trickled back down into the pulps, but also created a market for what would later be called *noir* fiction, a term that derives from Marcel Duhamel's 'série noire' books which Gallimard began publishing in France at the end of the Second World War, translations of the harder-edged, more cynical and oppressive writers like James Hadley Chase and Peter Cheyney, and newer names like Cornell Woolrich, David Goodis and Jim Thompson.

In Woolrich's fiction, from his early stories in such pulp magazines as *Dime Detective* or *Detective Fiction Weekly*, to the six novels he published in the early 1940s with their trademark 'black' titles, fatalism reaches almost metaphysical proportions. While a fear of the night or the dark may occasionally be linked to voodoo curses and mysterious powers of prophecy, the suffocating feeling of an inescapable destiny is typically written into the lockstep forms of Woolrich's narratives: murders that seem to follow an obscure logic, interlaced with futile attempts by the police to stop them, or the frantic attempts to clear the name of a condemned man in the last few hours before his execution. In Woolrich's histrionic universe, there is always one last turn of the screw that pins his protagonist to an inconsolable future: Julie Killeen in *The Bride Wore Black* (1940) avenges her husband's murder only to discover that she has killed the wrong men; Walter Lynch in 'The Death of Me' (1935) commits murder in order to hide the fact that he has switched identity with a corpse so as to escape his debts, but finds that he is a murder suspect whichever name he claims; and in *The Black Angel* (1943) Alberta Murray's attempt to save her husband from the electric chair results in her falling in love with the real murderer. False accusation is likewise one of the staple elements of former pulp-writer David Goodis's novels, producing identities that are in free fall and sexual relationships that are perpetually on the rocks. But here the focus is upon how the protagonists experience and endure guilt and failure. In Goodis's 1951 bestseller *Cassidy's Girl*, for example, the hapless anti-hero is wrongfully blamed for bringing about the deaths of those in his care in two separate incidents. But, far from resisting these injustices, he actually seems to welcome them, as if their repetition somehow confirmed his fundamental belief that he is a mere 'letdown artist' who gets 'kicked around' because he deserves it.[35] Similarly, in the *noir* classic *Dark Passage* (1946), Vincent Parry, who has mistakenly been convicted of having murdered his wife, escapes from prison and takes on a new identity, yet finds that he really has become a murderer when he kills a blackmailer in a struggle. Worse still, in a confrontation with the woman who is his wife's true killer, she throws herself out of a window, making it impossible for him ever to prove his innocence. Parry must remain a fugitive for the rest of his life and it remains an open question whether he can finally be reunited with Irene Janney, the girl who has helped him and whom he now loves. In a Goodis novel happiness is likely to be fleeting, precarious, and always unconvincing.

If the men in Goodis's fiction are paranoid in the extreme, then in Jim Thompson's they have become thoroughly demented and the descent into the nether world of Norman Bates in Robert Bloch's *Psycho* (1959) and thence of Francis Dolarhyde ('the Tooth Fairy') and Hannibal Lecter in *Red Dragon* is about to begin. Like Goodis, Thompson wrote chiefly for the new, sleazy 'paperback original' market that drove out the pulps in the 1950s. His work was more diverse than his reputation sometimes suggests and includes a fair amount of fictionalised autobiography. But in the majority of books the storyline soon slides over into the obsessive and the downright crazy. So when the '[t]wo big, bad, brainy bank robbers', as the intrusively omniscient narrator of *The Getaway* (1959) mockingly dubs them, at last escape being pursued and double-crossed they arrive in what appears to be a South American vision of hell, a country that eats away at its resident's money so efficiently that they can only survive by murdering their partners.[36] Here, in a Swiftian spin on James M. Cain's favourite device of having lovers whose conspiracy turns sour, Carol and Doc pretend to cheerily toast their new-found freedom 'to the strains of *Home Sweet Home*' and wait to see who will try to kill the other first.[37] As his taste in satire indicates, Thompson excelled at evoking the claustrophobia of madness, its bright infernal logic and amoral compulsions. This is the inner realm of all those who 'started the game with a crooked cue', men like Deputy Lou Ford in *The Killer Inside Me* (1952)[38] or his double, sheriff Nick Corey, in *Pop.1280* (1964) or the schizophrenic door-to-door salesman Frank Dillon in *A Hell of a Woman* (1954). In each case what starts out as a disarmingly upfront first person narration is revealed as something far more impenetrable and unsafe, enmeshed in its own craziness to the point where it is no longer really clear what kind of entity is doing the speaking. And as a sign of this indeterminacy, it is not unusual for their stories to be told from the other side of the grave.

Where earlier writers like Ernest Raymond in *We, The Accused* (1935) would seek to engage the reader's sympathies for their murderous protagonists, Thompson does not attempt to elicit our concern for the likes of Lou Ford. Instead he prefers to place us in the uncomfortable position of colluding in their contempt for the suffocating small-town mentality that envelops them, while leaving us in no doubt as to just how dangerous they are. This underscores an important feature of the contemporary thriller: no matter what clinical label these killers wear, they remain essentially monsters, indifferent to the diagnoses they inhabit. In the words of Troy Louden, the 'criminal psychopath' in Charles Willeford's *Sideswipe* (1987), 'What it means is, I know the difference between right and wrong and all that, but I don't give a shit.'[39] To that extent the confessions of figures like Lou Ford are unreadable, beyond interpretation – a striking reversal of the scientific move over the past 150 years to replace the notion of monstrosity by the categories of perversion and psychopathology. In a sense, the 'genius' of Hannibal Lecter lies in his clinical mastery of these psychiatric categories, and his transcendance of them as a kind over-worldly meta-monster. Indeed, it is scarcely an exaggeration to say that today all crime fiction can be identified according to the stance it adopts in relation to the idea of the monstrous.

Thompson was not the only writer implicated in this development. Mickey Spillane's early Mike Hammer books which sold in huge numbers in the 1950s deliberately imagined the villain as terrifyingly, grotesquely sub-human in order to justify her death at Hammer's hands: Juno Reeves, the muscular transvestite in *Vengeance is Mine* (1950), for example, or the dis-figured Lily Carver, 'a horrible caricature of a human' in *Kiss Me Deadly* (1952).[40] And to fully grasp the nature of this deep-rooted phenomenon, one would need a cultural history of the serial killer in the popular imagi-nation – a history that forms the premise of Caleb Carr's nineteenth-century thriller *The Alienist* (1994).[41] As Carr's novel suggests, the monstrous – even in its earliest incarnations – is that which resists or challenges scientific expertise, a kernel of pure unmotivated evil that will always lie just outside official knowledge.[42] In a general way, this unbridled monstrosity invokes the nether side of progress or, in texts like Brett Easton Ellis's *American Psycho* (1991), the 'bad conscience' of late twentieth-century affluence. Yet it seems doubtful whether the monstrous can finally be reduced to a single template, a univocal meaning. In Petit's *The Psalm Killer*, for example, the terrifying sequence of murders that runs throughout the book is ultimately inseparable from the murky inner story of covert British operations in Northern Ireland, despite the intricate sexual aetiology of these crimes. If the humanly fallible expertise that is pitted against the serial killer is deeply complicit in the hu-man monster's creation, each case nevertheless has its own peculiar history of naivety and miscalculation.

The shifting registers associated with the monstrous are particularly clear in James Ellroy's writing where the preoccupation with serial murder and sex-ual mutilation in novels like *Because the Night* (1984) or *Blood on the Moon* (1984) gives way to a sustained ransacking of Los Angeles's corrupt histori-cal past that takes the unsolved 1947 Black Dahlia murder case as its entry point into a world of vice, blackmail, and rogue cops. Within this intensely precarious male universe, the protagonists' lives are connected through a web of criss-crossing secrets and half-truths shadowed by a threat of homo-sexual violation so savage that, in *The Big Nowhere* (1988) at least, rape and murder slide into vampirism or cannibalism. If Ellroy reproduces his-tory with a vengeance, however, it soon becomes clear that the serial killer narrative is too slender to accommodate this grander nightmare vision and, in his later work, Ellroy has been driven to depict twentieth century America as itself inherently monstrous, a story of 'bad white men doing bad things in the name of authority' again and again.[43] With their telegraphic, stac-cato rhythms, in places as fractured as any prose experiment by William S. Burroughs, Ellroy's edgy sentences in *White Jazz* (1992) or *American*

*Tabloid* (1995) represent a watershed in the thriller: a paranoiac political history as pungent as a horror comic or sleazy magazine.

But not all contemporary thrillers conflate the criminal with the monstrous in this overblown manner. The villains in novels as different as those of Patricia Highsmith or Elmore Leonard are scarcely less dangerous or less vindictive than their counterparts in James Ellroy or Jim Thompson and, although they tend to operate in a comparatively minor key, they do not invariably do so. Raymond Gidre's pursuit of Jack Ryan down a town centre street in Leonard's *Unknown Man #89* (1977), blasting out plate-glass store windows with his pump action shotgun, is a scene that Ellroy might well have imagined; and Leonard's psychopathic killers such as millionaire Robbie Daniels in *Split Images* (1981) or ex-con Teddy Magyk in *Glitz* (1985) are unspectacularly chilling adversaries whose creepy efficiency should not be underestimated. These men are *ordinary* monsters, but no less menacing or uncompromising in their criminality for all their mundane qualities. There is a parallel here with another, related type of thriller, those criminal capers in which the hard-nosed professionalism of the gunmen shades into a willing, if rather deadpan, sadism where any act that is deemed necessary will be carried out, whatever the cost. In Richard Stark's 'Parker' series or Lawrence Block's *Hit Man* (1998) or *Hit List* (2000), career criminals find themselves compromised or stymied and are forced to resort to non-routine uses of violence in order to set matters right.[44] Block's lone assassin Keller is exceptionally good at his job (expertise turned monstrous), but muddles through the rest of his life, fantasising about moving out of New York and living differently, reveries that are triggered by observing the men and women he has been contracted to kill. In fact, except for an occasional murder every couple of months, Keller's life is so uneventful that he thinks of himself as a retiree.

Curiously, what all these novels share is a marked lack of interest in criminal psychology as this would normally be understood. In Elmore Leonard's marvellous *LaBrava* (1983), for instance, the villain Richard Nobles (a literary cousin of Raymond Gidre) is typed as 'sociopathic' quite early on, and his Cuban accomplice privately dubs him 'the Monster from the Big Scrub', a 'swamp creature on the loose'.[45] But, unlike Jim Thompson's Lou Ford, there is no sense that Nobles's place among the 'endless files of psychiatric literature' has any real bearing on how the reader is to understand him.[46] Leonard is far more concerned with practical dilemmas and, if his characters rarely agonise about moral consequences, they do suffer from performance anxieties. How people manage to psych themselves up under extreme conditions is clearly what intrigues him and this provides the pretext for a variety of fantasy scenarios in which his characters try out actions and identities, intensifying the rhythms of suspense and, at the same time, connecting up with the reader's own fantasy investment in his narratives. Yet though this lends sharpness and humour to his writing, it adds much less psychological depth than one might expect. For all the exactness of Leonard's wary, hard-nosed street talk and tacky urban realism, there is hardly any detailed exploration of motive here, and scant regard for origins. Much the same is true of other, very different writers. Patricia Highsmith has noted that, while her 'criminal heroes' are 'psychopathic or neurotic', they are also 'fairly likable, or at least not repugnant'.[47] Her most successful creation, the murderer Tom Ripley, is however something of a mystery man. We learn very little about his past, apart from a brief glimpse of his difficult childhood with the contemptuous Aunt Dottie who brought him up. Instead, Highsmith describes the way in which Ripley is flooded by feelings of hurt and humiliation that feed his paranoia, 'swelling' into a 'crazy emotion of hate, of affection, of impatience and frustration' that impedes his breathing.[48] But these sudden intensities are quickly absorbed into Highsmith's impassive, deceptively transparent prose in which characters and events turn out to be far more elusive than they appear at first sight. Mundane occurrences can slide imperceptibly and irretrievably out of control, producing a fiction of nagging indirection in which we are made to feel that 'surveillance and introspection' come down to 'the same thing'.[49]

Highsmith is one of the very few women writers to make the world of the thriller her own and her work is a reminder of just how closed to outsiders that world has been. While there are now lesbian, Hispanic and many other variants of the hardboiled private eye, for example, the mainstream thriller has remained largely immune from such developments and the genre has attracted relatively few minority writers. So it is appropriate to close with two recent texts that seem less comfortable with the thriller's sexual premises and that have tried to tackle its blind-spots head on. Susanna Moore's controversial *In the Cut* (1995) starts from a woman's fixation upon male argot and male power, embedding it within the growing panic that a serial killer brings to her downtown New York neighbourhood. Part confession, part investigation, *In the Cut* records a teacher of creative writing's search for a working knowledge of the precinct that polices and gives shape to her desires, itemising the strange equivalences that resonate throughout street slang – in which 'to lash' is 'to urinate' and 'gangsters' are a woman's breasts – until she comes to a point where an official interrogation turns into intercourse and the phrase 'Give it up' is no longer a demand for information but has become an explicit sexual command.[50] The woman's narration is as dangerous and doomed as anything in Jim Thompson, but it is the delicate anatomical precision with which she probes the blind alley of passion that distances this compulsive novella from its pulp antecedents. By contrast, *The Long Firm* (1999), Jake Arnott's saga of East End gangsterdom, takes a leaf out of James Ellroy's unsavoury book to rewrite the secret history of London in the sixties and seventies as an organised criminal pursuit in which anything goes. But for Arnott homosexuality provides the code and the allure behind this world in a way in which it could never do for Ellroy. Indeed, in the end the various personae of Harry Starks, the queer racketeer whose story animates each of the novel's five narrative voices, finally vanish into the myth that he has so carefully cultivated, a Houdini-like figure who leaves behind a backwash of rumour, disinformation and awe. How far *The Long Firm* and *In the Cut* point towards a more heterodox future for the thriller remains to be seen. Yet in the sharply opposed cultural logics revealed by their respective dénouements, Arnott and Moore seem to promise that the thriller is likely to continue to flutter between the dead-end and the mythic for some time to come.

## NOTES

1 See, for example, Jack Adrian, 'Robert Ludlum', *The Independent, The Wednesday Review*, 14 March 2001, p. 6.
2 Quoted on the cover of the 1990 Dell paperback edition of *Red Dragon*.
3 Quotes from the *San Diego Union-Tribune*, the *Philadelphia Inquirer*, and *New York Newsday* cited on the cover 1993 Avon paperback edition.
4 'Introduction' to Dorothy L. Sayers, ed., *The Omnibus of Crime* (New York: Payson & Clarke Ltd., 1929), p. 19.
5 R. Austin Freeman, 'The Art of the Detective Story' (1924) in Howard Haycraft, ed., *The Art of the Mystery Story: A Collection of Critical Essays*, 2nd edn (1946; New York: Carroll & Graf, 1983), p. 9.
6 Sayers, *The Omnibus of Crime*, pp. 15, 21, 32. For more detailed discussion of this point, see David Glover, 'The Writers Who Knew Too Much: Populism and Paradox in Detective Fiction's Golden Age', in Warren Chernaik, Martin Swales and Robert Vilain, eds., *The Art of Detective Fiction* (London: Macmillan, 2000), pp. 36–49.
7 Valentine Williams, 'How Thrillers Are Made', *John O'London's Weekly*, 7 September, 1935, pp. 765–72. Like Edgar Wallace, Williams was a former Reuters and *Daily Mail* reporter who turned to thriller writing. A brief biography can be found in Donald McCormick, *Who's Who In Spy Fiction* (London: Sphere, 1977), pp. 231–2. For a more recent discussion of verisimilitude that concurs with Williams, see Steve Neale, 'Questions of Genre', *Screen* 31 (1990), 45–66.
8 Chris Petit, *The Psalm Killer* (1996; London: Pan Books, 1997), p. 12.
9 Dashiell Hammett, *The Dain Curse* (1929; London: Pan Books, 1975), p. 93.
10 Gilles Deleuze, 'Philosophie de la Série Noire', *Arts et Loisirs*, 18 (1966), 12–13. For a discussion of Hammett's 'homely' metaphor, see Steven Marcus, 'Dashiell Hammett and the Continental Op', *Partisan Review*, 41 (1974), 370–2.

11 See John G. Cawelti, *Adventure, Mystery, and Romance: Formula Stories as Art and Popular Culture* (Chicago: University of Chicago Press, 1976), p. 39.

12 For a useful short history of mass market literature in the late Victorian and Edwardian periods that glosses many of these long-forgotten terms, see M. J. Birch, 'The Popular Fiction Industry: Market, Formula, Ideology', *Journal of Popular Culture* 21 (1987), 79–102. On the origins of pulp magazines, see Tony Goodstone, *The Pulps: Fifty Years of American Pop Culture* (New York: Chelsea House, 1970), pp. ix–xvi.

13 Edgar Wallace, *Sanders of the River* (1911; Garden City, NY: Doubleday, Doran, 1930), p. 3.

14 Ezra Pound, *ABC of Reading* (1934; New York: New Directions, 1960), p. 9.

15 Edgar Wallace, *White Face* (London: Hodder & Stoughton, 1930), p. 45.

16 Edgar Wallace, *The Hand of Power* (1927; New York: The Mystery League, 1930), p. 319.

17 Founded by the writer H. L. Mencken and drama critic George Jean Nathan, the first (April 1920) issue of *The Black Mask* was an 'All-story magazine' aimed primarily at male readers. As early as December 1922 it began to publish stories by Dashiell Hammett and Carroll John Daly and between 1926 and 1936, under the editorship of Captain Joseph T. Shaw, became the flagship for the new hardboiled style of crime writing. See William F. Nolan, *The Black Mask Boys* (New York: George Morrow & Co., 1985), pp. 19–34.

18 Quoted in William F. Nolan, *The Black Mask Boys* (New York: George Morrow & Co., 1985), p. 36. Carroll John Daly's Terry Mack and Race Williams made their first appearances in the May and June 1923 issues of *Black Mask* respectively.

19 See Erin A. Smith, *Hard-boiled: Working-Class Readers and Pulp Magazines* (Philadelphia: Temple University Press, 2000).

20 Carroll John Daly, *The Snarl of the Beast* (New York: Edward J. Clode, 1927), p. 12.

21 Dashiell Hammett, *Red Harvest* (1929; London: Pan Books, 1975), p. 105.

22 Dashiell Hammett, 'The Scorched Face' (1925) in *The Big Knockover and Other Stories* (Harmondsworth: Penguin, 1969), p. 99.

23 Slavoj Žižek, *Enjoy Your Symptom! Jacques Lacan in Hollywood and out* (New York and London: Routledge, 1992), p. 157.

24 Hammett, *Red Harvest*, p. 5.

25 W. R. Burnett, *Little Caesar* (1929; London: Zomba Books, 1984), p. 82.

26 Sean McCann, *Gumshoe America: Hard-Boiled Crime Fiction and the Rise and Fall of New Deal Liberalism* (Durham, NC and London: Duke University Press, 2000), p. 110.

27 Hammett, *Red Harvest*, p. 8.

28 Paul Cain, *Seven Slayers* (1946; Berkeley, CA: Black Lizard Books, 1987), p. 123.

29 Paul Cain, *Fast One* (1933; Harpenden: No Exit Press, 1987), p. 44. For a reading of Dinah Brand as masculine, see Erin A. Smith, *Hard-boiled*, pp. 162–4.

30 William Faulkner, *Sanctuary* (1931; New York: Vintage Books, 1993), p. 219.

31 In Britain, there were some important parallels at roughly the same time. In Francis Iles's (Anthony Berkeley Cox) innovative *Malice Aforethought* (1931) the murderer's plans are revealed in the novel's first sentence and the suspense lies in not knowing whether or not he will be able to carry out his crime successfully. And in Agatha Christie's *The ABC Murders* (1936), the Poirot narrative is intercut with

glimpses of a mysterious and suspicious figure who seems to be implicated in the apparent serial killings, though this finally turns out to be a ruse. For precursors, one might look back to Marie Belloc Lowndes's Jack the Ripper novel *The Lodger* (1913).

32 James M. Cain, 'Author's Preface' to *Double Indemnity* (1945) in *The Five Great Novels of James M. Cain* (London: Picador, 1985), pp. 235–6.

33 James M. Cain, *The Postman Always Rings Twice* (1934) in *The Five Great Novels*, pp. 34–5.

34 Faulkner, *Sanctuary*, p. 317.

35 David Goodis, *Cassidy's Girl* (1951; Berkeley, CA: Black Lizard Books, 1987), p. 146–7.

36 Jim Thompson, *The Getaway* (1959; London: Zomba Books, 1983), p. 98.

37 *Ibid.*, p. 115.

38 Jim Thompson, *The Killer Inside Me* (1952; London: Zomba Books, 1983), p. 248.

39 Charles Willeford, *Sideswipe* (1987; London: Victor Gollancz Ltd., 1988), p. 50.

40 Mickey Spillane, *Kiss Me, Deadly* (1952; New York: Signet Books, 1953), p. 152.

41 See Mark Seltzer, *Serial Killers: Death and Life in America's Wound Culture* (New York and London: Routledge, 1998).

42 According to Michel Foucault, the monstrous is historically the oldest of the three 'figures' out of which the modern notion of 'abnormality' was constructed in the late nineteenth century. See Michel Foucault, *Les Anormaux: Cours au Collège de France, 1974–1975* (Paris: Gallimard/Seuil, 1999).

43 Ellroy has used this phrase on a number of occasions. See, for example, his interview with Edward Helmore in *The Guardian G2*, 20 April 2001, pp. 4–5. In a review of *The Cold Six Thousand* (2001), Gérard Meudal has hinted at a psychoanalytic explanation for this shift of focus in Ellroy's writing; see 'Machine diabolique', *Le Monde des livres*, 13 April 2001, p. 2.

44 'Richard Stark' is a *nom de plume* of crime writer Donald E. Westlake. The 'Parker' series began with *The Hunter* in 1962 and these novels still appear from time to time. *Backflash* was published in 1998.

45 Elmore Leonard, *LaBrava* (1983; Harmondsworth: Penguin, 1985), pp. 46–7, 65.

46 The phrase occurs in *The Killer Inside Me* when Lou Ford is revisiting his father's old office. Ford *père* was a doctor whose shelves are filled with volumes by Krafft-Ebing, Freud, Jung, Bleuler or Kraepelin. In a strangely Oedipal moment, Lou both asserts that these books contain '[a]ll the answers' and yet approvingly emphasises the typicality of his image in the mirror ('Maybe friendlier looking than the average.'), suggesting that his acceptance of such diagnoses is merely a ruse. See Thompson, *The Killer Inside Me*, pp. 131–2.

47 Patricia Highsmith, *Plotting and Writing Suspense Fiction* (London: Poplar Press, 1983), p. 46.

48 Patricia Highsmith, *The Talented Mr Ripley* (1956; Harmondsworth: Penguin, 1979), p. 87.

49 Terence Rafferty, 'Fear and Trembling', *The New Yorker*, 4 January 1988, p. 75.

50 Susanna Moore, *In the Cut* (1995; London: Picador, 1996), p. 120.

# 9

LEROY L. PANEK

# Post-war American police fiction

Like the poor, in the world of crime fiction cops have always been with us. From the beginning we find Sergeant Cuff, Inspector Bucket, M. Lecoq, to say nothing of Poe's Prefect, or Doyle's Lestrade. In the Golden Age they multiply – Inspectors Alleyn, Appleby, Grant, and Parker, to name only a few. Across the Atlantic, Ellery Queen's dad was a cop, and even Dashiell Hammett portrayed police officers in a sympathetic light in his early stories. But nobody claims that the presence of a police officer makes police fiction. Indeed, in most detective fiction written before 1950, police officers play a decidedly subordinate role – as foils or representatives of the state clearing the boards at the end. Even if main characters wear badges, the fact that they are cops has no impact on their characterisation; they act like any other amateur or private detective, unfettered by bureaucracy and law.

And then things changed. Post-Second World War and then post-Vietnam, transformations in American society had a lot to do with the change. New concerns about crime, civil rights, drug abuse, urban terrorism, previously unknown levels of violence, and acute attention to the role of the police changed things. For the first time ever, writers began to examine real cops and the fascinating, tedious, traumatic, and thankless job they do and the ways in which their employment makes an impact on them. Television had something to do with the change. Jack Webb's *Dragnet*, on radio in 1949 and then on television in 1952, projected a new image of the police officer and served as the precursor to scores of police dramas that appeared on network television in the ensuing decades. Along with these, other currents in popular fiction influenced the emergence of the police novel. The spy hero was made redundant by the collapse of the Soviet Union and thriller writers needed someone else to fill the void. Techno-thrillers like Tom Clancy's *Hunt for Red October* (1982) emerged as a popular form. Added to this was the recognition that while they continue to appeal to readers, amateur sleuths and private eyes have little relevance when it comes to the real criminals and real crime in the last half of the twentieth century. For those one needs cops.

But the police novel began slowly. Until the mid-1980s, police novels formed a very small pocket in the garment of crime fiction. Moreover, the few critics who found them worthy of comment defined the genre by applying to the police novel the criteria of the detective story developed in the 1920s and 1930s – the need for clues, for a surprise ending, and all of the other conventions adhered to by critics and writers alike. Thus the notion formed that the 'police procedural' should be a standard mystery novel in which police work influenced the ways in which characters behave and also provided the ancillary furniture necessary to stretch the surprise detective plot into the length of a novel. This definition never quite worked. From early on it left such important and influential fiction as McKinley Kantor's *Signal Thirty-Two* (1950) and then Joseph Wambaugh's *The New Centurions* (1970), *The Blue Knight* (1972), and *The Choirboys* (1973) outside the genre. The restrictive definition, moreover, overlooked the fact that from the late 1960s onwards the police novel began to appear in a variety of forms from the standard whodunit to the thriller and even to the love romance. And regardless of their narrative structure, all of these forms focused on the same essential point – that crime and police work have a unique impact on the way men and women work as well as the way they live.

While the police novel's origins can be found at mid-century, most of its practitioners began from or after the 1980s: Joanna C. Hazelden's list of police fiction posted on the Chicago Public Library's website (2002) cites thirty-nine police writers who began writing after 1984 compared to nine whose first works appeared between 1970 and 1983, and six who began writing police fiction in the 1950s and 1960s. And such significant recent writers as Robert Daley, Ridley Pearson, Patricia Cornwell, and Dan Mahoney do not appear on her list. No matter how slowly it started, however, the police novel began immediately following the Second World War and its apprenticeship extended from the publication of Lawrence Treat's *V as in Victim* in 1945 roughly to the publication of Joseph Wambaugh's *The Choirboys* in 1973.

For Treat, *V as in Victim* was simply another attempt to provide the kind of variety within a pattern that drives the market for detective mystery novels. In *V as in Victim* he introduced a pair of New York police officers, Mitch Taylor and Jub Freeman. With Freeman Treat simply carried on the tradition of scientific detection begun at the turn of the century by his character's namesake, R. Austin Freeman. With Mitch Taylor came the innovation: Taylor possessed traditional, routine police wisdom combined with cynicism, exhaustion, and the attitudes and values of the lower middle class. In short, in Mitch Taylor Treat introduced a character who mirrored the background, attitudes, and aptitudes of real police officers.

Unlike Treat, the second of the pioneers, Hillary Waugh, set out to make himself a police writer. Waugh wrote one novel (*Last Seen Wearing*, 1952) about Chief Frank Ford, eleven novels about small town police chief Fred Fellows, and three novels about New York Police Department detective Frank Sessions. In his books Waugh often brought in an area of crime that had generally been taboo in mystery fiction – but which frequently is the business of real police – sex crime. Thus, for example, he introduced murder as a consequence of adultery in *Sleep Long My Love* (1959), rape and murder in *The Young Prey* (1969), and the murder of a prostitute in *Finish Me Off* (1970). He also featured the routines that are the staple of police work and can only be accomplished by groups rather than individuals: in *Sleep Long My Love*, for example, the members of the Stockford Police Department sort through vehicle registrations, canvass shops, and check out all of the employees of every business in the area of the murder. The hero's ingenuity, then, focuses on finding the procedure that will uncover the criminal in the anonymous and transient society that had become a feature of late twentieth-century life.

As important as Treat and Waugh may be for breaking ground, Ed McBain ensured the popularity of the police procedural novel with his series of books about the 87th Precinct which began with *Cop Hater* in 1956. Unlike the earlier writers, McBain chose to depict a team of officers. Thus in the 87th Precinct saga, while primarily focusing on Detective Steve Carella, McBain introduced a number of detectives (Arthur Brown, Cotton Hawes, Bert Kling, and Meyer Meyer) who play substantive roles in most of his narratives. McBain went to some pains to portray the 87th Precinct and its officers as a real place inhabited by real people. He emphasised the procedural aspect of police work by including facsimiles of routine bureaucratic forms: *Cop Hater*, for example, includes copies of a pistol permit, a ballistics report, a coroner's preliminary report, and an arrest/conviction report. More important than these, as George Dove has pointed out in a number of places including his *The Boys from Grover Avenue* (1985), were the police motifs McBain established in his books – the overworked force, the hostile public, the burned out cop, the alienation from normal life, etc.

The other prominent police author of the first period was Elizabeth Linington who published under her own name and as Anne Blaisdell, Lesley Egen and Dell Shannon. Linington combined heroes like Lieutenant Luis Mendoza of the Los Angeles Police Department with the same view of routine, efficient, and dedicated police work dramatised by Jack Webb in *Dragnet*, *Badge 714* (1951), and *Adam 12* (1968). Indeed the cover of Bantam's edition of her 1976 *Streets of Death* pictures Los Angeles Police Department badge 714, Webb's Detective Joe Friday's badge number. Like McBain, Linington was a commercial writer, experienced in other popular forms. Both were prolific writers whose police books barely reached novel size. Indeed many of McBain's books read like embellished short stories. While each writer strove to present police work in a realistic light, each also showed romantic tendencies. Thus, McBain may nod towards the collective hero of the detective squad, but he inevitably comes back to the idealistically portrayed Steve Carella, and Linington provided a refuge from the mean streets by endowing her Lieutenant Mendoza with independent wealth and an idyllic home life.

The other notable phenomenon of the 1950s and 1960s was the reflection of the drive for African American civil rights in the introduction of black police officers. With Coffin Ed Johnson and Grave Digger Jones, Chester Himes introduced black police detectives in the late 1950s, followed in 1970 by Ernest Tidyman's character Shaft. In each case, however, the characters are more like hardboiled private eyes than police officers. This was not the case with John Ball's Virgil Tibbs in *In the Heat of the Night* (1965). Here Ball introduced some rudimentary police procedure and forensics and contrasted them with the slip-shod practices and racism found in a small southern town.

But events in the United States in the 1960s changed the country and its police profoundly. In 1964 Congress passed the Civil Rights Act which outlawed job discrimination on the basis of race or sex. That had an impact. In the same year, the US Supreme Court decided against the state in *Escobido v. Illinois* and followed two years later by deciding against the state in *Miranda v. Arizona*. Both cases resolutely established suspects' rights to counsel and protection from self-incrimination. That had an impact. Following an altercation at a routine traffic stop, the Los Angeles community of Watts erupted in riot, fire, and pillage in 1965. And after the assassination of Dr Martin Luther King in 1968, major cities across America experienced the same urban conflagration. That had an impact. So did the assassinations of Jack and Robert Kennedy. Like these murders, in the 1960s Americans experienced new and shocking varieties of crime: from 1962 to 1964 the Boston Strangler made national headlines; in 1966 Richard Speck murdered eight nurses in Chicago; in the same year Charles Whitman randomly shot people at the University of Texas; in 1968 the first of the still unsolved Zodiac killings took place near Los Angeles; and the next year Charles Manson and his followers murdered Sharon Tate. Crime and the dark world of criminals had its literary repercussions, too. Truman Capote undertook what he saw as a new kind of fiction with *In Cold Blood* (1965), Vincent Bughosi anatomised the Manson Family in *Helter Skelter* (1974), and finally Norman Mailer examined murderer Garry Gillmore in *The Executioner's Song* (1979). That had an impact. In response to the needs of this wave of horrific crime, the FBI, among other things, established a computerised database of fingerprints and opened its profiling unit. That, too, had an impact. Finally, in 1968 at the Democratic Party's national convention Chicago police physically confronted demonstrators in what was later termed a 'police riot'.[1] And in 1972 investigators in New York City issued the Knapp Report that documented the widespread corruption in the country's largest police force.[2]

Because of the new ways in which Americans came to view crime and the police, the police novel changed. While New York and Los Angeles dominated earlier fiction, by the mid 1990s there was scarcely a major city in the United States that had not been used as the setting of a police novel or series of novels: for example, Rex Burns's Denver, Michael Z. Lewin's Indianapolis, John Sandford's Minneapolis, Jon A. Jackson's Detroit, Bill Crider's Dallas, and J. A. Jance's Seattle. And by way of contrast, writers reached outside of the cities to describe different kinds of police work and different kinds of pressures acting upon non-urban police. Thus Tony Hillerman uses Native American reservations in the southwest, and Alaska determines the way in which Sue Henry's Trooper Alex Jensen does his job. Indeed, contrasting places became a useable method of elaborating on police procedures for a number of writers like Archer Mayor who contrasts the police of Brattleboro, Vermont and Chicago in *The Skeleton's Knee* (1993). While it does not reflect the same kind of variety as the exploration of new settings, the new police novel began to explore the complexity of police organisations. The modern police force can possess a mind-numbing number of specialised departments – traffic, robbery/burglary, fraud, homicide, juvenile, public morals (prostitution and gambling), internal affairs, public relations, crime laboratory, K-9 unit, police artists, bomb squad, SWAT team, and patrol (which can be foot, bicycle, automobile, horse, boat, helicopter and fixed-wing aircraft). And this leaves out communications, payroll, and maintenance. While most writers portray homicide detectives, a few go further afield – bloodhound handlers form part of the substance of Sherri Board's *Angels of Anguish* (1999), Robert Crais bases *Demolition Angel* (2000) on the Los Angeles Police Department's bomb squad, Patricia Cornwell centres her books in the Commonwealth of Virginia's medical examiner's office, and Nat Hentoff in *The Man from Internal Affairs* (1985) follows cops investigating cops.

In addition to this new use of geographical and departmental diversity, one of the most notable changes in the new police novel lay in the backgrounds of the writers. For one thing, they represented a generation loosened from the rigid formulaic demands of the detective story held by those who grew up with Christie, Queen, and Howard Haycraft. And as a consequence, in the 1980s and 1990s the police novel became a much more flexible form – one which could use the old clues and surprise pattern of the formal detective story but which could also employ the techniques of the psychological novel or the thriller. Additionally, while the police book was still the province of the professional writer, a number of the new writers were former police officers. Thus, along with Joseph Wambaugh, Dallas Barnes and Paul Bishop came from the Los Angeles Police Department, Enes Smith was a cop in Oregon, Robert Simms Reid was a cop in Montana, Terry Marlowe was on the Dallas force, Hugh Holman is a Chicago cop, and Joseph McNamara was police chief in San Jose, California. And with Robert Daley, Bob Leuci, William Caunitz, Bill Kelley, Ed Dee, Michael Grant, Dan Mahoney, and maybe John Westerman (who worked on Long Island), alumni of the New York Police Department almost formed a school of their own.

In some ways, the new police novels followed leads established by writers in the 1950s, but embellished them because they generally wrote longer books and because fiction after the 1960s permitted hitherto unimaginable frankness. In depicting police procedures, for instance, one finds longer and more detailed descriptions of the things police officers do. Thus while McBain includes facsimiles of routine reports, a number of the later writers show their characters awash in paperwork – filling in DD5 sheets, accounting for each bullet fired from weapons, etc. William Caunitz in *Black Sand* (1989) shows the response of the working police officer to compiling these reports:

> Teddy Lucas read the report typed under 'Details of the Case' on the bottom of the DD5 Supplementary Complaint Report, commonly called simply the five, the detective form used to report all phases of an investigation. He checked the crime classification code to insure that the fairy tale complied with department policy and procedures and, satisfied that it did, affixed his signature in the space provided at the bottom of the report.
>
> I've become a goddamn fiction editor, he thought . . .[3]

On top of the same kind of paperwork required of officers in older novels, cops after the 1960s have become the victims of 'management'. Thus Rex Burns in *Strip Search* (1984) comments on this new police procedure:

> Modern police management worshiped quantification and statistics were forever being updated and refined and compared. If homicides declined a percentage point or two, crime was being beaten. If they went up, the bad guys were winning. There were figures on the ratio between solved and unsolved cases in every category, and a red pencil marked a quantifiable line between acceptable and unacceptable. There was even an annual time study of the number of crime reports divided into the total man-hours available for each division and section. The result indicated the average amount of time that could be allotted to each crime. In Homicide, it was sixteen hours.[4]

But as a counterpoint, writers also have their heroes report to the readers the painful and pessimistic litany of police statistics – that most crimes are not solved, that most property is never recovered, that most victims never receive justice.

And because publishers would now permit it, after the 1970s police novels describe the horrific details that form part of police routine. With the Y cut made in the torso and the sawing open of the skull, the description of the autopsy became a convention. And after the seventies police writers regularly describe the details of violent death – mutilated genitals, post-mortem secretion of faeces and urine, the growth of maggots in decaying flesh. And they describe the ways cops try to cope with this – from rubbing Vicks Vapo-Rub under their noses, to smoking cigars, to chewing rubber bands.

Like the books of the first two decades, the new police novel continued to demonstrate that cops work in uncomfortable and inevitably seedy conditions. In this respect, one of the most apparent aspects of all police novels is the attention paid to weather. The opening pages of most police novels make some acknowledgement of foul weather, which is too hot or too cold or too wet for human comfort. This, of course, recognises that, like letter carriers, police have to work in all sorts of climactic conditions. And if the weather is foul, the place where cops work, the police station, is just as nasty. While over the past few years writers acknowledge that their police officers have computers, beepers, and cell phones, the station is at best a depressing place to work. Thus in Michael Grant's *Line of Duty* (1991):

> The atmosphere in a police department facility can be depressing enough in the daytime, but at night, without the distraction of ringing telephones, clicking typewriters, and constant chatter, the shabbiness of the surroundings is even more glaring. The ubiquitous bile-green paint, broken window shades, and cheap metal furniture did nothing to alleviate the sense of squalor.[5]

And the places police officers visit in their encounters with criminals and their victims are worse, far worse.

Additionally, in the last quarter of the century one of the things that served as the basis for the police procedural book when it began – the team – changed. George Dove in *The Police Procedural* (1982) makes the point that the concept of officers working as a team to solve crimes defines the sub-genre.[6] Beginning in the 1970s, however, the fact that police officers work within an organisation becomes one of the chief impediments to solving crimes. Robert Daley makes the point in *Tainted Evidence* (1994) that 'The role of headquarters, as he saw it, was to screw cops for the sake of political expediency, and he foresaw getting screwed over what had happened tonight'.[7] External and internal politics become two pervasive themes. Indeed, some of the new writers like Daley depict the operation of police officers against the background of a bureaucratic and politically charged system. Universally writers demonstrate the debilitation caused by politicians meddling in police business. Some politicians are corrupt as in Joseph McNamara's *Fatal Command* (1987) where politicians cause an able police chief to neglect and ignore his duty. All politicians are self-serving. Consequently, as in Lawrence Sanders's *The First Deadly Sin* (1972), one of the police hero's jobs becomes keeping sensitive and complicated investigations out of their hands. Internal politics form a second dilemma for the officer intent on solving cases. A series of novels including Dorothy Uhnak's *False Witness* (1981), Jack Early's *Donato and Daughter* (1988), Bob Leuci's *Captain Butterfly* (1989), Michael Grant's *Line of Duty*, and William Caunitz's posthumous *Chains of Command* (1999) make individual ambition within the police hierarchy a central theme. On top of this, in recent New York books writers confront the issue of whistle-blowing as well as the Knapp Commission inspired institution of Field Associates, police officers recruited to spy on their colleagues. In all, for the past thirty years police writers have both made a point about the corrosive nature of large department police work and added the techniques of the novel of political intrigue to the story about crime, criminals, detection, and solution.

Like the conflict between the need for a complex organisation to police America's cities and the need for individual intelligence, initiative, insight, and bravery, the introduction of modern forensic techniques also presents opportunity for both narrative elaboration and tension. For a number of writers, descriptions of police science provide a fascinating opportunity to either build plots or embellish them. Computers, for instance, form the basis for the plot in Barbara D'Amato's *KILLER.app* (1996) where malefactors place Trojan Horse programs in the Chicago Police Department's computer system. And Ridley Pearson's *Chain of Evidence* (1995) culminates in the hero's attempt to breach the 'firewall' of a computer system in order to obtain crucial evidence. Wambaugh based *The Blooding* (1989) on the discovery of and use of DNA as a foolproof tool for identification. Because her hero is a scientist, Patricia Cornwell pays careful attention to scientific method and scientific instruments in her books. In *Postmortem* (1990), for instance, she goes to some pains to describe the science underlying the discovery of the criminal's identity, including using similes to help readers visualise laboratory instruments – comparing the size of one, for instance, to that of a microwave oven. Shuffling through police books written in the last decades of the century one finds appearances of or allusions to every imaginable forensic specialty from dentistry (see Faye Kellerman's *Sacred and Profane*, 1987), to botany (see Robert Simms Reid, *Cupid*, 1990), to entomology (see Michael Connelly,

*Black Ice*, 1993), to anthropology (see Martin Cruz Smith's *Gorky Park*, 1984). And psychologists and psychiatrists make regular appearances to introduce the newly discovered technique of profiling.

While some writers like Cornwell emphasise the utility of forensic techniques in detection, other police writers have their doubts about them. First of all, there is scepticism about the worth of scientific evidence. Regarding the old stand-by, the paraffin test, in *The New Centurions* Wambaugh's character comments that it is:

> Not worth a shit . . . Only in the movie whodunits. A guy can have nitrates on his hands from a thousand other ways. The paraffin test is no good.[8]

On top of this, obtaining scientific evidence costs money in budget-strapped departments. Thus in Caunitz's *Black Sand* when discussion turns to dental evidence:

> . . . the kicker is that we have to pick up the tab, which means getting the borough commander's approval for the expenditure of department funds.[9]

And when the question of whether to submit samples for DNA analysis arises the cops in J. A. Jance's *Breach of Duty* (1999) note that 'As you well know, those kinds of tests are prohibitively expensive'.[10]

With psychological profiling the case is equally problematic. Some writers use the creation of a psychological profile as the basis for their books and the solution to the crimes committed in them. Leslie Glass, for example, in *Burning Time* (1993) portrays a psychiatrist whose profile of the serial killer helps the police catch him. Cornwell views profilers in the same light: 'Profilers are academicians, thinkers, analysts. Sometimes I think they are magicians.'[11] Often, however, the utility of profiling in identifying and apprehending criminals is not so clear. Thus, in *The Silence of the Lambs* (1988) Thomas Harris uses profiling as yet another of Hannibal Lecter's ruses. While she speaks highly of profiling, in Cornwell's *Body Farm* (1994) profiling does not lead to the identity of the killer. Dan Mahoney mentions the FBI's profiling unit in *Black and White* (1999) but his detectives do not use its resources, and in William Bayer's *Wallflower* (1991) the detective finds that even the FBI's expert does not believe in the profile he presents. As it turns out, profiling plays a number of roles in the contemporary police novel. To be sure it reflects current law enforcement practice (one currently being challenged in the courts) and, additionally, it provides a simple method of characterising and explaining criminals and their behaviour in a genre more concerned with effects than causes. Profiling, like forensic science, however, also tends to contradict a basic tenet of the traditional detective story or thriller – that crime is ultimately solved by the reason, initiative, and bravery of an individual, or, in some cases, heroic individuals. Finally, in many police novels profiling breaks down to a label for the knowledge possessed by the police officer, like Detective Rocco in Richard Price's *Clockers* (1992), who knows from long experience as a cop the ways criminals look and behave.

Extending the notion that police work endows individuals with special insights is the almost universal theme that police work sets individuals apart from society and makes them, ultimately, a misunderstood and persecuted minority. Beginning with the omnipresent acronyms, police books provide bits of 'coptalk', jargon based on contractions ('perp' for 'perpetrator'), slang, vulgarity, and profanity. In their vernacular, cops are cops and everyone else is a 'citizen' except for those who are 'mutts', or 'alligators', or 'scumbags', or 'turdbirds', or 'snakes', or 'skels', or 'scrotes'. The communal experience of excitement, boredom, danger, stress and plodding routine as well as serving as witnesses to the worst effects of human depravity separates police officers from everyone else in society and forms a bond that penetrates all aspects of their lives. In *Cupid* Robert Simms Reid explains it this way:

> There was a time when I could separate my work life from my life in general. I had my life, and then I had the things that happened to me on the job . . . Then work and life started to join, but for a while I could see it happening and still keep work at the station. At first I tried to avoid talking to my friends – even my wives – about work because I didn't want them to think I was showing off, trying to be a TV cop. Then I wanted to tell them what it was like, but explanations eluded me. And after I became a detective, I couldn't tell them what it was like – really like – because they had no right to know. Not some kind of warped macho-cop right to know shit, no kind of theatrical-code garbage like that. It was a matter of privacy, my privacy and the privacy of my victims.[12]

Police work exempts officers from the pleasures of common humanity – friends, family, sleep, relaxation. Cynicism is epidemic, alcoholism is usual, divorce is universal, and the only life is that at the station – indeed, many characters refer to it as the 'station house', or just 'the house'. Reflecting on this, one of Michael Grant's characters exclaims 'This job has beaten the shit out of me for the last time. I am a victim of police brutality'.[13] Added to the isolating impact on the individual of police work, from the 1970s onwards characters mourn the fact that things have changed.

Like the world, the cop's job changed in the last quarter of the twentieth century. For one thing, the paramilitary discipline formerly the hallmark of police departments has gone by the board:

It's not like the old days . . . when a desk officer told a cop to shit, and the cop asked how much would you like, sir. The new breed is young, most have never been in the service, and only a few of them have heard terms like "military discipline" and "military courtesy".[14]

And with military discipline, seemingly everything else has disappeared. Modern management methods diminish the value of the individual police officer – and progress has banned (but not displaced) one of the cops' traditional methods of handling crime:

"Damn, how did they ever catch anyone in the old days?"

"It was easy," Shannon answered. "They didn't have computers to drown them in useless information."

"Yeah, and they had investigative tools not available to us," Rose said.

"Like what?" Velez asked.

Rose smiled slyly. "They could beat the shit out of a suspect until he told them what they wanted to know."[15]

And the job has changed because law and society have forced police departments to change their personnel practices:

No more captains and lieutenants. They want civilian managers in charge of police operations. A pork barrel like the Board of Ed. Just take a look at what's happening in the Job today. We have cops with yellow sheets. Cops who cannot communicate in the English language. We're forced to hire females. Some of them don't weigh a hundred pounds soaking wet; they can't reach the accelerators of radio cars; don't have the physical strength to pull the trigger of their service revolvers. We were forced to lower the height requirement to accommodate women and Hispanics. We're becoming a department of goddamn dwarfs.[16]

Indeed, the role of women in police work has become one of the major themes of the new novel.

Before Dorothy Uhnak's Christie Opara (introduced in 1968) women did not play a significant role in police novels. With the passage of civil rights legislation, however, police departments had to accept women into their ranks. From Uhnak onwards the trauma of this change and the challenge of incorporating women into formerly all male organisations became a major theme. Writers reflect the anger and fear felt by policemen when confronted with the reality of women colleagues. These range from reservations about women's physical abilities to do police work, to concerns about romantic relationships like those Daley portrays in *Cop Killer* (1978), to the sarcastic observation in Kelly and LeMoult's *Street Dance* (1987) that most crimes are committed by men:

"And now we got women cops . . ." He shrugged. "You and me know what that's all about. It's a fucking joke, that's what it's about. What we oughta do is tell the bad guys 'Look, we gotta have women on our side, so you guys should have women criminals just to make it fair.'"

He laughed. "I'll have to tell the Spring Man about that one. From now on, the Mafia's got to have fifteen percent women or we call off the game."[17]

There also exists the fear that women police officers will endanger their male partners. Thus in *The New Centurions* one of the most sensitive of the characters says:

With some of the other policewomen there was no difference, except you had to be more careful and not get involved in things where there was the slightest element of danger . . . . because a policewoman was still a woman, nothing more, and you were responsible for her safety, being the male half of the team.[18]

And Wambaugh also points out that women cops can be a danger to themselves by over compensating:

The director of security had once warned her that women in police work frequently take great risks because they don't want to call for backup from the men until they're sure they need it. But by then, it's often too late. He'd warned that many female cops had been needlessly injured and even killed, for fear of seeming to be the damsel in distress.[19]

Nonetheless, a number of writers describe the ways in which women adapt to and succeed in a world formerly defined by men. They make adjustments. Thus Lynn Hightower's hero notes that "My observation is that women smile no matter what . . . You're a cop. Don't smile when people are giving you grief".[20] And they help each other. In *Diamond in the Buff* (1989) Susan Dunlap's hero acts as mentor to new female recruits helping them adapt to the mores of an all male environment:

After the last ceremony when new officers were sworn, I had taken a couple of the women aside and said, "Berkeley's a small town. There are going to be times when you roll out and find the corpse of a friend's mother, or child, or the friend himself. You're going to feel like shit. But no matter how bad you feel, how justified that is, remember this: Women cops don't cry. A guy cries, people think that's a sign he's human, but a tear rolls down a woman officer's cheek, she loses credibility forever.[21]

After 1968 a number of writers feature women heroes. And these heroes respond to crime and violence in a variety of ways. These range from April Wu's sympathy for victims in Leslie Glass's novels, to detectives Marti McAlister's and Deb Ralston's juggling family and job in Eleanor Taylor Bland's and

Lee Martin's books, to Kay Scarpetta's expertise and courage in Cornwell's novels, to the toughness and drive of Bob Leuci's hero in *Captain Butterfly*, to Jack Early's Dina Donato whose ambition is to become New York's first female Chief of Detectives in *Donato and Daughter* (1989). Some of these women respond to the physical and intellectual challenges and dilemmas of police work the same way men do and some do not. And that is the point.

More than women, more than serial killer and terrorist plots, more than anything, the law defined the police novel as it came to be written in the last quarter of the century. In other forms of the crime story the law is either implicit or something to be ignored or bent. Not in the cop novel. This was not always the case; it was something that happened after the 1960s. The change can be seen by looking at a passage about suspects being questioned in McBain's 1956 novel *Cop Hater*:

> Actually, they had said a hell of a lot more than they should have. They'd have been within their rights if they'd insisted on not saying a word at the lineup. Not knowing this, not even knowing that their position was fortified because they'd made no statement when they'd been collared, they had answered the Chief of Detectives with remarkable naivete.[22]

This simply could not have happened after the US Supreme Court's decisions in *Miranda* and *Escobido*. And those decisions, as well as decisions with respect to search and seizure (like the 'fruit of the poison tree' doctrine that holds that an illegal police act taints any and all evidence developed subsequent to that act), resonate through police novels from the 1970s onwards. A glance at a few titles shows this: Charles Brandt's *The Right to Remain Silent* (1988), Barbara Paul's *You Have the Right to Remain Silent* (1992), J. A. Jance's *Without Due Process* (1992), Ridley Pearson's *Probable Cause* (1990), Pearson's *Chain of Evidence* (1995), Harry Levy's *Chain of Custody* (1998), Robert Daley's *Tainted Evidence* (1993), Archer Mayor's *Fruits of the Poisonous Tree* (1994), and Patricia Cornwell's *Body of Evidence* (1992). After the 1960s courts across the country increasingly enforced Constitutional guarantees with respect to self-incrimination, privacy, and property rights. Suspects could not be questioned without being apprised of their rights, probable cause became more rigidly defined, and search warrants became a necessity in a wider variety of situations – in Rex Burns' *Strip Search* the detectives need to procure a warrant to search a trash dumpster and in Pearson's *Probable Cause* the characters discuss the legality of obtaining hair from a suspect's dog without a warrant. Brandt's *The Right to Remain Silent* (1988) depicts the new climate by comparing police procedures in 1961 and 1976. Simply put, novels after the 1970s show that the new guarantees provided by the courts for individual and property rights irritate and bewilder police officers. As Lawrence Sanders's hero put it '. . . recent court decisions, particularly those of the Supreme Court, had so confused him – and all cops – that he no longer comprehended the laws of evidence and the rights of suspects'.[23] An instructor at the Police Academy in *The New Centurions* tells recruits that:

> You're going to be upset, confused, and generally pissed off most of the time, and you're going to hear locker room bitching about the fact that most land-mark decisions are five to four, and how can a working cop be expected to make a sudden decision in the heat of combat and then be second guessed by the Vestal Virgins of the Potomac . . .[24]

Perhaps most telling is the following interchange from Joseph McNamara's *Fatal Command*:

> "Back in 1966 a guy named Danny Miranda was arrested in Arizona on a rape charge. The cops questioned him in the station house and he confessed to the crime. The U.S. Supreme Court overturned the conviction because the cops hadn't told him he had the right to a lawyer and the right to remain silent. They made it a national rule. That's why we carry those little cards to read to suspects."
> "But was he guilty?"
> "Oh, yeah. But that wasn't relevant, as they say."
> "Did they, you know, beat a confession out of him? Or scare him into confession?"
> "No."
> "And the confession, I mean, was it correct, truthful?"
> "True as true can be.'"
> "I wonder if the woman who was the victim felt as vulnerable as I do."[25]

All of this had consequences for the detectives in the police novel. They devise ways to circumvent the law. Thus, in *The Blind Pig* (1978) Jon Jackson describes the 'Tennessee Search Warrant', where an unseen cop answers 'come in' when a partner seeks admission to a private residence. There is the need to take cryptic notes and hide them from defence attorneys during pre-trial discovery. There is the bogus 911 emergency telephone call giving police probable cause to enter anywhere. And also many writers agree, because they feel hamstrung by the courts, from Wambaugh's Bumper Morgan to Dan Mahoney's Brian McKenna, cops lie to make arrests and convictions. Either that or they surreptitiously take matters and justice into their own hands. Sometimes cops like Kelly and LeMoult's Vince Crowley in *Death Spiral* (1989) go off on their own and avoid reporting to supervisors. Sometimes, as does Tony Scanlon in Caunitz's *Suspects*, cops use their own sense of justice to determine who is or is not arrested. Sometimes, as in Mahoney's *Black and White* in which serial killers are bounced between jurisdictions to ensure capital punishment, cops work the system to ensure the justice the courts will not ensure. Sometimes, as in Anthony Bruno's *Bad Guys* (1988), the vigilante cop becomes the hero. And in books about terrorists in which police act in a paramilitary capacity, questions about law and the courts go by the board. Whatever the technique heroes employ, in the new police novel the courts become just as much an adversary as the conniving ambition embedded in the police hierarchy and the pressures of the job. And, of course, there is the principal struggle with crime and criminals.

Unlike the classical detective story, in the police book the world of the novel is not made whole again. Unlike the hardboiled story, in the police novel the hero finds little enduring sense of having symbolically achieved even a small fragment of justice. In the police novel heroes rarely struggle with the ontology of crime. Sometimes detectives find out about the horrifying childhoods of criminals, but most writers simply label their villains as sociopaths and leave it at that. As James Lee Burke puts it in *Heaven's Prisoners* (1989) 'What produced them? Defective genes, growing up in a shithole, bad toilet training? Even after fourteen years with the New Orleans police department, I never had an adequate answer.'[26] Police novels deal with effects and not causes. And they deal with the impact of those effects on police officers. Indeed, it makes many characters believe they are witnessing the decline and death of American civilisation. This spans the decades. Thus in *Yesterday is Dead* (1976) Dallas Barnes's hero observes that:

> . . . within a few years, maybe a decade, the system would fall riddled with corruption and the incurable cancer of self-righteousness.[27]

In the eighties William Caunitz's hero decries the fact that:

> . . . we've fucked up our criminal justice system; we've fucked up our ozone layer; we've fucked up our ecological balance; and now, we're fucking up sex.[28]

And in the 1990s Lillian O'Donnell includes the following in *Pushover* (1992):

> Like Norah, Ferdi Arenas was particularly disturbed by what was happening to children. They were being randomly murdered on the streets, in cars parked in their home driveways, and even in their own homes. A society that cannot protect its young is marked for extinction.[29]

In *Strip Tease* (1993) Carl Hiaasen sums up this belief in a conversation between two cops:

... "I remember what you told me a long time ago –"
"The world is a sewer and we're all dodging shit."
"Very uplifting, Al. I'm surprised Hallmark hasn't bought up the copyright."
"Words to live by."
"You know what's sad? I'm beginning to think that you're right. I'm
   beginning to think there's no hope."
"Of course there's no hope," Garcia said, "but don't let it get you down."[30]

This kind of attitude can be found in most contemporary police novels. Depravity, cruelty, greed, and the dark abscesses of the soul confront the police with evil beyond their capacity to restrain or understand. Police officers both witness the effects of crime and endure the constraints of pettifogging rules, the distrust of the public along with personal demons created by the stress of their occupation. From the very beginning, however, the single most enduring theme of the police novel has been the solace provided to the individual by belonging. This, of course, exists in the theme of 'brotherhood' mentioned in virtually every book – the identity and meaning brought to the individual by belonging to the extended family of police officers. Being a police officer, however, also means belonging to something with altruistic and ultimately transcendental purpose. In spite of rules and incompetence, in spite of the all too obvious frailties of its members, for the heroes of police books being a police officer means being part of an organisation which both serves society and participates in the larger struggle of good versus evil. As Robert Daley puts it in *A Faint Cold Fear* (1992) 'Douglas had been a cop a long time. Reality had smothered his idealism long ago. Nonetheless he still believed in absolutes. There was good on one side and evil on the other . . .'.[31] In the police novel ordinary men and women become heroes because they maintain and act upon that belief. And in that lies the fundamental satisfaction so many readers seek.

## NOTES

1 See *Rights in Conflict: the violent confrontation of demonstrators and police in the parks and streets of Chicago during the Democratic National Convention of 1968. A report submitted by Daniel Walker, director of the Chicago study team, to the National Commission on the Causes and Prevention of Violence* (1 December 1968).
2 See *Report of the Commission to Investigate Allegations of Police Corruption and the City's Anti-Corruption Procedures* (26 December 1972).
3 William Caunitz, *Black Sand* (1989; New York: Bantam, 1990), p. 61.
4 Rex Burns, *Strip Search* (New York: Viking, 1984), p. 89.
5 Michael Grant, *Line of Duty* (New York: Doubleday, 1991), p. 248.
6 See George N. Dove, *The Police Procedural* (Bowling Green, OH: Popular Press, 1982), p. 2.

7 Robert Daley, *Tainted Evidence* (New York: Warner, 1994), p. 68.
8 Joseph Wambaugh, *The New Centurions* (1990; New York: Dell, 1972), p. 119.
9 Caunitz, *Black Sand*, p. 205.
10 J. A. Jance, *Breach of Duty* (New York: Avon, 1999), p. 219.
11 Patricia Cornwell, *Postmortem* (New York: Avon, 1990), p. 73.
12 Robert Simms Reid, *Cupid* (1990; New York: Bantam, 1991), p. 116.
13 Grant, *Line of Duty*, p. 344.
14 William Caunitz, *Suspects* (New York: Bantam, 1987), p. 186.
15 Grant, *Line of Duty*, p. 117.
16 William Caunitz, *One Police Plaza* (New York: Crown, 1984), pp. 263–4.
17 Bill Kelly and Dolph LeMoult, *Street Dance* (New York: Charter, 1987), pp. 170–1.
18 Wambaugh, *New Centurions*, p. 270.
19 Joseph Wambaugh, *Finnegan's Week* (New York: Bantam, 1994), p. 311.
20 Lynn Hightower, *Flashpoint* (New York: Harper Collins, 1995), p. 168.
21 Susan Dunlap, *Diamond in the Buff* (New York: St Martin's, 1989), p. 78.
22 Ed McBain, *Cop Hater* (1956; New York: Signet, 1973), p. 86.
23 Lawrence Sanders, *The First Deadly Sin* (1972; New York: Berkeley, 1980), p. 473.
24 Wambaugh, *New Centurions*, p. 20.
25 Joseph McNamara, *Fatal Command* (New York: Fawcett, 1987), p. 132.
26 James Lee Burke, *Heaven's Prisoners* (New York: Pocket Books, 1989), p. 27.
27 Dallas Barnes, *Yesterday Is Dead* (New York: Signet, 1976), p. 214.
28 Caunitz, *Black Sand*, p. 106.
29 Lillian O'Donnell, *Pushover* (New York: Fawcett, 1992), p. 94.
30 Carl Hiaasen, *Strip Tease* (New York: Knopf, 1993), p. 117.
31 Robert Daley, *A Faint Cold Fear* (New York: Warner, 1992), p. 451.

# 10

## MARTIN PRIESTMAN

# Post-war British crime fiction

When Julian Symons published his classic study *Bloody Murder* in 1972, his forecast of a 'declining market' for straightforward detective fiction seemed reasonable.[1] The once pre-eminent formula of crime, false trails and triumphant solution by a brilliant detective either looked very old-fashioned or had started to be replaced by other sources of interest, such as espionage or psychological suspense. At the time of writing, 2002, things look different. Detection is once more flourishing and, without sacrificing its traditional complement of early-discovered corpses, red herrings and surprise solutions, now enjoys a critical esteem in the 'respectable' marketplace that would have been unthinkable a few decades ago. Books have also at least doubled in length: from the 200-odd pages which remained statutory up to the 1970s, many detective novels now weigh in at around 500. Some of this additional weight is taken up with the detective heroes' personal and working relationships; some with an equal filling-out of a large cast of suspects and other characters; and some with a range of consciously 'literary' techniques, such as the deliberately confusing opening which shuffles a variety of viewpoints, settings and even time-periods before our eyes, engaging our readerly alertness from the start in a quest to discover what is going on. In other words, present-day detective novels ask to be treated as serious books in their own right, rather than as the 'escape from literature' they were once expected to be.[2]

A mapping of how this change came about in the decades between 1940 and 2000 seems particularly needed for British crime fiction, on whose post-war developments there has been very little synthesising criticism since Symons, and which is still too often seen as an indecisive hangover from the privileged fantasy-world of the pre-war 'Golden Age', or as palely reflecting trends which really belong to America. While the most important development, that of the 'police procedural' (though this can be an over-limiting term), parallels that in the USA, the British version has its own home-grown points of origin and has developed in very different directions.[3] Perhaps because it is still rapidly evolving and has no clearly defined 'golden' past of iconic stereotypes to look back on, police fiction has a far lower profile in critical circles than amateur or private eye detection. But the story of British detective fiction since the Second World War is largely the story of how middle-ranking career police officers – usually detective inspectors – came to be taken seriously.

The longevity of Agatha Christie and many of the other Golden Age writers discussed in Chapter 4 ensured their continuing domination of public perceptions of British detection from the 1940s until as late as the 1970s.[4] Some younger writers who began their careers in the 1940s continued in their mode, often accentuating its already strong element of self-parody: arguably, the dark context of the Second World War and its aftermath produced a paradoxical urge both to seek the comforts of the traditional form and to demonstrate their artificiality. Thus Edmund Crispin's whodunits featuring the Oxford Literature Professor Gervase Fen jokily brandish an array of 'literary' credentials at every turn, self-consciously signalling that they are aimed at those more interested in books than actual crime while absolving themselves of any responsibility towards realism or emotional empathy. The element of deconstructive spoofery to be found in Golden Age writers such as Michael Innes and John Dickson Carr (whose similarly-named Gideon Fell at one point observes that 'We're in a detective story, and we don't fool the reader by pretending we're not') is taken even further when Fen declares 'I'm the only literary critic turned detective in the whole of fiction' or proposes a left turn in the middle of a car chase because 'Gollancz is publishing this book'.[5] The sense of literary and crime-solving obsessions as mirror-reversals of each other is brought out in Fen's comic relationship with a Chief Constable who is as keen a literary critic as Fen is a detective: indeed, Crispin explains that it is their very amateurism which makes them excel more in these roles than their professional ones.[6]

Fen is, however, virtually the last of his breed; in general, the fantasy of the amateur sleuth – based on the rapidly receding idea of a leisured class – gave way to the realistic recognition that the investigation of serious crime was the province of the police. Christianna Brand's *Heads You Lose* (1941) continues the tradition of macabrely punning titles favoured by such Golden Age writers as Ngaio Marsh: here the reference is not only to the bizarre toss-up as to who will be killed (the main victim seals the fate she describes by saying she would not be seen dead in a ditch wearing a certain hat), but also to the fits of madness which have driven the otherwise decent and respectable culprit to kill and then (the third meaning) behead them. Brand's novel epitomises the classic 'house party' structure where an intimate group of well-heeled suspects turn the inquiry into a high-spirited if somewhat hysterical game which perversely – since it results in the elimination of at least one of them – cements their solidarity in class and/or familial terms.[7] Unlike such genteel Scotland Yard inspectors as Marsh's Alleyn or Innes's Appleby, however, Brand's series-detective is the local police inspector, 'Cocky' Cockrill. With subliminal echoes of Gaboriau's lower-class but self-assured Lecoq – appropriately birdlike features and a hat worn Napoleonically sideways – Cocky is a 'character' who can be trusted rather than condescended to, because most of the cast know him from their childhood. Even so – echoing another nineteenth-century forebear, Sergeant Cuff – Cockrill acts more as a midwife of the truth which the group are discovering for themselves than as an implacable external accuser.[8] Brand's later *Green for Danger* (1944) brings the wartime context to the centre of the action, when Cockrill discovers that the murder of a military hospital surgeon, which seems to arise from a traditional-style love-triangle, is actually the misdirected revenge of a nurse deranged by her mother's death in an air-raid.

In the novels of Julian Symons, the police often represent the best that detection can offer, but are then used to show the fallibility of detection itself. At the end of the early, traditional-seeming whodunit *A Man Called Jones* (1947), the indicatively-named Inspector Bland sends the ex-suspects to sleep with his closing explanation of the case, only to be confronted in the last line with the arrival of a character whose non-existence was its linchpin. The accepted police theories are similarly thrown into question in the last few words of *The Thirty-First of February* (1950) and *The Colour of Murder* (1957). In *The Man Who Killed Himself* (1967), the plodding local inspector uses the false evidence planted by the killer to arrest him for the murder of one of his own aliases. As in many of Symons's books, names such as Clennery Tubbs and Major Easonby Mellon indicate a stance of ironic detachment from the world depicted which suggests a sub-Marxist or absurdist critique of bourgeois society in general: an impression further confirmed by the number of Symons characters who end up terminally mad.

While his own one-off *coups* have no room for a series-hero, Symons as a critic had high praise for Colin Watson, whose Inspector Purbright represents a further step towards providing police heroes with a small-town provincial beat rather than summoning them from Scotland Yard.[9] Nonetheless, Watson's 'Flaxborough Chronicles' owe much to a tradition of provincial comedy whereby nothing can be taken quite seriously. The first Flaxborough novel, *Coffin Scarcely Used* (1958), concerns the misdeeds of a cabal of town worthies with names such as Carobleat, Gwill and Gloss, who run a brothel under the disguise of antique furniture advertisements in the local paper, and then fall out over the proceeds. A similar mixture of civic and sexual shenanigans appears in *Broomsticks Over Flaxborough* (1972), where a trio of local bigwigs exploit the credulity of a witchcraft coven for sexual purposes un-der satanic disguise, while *Hopjoy Was Here* (1962) deploys the absurdist device – also used in Graham Greene's *Our Man in Havana* (1958) and John le Carré's *The Tailor of Panama* (1996) – of a spy who fabricates the sinister activities he is meant to be spying on. As the title of his 1971 study *Snobbery With Violence* suggests, Watson is critical of the class-elitism underlying the Golden Age whodunit; nonetheless, the cocoon of provincial absurdity in which Purbright and his comically galumphing Sergeant Love are wrapped protects the reader from having to take them entirely seriously.[10] Distanced in a different way is H. R. F. Keating's Bombay-based Inspector Ghote, whom his author intended to call 'Ghosh' – presumably to suggest comic bewilder-ment – until informed that the name came from the wrong part of India.[11] Keating did not in fact visit India until 1974, making the Ghote series a fascinating repository of current British ideas about it rather than a direct representation. *The Perfect Murder* (1964) involves two apparently separate cases: the near-murder of a rich businessman's secretary, Mr Perfect, and the theft of one rupee from a politician's office. Both cases clearly embody the kind of lovable ineptitude thought appropriate to the recently independent ex-colony: the much-repeated phrase 'Perfect Murder' is belied by Perfect's eventual recovery, while the fact that Ghote is told to give the missing rupee case equal 'top priority' gestures at the excessive kowtowing to authority we might expect from a state only just learning to police itself. A certain European paternalism towards the new republic is also conveyed in Ghote's touching reliance on a German-English textbook of policing methods, and by the comparatively gigantic stature of a Watson-like Swede who rescues the diminutive inspector from several scrapes.[12]

Also from the early 1960s, Nicolas Freeling's Netherlands-based Inspector Van der Valk series uses Simenon's Maigret as a model to explore rather more serious issues, from the pornography racket of *Love in Amsterdam* (1962) to the legacy of Nazi death-camps and the prehistory of the Vietnam War.[13] Perhaps because of his 'foreignness', rather than in spite of it, Van der Valk's adventures give a satisfying sense of moving into uncharted yet disturbingly credible areas of modern life. The image of the outwardly placid and affluent modern state as concealing various kinds of festering malaise, with a not-always scrupulous career policeman as its necessary defender, may have been easier to accept in a foreign rather than a British context, where various class assumptions would still, in the 1960s, need to be negotiated. Also widely read in Britain, the South African James McClure's novels featuring the white Inspector Kramer and loyal black Sergeant Zondi (starting with *The Steam Pig*, 1971) effectively gestured at some of the horrors of the Apartheid system without entirely divorcing themselves from it.

Another kind of foreign country could be found in a past where – it was understood – life was rougher and sleazier than now, and modern attitudes to policing were still struggling to be born. Peter Lovesey's *Wobble to Death* (1970) and *The Detective Wore Silk Drawers* (1971) are set in the doubly removed realm of Victorian sport: marathon racing and bare-knuckle boxing respectively. Lovesey's doggedly unimpressible Sergeant Cribb ('steal' in thieves' slang) offers a similar kind of reassurance to Dickens's presentation of the police in his articles in *Household Words* (1850–3), combining solid lower-middle-class respectability with an initimate knowledge of the criminal world.[14] In *Waxwork* (1978) the blocking of Cribb's promotion, clearly on grounds of social rank, ends the series on a note of class bitterness which might have been harder to convey in a more contemporary setting. The reassurance that the evils being investigated are well in the past has been drawn on more recently in Ellis Peters's and Lindsey Davis's series featuring the mediaeval monk Brother Cadfael and the Roman imperial agent Marcus Didius Falco.[15]

The name of Peter Dickinson's Inspector Pibble – in an underrated series starting with *Skin Deep* (1968) – can be added to those of Cockrill, Purbright and Cribb, to confirm a common image of police investigators up to the 1970s as lower-middle class and faintly patronisable. From about then, however, the dominant inspectorial names acquired a different resonance: Dalgleish, Wexford, Dalziel, Laidlaw, Wycliff, Resnick, Morse, Rebus. The last two names appropriately denote kinds of secret code; the others have Celtic, foreign or historical associations which bestow other kinds of dignity. Though most of these detectives are from similar backgrounds to their forebears, their names now suggest a class-transcending potential for heroism.

In this, they owe more than is sometimes recognised to the George Gideon series with which J. J. Marric (i.e., John Creasey) virtually founded the British 'police procedural' mode in the 1950s. *Gideon's Day* (1955) sets the pattern by presenting a brief period in the life of the Metropolitan CID's offices at Scotland Yard as overseen by Superintendant (later Commander) Gideon. Some elements look old-fashioned from today's viewpoint: a Chinese drug trafficker threatens teenage lives and indeed 'Christian civilisation' with nothing stronger than marijuana reefers.[16] But, while most officers are as pure at heart as the Dixon of Dock Green who is normally taken as embodying a naive, prelapsarian faith in the British bobby, the series does confront such issues as police corruption, work-induced strains in the hero's marriage and family, and current social problems as direct causes of crime (as in the slum-clearance delays which motivate the serial arsonist of *Gideon's Fire*). The crimes, too, seem strikingly modern: serial killing and child sex-abuse are treated as regular occurences rather than with the drop-everything-else horror that has come to dominate much crime fiction since the 1980s.[17]

At the same time, considerable comfort can be gained from Gideon's bird's-eye view from the very top of the Metropolitan Police ladder, reassuring us that the crimes surveyed are the *only* serious crimes in the whole of Greater London in the given period. Also, by revealing many of the culprits' identities early on, the novels shift our attention to the process rather than the magic of policing. We feel it is only a matter of time before most are caught – though, in line with procedural realism, a significant number also escape. Because Scotland Yard is itself Gideon's home patch, the standard contrast between local plods and the smooth operator from London is dissolved in favour of a comprehensible, meritocratic promotion structure where class is simply not an issue. Instead, Gideon is vested with such class-transcending traits as an imposing physique and a name whose biblically heroic connotations are evident from the first sentence, when he is about to sack a bribe-taking officer: 'The wrath of Gideon was remarkable to see and a majestic thing to hear.'[18]

To varying degrees, many of the most important British crime writers from the mid-1960s onwards have grafted Creasey's procedural model on to that of more traditional detective fiction. Though it is not unknown for criminals' identities to be revealed early on, enough secrets are retained to invest the hero with the mantle of detective genius, discreetly concealed under the plain clothes of the Detective Inspector (or above) somewhere outside London. By and large, the movement towards greater class-inclusiveness continues, not only by way of the wide range of cases the police are naturally expected to tackle but also because of the genre's increasingly confident probing of the dynamics of day-to-day workplace relationships. Since working within a meritocratic structure has become the common experience of a great deal of the population – women now very much included – it is arguable that a major part of police fiction's appeal lies in its reflection of this shared experience, interleaved with the kind of high drama which also permits an escape from it.

P. D. James's *Cover Her Face* (1962), Ruth Rendell's *From Doon with Death* (1964), Reginald Hill's *A Clubbable Woman* (1970) and Colin Dexter's *Last Bus to Woodstock* (1975) mark the first appearances of police heroes who have continued to be massively successful. Rendell's Wexford and Burden, Hill's Dalziel and Pascoe, Dexter's Morse and Lewis are bonded from the first into the lopsided duos which combine the traditional appeal of the Holmes-Watson format with a more contemporary recognition that most detectives do in fact operate within police teams. James's Dalgleish is a partial exception, descending on the usually rural crime-scene from Scotland Yard with a more shifting rota of sidekicks, and rising ever-higher in the ranks; but Morse and Wexford are fixed permanently at Inspector (later Chief Inspector) level in the regional towns of Oxford and the fictional Kingsmarkham, while Dalziel's broader brief as Superintendant of Mid-Yorkshire CID is grounded by a strong emphasis on his local knowledge. Despite variations, all four writers aim to present police work as collective, grim and often untidy, rather than as merely an elegant intellectual exercise.

In all of these first novels the victim is a woman, and Hill's punning title *A Clubbable Woman* – suggesting that a woman is murderable insofar as she is sociable – has a broad relevance to all of them. A housemaid trespasses too far on the goodwill of her upper-class employers; a housewife's social life is so restricted that a private correspondence is rightly assumed to point straight at her murderer; another housewife snoops on her neighbours' affairs out of boredom; a young woman is killed because of a casual sexual encounter. Except in the last case, the victims are technically 'innocent' sexually, but have somehow aroused dangerous passions in others. The murderers are also all women: a jealous rival, a mother defending her family from a misalliance, a lesbian admirer and, in the most dubious case, the victim herself persuading a reluctant male to pull a trigger for a joke. Though the prospect of male sexual violence is entertained in all these cases – in three of them a youth's obsession with the victim has put him close to the murder scene – the 'women beware women' motif shifts our gaze at the last moment towards the more comforting idea of women protecting society from their own sex's transgressions. It is arguable that the first choice of a female victim by four such different writers is more than coincidence, and responds to the disturbances of the 'sexual revolution' of the 1960s and 70s. New uncertainties about the traditional social restrictions of marriage, and about the younger generation's more casual attitude to sex, merge with a pre-feminist instinct that women who test these boundaries deserve some kind of retribution, perhaps as a substitute for the more overt moral sanctions of earlier times.

Some sense of how these writers have gone on to develop their scenarios can be given by comparing the books – not always their best – they produced in or about the millennium year 2000. P. D. James's Dalgleish has published poetry and risen to the Gideon-like height of Commander (from which, rather improbably, he continues to be assigned to individual cases), and his crime-scenes have moved on from the Christie-esque country-house of *Cover Her Face* to various kinds of workplace, often still great houses but now devoted to such dignified spheres of work as medicine, publishing, the law or the church. As James's novels have grown longer while retaining a straightforward 'whodunnit' structure, the increased space given to the inner thoughts of most of the characters can lead to a sense of having been tricked when one of them turns out to be guilty. Accordingly, in *Death in Holy Orders* (2001), the murderer of three people in what is essentially an old-style inheritance plot needs to be fitted out with a series of philosophical justifications from committed atheism to despair at the decline of civilised culture, in order to match his crime with what we know of his thoughts. A widower, Dalgleish commences the second of two rather wan affairs with innocent parties, but in general continues to follow a line of superior detectives going back to Poe's Dupin, with a cultured rapport with his well-bred suspects offsetting his scientific sharpness, an effortless ascendancy over the local police, a largely inviolate private life, and a series of upward-gazing sidekicks – always with the same surname initial but progressing from the dim Sergeant Martin to the far better realised, working-class Kate Miskin, who first appeared in *A Taste for Death* (1986). The growing tendency of other crime writers to use recent publicly-reported events as a springboard for social criticism has been largely resisted by James, unless to put a conservative spin on them. Thus, where Minette Walters's *The Shape of Snakes* (2000) is angrily based on the inadequate police investigation of the murder of the black teenager Stephen Lawrence, *Death in Holy Orders* alludes to the Lawrence case in passing, but in sympathy with police dissatisfaction at being labelled as institutionally racist.[19]

Despite their shared status as reigning 'Queens of Crime', their peerages and their personal friendship, Ruth Rendell's work differs markedly from James's. Far more prolific – she also writes non-series psychological thrillers under her own name and as Barbara Vine – she tends to use the Wexford series to explore various current issues, from militant feminism to modern slavery to environmental protest. With the fictional Kingsmarkham as a microcosm, she follows Colin Watson in sometimes condescending to its small-town manners and values. This is particularly evident in the lower-middle-class bigotry of Wexford's sidekick Sergeant (and upwards) Burden, but also in a certain stylistic brittleness which teeters on the brink of satire without ever quite falling in. Following recent news cases, *Harm Done* (1999) deals with anti-paedophile hysteria in the town's small sink-estate, whose tensions Rendell explores with a laudable attempt at class-inclusiveness, though her ear for working-class speech seems to be drawn more from media-speak than the street: thus the mob leaders call themselves 'The Kingsmarkham Six', a locution normally applied to the wrongly imprisoned.[20] This somewhat misjudged tone contrasts sharply with the other main case, a grippingly-disclosed story of domestic abuse in the kind of middle-class setting Rendell can handle with accurate ease. Wexford himself follows Purbright and other small-town police heroes in being happily married.

In *Last Bus to Woodstock*, Colin Dexter's experience as a setter of school exams and crossword puzzles emerges in Morse's detection of a hidden message encoded in the spelling mistakes of an apparently innocuous letter, and in the way a Latinate *Times* crossword clue draws his attention to the victim's missing brassière. Morse's own name gestures towards this world of encryption, in which the truth can be unearthed from the most unlikely messages given a sufficient hold on precise linguistic rules. His somewhat pedantic erudition is given a particular pathos by its Oxford setting, in a world of learning to which he will never belong but from which he cannot avert his gaze. Counterbalancing this side of his character is a 'common man' side, signalled by his love of pubs, mean cadging of drinks and lifts, and salacious interest in the women in the case, with one of whom he often has a shortlived affair. In *The Remorseful Day* (1999) little has changed, from the pouncing on a split infinitive[21] to the lingering presentation of the female victim as sexually available at the time of death. However, such similarities pale in relation to the event which made the novel's publication something of a national news story: the death of Morse himself after a long illness. Though Dexter is clearly making a bid for some of the tragic depth of hardboiled fiction – having him arrest his lover in the first novel, and die a lingering death in his last – there is something about the self-satisfied unchangingness of Morse's world-view, and the novels' patent lack of interest in the other characters, which makes them hard to take as seriously as they seem to ask, or as the acclaimed TV series somewhat loosely modelled on them.[22]

If Rendell often seems to condescend to poorer realms from a middle-class heartland, Reginald Hill's novels move in the opposite direction. Brilliantly grounded from the start in rumbustiously working-class speech and attitudes, they have become increasingly ambitious in dealing with a range of serious socio-political issues and with the world of high literary culture, as in the elaborate pastiches of Virgil and Homer in *Arms and the Women* (2000), whose opening not untypically reads more like a postmodernist experiment with fragmented narrative than the start of a detective story. Such balancing acts are firmly held together by the three-way relationship between the Falstaffian Chief Superintendant Dalziel, foul-mouthed, boozy and sex-obsessed, but always finally turning up trumps both in intelligence and compassion; Pascoe's wife Ellie, who represents everything high-minded and politically correct but is fallible enough to be endearing; and the quiet, educated Inspector Pascoe, whose attempt to steer a middle course between them makes his the central consciousness. A fourth, increasingly important member of the cast has been the gay Sergeant Wield, whose acceptance by Dalziel despite a barrage of crude jokes provides a continual test-case of the path between progressive social values and earthy wit Hill manages to tread, usually unerringly. Where James tends to use wit as a mark of villainy, Rendell's terse style implies a generally humorous outlook without breaking into actual jokes, and Dexter's salacious jests are often somewhat short on good humour, Hill's novels are built up out of a succession of comic dialogues which – though some remarks are clearly feeds to the punchline – are both thought-provoking and genuinely hilarious.

In some novels by the above four writers, and in many by younger ones, two major new themes emerged in the 1980s: the serial killer and child-abuse. Partly based on real popular fears aroused by a growing number of actual reported cases, the serial-killer motif also offered its own narrative satisfactions. The traditional-style investigation of the early murders is constantly intercut with the tension of trying to prevent the next, and it is almost mandatory that the chief detective figure eventually finds her or himself under threat, allowing the whole case to climax in a dramatic personal confrontation with the unmasked monster – whose anonymous thoughts have often been conveyed to us in brief, chilling interludes between chapters. The fact that the serial killer's motive is usually sexual addresses another significant development of these decades. Whereas the novels we have considered from the 1960s and 1970s generally suggested that their female victims partly invited their own deaths, and their murderers received a certain sympathy, in the serial-killer novel all blame is shifted completely from the victims to the male killer, whose inability to cope with his sexual urges in a liberated way has put him completely beyond the human pale. It has become important to blame, not sexual activity itself, but the self-repressions which turn male desire into violence. While a final account of these repressions may evoke a kind of sympathy, it is only the kind we feel for monsters who must be hunted down and killed.

Some of these points also apply to the theme of domestic – most usually child – abuse. Generally kept hidden until the end, the revelation of such abuse often now fulfills the cathartic function of the more complex but less emotionally engaging revelations of the traditional whodunnit. Stimulated, once again, by popular concern over many actual cases, the child-abuse theme also condenses into a kind of shorthand the many long-noted similarities between detective fiction and psychoanalysis, with the detective or analyst slowly peeling away layers of deception from a core of infantile sexual anxiety. Where classical Freudians from Marie Bonaparte to Charles Rycroft followed their master in suggesting that the reader-child's own Oedipal sexual feelings for a parent are both gratified and concealed in the whodunit structure (with the roles of killer, victim and sleuth divided between parents and child according to taste), this recent strain of crime fiction follows more recent revisionist accounts suggesting that Freud himself either obscured or misread evidence of real parental abuse of his patients.[23] The result is a sub-genre with strong ideological, generally feminist, implications: though the victim of abuse is usually technically guilty of something, that guilt is then transferred to the abuser, usually a father or other male authority-figure representing the patriarchal power-structure of the traditional family.[24]

Both these motifs are so firmly entrenched in the crime fiction of the 1980s and 1990s that, in what follows, I shall just indicate rather than dwell on them. In the opening books of two of the most effective 1980s police series, they chime in with other markedly dystopian elements. Ian Rankin's *Knots and Crosses* (1987) and Michael Dibdin's *Ratking* (1988) introduce Inspectors John Rebus and Aurelio Zen, both of whom are seen to battle with some nightmarish aspect of the political system as well as specific villains. In line with these concerns, both are presented to us in close-up before the main case is fully under way, and are tormented by a past history whose revelation is intimately related to the case's solution. Something is rotten in the state, and the Hamlet-like sense that it is at once social and personal owes much to the figure of the American private eye, from whom Rebus and Zen also borrow a state of chronic job-insecurity whereby their promotions seem blocked or they find themselves repeatedly posted away from their home beat. The American genre also suggests their usual location – the threatening cityscape – as well as the sense that the evil at the heart of the case cannot be removed by the identification of a single individual. Perhaps in response to the 1980s' domination by the strongly right-wing Thatcher and Reagan governments, much of the decade's crime fiction explores the fracture between glossy, wealth-driven appearances and hidden histories of oppression and abuse.

Rankin's *Knots and Crosses* combines a classic serial-killer plot with the idea of high-level corruption, in a hushed-up military training scheme whose extreme mental cruelty has driven Rebus from the SAS into the police, and the killer over the edge via a traumatic moment of sexual self-recognition. Rebus's name denotes a code in which images or objects replace words, and the fact that the killer communicates with him using the symbolic knots and crosses of the title suggests, along with several references to Stevenson's *Dr Jekyll and Mr Hyde*, that they are linked as two halves of the same personality. All this, plus further levels depicting the grimy tedium of police work, and Rebus's almost inevitable drink problem and broken marriage, makes this novel an ambitious compendium of genre motifs from the realistic to the ludic. Subsequently, Rebus's anguished metaphysical baggage has given way to an increasingly full world of working and transiently sexual relationships, while exploring such serious issues as the traffic in East European refugees (*The Hanging Garden*, 1998) and child-abuse (*Dead Souls*, 1999), and increasingly centring round Rebus's Moriarty, the imprisoned underworld boss Big Ger Cafferty, who emerges from jail in *Set in Darkness* (2000) to best Rebus in a case involving property speculation around the site of the new Scottish Parliament.

Like Rankin's outwardly prosperous Edinburgh, Dibdin's various Italian locations are half-familiar to a fair majority of readers, but chiefly identified with culture or tourism, so that there is an inbuilt sense of enthralling discovery in the exposure of these places' festering underbellies. Posted to Perugia by various string-pulling politicos, Zen's inquiries into the kidnap of a telecommunications tycoon are divided between disentangling the lies of the tycoon's family and circumventing a network of jurisdictional rivalries within the police system itself. The realisation that the family have little wish to pay the ransom revives memories of Zen's own lost father and of the (real-life) terrorist kidnap of prime minister Aldo Moro, whose whereabouts Zen was prevented from investigating by the powerful state forces which have since stymied his career. Our sense of ambivalence over the kidnapped father is exacerbated by a daughter's revelation that he routinely abused her. Though Zen solves the case – which soon becomes one of murder – there is little sense of triumph: the title of *Ratking* refers to the composite creature formed by many rats with enmeshed tails rather than to a single mastermind. This image of all-pervasive complicity among the powerful could stand equally for all the other Zen novels, not least *Blood Rain* (1999), where the Mafia itself becomes a pawn in a government-led game which seems to result – though he is revived in *And Then You Die* (2002) – in Zen's own murder.

The six writers I have been discussing are by no means the only ones to feature police detectives. P. D. James's pairing of a smooth cultural insider from Scotland Yard with a working-class female career detective has been taken much further in Elizabeth George's pairing of Inspector Thomas Lynley, eighth Earl of Asherton, with the grim-faced Sergeant (and upwards) Barbara Havers. Somewhat comically embodying the widely-held American view that the aristocracy is still a vital force in British life (or even fantasy), Lynley is accompanied by an impossibly top-drawer collection of friends and lovers also engaged in policing or forensics, but despite this the novels are excellently written and the various British settings are carefully researched. Often more daring than James in subject-matter – her first novel, *A Great Deliverance* (1988), involves the now-standard child-abuse motif which James has largely avoided – George's novels also cover a greater range of modern British life in class and other terms, as witness *Deception on his*

*Mind* (1997) which is partly and quite convincingly set in an Asian community. If George's ear for English idiom sometimes fails her it is not for want of careful checking.[25]

Most home-grown police series now confine their inspector heroes to a local patch. Where this is small-town or rural, like W. J. Burley's Cornish-based 'Wycliffe' or Caroline Graham's 'Barnaby' series, Rendell's solid, married Wexford often supplies the model. One of Wycliffe's woman officers is called Burden and the killer in *Wycliffe and the Schoolgirls* (1976) is called – in somewhat perverse tribute – Rendell; while Barnaby's assistant Troy outdoes the original Burden in petty-minded bigotry (though Graham's dedication of *The Killings at Badger's Drift* (1987) to Christianna Brand points to her more traditional affiliation to the country village whodunit). R. D. Wingfield's Inspector Frost resembles Morse in his frequent run-ins with superiors, dirty mind, ill-treatment of sidekicks and possession of a host of minor vices from chronic unpunctuality to incessant smoking in sacrosanct places, but the series also owes much to Colin Watson in its comic orientation and its creation of a town – Denton – too large to be pretty but too small be identifiable. Differing from Morse in his preference for hunch over logic and chaotic absorption in a flood of cases rather than in worrying at the details of a single problem, Frost is roughly halfway between Purbright or Wexford and an urban maverick like Rebus: while routinely sloppy and ill-behaved, he holds the George Cross for bravery, and, while projecting himself as sexually on the loose, is forlornly widowed rather than angrily divorced.[26]

In more fully urban settings Rankin's Rebus has many pre- and post-echoes. William McIlvanney's two Laidlaw novels (the somewhat over-written *Laidlaw*, 1977, and much more powerful *The Papers of Tony Veitch*, 1983) did not become a series, but created an influential symbiosis between a crime-ridden yet vital Glasgow and the divorced, hard-drinking but intellectually literate hero. Christopher Brookmyre's more recent witty novels, beginning with *Quite Ugly One Morning* (1996) and often featuring the guerilla journalist Jack Parlabane, are set in a similarly envisaged Glasgow. Where Laidlaw reads Camus and Rebus relates everything to his encyclopaedic knowledge of rock music, John Harvey's equally divorced, Nottingham-based Charlie Resnick (Starting with *Lonely Hearts*, 1989) favours jazz. These obsessive, lonely hobbies come across as much-needed badges of identity in the anonymity of the big cities which are, nonetheless, perhaps better celebrated here than in most 'straight' British novels. In some cases, the whiff of corruption which spices many if not most urban procedurals goes beyond the odd bad apple: G. F. Newman's *Sir You Bastard* (1970) and Irving Welsh's *Filth* (1998) present the force as completely corrupt, anti-heroes included.

At the opposite end of the crime-writing spectrum, Robert Barnard's Perry Trethowan of Scotland Yard (from *Sheer Torture*, 1981) surveys urban sleaze – e.g. the pornography racket in *Bodies* (1986) – from the wittily urbane standpoint of the Golden Age.

Though not technically part of the police force, a new type of 'official' detective has emerged since the 1980s in the shape of the psychological profiler, who revives something of the mystique of Sherlock Holmes in his near-uncanny ability to identify serial killers through the pattern of their crimes. Alongside her two series featuring the lesbian journalist Lindsay Gordon and the private eye Kate Brannigan, Val McDermid's *The Mermaids Singing* (1995), *The Wire in the Blood* (1997), *A Place of Execution* (1999) and *Killing the Shadows* (2000) constitute a recognisably separate sequence in their exploration of this idea, although only the first two centre round the series-hero Tony Hill. While the first follows a very similar pattern to Rankin's *Knots and Crosses* – a series of murders (though these involve far more horrific and sexualised torture) designed to lure the profiler-hero towards a culminating attack from which he only just escapes – *Killing the Shadows* plays more intricate games with the form, offering us snippets of serial-killer novels whose authors are then murdered, for reasons connected to a case modelled on the notorious failure of profilers to entrap the lead suspect in the real-life murder of a young mother on Wimbledon Common.[27] What makes the novel effective is that, while never lapsing into actual parody, it treats the ever-more grizzly conventions of the profiler/serial-killer genre as so well-worn that there is little left to do other than play literary tricks with them.

While police or related detectives preponderate, post-war British crime fiction has featured other types of protagonist. The male 'amateur' is virtually defunct as a series-hero and even men like Crispin's Professor Gervase Fen, whose day-job in one of the cultured professions leaves him leisure to solve crimes on a series basis, have become increasingly rare, despite the fair success of Simon Brett's usually-'resting' actor Charles Paris.[28] More standard has been the non-series hero whose demanding day-job plunges him into a particular one-off case, such as the jockeys and other hard-working, hard-fighting heroes of Dick Francis.[29] Though the main new developments in another sub-genre – women and black private eyes – have made most impact in America, brief mention is worth making here of Reginald Hill's black private investigator Joe Sixsmith and a longer list of female ones, including Antonia Fraser's Jemima Shore, Liza Cody's Anna Lee, Gillian Slovo's Kate Baier, Sarah Dunant's Hannah Wolfe and P.D. James's Cordelia Gray – arguably the first successful female private eye in *An Unsuitable Job for a Woman* (1972), but then dropped by the author after one more outing.[30]

While seizing a traditional bastion of fictional maleness, such heroines exploited the private eye's outsider status to show how society is stacked in favour of male, as well as financial and political, power; the main drawback being that, once the initial fun is over, the private eye remains a figure of fantasy. By the 1990s, new forms of empowering investigative roles for women were being sought. Strangely, despite the TV success of such figures as Jane Tennison in Lynda LaPlante's *Prime Suspect* series,[31] few fully-empowered British police heroines have so far emerged in print; although P. D. James and Elizabeth George have both created memorable sidekicks in Inspectors Kate Miskin and Barbara Havers, these are both firmly overshadowed by very traditional male authority-figures. The same can be said of Rebus's main sidekick Siobhan Clarke: growing in importance throughout Rankin's series, an internal logic forbids her overtaking the hero himself.

One successful type of female maverick – in realistic terms more credible than the private eye but with a similar ambivalence between working for hire and for principle – is the journalist, as represented in McDermid's series featuring Lindsay Gordon (from *Report for Murder*, 1987), whose championship of lesbian-related causes leads her into a more general championship of minority victims; and in Minette Walters's second novel *The Sculptress* (1993), whose heroine combats entrenched prejudice against an overweight supposed murderess. Lawyers, too, combine a solid professional status with a regular opportunity to encounter criminal cases which may require further investigation, as with Frances Fyfield's two series-heroines, the barrister Helen West and solicitor Sarah Fortune. Fortune's cases usually arise from her somewhat improbable sexual generosity to a string of lame ducks, while West's on-off affair with a policeman gives her adventures more of a detective element; however, Fyfield's frequent theme of a male sexual abuser's obsession with a single victim is generally revealed early on, making these books more tales of gothic pursuit than straightforward detective stories.[32]

Looking back at Julian Symons's 1972 vision of the detective novel as a declining market, we may say that he greatly exaggerated its demise. At the same time, his preference for the term 'crime novel' to describe future developments has been borne out by the strong admixture of other elements to what remains a remarkably resilient formula of crime, investigation and solution. If some of the pleasures of the incredibly ingenious final revelation have been sacrificed, these have been replaced by increasing attempts to make the solution mean something in emotional, social or political terms. The decision by many writers to base their plots on real events in the public sphere – anti-paedophile riots, psychological profiling failures, anti-Mafia drives, the new Scottish Parliament – often involves an intelligent rethinking of those events' implications from credible but unexpected angles. Against the often radical implications of these diagnoses can be set a continuing, perhaps increasing, trust in the normal agencies of law enforcement as offering at least the best hope of a remedy for the ills identified. At the start of the third millennium, the market for what the French have always called *le roman policier* remains as buoyant as ever.

## NOTES

1 Julian Symons, *Bloody Murder: From the Detective Story to the Crime Novel: A History* (1972). The 2nd edition (Harmondsworth: Penguin, 1985), p. 235, reaffirms this view.

2 See Marjorie Nicolson, 'The Professor and the Detective' (1929), reprinted in Howard Haycraft, ed., *The Art of the Mystery Story: A Collection of Critical Essays* (1946; reprinted New York: Carroll & Graf, 1983), p. 133.

3 See George N. Dove and Earl F. Bargainnier, eds., *Cops and Constables: American and British Fictional Policemen* (Bowling Green, OH: Popular Press, 1986).

4 Christie died in 1976; Margery Allingham in 1966; Anthony Berkeley Cox in 1971; Nicholas Blake (C. Day-Lewis, the Poet Laureate) in 1972; John Dickson Carr in 1977 and Ngaio Marsh in 1982.

5 See John Dickson Carr, *The Hollow Man* (1935; Harmondsworth: Penguin, 1951), pp. 186–7; Edmund Crispin, *The Gilded Fly* (Harmondsworth: Penguin, 1944), p. 65, and *The Moving Toyshop* (Gollancz, 1946; Harmondsworth: Penguin, 1958), p. 87. Victor Gollancz was the mid-twentieth century's leading publisher of left-wing books as well as much crime fiction.

6 Crispin, *The Gilded Fly*, p. 17.

7 See Nicola Humble, *The Feminine Middlebrow Novel, 1920s to 1950s: Class, Domesticity, and Bohemianism* (Oxford University Press, 2001), pp. 183–91, for an interesting discussion of the eccentric family in detective fiction.

8 For more on Lecoq and Cuff, see pp. 64–5 and 34 of this book.

9 See Symons, *Bloody Murder* (1985), p. 189.

10 Colin Watson, *Snobbery with Violence* (London: Eyre and Spottiswoode, 1971).

11 See H. R. F. Keating, *Inspector Ghote: His Life and Crimes* (London: Hutchinson, 1989), p. 1.

12 While aware that Keating's account of India is based on reading rather than experience, Meera Tamaya argues in *H. R. F. Keating: Post-Colonial Detection: A Critical Study* (Bowling Green, OH: Popular Press, 1993) that it captures its historical post-imperial moment very effectively.

13 See *Double Barrel* (1964) and *Tsing-Boum* (1969). Partly thanks to a popular TV series (BBC, 1959–63), Maigret epitomised the *noir*-ish post-war appeal of European policing at a time when the Continent was still, for many, 'over there'.

14 In his articles on the Detective Police (see also p. 42), Dickens alters real officers' names slightly to bring out the drama of their trade, for example to Wield, Whichem (bewitch 'em) and Stalker.

15 Starting with Ellis Peters, *A Morbid Taste for Bones* (1977), and Lindsay Davis, *The Silver Pigs* (1989).

16 J. J. Marric (John Creasey), *Gideon's Day* (1955; London: Hodder & Stoughton, 1964), p. 38.

17 They are treated separately in *Gideon's Fire* (1961) and combined in *Gideon's Day*.

18 Marric, *Gideon's Day*, p. 7.

19 See P. D. James, *Death in Holy Orders* (London: Faber, 2001), pp. 200–1. Stephen Lawrence was murdered in 1993 in what the police at first failed to treat seriously as a racist attack, leading to a failure to convict the clearest suspects. The subsequent MacPherson Inquiry criticised the police for 'institutional racism'.

20 See Ruth Rendell, *Harm Done* (1999; London: Arrow, 2000), p. 181.

21 In the paperback edition of *The Remorseful Day* (London: Pan, 2000), p. 14, the dreaded split infinitive is unfortunately surrounded by a series of typesetting howlers which make its context ungraspable.

22 See p. 241 of this book.

23 See Marie Bonaparte, *The Life and Works of Edgar Allan Poe* trans. J. Rodker, (London: Hogarth, 1949), p. 156; Charles Rycroft, 'Analysis of a Detective Story' in *Imagination and Reality: Psycho-Analytical Essays, 1951–1961* (London: Tavistock Press, 1968), pp. 114–16. For the revisionist account of Freud, see for example Jeffrey Masson, *The Assault on Truth: Freud's Suppression of the Seduction Theory* (New York: Farrar, Straus & Giroux, 1985).

24 This theme is not unique to the 1980s and 1990s: it also hovers disturbingly over such early Sherlock Holmes stories as 'A Case of Identity' and 'The Speckled Band'.

25 See interview in Paul Duncan, ed., *The Third Degree: Crime Writers in Conversation* (Harpenden, Herts: No Exit, 1997), p. 94.

26 The two first novels, *Frost at Christmas* and *A Touch of Frost*, were both published in 1990 but written earlier, 1984 and 1987. Frost really came to prominence through the ITV series from 1992, starring one of the country's best-loved comic actors, David Jason. As with the similarly popular John Thaw's Inspector Morse, the highly sleazy comedy of the books is sacrificed to the star's determination to adopt expressions of angrily resentful concern, whatever the nature of the case.

27 Rachel Nickell, murdered in 1992.

28 Starting with *Cast, In Order of Disappearance* (1975).

29 Starting with *Dead Cert* (1962).

30 For first novels in the series mentioned, see Reginald Hill, *Blood Sympathy* (1985); Antonia Fraser, *Quiet as a Nun* (1977); Liza Cody, *Dupe* (1980); Gillian Slovo, *Morbid Symptoms* (1984); Sarah Dunant, *Birth Marks* (1991).

31 An occasional drama series beginning with *Prime Suspect* (ITV, 1991). See too the heroines of such TV series as *Juliet Bravo* and *The Gentle Touch*, both from 1980.

32 See, for example, *Shadow Play* (1993), *Perfectly Pure and Good* (1994) and *Staring at the Light* (1999).

# 11

MAUREEN T. REDDY

# Women detectives

Until quite recently, the story of the development of crime fiction was most commonly told as a movement from man to man, beginning with Edgar Allan Poe, then Arthur Conan Doyle, followed by Dashiell Hammett and so on. Fittingly enough, critics of the genre most concerned with mysteries, secrets, and deceit thus misrepresented its true story by writing women, both writers and detectives, out of its history until they appeared, seemingly from nowhere, first in the Golden Age and then again with the rise of feminist crime fiction in the 1980s. That distorted and partial history began to undergo revision in the late 1980s, as feminist critics discovered lost women writers such as Seeley Register and Anna Katherine Green and also began to look at gothic and sensation fiction for the roots of the genre. It is now widely acknowledged that the woman writer and the woman detective have as long a history in crime fiction as do their male counterparts.

Ann Radcliffe's wildly popular gothic novel, *The Mysteries of Udolpho* (1796), follows the classic gothic plot of an innocent young woman, orphaned and thus alone in the world, trapped in a mysterious and frightening place by a dangerous, threatening man. Because the central character, Emily, occupies such a precarious position throughout the text, readers are most likely to recall her as the victimised, passive heroine of the novel, with her rescue by one man and her eventual happy marriage to another the chief plot points. However, Emily also acts as a detective throughout the novel. Far from passively accepting her imprisonment by the vile Montoni, she consistently resists and defies him, capitulating to his (financial) demands only in an attempt to save her aunt's life. She courageously explores Udolpho, trying to uncover the truth of Montoni's past and of his present activities, searching for her aunt, and looking for possible avenues of escape. Emily's detecting inspires Catherine Morland's activities in *Northanger Abbey* (1817, but written c. 1798), Jane Austen's delightful send-up of, and tribute to, gothic novels and their female readership. Sensation fiction, a Victorian development from gothic fiction, includes few female detectives in comparison with its vast number of female victims and villains but contributed to the rise of detective fiction generally by centring on secrets, deceit, and murder. Wilkie Collins's *The Woman in White* (1860), considered the first sensation novel, is exceptional in its depiction of a partnership between a male detective, Walter Hartright, and a female one, Marian Halcombe. Significantly, Collins's male detective finds success and romantic love, but Marian is debarred from romantic fulfillment. Collins makes much of Marian's lack of physical attractions, repeatedly contrasting this highly intelligent woman with her less intelligent but far more lovely half-sister, thereby upholding an already-familiar stereotype.

Mary Elizabeth Braddon's still widely read *Lady Audley's Secret* (1862) features a female villain and a male detective (Robert Audley) at the centre of a plot that is a clear precursor of detective fiction in its attention to the process of detection: the reader and Robert together uncover clues that lead inexorably to Lucy's unmasking. Robert Audley presages Sir Arthur Conan Doyle's Sherlock Holmes in both his conception of himself as rigorously analytical and scientific in his methods and his relentless pursuit of the villain.

The astonishing and persistent popularity of the Holmes stories may owe something to the position of women within them: dark, disruptive, inexplicable presences who either require male protection or pose threats to masculine order that must be contained, women can never act as detectives themselves in a Holmesian world. Even the woman Holmes most admires, Irene Adler, his equal in disguise and in logical thought, is not allowed to put her obvious gifts in the service of detection. Although a number of woman-authored stories featuring female detectives appeared at roughly the same time as Doyle's Holmes stories, none attained the popularity of Holmes, which may be interpreted as testimony to the dominance of bourgeois, patriarchal ideology. Characters such as Catherine Louisa Pirkis's Loveday Brooke (in *The Experiences of Loveday Brooke, Lady Detective*, 1893–1894) and Mrs L. T. Meade's Florence Cusack (four stories in *Harmsworth Magazine*, 1899–1900) remain little known. These women detectives should be read as precursors of the boom in feminist detective fiction nearly 100 years later, especially since they arose during the first wave of feminism. In particular, Loveday Brooke deserves more attention, given Pirkis's emphasis on the obstacles the detective must overcome to do her job. A thirtyish single woman, Loveday sees herself as a logical, unemotional, professional person, but others frequently challenge her right to detect, seeing her as too 'lady-like' for such work. Unlike the many other female detectives who briefly appeared in print in the 1890s, and whose detective adventures generally ended with the protagonist's marriage, Loveday avoids romance and keeps working.

While there were many women writers of mystery fiction in the years between Sherlock Holmes and the first appearance of feminist detectives in the 1970s, most of these writers created male detectives, as did virtually all male writers of mystery fiction. The few series that did feature women sleuths in those decades tended to make their protagonists nosy spinsters or the helpmates of male detectives. Significantly, the very few writers who violated those norms created amateur detectives, such as Margaret Tayler Yates's Davvle McLean, a journalist who first appears in *The Hush-Hush Murders* (1937). Agatha Christie began her long career in crime fiction with a male detective, Hercule Poirot, introducing her second most celebrated series detective, Miss Jane Marple, ten years later in *Murder at the Vicarage* (1930). Miss Marple, an elderly woman of independent means in the tiny village of St Mary Mead, uses the spinster stereotype to her advantage. Indeed, a lifetime of nosiness – which might also be called close observation – constitutes her special power as a detective, although the local police see her as an 'interfering old pussy'. Miss Marple seldom gets official credit for the mysteries she solves in the twelve novels and twenty-one short stories in which she appears. In a pattern similar to Christie's, Dorothy L. Sayers began with a male detective, Peter Wimsey, and only later had Peter's love interest, Harriet Vane, investigate also (in *Gaudy Night*, 1935).

The rise of hardboiled fiction in the 1920s in the United States and its eventual dominance in critical opinion ensured that female detectives would be relegated to the ranks of amateurs and seen as marginal in the development of the crime fiction genre. Among other things, the hardboiled represents an intensification of the crime novel's commitment to a particular variety of realism that depends heavily on a tough, uncompromising surface verisimilitude. At the time, women were debarred from most law enforcement positions and were unlikely to be found working as private detectives; they thus are also debarred from the world of the fictional private eye. The intense masculinity of the hardboiled, its centralisation of an alienated male consciousness and its positioning of women as either dangerous, seductive villains or nurturing but essentially insignificant helpmates simultaneously reproduce and explain the very same cultural myths that made female professional private eyes unlikely outside the novel as well. Defining itself against the Golden Age detective fiction that flourished at the same time, the hardboiled thus positioned the Golden Age sleuths and their readers as feminine, indeed as little old ladies who could not tolerate a dose of the truth. Raymond Chandler's much-quoted 'mean streets' definition of the hardboiled hero in *The Simple Art of Murder* insists on the detective's maleness: 'The detective in this story must be such a man. He is the hero. He is everything. He must be a complete man and a common man, yet an unusual man.'[1] 'Man' here is not a generic human being, but the designation of a single sex; as Kathleen Gregory Klein has pointed out, substituting 'woman' and 'she' in this description creates absurdity.[2] Looking back at his Philip Marlowe stories, Chandler reiterates this essential masculinity in the introduction to *Trouble Is My Business* (1950). Hardboiled writers, he says, do not believe in the inevitability of justice:

> The stories were about the men who made that [justice] happen. They were apt to be hard men, and what they did, whether they were called police officers, private detectives, or newspaper men, was hard, dangerous work. It was work they could always get. There was plenty of it lying around. There still is.[3]

That work was not 'lying around' for women, however, in life or in fiction. The pattern of a male detective relentlessly pursuing a female opponent whose villainy consists entirely in the danger she poses to men and to patriarchal order, including inheritance, that we see in *Lady Audley's Secret* is a staple plot of hardboiled detective fiction and of *film noir*. While Braddon's novel subtly critiques that obsessive masculine pursuit, the hardboiled glorifies it, repeatedly positioning women as the dangerous Other that must be contained and controlled.

Dorothy L. Sayers's 'Introduction' to *The Omnibus of Crime* (1928) acquiesces in the exclusion of women from the role of protagonist in detective fiction, asserting that fictional female detectives, few as they were, 'have not been very successful.'[4] These detectives, she claims, have been either 'irritatingly intuitive' or foolishly 'active . . .walking into physical danger and hampering the men engaged on the job'. She concludes that 'better use has been made of women' as amateur detectives in fiction, as the female private eyes are too concerned with marriage, too young, and too beautiful. For all these reasons, they are simply unbelievable to Sayers, and perhaps to most readers as well:

> Why these charming creatures should be able to tackle abstruse problems at the age of twenty-one or thereabouts, while the male detectives are usually content to wait till their thirties or forties before setting up as experts, it is hard to say.

Actually, it is quite easy to say. Perhaps most important is the social demand that women, to be interesting, must be desirable objects to men, hence young, beautiful, and marriageable. With men the presumed major audience of most detective fiction, and detective fiction, like other forms of popular culture, likely to encode the prejudices and fantasies of its target audience, the female detectives' youth, beauty, and interest in men (signalled by their desire to marry) all make complete sense. Socialised to patriarchal ideals, women are likely to identify with a masculine reading position as well; as Simone de Beauvoir argued, woman is Other even to herself.[5] Then, too, the men 'set up as experts' after jobs and experiences that prepared them for private detective work, but those forms of preparation were not open to women, who consequently are depicted as going into the private eye business very young. The trends in female private detectives Sayers critiques here find their logical culmination in the sexpot private eyes of the late 1950s and 1960s, meant to appeal to male fantasies, such as Henry Kane's Marla Kent, who debuted in the aptly titled *Private Eyeful* (1959).

A field consisting of increasingly cartoonish female professional private eyes and increasingly stereotypical nosy spinsters along the lines of Christie's Miss Marple began to change forever with Amanda Cross's first Kate Fansler book, *In the Last Analysis* (1964). This series's debut coincided with the beginning of the second wave of the feminist movement, marked in the United States by the publication of Betty Friedan's *The Feminine Mystique*. While the plots and structure of the first two books in the Kate Fansler series are highly traditional, as is their conception of the role of the amateur detective – to right wrongs the official system of justice cannot or will not address and thereby to restore order – the third book in the series, *Poetic Justice* (1970) breaks that pattern. Beginning with this third novel, Cross begins to move away from the traditional mystery's progression from disorder to order and instead incorporates challenges to the very idea of social order in her plots, demonstrating some of the ways in which the status quo depends on women's continuing oppression. Thematically, the novels, most of which are set in the academic world in which Kate works as an English professor, tend to focus on feminist concerns and to include feminist critiques of culture, with particular attention to the significance of work and friendship in women's lives, a direct challenge to other popular fiction's centralisation of romance. Kate becomes more active as a detective as the series progresses and more confident in her own authority; at the same time, Cross's depiction of Kate diverges ever more sharply from male models. While she was writing the Kate Fansler series under the pseudonym Amanda Cross, the author also published a number of important works of feminist criticism and theory under her own name, Carolyn Heilbrun, a doubled career that suggests the deliberateness with which she revised the crime novel.

In 1972, when Cross had four Fansler novels in print, P. D. James published the first modern novel to feature a female private detective, *An Unsuitable Job for a Woman*. At twenty-two, Cordelia Gray, James's protagonist, is as young as the fictional female private detectives Sayers mocks, but in contradistinction to these forebears is far from being an expert at anything. We learn that she became an independent investigator almost accidentally, when her hapless partner committed suicide and bequeathed her the failing detective agency and a gun. *An Unsuitable Job for a Woman* combines a mystery plot with the structure of (female) *bildungsroman*, as the novel interweaves the story of Cordelia's development into an adult professional detective with the investigation she is hired to handle. Like the male hardboiled detectives, Cordelia is solitary and alienated from her surroundings; also like them, she repeatedly encounters resistance to her investigation and challenges to her authority. Unlike them, however, these conditions result directly from her gender, a fact that the novel's title underscores. Various characters question Cordelia's right to work as a detective, insisting that such work belongs to men; Cordelia herself is plagued by doubts. By the end of the novel, however, a more mature and confident Cordelia than the one we meet as the novel opens asserts her right to investigate and indeed to choose whatever work she wishes, relying in part on fantasies of her long-dead mother's approval. This novel has all the hallmarks of a first book in a planned series, but in the event James did not return to Cordelia Gray for ten years, publishing the second book in the series, *The Skull Beneath the Skin*, in 1982. The Cordelia we find in *Skull* differs radically from what readers might expect based on the final chapters of *An Unsuitable Job for a Woman*. In the second book, Cordelia makes silly mistakes, gets herself (and others) into dangerous situations due to her foolish miscalculations, and even fails to solve the novel's central mystery. By the end of this book, Cordelia retreats into finding lost pets, a speciality more suited than solving murders to conventional ideas about appropriate work for young women. James herself, apparently happily, turned away from Cordelia and back to her main series character, police detective Adam Dalgliesh. Feminist critics have offered a variety of explanations for this disappointing end to a promising new series, with Nicola Nixon's argument that Cordelia's diminution parallels James's own retreat from feminism most persuasive.[6]

The brief, disappointing history of the Cordelia Gray series may explain why James is so seldom acknowledged as the creator of the first modern female private eye, a distinction usually given to Marcia Muller, whose Sharon McCone series begins with *Edwin of the Iron Shoes* (1977). James published *An Unsuitable Job for a Woman* when feminist ideas were just beginning to gain popular attention and wide currency through such vehicles as *Ms* magazine. By the time Muller's first book came out, liberal feminist ideas had seeped into public consciousness, with the dominant ideology adjusting ever-so-slightly to accommodate some of those views. For example, women had begun to enter the workplace in positions previously held exclusively by men and there was general, if grudging, agreement that equal work deserved equal pay (not that there was any agreement about what constituted equal work or that equal pay was actually forthcoming). The more radical and revolutionary insights of feminism – those requiring structural change, as opposed to comparatively minor adjustments within the existing structure – continued to be treated as threatening and/or ridiculous by the mass media, the source of most people's information and thus a significant shaper of public opinion. A substantial readership was ready for the liberal feminism of Muller's series in 1977, primed to accept a woman as a private eye. Significantly, the first book to feature a radical feminist detective, M. F. Beal's *Angel Dance*, also appeared in 1977, but plunged almost immediately into obscurity, beloved by feminist critics to this day but read by almost no one else, then or now.

Muller's McCone is thus not the first modern female professional detective, but she is the first to remain at the centre of an ongoing series (of twenty-two books as of this writing). One of Muller's most important early contributions was to demonstrate that genre boundaries could be pushed a bit without changing the form entirely and thus destroying its pleasures, even though the female – and recognisably feminist – consciousness at the centre of Muller's novels necessarily calls into question all the conventions of the hardboiled tradition. Instead of leaving those conventions intact and simply dropping a female into the main role, the strategy Lillian O'Donnell adopts with the police procedural in her Norah Mulcahaney series (begun with *The Phone Calls* in 1972), Muller foregrounds the conflicts between Sharon McCone's gender role and her work role.

Although created in the late 1970s, Sharon McCone is best considered an invention of the 1980s, as the second Muller novel to feature her did not appear until 1982, but was then followed by more or less annual instalments. Because of this publication history, Muller ought to be considered alongside Sara Paretsky, Sue Grafton, and Liza Cody, all of whom began series in the early 1980s and continued them through most of the decade. Sally Munt sees the 1980s as the heyday of feminist crime fiction, a boom that Munt attributes to the dominance of Thatcherism and Reaganism, both of which 'reified an individualist, urban culture' and led to popular fiction that gave women 'a fantasy of individualized power and control'.[7] These series offer more than that fantasy, however, particularly in their shared interest in remapping the terrain originally staked out by the hardboiled.

While these series do indeed borrow many of the conventions of the hardboiled, they do so finally to turn those conventions on their heads. For instance, these series – and the many others that followed them – all focus on solitary central characters, as do hardboiled novels. However, solitariness for a woman has far different meanings than does solitariness for a man, as historically women have been defined by their relationships with men and have been refused the right to self-definition. In addition, unlike their male precursors, these female detectives try to ameliorate that solitariness by creating strong networks of friendship that do not merely duplicate family structures. Each of the detectives gives considerable thought to her relationships with others, working out the ethics of friendship and caring in ways indebted to feminism's insight that the family is the primary social institution in the oppression of women. Unlike the male detectives, the solitariness of the female detectives is not presented as a badge of honour but as a condition dictated by prevailing gender definitions. Of all these detectives, only Sharon McCone displays serious interest in a continuing heterosexual relationship, and only Muller tries to link crime plots with romance plots, however revised. For the other detectives – Paretsky's V. I. Warshawski, Grafton's Kinsey Millhone, and Cody's Anna Lee – relationships with men are always possible threats to their hard-won autonomy and independence.

More significantly, these series' novels tend to link a particular investigation – of insurance fraud, of murder, of a missing person – to wider social problems that are usually related in fairly direct ways to women's continuing oppression. While the male-authored hardboiled novels repeatedly invoke a world whose corruption and decadence threaten to engulf us all, with the hero standing alone against the forces of evil, the feminist revisions particularise that corruption as gender specific. In *Tunnel Vision* (1987), for example, Paretsky has V. I. set out to investigate a case that expands rapidly, bringing together financial fraud, political corruption, child sexual abuse and wife-battering, all closely related to women's subordination, economically and socially, to men. In place of the hardboiled's justification of continuing male dominance through the spiderwoman figure whose sexuality poses a danger to men and thus to the culture as a whole, feminist crime novels explore the results of that dominance. In those cases where the villain turns out to be female, she is never a seductress in search of power and money, but either a patriarchal enforcer (such as V. I.'s aunt in *Killing Orders*, 1985) or a woman trying to end or avenge her own victimisation (as in Grafton's *'F' is for Fugitive*, 1989).

The violence that marks the hardboiled tradition also undergoes analysis and revision in the feminist series. Graphic descriptions of violence abound in the hardboiled, with the detective repeatedly proving his heroism (and masculinity) by physically destroying others, with that destruction lovingly detailed so that readers participate vicariously in his triumph. A man acting violently is behaving within gender boundaries, but a woman behaving violently obviously is not. Rather than accept the violence and manliness equation or eschew violence altogether in a 'soft boiled' stance, the feminist detectives examine the meanings of violence and treat physical violence as an option they sometimes must use, but prefer not to. None of the detectives glories in her physical triumph over an adversary, nor do they leave the field of detection littered with the bodies of their opponents. Instead, each of them acts violently when necessary – usually in self-defence or in the defence of another – and understands that violence as having a lasting impact on her. There is an ambivalence toward violence even in Paretsky's series, which tends to be more graphic in its descriptions of violence than the other series. That ambivalence extends to guns, which are a staple of the hardboiled and seldom seriously interrogated. In each of the feminist series, however, the detective considers the social meanings of guns and hesitates before purchasing one, worrying about her own capacity for violence and the ease with which violence escalates when guns are involved.

Probably the most important distinction between the hardboiled and feminist revisions of it lies in the theme of fighting back, not only against violence but against all attempts at external, particularly patriarchal, control. Hardboiled detectives repeatedly encounter obstacles and traps meant to render them ineffective; their female counterparts encounter those same obstacles, but also the more generalised obstacle of gender limitations and social attempts to control and contain women. Liza Cody's second Anna Lee book, *Bad Company* (1982), extensively explores the consequences of fighting back against that containment. Anna tries to thwart a kidnapping and instead is kidnapped herself, held captive with the original victim, Verity, for two-thirds of the novel. From the start, Anna must fight not only against the four thugs who hold them prisoner, but also against Verity, who objects to Anna's every action for fear of worse mistreatment by their captors. Verity represents society's good girl, accepting her own powerlessness in the hope that those who control her will treat her less cruelly than otherwise. Anna, in contrast, believes that accepting powerlessness leads to spiritual and possibly even physical death and therefore fights back constantly. Anna's determined resistance ultimately leads to better conditions for both of the women, but Verity clings to her role of good girl even after they are released, suggesting to interviewers that Anna was worse than the thugs. This novel operates as an allegory of feminist resistance to patriarchy's attempts to enclose and silence women, with Verity standing in for anti-feminist women who persistently cast their lots with men.

The other series featuring female detectives incorporate similar feminist critiques of gender roles and social constraints, with the detectives often reflecting on their own roles and occasionally even comparing themselves to their fictional male counterparts, as if to point the contrast while also making the connection with an identifiable tradition. In *Killing Orders* (1985), for instance, Paretsky has V. I. imagine about how nice it would be to have a bodyguard and then think, 'Of course, a hardboiled detective is never scared. So what I was feeling couldn't be fear. Perhaps nervous excitement at the treats in store for me'.[8] Paretsky's V. I. and Grafton's Kinsey come closest to the hardboiled tradition in their language, adopting the sarcastic verbal style of the tough-talking male detectives. That talk seems to be a way of projecting an image of mental and physical toughness, as V. I.'s narrative voice is quite distinct from the way she speaks to her adversaries. Kinsey's voice is consistently tougher than V. I.'s; Scott Christianson reads Kinsey's wisecracking and tough talk as a deliberate appropriation of male power. Christianson identifies language as the hardboiled tradition's distinguishing feature and thus positions Grafton more centrally within that tradition than do most critics. He asserts that Kinsey's tough talk is 'an exercise of power – the power to express her emotions and sensibilities, and power over situations and circumstances'.[9]

By the end of the 1980s, each of these series was firmly established, with seven books in Grafton's, ten in Muller's, and five each for Paretsky and Cody. Other series featuring female private detectives had also begun, but these four remained the most important, with Grafton's by far the most popular. During this same period, an astonishing number of series with female protagonists, amateurs and police, also came into print, the way paved for them by the success of these female private eye novels. These writers proved that there was a readership hungry for strong women detectives and at the same time pushed the boundaries of what was acceptable in crime fiction.

Perhaps the most interesting development in this boom of female detectives in the 1980s was the lesbian detective novel, with Katherine V. Forrest's Kate Delafield series one of the most important. Unlike most of the other lesbian detective series of the 1980s, Forrest's does not begin with a coming out story; as the series begins, Kate's lesbianism is an established fact that readers simply have to accept. Together, the three novels in this series published in the 1980s – *Amateur City* (1984), *Murder at the Nightwood Bar* (1987), and *The Beverly Malibu* (1989) – begin a long-overdue feminist revision of the police procedural. While Kate is perhaps the least radically feminist of the lesbian detectives created in this period, she is by far the least conventional of the female police officers of the 1970s and 1980s, precisely because she is a lesbian. Although Forrest's plots are traditionally structured – a crime is committed and then the novel follows Kate's procedure as she painstakingly gathers evidence to solve that crime, arresting the perpetrator toward the end of the novel – Kate's struggles to reconcile her personal values and her sexuality with her job form a powerful continuing theme across the novels and constitute an interrogation of policing itself.

Forrest's novels were published by the Naiad Press, which played a crucial role in bringing lesbian mysteries to prominence in the 1980s. In addition to Forrest, Naiad published books by Nikki Baker, Lauren Wright Douglas, Vicki P. McConnell, and Claire McNab. Other lesbian crime series were also published by small feminist presses, such as Seal and Firebrand, which suggests that major houses initially were uninterested in publishing this work. Most of the lesbian detectives of the 1980s are amateurs, but that is where their resemblance to their Golden Age sisters ends. Like other feminist crime fiction, these novels tend to link the particular crime under investigation to wider social issues involving women. Barbara Wilson's second Pam Nilsen book, *Sisters of the Road* (1986), for example, focuses on the continuum of women's sexual oppression, presenting multiple views of what precisely constitutes that oppression. That inclusion of divergent views, with no hierarchical ordering of them, is typical of lesbian crime fiction of the 1980s. This fiction picks up on the hardboiled's treatment of women as dangerous to men but redefines the threat from a lesbian perspective, suggesting that women's real danger lies in the radical threat lesbians pose to the status quo through rejecting the assumption that patriarchal order is desirable and insisting on the value of women's relationships with other women. Many lesbian crime novels of the 1980s completely resist closure, repeatedly violating the genre's demand that the crime be solved for justice to be served. Wilson's first novel, *Murder in the Collective* (1984), implies that solving the crime actually undermines the possibility of justice.

By the late 1980s, the boom in lesbian crime fiction had reached the major publishing houses, an acknowledgement of the genre's crossover success. Two of the most popular – and mainstream-published – American lesbian detective series of the 1990s feature private eyes, Sandra Scoppettone's Lauren Laurano and Phyllis Knight's Lil Richie, with both series treating the detectives' lesbianism as a non-issue, apart from some comments about continuing homophobia, and generally focusing on cases unrelated to the detectives' sexuality. These series tend not to push genre boundaries, but to work within the established conventions, showing lesbians as just like any other detectives. Val McDermid's journalist/amateur sleuth Lindsay Gordon, who first appeared in *Report for Murder* (1987), remains among the few British lesbian detectives, with cases that often connect with larger social issues.

In the 1980s, 207 new series by women writers began, with the huge majority featuring female protagonists; about half of those series began in the final three years of the decade. Despite this boom, however, the 1980s produced no crime novels featuring black women as detectives by women of colour, although such detectives did feature in two series by Marcia Muller. Generally, white lesbian detectives represented the group furthest from traditional centres of power in crime fiction. In the 1990s, that changed; as of this writing, there are thirteen established series by black women writers with black detectives, and several more by and about other women of colour.

Much as the white feminist writers who created detective series in the 1980s significantly altered the genre by incorporating feminist themes, questioning the conventional plot's restoration of order, and centralising a female consciousness, women of colour had a transformative impact on the genre in the 1990s. Like the white feminist writers, these writers challenge the definitions of order and justice on which crime fiction has traditionally operated. Additionally, together they expose the limits of that earlier white feminist revision of detective fiction by addressing issues of race and class as well as gender, with all of their series treating racism as a fundamental fact of life and as an absolutely central component of the dominant ideology. While the white feminist writers critique the intense masculinity of the hardboiled tradition, for instance, the women writers of colour critique both that masculinity and the normative whiteness of the genre.

The largest group of women of colour now writing and publishing crime fiction are in the US; it is their work that has had the greatest impact on the genre thus far. The majority of black female detectives created by these writers are amateurs, with only one professional private eye series currently in print, Valerie Wilson Wesley's Tamara Hayle books, which began with *When Death Comes Stealing* (1990). Wesley's novels for the most part fit the revised hardboiled formula familiar from the feminist novels of the 1980s, with just a few significant differences. The two features that tie this series to those by other black women writers and distinguish it from the series by white feminist writers are Wesley's attention to race and racism and also her depiction of Tamara as a single parent. Virtually all of the black women detectives are parents or otherwise have daily responsibility for children, a circumstance that ties them to black community concerns and sharply differentiates them from their solitary white counterparts. Like most professional private eyes in fiction, Tamara comes from a law enforcement background, but left the police force and set out on her own when she decided that the police's institutionalised racism was irremediable. In that first novel, Wesley has Tamara describe an incident in which her pre-teen son, Jamal, was hassled by white police officers who saw their terrorising of him and his friends as a joke. She left the police force in order to maintain her son's respect, recognising that she is able to tolerate racism directed at herself but cannot countenance racism directed at her son.

That righteous distrust of the police is shared by most of the black women detectives, with all but one of the series incorporating direct commentary on the racism of police forces in general and specific examples of racist actions by officers. The sole exception is Eleanor Taylor Bland's Marti MacAllister series of police procedurals, which is especially interesting given the pains other series with black police protagonists give to explaining why any black woman would remain committed to an institution so steeped in racism as the police. In a move thematically parallel to Katherine V. Forrest's explanation of Kate Delafield's police career – Kate decides first to become and then to stay a police officer despite the entrenched heterosexism and sexism of police forces because she decides that a police force with a lesbian cop is better than one without her – several of the black police officer protagonists have personal and social reasons for joining the force along with a crusading attitude towards ameliorating the racist attitudes of the police. One series begins as the protagonist's career with the police ends when she comes to realise that she cannot alter entrenched attitudes: Grace Edwards's Mali Anderson is an ex-cop with a pending wrongful dismissal and discrimination suit against the NYPD when she is introduced in *If I Should Die* (1997). Bland's Marti occasionally reflects on her position as the sole woman and one of only two black detectives on the force of a Chicago suburb, but the series as a whole never suggests that police forces in general are both racist and sexist. In an essay on her series, Bland says that she chose to make her detective a police officer 'because I wanted to write mysteries about a real woman with a real job, with legitimate authority, who functions within the constraints of that authority. I wanted to write about a good cop.'[10] This essay juxtaposes an account of Bland's nephew's death under 'questionable circumstances, while in the custody of the [LA] police department' with an explanation of why she writes, saying that her detective is 'my insistence that there is good in this world, that there are good people'.[11]

Given the facts of book publishing and selling, it is probably fair to assume that black women writers' core audiences are likely to be predominantly white, and to varying degrees each of the black women crime novelists includes some acknowledgement of that probability in her work. Several of these writers go into more detail about the workings of racism than would be strictly necessary for an audience composed mainly of people of colour and offer direct commentaries on race matters that only make complete sense if read as directed at white readers. For example, the issue of colourism comes up frequently, with the authors having characters comment on exact shades of skin colour and on the 'desirability' of light skin in a racist culture. Barbara Neely's Blanche White series, with a black domestic worker/amateur detective as the protagonist, includes as its second instalment a novel whose plot revolves around social class among blacks and the disparate impact of colourism on women and on men (*Blanche Among the Talented Tenth*, 1994). On the whole, Neely's series is far more overtly political than any of the other series by black women, with Blanche deeply committed to the emancipatory project of black women's liberation from racism, sexism, heterosexism, and classism. Blanche's special power as a detective is her invisibility to white people and to black upper-class people, an invisibility rooted in her hypervisibility as a type. That is, most people who look her way see not Blanche, an intelligent, thoughtful, politically astute feminist, but a generic black woman, a servant. Consequently, people speak openly in front of Blanche, behaving as if she simply does not exist as a hearing, thinking person but only as a function. The first book in the series, *Blanche on the Lam* (1992), depicts Blanche as hiding in plain view, a possibility created by racism.

While not all the black women writers of current series share a single political perspective, their works do share a number of characteristics that together suggest a basic ideological stance in contradistinction both to hardboiled ideology and to white feminist revisions of that ideology. In brief, these characteristics include a black female consciousness in the central position in the text, with that consciousness both demonstrably connected to a wider black community and shaped by it; emphasis on the political dimensions of friendship between black women; attention to black women's roles as mothers, of their own children and of other black children; scenes of instruction on the intersections of race and gender; use of a specifically race-based invisibility/hypervisibility theme; and narrative interest in colourism and class issues among people of colour, particularly their impact on black women. A few books by different writers or a single series that incorporated these features might be of only passing interest, a kind of footnote to the hardboiled and classic traditions in crime fiction. The sheer number of series that share these features, however, carries weight and suggests a wholesale revision of crime fiction traditions even larger in scope than the feminist counter-tradition in crime created by white feminist writers in the 1980s.

The influence of these black women writers can already be seen in series by white feminist writers, which are increasingly likely to tackle race and racism, not always with good results. Whereas in the 1980s the white women detectives never reflected on the myriad ways in which their race offers them privileges that complicate gender discrimination, that topic now occurs with some frequency. The novel by a white woman about a white detective that comes closest to really examining intersections of race and gender is Linda Grant's *A Woman's Place* (1994), part of her Catherine Sayler series, which focuses on a white female private eye whose partner, Jesse, is a black male computer genius. This novel's plot revolves around sexual harassment and gender discrimination, with Jesse – the sole black character in the novel – going undercover at a software company. Catherine remarks that 'Jesse maintains that being black and a techie is the next best thing to being a fly on the wall'.[12] At one point, Catherine and Jesse argue about snuff pornography and its relation (or lack thereof) to sex, with Catherine insisting that it is not about sex at all, but 'about the same thing the Klan's about. It's just a different set of victims'.[13] A moment later, Catherine reflects on Jesse's failure to understand her position and thinks, 'On the other hand, I could never really understand how he felt as a black man. I could be outraged and appalled by racial hate crimes, but I didn't live with the subtle and not-so-subtle racism that could turn ugly at any time.' Catherine's thoughts here parallel race and gender instead of considering them as interactive; in her view, she is gendered and Jesse is raced. Consequently, she does not get to the next logical step of considering how her race is enabling for her as a private eye, but at least this novel offers some consideration of race. Other white feminist writers have begun to tackle race and racism in their series as well, with Sara Paretsky involving V. I. with a black police detective in several of her novels and examining some of the complications of interracial romance and Marcia Muller's Sharon McCone discovering in *Listen to the Silence* (2000) that she is in fact Indian, not mostly white and one-eighth Indian as she previously believed. This novel deals with race somewhat over-simply, treating it as a biological rather than a cultural fact. Black women writers' influence can be seen in other ways as well, as for instance in the use of more socially marginal characters as protagonists in white women's detective fiction. Probably the best example of this type is Liza Cody's second series, which focuses on Eva Wylie, a female wrestler from a deeply deprived background who sees Anna Lee as the enemy, no different from the police and other authority figures. Shifting the angle of vision from a middle-class white consciousness, as Cody does in *Bucket Nut* (1993), opens for reconsideration every element of crime fiction already revised by white feminist writers.

A still-new variation on this incorporation of marginal social positions is the 'girls just want to have fun' or 'tart noir' sub-genre. In this sub-genre, the silenced and controlled spiderwoman figure of the hardboiled now acts as the detective, recounting her madcap adventures (sexual more often than not) in books with titles like *Freeze My Margarita* (Lauren Henderson, 1998) and *What's a Girl Gotta Do* (Sparkle Hayter, 1994). These series signal a turning away from the serious political concerns of both white feminist detective series and black women's detective fiction, starting from the now-popular position that we live in a post-feminist age. From this standpoint, all legitimate feminist gains have already been made and it is time for women to stop being so serious and start having fun (with men) again. Charlotte Carter's Nan Hayes series is a fascinating bridge between the other series by black women writers and the tart noir genre. In the first book in that series, *Rhode Island Red* (1997), Nan – an educated black woman who chooses to make her living as a street jazz musician – attends little to race; the novel thus is oddly post-feminist, post-race-conscious in its plot and themes. With each successive book in the series, however, race assumes a more prominent place in the plot and in Nan's consciousness. By the third book, *Drumsticks* (2000), the plot is all about race and racism. In this novel, Nan sets out on her own to investigate a murder case assigned to a white police detective. She tells this man that she doubts witness accounts of the shooting he has been assigned because people in the crowd probably assumed they saw 'the policeman's favorite citizen': 'That ubiquitous black man who does everything when nobody's looking. He kidnaps little children, he hijacks vegetable trucks, he fucks up the Internet – just causes no end of trouble for law-abiding people.'[14] Nan even gets a black male police detective to help her by appealing to racial solidarity over police fraternity.

Another variant of post-feminist crime fiction, the medical/police investigation of serial killers with a woman doctor as the detective began in 1990 with Patricia Cornwell's *Postmortem*. That book, which introduced Dr Kay Scarpetta, Chief Medical Examiner for the Commonwealth of Virginia, won slews of awards, became a huge bestseller, and continues to spawn imitators. The pattern in the Scarpetta series includes highly detailed descriptions of the bodies on which Kay performs postmortems, FBI involvement in tracking serial killers, endangerment of the detective, and her ultimate triumph over the forces of evil, at least as manifest in one criminal per book. Cornwell's extremely conservative Republican politics are obvious throughout the Scarpetta series (eleven books as of 2001), particularly in her nearly worshipful portrayal of the FBI, her admiring treatment of her gun-toting central character, and her lavish descriptions of the lifestyle Scarpetta's wealth affords her. Kathy Reichs's Dr Tempe Brennan series, which began with *Déjà Dead* in 1997 and includes four books as of this writing, is close to Cornwell's in conception but less conservative and less self-indulgent. Like Cornwell, who worked as a secretary for a medical examiner's office and then as a police reporter, Reichs evidently draws heavily on her own life. Her main character even has the same job – forensic anthropologist in North Carolina and Montreal – as Reichs herself.

It is of course impossible to predict which of these current trends in women's detective fiction will persist or how they will change. However, given all the changes wrought recently by women creators of female detectives, it seems certain that women will continue to have a significant role in shaping crime fiction. Any new history of the genre will have to take women detectives into account or risk being laughably incomplete.

## NOTES

1 Raymond Chandler, 'The Simple Art of Murder' (1946), in Howard Haycraft, ed., *The Art of the Mystery Story: A Collection of Critical Essays* (New York: Carroll & Graf, 1983), p. 237.
2 Kathleen Gregory Klein, *The Woman Detective: Gender and Genre* (Urbana: University of Illinois Press, 1988).
3 Raymond Chandler, *Trouble is My Business* (New York: Vintage, 1992), p. viii.
4 Dorothy L. Sayers, 'The Omnibus of Crime', in Haycraft, ed., *Art of the Mystery Story*, p. 79.
5 See Simone de Beauvoir, *The Second Sex*, trans. H. M. Parshley (New York: Random House, 1974), pp. xx–xxv.
6 Nicola Nixon, 'Gray Areas: P. D. James's Unsuiting of Cordelia', in Glenwood Irons, ed., *Feminism in Women's Detective Fiction* (Toronto: University of Toronto Press, 1995), pp. 29–45.
7 Sally R. Munt, *Murder by the Book? Feminism and the Crime Novel* (New York: Routledge, 1994), p. 201.
8 Sara Paretsky, *Killing Orders* (1985), p. 215.
9 Scott Christianson, 'Talkin' Trash and Kicking Butt: Sue Grafton's Hard-Boiled Feminism', in Irons, ed., *Feminism in Women's Detective Fiction*, p. 130.
10 Eleanor Taylor Bland, 'Marti MacAllister: Good Cop. Bad Cop – Fact vs. Fiction', *Mystery Reader's Journal*, 14:2 (1998), p. 16.
11 *Ibid.*
12 Linda Grant, *A Woman's Place* (New York: Scribner's, 1994), p. 14.
13 *Ibid.*, p. 51.
14 Charlotte Carter, *Drumsticks* (New York: Mysterious Press, 2000), p. 29.

# 12

ANDREW PEPPER

# Black crime fiction[1]

To write about black[2] crime fiction, as opposed to white or any other kind of crime fiction, is to write about a body of writing that does not exist, or rather does not exist in isolation from, and has not developed outside or beyond the parameters of, these other kinds of crime fiction. Crime fiction, like all cultural practice, informs and is informed by its cultural and political contexts; so that just as the idea that 'blackness' or 'whiteness' ever described natural essences or biologically pure categories has been well and truly dismissed, the idea that the term 'black' (or indeed 'white') crime fiction refers, or has ever referred, to a rigidly defined and uniform practice, needs to be resisted. But this is a chapter on black crime fiction, nonetheless, and its very existence in a book of this nature testifies to the continuing significance of race as a trope of difference both in Britain and the United States. After all, who could argue with any conviction that categories like 'black' or 'white' in the US and Europe are suddenly of no consequence, when much of the anecdotal evidence points to the contrary? For however problematic 'race' as a biological category might be, belief in the existence of race, like a belief in the existence of witches, as Kwame Anthony Appiah remarks, 'continues to have profound consequences for human life'.[3] Or as Howard Wincant puts it:

> As we watch the videotape of Rodney King being beaten up by Los Angeles police officers; compare real estate prices in different metropolitan neighbour-hoods; select a radio channel to enjoy while we drive to work; size up a potential client, customer, neighbour, or teacher, we are compelled to think racially, to use racial categories and meaning systems into which we have been socialised.[4]

The trajectory of this chapter is, therefore, underwritten by a deliberately contradictory logic. The emergence and development of black crime fiction, predominantly in the United States but also in Britain, cannot be understood in isolation, as an entirely separate or uniform cultural practice. Nor, however, can examples of black and white crime fiction be unproblematically collapsed onto one another, as though to suggest a distinctive black culture and identity is itself a fiction, or that racial differences themselves are semantic rather than tangible and without 'profound consequences for human life'. Still, rather than trying to map out a detailed account of the origins and development of black crime writing in the United States and elsewhere – a task that has already been undertaken by Stephen Soitos in his book *The Blues Detective*,[5] and anyway requires far more time and space than is permitted here – this chapter will attempt to engage with, and untangle, a narrower question arising from the aforementioned contradiction; namely, whether or to what extent black crime writers can use the codes and conventions of a complex, ideologically conflicted genre to retrieve and promote what Michael Eric Dyson has called 'an enabling solidarity' without falling victim to a problematic racial essentialism or placing 'an ideological noose of loyalty around the necks of critical dissenters from received ideas about racial unity'.[6]

Certainly the rise to generic prominence of increasing numbers of black crime writers, particularly in the United States (which will be the predominant focus of this chapter), and the subsequent and inevitable re-articulation of black culture(s) and identities as multiple and heterogeneous, is part of this process. Still, the question of whether this kind of appropriation – of a genre whose codes and conventions have, largely, been shaped by a set of white, male discourses – can be unproblematically utilised for subversive or utopian ends, is not so clear. Nor is it clear whether the genre, and the potentially empowering figure of the detective, can be used as vehicles for overturning existing social hierarchies and furthering a culturally or politically transgressive agenda. And what happens when the already alienated figure of the detective is re-constituted as, say, black or, for that matter, as female or gay? Does this kind of shift necessarily radicalise the genre? And do we need to think about formal as well as thematic issues? In other words, can a crime novel be thematically subversive, yet formally reactionary, and what are the implications of this uneasy conflation?

Attempts to engage with such questions have fallen into a number of camps. The first, broadly influenced by contemporary work in post-colonial and African-American cultural theory, argues that the act of generic appropriation is subversive if it entails the radical re-articulation of that genre's codes and conventions. This position draws upon the work of, among others, Henry Louis Gates and Houston A. Baker and their influential efforts to delineate a transformative African-American tradition or aesthetic based on the premise of 'signifying'[7] or a 'blues ideology'[8] (processes by which Euro-American forms are ironically re-worked through the lens of

African-American folk culture). Stephen Soitos, for example, suggests that in so far as African-American writers reject the white myth of the lone hero and utilise the tropes of a black vernacular culture, their project is generically and ideologically subversive.[9] A second cluster of critics, meanwhile, adopting a broadly Marxist approach and taking up an opposing position, focus on the ways in which ideology functions through and on the crime novel and determines or at least 'hails' both the subject in the fiction and the reader. Hence Stephen Knight, Dennis Porter and Ernest Mandel, though by no means offering a uniform analysis, nonetheless argue that the crime novel, in whoever's hands, is at best a conservative genre that reflects the needs and desires of its predominantly middle-class readership in so far as it ultimately depends upon a restoration of the status quo and a reaffirmation of the existing social order.[10]

However, constituting the crime novel as either exclusively reactionary or subversive, hegemonic or counter-hegemonic, is problematic, because it overlooks the extent to which the genre, particularly in its harder-boiled American guise, is shot through with an uneasy mixture of contradictory ideological inflections or, rather, is coded to both resist and re-inscribe the dominant cultural discourses. The cultural politics of the hardboiled detective, after all, have always been deeply ambivalent. At once an alienated maverick whose interventions are necessary because the law is shown to be corrupt or inadequate, he or she is outside of the dominant social order and yet is a crucial part of the machinery by which social control is maintained and existing hierarchies policed. The idea, therefore, that a set of transformative 'black tropes' (to use Soitos's term) are able to irrevocably defuse all of the genre's reactionary elements is deeply problematic. Paul Cobley, for example, notes that Himes's Harlem Cycle depicts two violently conflicted black policemen who, trapped in a racially oppressive system which they themselves are responsible for upholding, could never hope to map themselves back into a long tradition of African-American culture or parodically reinvent themselves as 'tricksters'.[11] Nor, however, should it be assumed that crime fictions necessarily secure culturally dominant ways of perceiving the world, or invite readers to do likewise. Jim Collins makes the point that crime fictions also foreground social disintegration and undermine the tendency of narratives (and detectives) to achieve unproblematic control and closure.[12] Moreover, the disaffected, socially alienated detective and the failure of official legal mechanisms to make the necessary corrections are part of a cultural discourse that is disruptive rather than integrative. Anyway, as Scott McCracken argues, the assumption that readers consume crime fiction in order to secure or legitimise their own reactionary social and political views, and by implication are unable to construct politically or culturally transgressive meanings via their own interaction with the text, is more than a little patronising.[13]

A third approach, then, is needed, one influenced by work carried out in cultural studies and cultural materialism and able to acknowledge and unpack some of these ideological complexities. The cultural studies project in Britain, as Jonathan Culler argues, initially set about trying to recover and explore popular culture (as an authentic expression of 'the people') and then collided with European Marxism, which analysed mass, as opposed to popular, culture as ideologically oppressive (or an imposition on 'the people').[14] Black crime fictions, in these terms, might simultaneously give voice to the socially and politically marginalised and yet also re-inscribe a reactionary politics that, in part, informs racially determined relations of domination and subordination. It is our job, therefore, to investigate the resulting tensions – both formal and thematic tensions – and to consider how and whether such tensions are dealt with and closed off, and how and to what extent particular crime novelists, more so than others, bring the kind of competing ideologies already alluded to into messy, violent, unruly patterns that cannot be easily reconciled. In other words, novelists who neither resolve their narratives in neat, contrived ways, nor give their protagonists the kinds of secure, whole identities that enable them to transcend the materiality of their lives.

Certainly Chester Himes – whose so-called Harlem Cycle, a series of novels published initially in France between the late 1950s and late 1960s and featuring two black police detectives, Coffin Ed Johnson and Grave Digger Jones, working in Harlem – stands as an important benchmark in the development of black crime fiction, at least in so far as he immediately grasped the significance of these tensions, particularly in relation to his distinctively 'unheroic' black protagonists who could never hope to transcend the material conditions of racial oppression and discrimination operating on and through them. Inevitably, too, the law which they themselves must enforce is part of the institutionalised superstructure upon which racially-conceived relations of domination–subordination depend. Of course, one of the distinctive features of the hardboiled crime novel has traditionally been the problematic nature of notions like 'law' and 'justice'. Unlike the classical detective fiction of Christie and Sayers where the moral interventions of respectable middle- or upper-class investigators ensured a seamless restoration not just of law and order but also of the entire social structure, American novelists like Dashiell Hammett presented a world so corrupted and violent that their detectives could only ever hope to achieve partial understanding and a flawed, provisional justice. Himes's detective novels are riven with a similar set of complications but the extremity of this disjuncture once it has been mapped on to the canvas of a racially segregated Harlem is so intense that it threatens to shatter the already problematic equilibrium negotiated by the likes of Sam Spade and the Continental Op. This disjuncture also renders Coffin Ed and Grave Digger virtually impotent and incapable of exercising their will except through acts of uncontrolled and undirected rage.

This rage manifests itself, most visibly, in overdetermined moments of grotesque violence whose cumulative effect is to unsettle, if not directly assault, generic conventions and readerly expectations. But to use a boxing idiom, it is more appropriate to conceive of these 'assaults' as tentative jabs rather than roundhouse blows. Certainly much of the criticism on Himes's crime fiction has overlooked the subtlety inherent both in the way he manages to bend, without entirely breaking, the genre's codes and conventions, and in his politically and culturally ambiguous depictions of black culture(s) and identities in the United States. Himes's novels, according to James Sallis, his biographer (and a crime novelist in his own right), have been unfairly written off as 'potboilers' that 'pandered to excessive violence and grotesque characterisations'[15] (or critiqued from within the black community by those who felt that too much of his violence stayed within the ghetto and hence somehow let the dominant white culture off the hook), but his work has also been problematically situated – by Soitos for example – within a culturally vibrant and enabling African-American tradition of letters. And while Himes's crime fictions have been praised by Gary Storhoff for the ways in which they 'radicalised the social and political ideologies concealed by the detective fiction form'[16] they have also been criticised, by Woody Haut for example, for tending 'to be more conservative than they appear'.[17] What none of these positions acknowledges, however, is the artful way in which Himes takes and blends seemingly contradictory generic codes, cultural representations and political ideologies into a body of work that alludes to the possibility of social and generic upheaval and yet simultaneously re-inscribes the logic of a set of repressive discourses which have underpinned, and continue to underpin, racially-determined relations of domination-subordination.

If Himes lands stinging jabs, rather than heavyweight blows, then his targets are not just white racism and the institutional structures that affirm and replicate its logic, or Grave Digger and Coffin Ed's white superiors, or the codes and conventions of a genre shaped by a set of white, male discourses, or complacent white readers, but also reductive (and implicitly essentialist) attempts to pigeon-hole him as a 'black' writer or his black characters as 'positive' or 'empowering' role models or one-dimensional victims of white racism. As Himes himself said:

Maybe it was an unconscious protest against soul brothers always being considered victims of racism, a protest against racism itself excusing all their sins and faults. Black victims of crime and criminals might be foolish and harebrained, but the soul brother criminals were as vicious, cruel and dangerous as any other criminals.[18]

Certainly the task of juggling an array of competing ideas, ideologies and discourses, of drawing upon the traditions of crime fiction while simultaneously exploding them, of highlighting racial injustices in the context of black deviancies, of juxtaposing bitter irony, wild improbable comedy, coruscating social protest and astute political commentary, was a prodigious one. Eventually, perhaps, it grew to be untenable, and in the final (completed) novel in the Harlem Cycle, *Blind Man With a Pistol* (1969), at least some of the various balls that Himes had been trying to keep up in the air throughout the series fell around him. For sure, there is little of the grotesque humour that characterises much of the Cycle, and Coffin Ed and Grave Digger are virtually unrecognisable as the fearsome, albeit conflicted 'ace' detectives from earlier novels. Marginalisation has bred cynicism which has bred self-loathing. Long gone, it seems, is their violent panache and confident swagger. They ride into the novel 'practically unseen, like a ghostly vehicle in the dark, its occupants invisible',[19] and depart it, suspended from the department, firing their famed nickel-plated Colts at rats on a derelict building site. Along the way, they fail to discover who was behind a gruesome multiple stabbing or the murder of a white man, they leave in place a gambling syndicate that seems to implicate their superiors in the department, and they vent their frustrations, to no effect, on a crowd of black protesters, who eventually turn on one another. As the unrest spreads beyond the carefully demarcated borders of Harlem, the generic structures seem to crumble in Himes's hands, and the novel concludes not with some attempt to shore up its defences but rather with a blind man firing a pistol wildly and indiscriminately at people on a crowded subway car. Given the context for the novel, Harlem at the butt end of the sixties when black protest had fragmented and turned in on itself, the symbolic register of a black man firing a pistol in a crowded subway car has obvious resonance. Still, after such a dénouement, there didn't seem to be anywhere else Himes could go, at least within the genre. The fact that his follow-up novel, *Plan B*, an even bleaker tale in which his two protagonists finally turn on each other, was never finished is perhaps revealing.

Keen to implicate the generically radical with the politically radical, *Blind Man With a Pistol* has been praised by James Sallis and Gilbert Muller, among others, as the culmination or crowning achievement of his work as a crime writer,[20] and certainly the marginalisation of his two detectives, and the rage it produces, finds its most radical articulation in this final novel. But it is also something of an anomaly in the Cycle, a novel that takes Himes and the reader down a generic dead-end and short-circuits the genre's key structuring tension – to use Culler's phrase, the genre as expression *of* the people and imposition *on* the people – and diffuses it into a politics of nihilism and despair.

A more fitting culmination to the Cycle might be its penultimate instalment, *Cotton Comes to Harlem* (1964), in which Coffin Ed and Grave Digger hunt down the armed robbers who have made off with $87,000 collected from poor black families by the Back to Africa movement. Taking stock at the start of the novel, referring both to the robbery and, more generally, to the despair and anger that stalks the black residents of Harlem, Coffin Ed declares, barely able to contain his own bitterness:

> We've got the highest crime rate on earth among the colored people in Harlem. And there ain't but three things to do about it: Make the criminals pay for it – you don't want to do that; pay the people enough to live decently – you ain't going to do that; so all that's left is let 'em eat one another up.[21]

In such a world, 'crime' is symptomatic of a much deeper racial malaise, a violent, obscene tearing of the social fabric rather than a set of incidents to be investigated and rationalised, and capitulation to the kind of nihilism that stalks the final pages of *Blind Man With a Pistol* seems inevitable, especially given the almost monotonous list of daily horrors that pass under Himes's detectives' noses. 'Man kills his wife with an axe for burning his pork chop . . . man stabs another man for spilling beer on his suit . . . woman stabs man in stomach, no reason given . . . woman scalds neighboring woman with a pot of boiling water for speaking to her husband'.[22] Capitulation might seem inevitable, too, given their precarious position in the police department and the discrimination they have to endure. Neither Coffin Ed nor Grave Digger are immune from the kind of violence that is born of anger and frustration and, in their case, assumes a misogynistic nature. In one incident, for example, Grave Digger slaps an unco-operative informant 'with such sudden violence . . . she went sprawling on her hands and knees; her dress hiked up showing black lace pants above the creamy yellow skin of her thighs',[23] while Coffin Ed is 'a fraction of a second' away from crushing the same woman's windpipe when Grave Digger intervenes. Without doubt, there is a disturbing relationship, here, between male violence and female sexual objectification, but Manthia Diawara makes the point that Himes's portrayal of male-on-female violence is best understood not as a strategy designed to shore up a set of masculinities 'in crisis' but rather as another expression of black rage – 'a savage explosion on the part of some characters against others whom they seek to control, and a perverse mimicry of the status quo through recourse to disfigurement, mutilation, and a grotesque positioning of weaker characters by stronger ones'.[24]

Still, capitulation to the consuming nihilism of a dog-eat-dog anger is not, in the end, inevitable. Instead it runs up against another set of discourses that shape Coffin Ed and Grave Digger not as black men but as detectives or, rather, as black detectives. Though stretched to near breaking point, Himes's detectives manage to retain some sense of what this role or function stands for; hence their awareness that the extent of social injustice in Harlem cannot be used as an excuse for abjuring their duties as police officers, even when they come face-to-face with the robbery's prime suspect:

> Coffin Ed drew back to hit him but Grave Digger caught his arm. "Easy, Ed," he said. "Easy on this mother-raping scum?" Coffin Ed raved. "Easy on this incestuous sister-raping thief?"
> "We're cops," Grave Digger reminded him. "Not judges."
> Coffin Ed restrained himself. "The law was made to protect the innocent," he said.
> Grave Digger chuckled. "You heard the man," he said to Deke.[25]

The complexity of this exchange is all the more remarkable because of its compression, because what it means is left open for the reader to determine. Ed's rage is initially set against Digger's calmness but later on Ed's restraint and his defence of the law is unsettled by Digger's chuckle. But does Ed really believe the law was made to protect the innocent and is Digger's chuckle an attempt to further diffuse the situation or a hollow, bitter reaction, an implicit recognition of the validity of Ed's anger? Or is Ed merely justifying his own attack on the suspect on the grounds that he is guilty and hence undeserving of the law's protection? In which case, Digger's reaction could just be re-establishing solidarity with him, as long as the threats remain verbal not physical. Storhoff argues that the Harlem Cycle is best understood as a series of violent 'assaults' – on and by Himes's 'ace' detectives; on notions of order and coherence; on the codes and conventions of the genre; and particularly on the white reader.[26] This motif works to a point but, ultimately, it denies the subtlety of what is going on here. Himes is not 'assaulting' the reader (white or black) but rather forcing him or her into an active interpretative role. Against a backdrop of a city sliding towards racial apocalypse, readers must decide whether Ed and Digger are part of the problem or part of the solution, or indeed neither.

Faced by a situation in which an angry mob of Back to Africa supporters who have lost their money in the robbery run into a group known as Back to Southland, trying to recruit people to join a plantation-style regime based in

Alabama, a full-scale race riot beckons. At which point, Ed and Digger step in and defuse the tension using wry humour backed up by violent intent; so much so that we are told the 'white cops looked at [them] with the envious awe usually reserved for a lion tamer with a cage of big cats'.[27] But what to make of it – whether their actions constitute a 'victory' for black power over white racism or suggest that some kind of enabling racial solidarity might emerge – is not clear, especially since their intervention is overshadowed by their boss's decision to 'arrest every black son of a bitch in Harlem'[28] and prefigures their growing marginalisation within the department. Anyway, the idea that blackness operates as a trope of sameness connecting different people across time and space has already been exploded, at the start of the novel, by the implicit suggestion that the Back to Africa movement is a fraudulent organisation based on an untenable premise. As a character in Walter Mosley's *A Red Death* (1991) says, referring to a related organisation, 'I cain't see how them Africans could take kindly t'no American Negro. We been away too long, man. Too long.'[29]

Comparisons between Himes and Walter Mosley, a writer who entered the genre more than twenty years after Himes had departed it, simply on the grounds of a shared ethnic and national background, are both inevitable and, to some extent, problematic. Mosley himself is keen to distance himself from such a comparison, asserting that 'even though [Himes] wrote crime, I'm entering the genre in a different way'.[30] Unlike Himes, he grew up in the shadow of Civil Rights and perhaps as a reflection, his fiction is gentler, less polemical, the product of a more conciliatory era. Certainly his writing has gained the kind of mainstream recognition that Himes never achieved; the seal of approval bestowed on his work by Bill Clinton only augmented this appeal. Furthermore, the very act of focusing upon and therefore privileging these two novelists implicitly, and quite wrongly, suggests that Mosley re-activated a form or sub-genre that had lain dormant since Himes's departure. Still, while much has changed during the twenty years that separates Himes's departure from, and Mosley's arrival into, the genre, much has also stayed the same; black Americans are entering the middle classes in rapidly increasing numbers but a significant underclass also still exists; 'new' immigrant arrivals from Asia and Latin America have transformed the physical and cultural landscape of the United States but racial-ethnic divisions based on 'old' cleavages remain endemic. To this end, and not least because both writers have arguably made the most significant, innovative contributions to this particular sub-genre, comparisons are both inevitable and potentially revealing. One should not forget, too, that Mosley's five crime novels, featuring surrogate detective Ezekiel 'Easy' Rawlins, are set in Los Angeles between the end of the Second World War and the start of the 1960s, a period that both predates and overlaps with the implied 'present' of Himes's Harlem Cycle.

Compared to Himes, who operates in a much tighter hardboiled frame and whose fiction is more of a challenge to, than a continuation, of a tradition of African-American letters, it is tempting to treat Mosley's work as part of the ongoing project of re-writing and re-claiming the previously lost stories of black Americans themselves; as documents of what it was like to be poor, black and living in Los Angeles in the twenty years following the end of the Second World War; as testaments to the vitality and richness of black writing and music; and as novels which set out to debunk 'official' (white European) discourses and unsettle existing power structures. Mosley's use of a 'blues' idiom throughout his work is a reminder that African-American culture is not a knee-jerk reaction to white racism but rather a complex, sophisticated blending of European- and African-American discourses in which the hegemonic aspects of the former are, in part, reconstituted as counter-hegemonic affirmations of an enabling black culture. Using a distinctive black dialect, for example, connects Rawlins to a collective, though by no means unitary past and encourages him to reject demeaning, externally imposed identities. As Rawlins says, 'I could only truly express myself in the natural, uneducated dialect of my upbringing.'[31] The blues, to this end, is not just a type of music, but a subversive and thoroughgoing African-American expressive form, and Mosley's fiction, shaped in its image, describes the experiences, and voices the concerns, of those people the blues speaks about and to: poor blacks who struggle in different ways to navigate a path through a hostile, white capitalist world without losing a sense of who they are and where they have come from. When Rawlins wanders along Bones Street in Los Angeles, listening to the sounds drifting out of the bars, or hears Lips McGee blowing wildly into his horn, Mosley is reminding us of the rich tradition of blues music that continues to give meaning to black American lives. As Rawlins remarks, 'That horn spoke the language of my history; travelled me back to times that I could no longer remember clearly – maybe even times that were older than I; travelling in my blood, back to some forgotten home.'[32]

The past is not just a locus of enabling black signifiers, though. Understood in its wider American context, it is also satiated with the logic of chattel slavery and a long and bloody history of racial discrimination. This is a logic and history which Liam Kennedy, in an essay on Mosley's fiction in Peter Messent's *Criminal Proceedings*, argues, shapes and limits the contours of Rawlins's identity, and forces him to act in ways that unsettle and ultimately damage the utopian possibilities implicit in the kind of oral or vernacular tradition that Mosley is writing out of.[33] Rawlins may prefer the comforting anonymity of the margins, may prefer to attain agency through the minutiae of everyday life – the sanctity of home, the joys of family and friendship, the satisfaction of honest work – but his ability to do so, to live on his own terms, is constantly under threat. In *Devil in a Blue Dress* (1990), he loses his job; in *A Red Death* his home and business are taken from him, and in *White Butterfly* (1992) he must help the police in order to 'win' his family's freedom. To this end, it is the will to survive that motivates him, rather than a vaguely articulated desire to do what is right. Which is not to say that he is morally bankrupt; just that as a black man subject to the injustices of living in a hostile white-controlled world, he is forced to compromise any kind of moral 'code' simply in order to remain alive.

Certainly Rawlins's ability to operate as an individualist detective is undermined by the consequences of racism. Unlike Raymond Chandler's Phillip Marlowe who works alone and prefers it that way, Rawlins cannot function as a detective without the support and protection of friends like Mouse, who anyway pours scorn on the white myth of 'lone hero'. 'That's just a lie them white men give 'bout makin' it on they own', he tells Rawlins. 'They always got they backs covered.'[34] Perversely, however, Rawlins, in order to survive himself, is forced to act in ways that damage and compromise the very things he relies upon and values – like family, community, and friendship. The end of *A Little Yellow Dog* (1996), where Rawlins's self-interest and carelessness lead directly to Mouse's bloody death, seems, therefore, to be a fitting climax to the series. One wonders whether Mosley will ever return to chart Rawlins's passage into old age.

Neither powerful nor powerless, Rawlins and the other black characters in Mosley's fiction struggle to carve out a small slice of the good life for themselves – and often fail. In the same way, the novels' various black neighbourhoods, though poor and in places dangerous, are not represented as unremittingly bleak ghettos. Despite the dangers that confront Rawlins when he traverses the city, he remains captivated by its physical beauty – the fluffy white clouds making their way across pool-blue skies towards the snow-capped San Bernadino mountains – and for everywhere like Ricardo's bar, 'the kind of place you could get killed in'[35] – there are other places like John's, where black working-class men and women go to drink, gossip, laugh, fight and listen to music. It is here, too, that Mosley's social portraiture and racial politics collide. Rawlins is, simultaneously, an attractive figure, someone who is able to exercise a degree of autonomy despite the restrictions imposed upon him by the agencies of white power, and a slippery, self-serving fixer whose actions often have dire consequences for those closest to him. Similarly, Mosley portrays the wider black community in ways that both foreground the immense pride that many of his bla acters take in being 'black' and in the achievements of black culture yet acknowledge that both blackness and whiteness are best understood in multiple, fragmented, and *non*-mutually exclusive terms.

In other words, mapped onto the moral complexities of Rawlins's character is a portrait of Los Angeles in which the depth and extent of racial divisions neither secures black – and white – identities as fixed and homogeneous, nor obscures the numerous ways in which ethnic, class, religious and regional 'traces' rub up against and unsettle the kind of binary system upon which racial divisions ultimately depend. Differences of skin colour, of social class, of regional background and religious affiliation unsettle attempts to forge unproblematic links between Mosley's various black characters, while references throughout his novels to white, Mexican and Jewish working-class suffering as understood by African-Americans and vice versa serve to underline areas of common ground. Jewish characters like Chaim Wenzler in *A Red Death* and Abe and Johnny in *Devil in a Blue Dress* are either Holocaust survivors themselves or understand the suffering endured by Jews in the Nazi death camps and, by implication, black Americans living in a racist, discriminatory society. As a corollary, it should be noted that attempts to equate these experiences run up dead against a comment made by Jackson Blue in *A Red Death* about McCarthyite discrimination. Describing a list circulating in the business community naming blacks *and* Jews to be excluded from the workplace, Jackson makes the point that this kind of common experience does not, in the end, lessen the lasting significance of 'race' or, rather, race as a social construction:

> One day they gonna th'ow that list out, man. They gonna need some movie star or some new bomb an' they gonna th'ow that list away . . . But you still gonna be a black niggah, Easy. An' niggah ain't got no politician gonna work fo' him. All he got is a do'step t'shit in and a black hand t'wipe his black ass.[36]

Plot, for Mosley, is something of a Trojan horse, a containing structure that is arguably less interesting than what it conceals; less interesting than his rich portrait of a black American community and protagonist undergoing subtle but significant transformation. Moreover, in so far as all of his Rawlins novels (to date) revolve around a missing persons investigation, they tend to be, formally, more conservative than Himes's Harlem Cycle. In this regard, James Sallis is perhaps a more appropriate generic descendent of Himes, and certainly his five (to date) crime novels featuring black American private eye, Lew Griffin, are among the most formally innovative to be found in the contemporary genre. *The Long Legged Fly* (1992), *Moth* (1993), *Black Hornet* (1996), *Eye of the Cricket* (1997) and *Bluebottle* (1999) move quickly from familiar into unfamiliar terrain; a missing persons investigation in *The*

*Long Legged Fly* reaches an apparently successful conclusion when Griffin finds a black civil rights activist in a Louisiana sanatorium but he has no idea what drove her there; another investigation, in the same novel only four years later, ends in failure when the object of his search is murdered, again without real explanation; another has a bittersweet conclusion when Griffin finds the woman he's been asked to track down but has to tell her that her father has been killed in an apparently motiveless assault; and in yet another Griffin's own son disappears, only to turn up again – and disappear – in a later novel. Challenging the traditional structures of the form, Sallis's novels have no real beginning and no real end. His stories, like a blues or a jazz riff, are told and re-told, each variation similar but also different. Past, present and future merge; the future is reflected in the past and played out in the present.

The search for knowledge, or at least rational explanations – explanations that might reveal what drove the black civil rights activist in *The Long Legged Fly* into a sanatorium or what compelled a mixed race sniper in *Black Hornet* to kill people at random – is always limited and provisional in Sallis's work. Still, though nothing is ever clear-cut, connections do, perhaps, exist between these conditions, between the rage that, in part, underpins the sniper's actions and relates to his abandonment by a white father, and the self-hate that causes the black civil rights worker to bleach her skin. These feelings are ones that Griffin well understands – perverse, or to use Himes's term 'absurd', expressions of what it is like to be black American living in the kind of society where the casual beatings handed out by white police officers and vigilantes replicate, albeit in an infinitesimal way, the practices of institutions or even governments. Seen in this light, the incidents that Griffin is called upon to investigate, the people who have gone missing or been killed, are not disruptions to the status quo but rather are the status quo. Griffin's function as a black private eye, then, seems clear; as Ralph Willett observes, he can do no more than 'prevent individuals, including himself, from sinking into an abyss of drink, self-loathing and despair that terminates in death or madness'.[37]

Capitulation to alcoholism, despair and self-hate is not an inevitability, though. Survival tactics adopted by black Americans throughout the history of the United States, practices of signifying or mimicry, have exacted considerable damage, not least because having to wear masks, to see oneself through someone else's eyes and talk using their language is potentially alienating. As Griffin laments, 'That same masking remains in many of us, in their children's blood, a slow poison. So many of us no longer know who or what we are'.[38] To this end, Sallis is more sanguine than Soitos about the subversive possibilities inherent in the figure of the black detective. Like Himes and Mosley, he seems to implicitly acknowledge that survival rather than revolution is the ultimate goal. Still, double-consciousness, for Sallis, does also have positive connotations at least in so far as 'signifyin(g)', to use Gates's term, implicitly suggests the transformation of that which is being 'signified' or transformed into something that is culturally distinctive, something African-American, something that eludes white control. 'We're all tricksters', Griffin declares, more optimistically, in *Bluebottle*. 'We have to be. Dissembling, signifying, masking – you only think you have a hold on us, tar babies all.'[39]

The burden of double consciousness – recognised by W. E. B. Du Bois when he remarked in 1903, 'It is a peculiar sensation, this sense of always looking at one's self through the eyes of others, of measuring one's soul by the tape of a world that looks on in amused contempt and pity',[40] – is similarly voiced and also reconfigured in Barbara Neely's work: a series of novels featuring Blanche White, a plump, middle-aged African-American maid and amateur sleuth. The fact that Blanche's identity, in the eyes of her wealthy employers, is that of a cipher, a simpering Mammy figure whose function is to serve, may signify her lowly status and foreground the power relations that underpin such hierarchies, but 'signifyin(g)' also has a progressive meaning in so far as wearing masks is but one of the tactics that Blanche uses to outwit her employers. As someone for whom 'reading people and signs, and sizing up situations, were as much a part of her work as scrubbing floors and making beds',[41] Blanche is well versed in the practice of what Soitos calls 'double-consciousness detection'[42] and her invisibility in the eyes of her employers affords her the space and opportunity to turn her ratiocinative powers towards uncovering the web of murder and blackmail in which she, inevitably, finds herself implicated.

Yet just how radical this practice is, within the scheme of Neely's fiction, is open to question, and one could argue that her subversive political agenda is undermined by formal conventionality. Certainly Neely has mapped the fragmented, divisive racial and class politics of contemporary America on to a generic form that owes as much to Agatha Christie as it does to Dashiell Hammett. In *Blanche on the Lam* (1992), Blanche's movements from New York to rural North Carolina both reaffirm and undermine the logic of this shift. The clearly signalled association of the rural South with the practices of the Klan and the brutal suppression of the black population constitutes a radical departure from the conventions of the country house form, but the very fact that the crime and investigation take place in a self-contained world acts as a kind of screen, distancing the narrative, detective and reader from

such problems. The secure, ordered world promised by the kind (
lematic resolutions achieved in *Blanche on the Lam* is, of course, at
with the novel's racial politics, whereby the social hierarchies and power
relations are constantly being unsettled. Perhaps all one can really say is that
how these resolutions are interpreted, whether Blanche's 'triumphs' unproblematically re-inscribe the status quo or whether they suggest that 'success'
for poor blacks in the United States will always be limited and conditional,
depends as much on the politics of the reader as it does on the politics of
the author. Certainly, the mediating presence of a black female voice at the
heart of the narrative inevitably diffuses the impression of misogyny that
stalks the margins of black crime fiction in general. Currently, too, Neely is
but one name on a growing list of black female crime writers; a list which
also includes Nikki Baker, Elizabeth Taylor Bland, Charlotte Carter, Penny
Mickelberry, and Valerie Wilson Wesley.

The emergence, first of all of Mosley and then Sallis and Neely, from out
of Himes's shadow has reflected and anticipated two related situations: the
growing voice and visibility not just of African-American but also Latino
and Asian-American novelists in the genre (and in Britain black Caribbean
writers like Mike Phillips), and the ongoing transformation of national and
ethnic identities in the wake of changing immigration patterns, demographics
and inter- or intra-group relationships. Phillips, in particular, is interested in
the ways in which the diasporic identities of his protagonists, notably Sam
Dean (a black British journalist with family in the Caribbean and New York
City who features in most, if not all, of Phillips's crime writing[43]) overlap
with but also elide fixed national, ethnic and class definitions. The subversive
or utopian possibilities of such new configurations, alliances and identities
are alluded to but, as in the work of Himes, Mosley, Neely and Sallis, rub
against the reactionary tendencies embedded in the genre. In the end, their
fiction and characters are manifestations of an at times bewildering mixture
of attitudes, ideologies, politics and ambitions; moving between hegemonic
and counter- hegemonic positions, their detectives consciously subvert the
values of a dominant, white culture while simultaneously securing its not so
fluid boundaries. Overlapping and yet diverging cleavages of ethnicity, class
and gender further unsettle the cultural landscape, and in so far as the gaze of
'other eyes' does not and cannot bring the attendant tensions into clear-cut
resolution, these writers, both collectively and individually, portray a world
on the verge of violent disintegration. ⁃ *as docs orig. H.R fic*

These detectives, then, are unable to transcend their circumstances, the
materiality of their lives, in the same way as their generic predecessors, or at
least the more overtly heroic figures like Chandler's Marlowe. Yet damage

does not correspond with defeat and while their visions are by no means optimistic, nor are they resolutely apocalyptic. Neither utopian nor dystopian, their crime fictions may not be what bell hooks describes as 'radical postmodernist practice' (that which substantially re-configures relations between 'centre' and 'margin').[44] What emerges, instead, is a portrait of the United States beset by bitter racial, ethnic, class and gender conflict, nonetheless able to contemplate a present and future where 'difference' can be acknowledged and where traditional relations of domination–subordination can be, if not overturned, then at least unsettled.

## NOTES

1 For a fuller version of these arguments, see my own *The Contemporary American Crime Novel: Race, Ethnicity, Gender, Class* (Edinburgh: Edinburgh University Press, 2000).

2 In this chapter I use the term 'black' or 'black American' rather than 'African-American' except where the latter term has been employed by critics or novelists I am referring to (e.g. Soitos). This is because (i) it tends to be a term favoured by writers themselves; (ii) the term 'African-American' fails to acknowledge the 'diasporic' nature of black identities and, indeed, the extent to which black identities in the US are being recast by the arrival of significant numbers of Caribbean immigrants since 1965; and (ii) though I refer, mainly, to American examples, the term 'African-American' is not appropriate for discussing the concurrent development of black crime fiction in the UK and elsewhere. 'Black', moreover, is not used to suggest a homogeneous culture or identity but rather one defined in terms of its heterogeneity.

3 Kwame Anthony Appiah, 'Race', in Frank Lentricchia and Thomas McLaughlin, ed., *Critical Terms for Literary Study* (Chicago and London: Chicago University Press, 1987), p. 277.

4 Howard Wincant, 'Dictatorship, Democracy and Difference: The Historical Construction of Racial Identity', in Michael Peter Smith and Joe R. Feagin, eds., *The Bubbling Cauldron: Race, Ethnicity and the Urban Crisis* (Minneapolis: University of Minnesota Press, 1995), p. 31.

5 See Stephen Soitos, *The Blues Detective: A Study of African American Detective Fiction* (Amherst, MA: University of Massachusetts Press, 1996).

6 Michael Eric Dyson, 'Essentialism and the Complexities of Racial Identity', in David Theo Goldberg, ed., *Multiculturalism: A Reader* (Oxford and Cambridge, MT: Blackwell, 1992), p. 221.

7 See Henry Louis Gates Jr, *The Signifying Monkey: A Theory of Afro-American Literary Criticism* (Oxford and New York: Oxford University Press, 1988).

8 See Houston A. Baker, *Blues, Ideology and Afro-American Literature: A Vernacular Theory* (Chicago: University of Chicago Press, 1984).

9 See Soitos, *The Blues Detective*, pp. 27–51.

10 See Stephen Knight, *Form and Ideology in Crime Fiction* (London: Macmillan, 1980); Dennis Porter, *The Pursuit of Crime: Art and Ideology in Detective Fiction* (New Haven, CT: Yale University Press, 1981); Ernest Mandel,

*Delightful Murder: A Social History of the Crime Novel* (London: Pluto, 1999).

11 Paul Cobley, *The American Thriller: Generic Innovation and Social Change in the 1970s* (Basingstoke: Palgrave, 2000), p. 137.

12 Jim Collins, *Uncommon Cultures: Popular Culture and Post-modernism* (London and New York: Routledge, 1989), p. 34.

13 See Scott McCracken, *Pulp: Reading Popular Fiction* (Manchester and New York: Manchester University Press, 1996).

14 Jonathan Culler, *Literary Theory: A Very Short Introduction* (Oxford and New York: Oxford University Press, 2000), p. 42–3.

15 James Sallis, *Difficult Lives: Jim Thompson, David Goodis, Chester Himes* (New York: Gryphon Books, 1993), p. 74.

16 Gary Storhoff, 'Aggravating the Reader: The Harlem Detective Novels of Chester Himes,' in Jerome H. Delamater and Ruth Prigozy, eds., *The Detective in American Film, Fiction and Television* (Westport, CT: Greenwood Press, 1998), p. 46.

17 Woody Haut, *Pulp Culture: Hardboiled Fiction and the Cold War* (London: Serpent's Tail, 1995), p. 46.

18 Chester Himes, *My Life of Absurdity: The Autobiography of Chester Himes* (New York: Doubleday, 1976), vol. 2, p. 111.

19 Chester Himes, *Blind Man With a Pistol* (1969; London: Allison and Busby, 1986), p. 33.

20 Gilbert H. Muller, *Chester Himes* (Boston: Twayne, 1989), p. 105.

21 Chester Himes, *Cotton Comes to Harlem* (1964; London: Allison and Busby, 1988), p. 14.

22 *Ibid.*, p. 14.

23 *Ibid.*, p. 24.

24 Manthia Diawara, 'Noir by Noirs: Towards a New Realism in Black Cinema', in Joan Copjec, ed., *Shades of Noir: A Reader* (London and New York: Verso, 1993), p. 266.

25 Himes, *Cotton Comes to Harlem*, p. 97.

26 Storhoff, 'Aggravating the Reader' p. 47.

27 Himes, *Cotton Comes to Harlem*, p. 116.

28 *Ibid.*, p. 120.

29 Walter Mosley, *A Red Death* (1991; London: Serpent's Tail, 1992), p. 215.

30 Walter Mosley in Paul Duncan, ed., *The Third Degree: Crime Writers in Conversation* (Harpenden, Herts: No Exit Press, 1997), p. 150.

31 Walter Mosley, *Devil in a Blue Dress* (1990; London: Serpent's Tail, 1991), p. 17.

32 Walter Mosley, *A Little Yellow Dog* (1996; London: Picador, 1997), p. 152.

33 Liam Kennedy, 'Black Noir: Race and Urban Space in Walter Mosley's Detective Fiction' in Peter Messent, ed., *Criminal Proceedings: The Contemporary American Crime Novel* (London: Pluto Press, 1997), p. 50.

34 Mosley, *Devil in a Blue Dress*, p. 158.

35 *Ibid.*, p. 129.

36 Moseley, *A Red Death*, p. 230.

37 Ralph Willett, *The Naked City: Urban Crime Fiction in the USA* (Manchester and New York: Manchester University Press, 1996), p. 126.

38 James Sallis, *Bluebottle* (Harpenden, Herts: No Exit Press, 1999), p. 24.

39  *Ibid.*, p. 92.
40  W. E. B. Du Bois, *The Souls of Black Folk* (New York: Dover, 1994), p. 2.
41  Barbara Neely, *Blanche on the Lam* (1992; New York: Penguin, 1994), p. 3.
42  Soitos, *The Blues Detective* , pp. 33–7.
43  See, for example, *Point of Darkness* (London: Penguin, 1995) or *An Image to Die For* (London: Harper Collins, 1995).
44  bell hooks, *Yearning: Race, Gender and Cultural Politics* (London: Turnaround, 1991), p. 27.

# 13

NICKIANNE MOODY

# Crime in film and on TV

One of the decisive steps in developing narrative cinema took place through
the realisation of a dramatic crime on screen. Edwin S. Porter's commercial
success with *The Great Train Robbery* (1903) rests on his understanding of
a variety of different genres whilst bending and extending their conventions
in order to produce something new and exciting. Moreover, this was a narrative experience which was very much in keeping with the headlines of the
day. His film is often thought of as the beginning of the Western genre, but
it is the crime that provides the narrative impetus. This chapter will look
at films and television programmes which foreground crime and detection
relying on mystery and adventure archetypes, but it acknowledges that during the twentieth century crime features in practically all commercial genres.
Therefore, the choice of films and television programmes focuses on transitions in the representation of crime and detection on screen as a means to
understand the determinants of these changes.

*The Great Train Robbery* ends with the leader of the bandits facing the
camera and firing into the audience. The technical achievement that excites
film critics is an early style of parallel editing which tentatively suggests the
simultaneity of the events taking place.[1] Within ten minutes (it was one
of the longest films of its day) the audience are taken from the telegraph
office, to the train and its journey, the events of the hold up, the dance hall
where the posse is rounded up and then on the pursuit itself. The emphasis,
however, is upon the execution of the crime and the apprehension of the
criminals. Significantly the film was advertised as a re-enactment, and claims
for authenticity have continued to be a vital aspect of screen crime narrative.[2]

Charles Musser argues that Porter was influenced by the violent crime
genre imported from England during 1903 and he connects it to Sheffield
Photo's *Daring Daylight Burglary*, Walter Haggar's *Desperate Poaching
Affray* and R. W. Paul's *Trailed by Bloodhounds*.[3] The British film industry
soon learnt to play it safe in its representation of crime, relying on comedy
and well-established detective figures to defuse critical or unsettling crime

227

narratives. Christopher Redmond identifies *Sherlock Holmes Baffled* (1900), made for viewing on a peep-show machine, as the earliest example of a trend which for twenty years treats the great detective as a figure of fun.[4] D. W. Griffith, the film director who completes Porter's experiments with editing, made several Holmes comedies between 1911 and 1912 featuring Mack Sennett. A more serious treatment of Holmes is found in the adaptation of William Gillette's immensely popular 1899 play *Sherlock Holmes* for the screen in 1916. The success of the film led Maurice Elvey to direct a full length version of *The Hound of the Baskervilles* (1921) which is significant because it was followed by a series of over twenty-five shorter films continuing the pairing of Eille Norwood as Holmes and Hubert Willis as Watson. These films were remarkably faithful to the stories. Together the stars tackled individual cases in thirty-five-minute films which were ideal for cinema programmes. They were just as popular as the Basil Rathbone series of films made by Twentieth Century Fox during the 1940s which made the actor an iconic Sherlock Holmes.

Censorship for British and North American films in the inter-war period had very different presuppositions and this directly affects the representation of crime on screen. Film censorship in Britain was supervised by the Home Office and enforced by the British Board of Film Censors. From initial legislation in 1912 the Board gradually consolidated its power. According to Nicholas Pronay and Jeremy Croft, its operation was 'far-reaching, comprehensive and systematic and it imposed strict limitations upon what film-makers could show or tell the public through the potentially inspiring, inflammatory and powerful medium of the cinema'.[5] The government was interested in film as a medium of communication both before and after the war because social surveys had shown that regular film-goers were drawn from lower income and less educated social groups, particularly the urban working class. Such an effective level of censorship was achieved voluntarily, thanks to the board's power to grant exhibition licences. By the early 1930s the list of grounds upon which a film could be refused a certificate took the form of a list of ninety 'don'ts' classified into nine categories which included the administration of justice and the representation of crime as well as depictions of violence. Film-makers conformed to these restrictions because they could not afford any delay in gaining their exhibition licence and recouping production costs. Commercial film-making in Britain has always been precariously financed and insolvency a very real threat. Therefore, the depictions of blackmail, embezzlement, violence, adultery and abduction that spice up the social comedies and dramas of high society in North American silent films remained largely untouched by British film-makers. By the late silent era North American film had already begun to associate crime with the city and establish the social problem genre which gives a sense of particular modernity and realism to US sound films.

Censorship in North America also determined the depiction of crime in the cinema, but had a different cultural context. Debate about censorship of the film industry was prompted by the same concerns as in Britain. Various government and public authorities believed that audiences needed to be protected from unwholesome influences. Moreover, Kevin Brownlow's detailed consideration of this period makes it clear that there was a definite belief that censorship would ensure the continuation of law-abiding behaviour.[6] The body set up to control the scandal-ridden film industry in 1922, The Motion Picture Producers and Distributors of America Inc (MPPDA), held no legal standing but imposed self-censorship and a mechanism for dealing with transgressions. Headed by Will H. Hays, MPPDA was set up to control film employees as well as their products and to bring the industry into good professional standing. The Hays Code also comprised 'don'ts' and 'be carefuls' but stars were also obliged to accept moral clauses in their contracts. A report for the National Committee for the Study of Social Values in Motion Pictures published in 1928 characterised MPPDA's aims as being 'to establish and maintain the highest possible moral and artistic standards of motion picture production and to develop the educational as well as the entertainment value and general usefulness of the motion picture'.[7]

Nevertheless it is within the US silent period that the beginnings of the gangster cycle can be found. Crime appears in North American film because it claims moral and educational imperatives or connections with events of the day, a pattern repeated by the British social problem films of the 1950s. The US film industry in the 1910s throve on fictionalisations of court cases and famous crimes whereas British censorship regulations were ambivalent if not opposed to representing living persons on screen. Brownlow sees the origins of the 'underworld' film in D. W. Griffith's *The Musketeers of Pig Alley* (1912). In *The Biograph Bulletin* for the month of release the claim is made that the film shows 'vividly the doings of the gangster type of people'.[8] *The Wages of Sin* (1913) caused a great deal of controversy for the existing National Board of Censorship because it re-enacted a notorious murder associated with illegal gambling by featuring the 'gangsters' involved. *Into the Net* (1924) also had a real life endorsement as the screenplay was based on a story written by the Police Commissioner of New York. It focused on the White Slave Trade and the police force's apprehension of a gang kidnapping young women in Long Island. Despite these antecedents it is generally the commercial success of Josef von Sternberg's *Underworld* in 1927 which is seen as the start of representations of powerful gangsters. Up until this point, according to Brownlow, criminals were depicted as 'reassuringly disorganised, under constant attack from vigilant cops, liable to turn informer at any moment, their criminal activities restricted to a little mild burglary'.[9] In the 1910s, the police in film narratives oscillated between comic buffoons and detective heroes, with various city forces such as Detroit issuing their own list of film guidelines, which insisted upon moral endings to films featuring crime and preventing knowledge of criminal practices being shown to impressionable audiences.[10] *Underworld* establishes new dilemmas but, as Brownlow is quick to point out, the power and glamour of the gangster already had its narrative realisation in *The Penalty* (1920). *Underworld* is significant because it complicates the crime narrative by presenting it from the gangster's point of view. Despite sentimental moments, the film established the violence and immediacy of the screen gangster's world during the 1930s and confirmed its box office potential.

Profits for all the major US studios plummeted after the Wall Street crash. Warner Brothers were particularly hard hit with profits of $17.2 million in 1929 which fell to $7 million in 1930 and an eventual deficit of $7.9 million in 1931.[11] Warner Brothers, however, had two of the top grossing box office successes of 1931, *Little Caesar* and *Public Enemy*. From these two films in particular the studio consolidated a crime formula which kept it solvent and influential throughout the decade. The start of the Warners gangster cycle is *Doorway to Hell* (1930), modelled on the life story of Al Capone (actually arrested in 1931), which emphasises the young criminal's attempts to go straight and his execution by his peers. The film concentrates on the relationship between the city environment, crime and ways of managing the aspirational rise of the gangster before taking up a position of moral censorship, calling for the punishment of the outlaw. To explain this duality Andrew Bergman refers to *Little Caesar* as a 'success tragedy' conforming to the nineteenth-century ideals of the self-made man in a dramatically contemporary setting, thus sustaining wish-fulfilment in popular fiction without making it appear nostalgic.[12] *Little Caesar*, *Public Enemy* and *Scarface*, made a year later by Howard Hughes, all explore the criminal mind. They respond directly to the major issues of public debate and the popular imagination by addressing realistic and contemporary subjects in the life of the American city during the depression. Nick Roddick sees these films as using crime to give 'dramatic focus to the fairly ordinary problems or aspirations – poverty, unemployment, sexual inadequacy, alienation, ambition and greed' which are then construed as criminal motivations which resonate with modern industrial society.[13]

After the success of *Little Caesar*, over fifty other gangster films were made by Hollywood studios in the first half of the decade. They excited growing calls for censorship because it was felt that they showed disrespect for law enforcement and glorified the gangster.[14] Will Hays chose not to respond to these concerns for several years, stating 'the insistent message that "crime does not pay" as flashed from the screen is the most forceful proof of the success of self-regulation in the motion picture industry'.[15] The experimentation of early gangster films therefore soon became 'the dominant form of conventional realism' in Hollywood cinema, but they achieved this through their relationship with other types of narrative reinforcing the moral ambiguity of crime as a response to the depression.[16]

Warner Brothers as a studio is also well known for its social problem films, which became an important part of their corporate image and a means of delivery for thrilling yet morally contained narratives. These films emphasise that social problems are the root of crime, but whilst dwelling on environment and injustice they maintain material wealth and social status as approved social goals. The prison films of the early 1930s – *Weary River* (1929), *Numbered Men* (1930), *20,000 Years in Sing Sing* (1933), *The Mayor of Hell* (1933) and the most well-known and ambiguous example of the genre, *I Am a Fugitive From a Chain Gang* (1932) – represent crime in a manner that contributes to the gangster cycle. They investigate the criminal via the issues of rehabilitation, personal honour, the extremes of social status in Depression America and an enclosed world of criminality. In building up this representation of the criminal environment, these films are connected to two other groups. The 'shyster' films of this early period identified by Bergman do not just deal with the world of the lawyer but locate the intersections between crime and respectability within politics and newspaper offices.[17] Bergman distinguishes these films from the gangster cycle because they lack emotional complexity in the way that they develop the character of the main protagonist in relation to his associates and because they deal explicitly with corruption.[18] *The Mouthpiece, Lawyer Man, The Dark Horse* – all made by Warners in 1932 – and *Five Star Final* (1931), gave a broader definition and location to the criminal underworld evident in the gangster films. These types are complemented by a smaller group of films that depict everyday life suddenly invaded by the city's criminal activity. Films such as *The Star Witness* (1931), *Taxi!* (1932) and *The St Louis Kid* (1934) mark a change of perspective in that ordinary citizens are caught between the gangster and the law and have to work matters out for themselves. James Cagney emerges as a role model and hero for the unemployed and the poorly paid in the way that characters he plays during this decade respond to work pressures and moral dilemmas. Crime is seen as very close to mundane life and easy to detect, with law enforcement either absent, complicit or ineffective.

The clear and dramatic account of crime and the city found in films of the early sound era evolves into a new cycle of gangster films for the mid

1930s. They respond to a change in the economy as well as the tightening of the Hays Production Code in 1935. Since the Hays Office now explicitly forbade the glorification of the criminal, Warners reversed the roles, making the eponymous gangster-hunters clear heroes in *G-Men* (1935). The films remained concurrent with contemporary events but narratives were now related from the point of view of law enforcers and concentrated on protagonists who were police detectives or government agents. The approved 'war against crime' was enacted in *Special Agent* (1935) and *Bullets or Ballots* (1936), which continued to be popular and sustain the original gangster cycle because they contained morally ambiguous characters, particularly Cagney in *G-Men*. Rather than detection, narratives surrounding crime at this point focus on the moments of moral decision-making. Towards the end of the 1930s, Warner returned to the prison drama and became particularly concerned with the plight of city youth who were at risk from their environment. The most significant of these films is *Angels with Dirty Faces* (1938) which ends the gangster cycle and its response to a specific cultural climate. Cagney as the criminal with his own code of honour retains his moral superiority to the end, leaving *The Roaring Twenties* – made the next year – to look back almost nostalgically at the Depression years.

A broader interest in exploring psychological motivation found a creative niche within the crime genre. The treatment of crime in US film after the Second World War is visually and narratively very distinct from that of the 1930s. Warners had already made a version of Dashiell Hammett's successful novel *The Maltese Falcon* in 1931 as part of the new realism of the gangster cycle. However its re-working (for a third time) in 1941 illustrates a new trend in the treatment of crime, which is distanced from the sense of actuality and the linear tracing of an investigation that underpinned film-making in the previous decade. Rather than reality, these new films create an atmosphere of deliberate unclarity. Contemporary cinemas did not advertise these distinctive thrillers as *film noir*: the term was first used in 1946 by Nino Frank, a French film critic who used it to identify a new direction within Hollywood wartime cinema which continued to influence the crime thriller in the post-war period.[19] Frank originally grouped *The Maltese Falcon* (1941) with four films from 1944 – *Murder My Sweet, Double Indemnity, Laura* and *The Woman in the Window*. French film critics were interested in how these films with their pursuit of fatalistic, existential themes and elements of expressionism stood out from other Hollywood products. Of particular interest to these critics was the concentration on effect rather than realism, visually disconcerting the viewer as well as disrupting narrative logic and delivery.

French analysis connected this depiction of crime to print fiction. Although many of the gangster films of the early 1930s had been adapted from novels, *film noir* engages more directly with the style and thematic concerns of hardboiled detective magazine serials of the 1920s and 1930s. Hardboiled detective fiction, with its narrative focus placed on the unravelling of a conspiracy and the ramifications of urban betrayal, emerged as a distinct American formula through *Black Mask*, a monthly magazine founded in 1920 and continuing in print until 1951. *Black Mask* originally published classical detective stories but developed a distinctive style for its American audience. The shared attitude of growing disbelief in stable social order which is found in these stories is a response to the aftermath of the first World War accentuated by the experience of prohibition and the depression. The stories concentrate on representing a world obsessed by greed, violence and power which exists at every level of society. The formula developed by this specific magazine is complemented by the vernacular style of the narrative. The stories are also interested in a different type of criminal investigator, his professionalism in a corrupt world and his ability to resist the temptations of the city. There is also the development of an additional character type to the classical formula, that of the *femme fatale* or female betrayer. Ultimately, however, *Black Mask*'s hardboiled formula sees crime as endemic to the city. Its style and preoccupations would be realised on screen during the 1940s when *film noir* gave visual form to the dark urban settings of these narratives and their inexplicable and unexpected violence.

The altered appearance of the crime film can frequently be associated with changes in generic affiliation. The distinct trend in the representation of crime that is identified by the term 'hardboiled' points to a blending of different elements of horror, gangster, mystery and the social problem film, resulting in a new narrative location and impetus for the crime drama. The combination exaggerates the moral ambiguity found in the previous decade and systematically tempts the male protagonist, who is clearly tainted by his proximity to crime even though he is the only one able to move between social strata and the dual worlds of crime and respectability. Crime is depicted as a series of escalations rooted in the illicit, often violent, pursuit of money. The investigator frequently encounters violent death which, in contrast to the earlier gangster film, is now eroticised in a way which further disrupts earlier demarcations between good and evil. The crime thriller returns to hardboiled fiction in order to privilege the exotic milieu of corruption over the solution and negation of crime that is offered by the classical detective formula.

Alongside Alfred Hitchcock's work in Hollywood from 1940, *film noir* begins to foreground the psychology of crime.[20] Frank Krutnik's analysis points to the way in which *film noir* emphasises how characters in films such as *The Postman Always Rings Twice* (1946) become drawn to crime and its consequences through an inner flaw.[21] Such interest gives rise to two key conventions, the flashback and the voice-over, which are used with increasing complexity and disorientation in films such as *The Killers* (1946), *The Locket* (1947) and *Sorry, Wrong Number* (1948). Crime is portrayed much more subjectively than hitherto. These examples and *The Dark Mirror* (1946) also illustrate *film noir*'s preoccupation with female criminality, sexual transgression and neurosis. Therefore, rather than sharing the previous decade's insistence on environment as the root of criminal behaviour, *film noir* locates it within the individual.

British film-makers in the 1940s were coming to terms with a period of stability for the industry and a relaxation of censorship. Both new experiences were the result of the Ministry of Information's control over British film production during the war. Their propaganda objectives added a fourth category of censorship to the pre-existing political, moral and social considerations. Cultural censorship which aimed to increase realism and motivate the British public to contribute to the 'people's war' gradually undermined the tenets of the other three criteria. The limitation of subject-matter and realism in the portrayal of violence, use of bad language and the representation of authority were all revised. The genre that evolved and became commercially successful in the 1950s was the social problem film. The main exponent of this was the direction and production team of Basil Dearden and Michael Relph, who were first brought together by the Ministry of Information.

In an article for *Screen*, John Hill identified a cycle of films which can be grouped together because they see crime linked to a social problem that can then be dealt with at a local and personal level.[22] Hill argues that they are distinctive because they share common characteristics in the way that they frame and narrate these events. Their narratives imply that a solution can be found to the problem. Therefore, the crime is narrated in retrospect or the telling of the events constitutes the solution itself, as a warning which will save others from the same fate. *Good Time Girl* (1948), which is often seen as the first of these films, has an initial scene which is completely separate from the actual story. The drama is introduced by the probation officer who tells the protagonist's story in order to bring another potential juvenile delinquent to her senses. The films are largely focused on juvenile crime and disorder but they also consider divorce, race relations, the black market, gambling, prostitution and blackmail as social problems, as well as the criminal underworlds associated with them.

Hill stresses that the problems that are narrated are not represented as those of broader society. The issue being explored becomes the problem of a mother, a policeman, a doctor or an ordinary family. Crime is never the problem of the criminal, but of those whom it affects. Therefore, *I Believe in You* (1952) is structured by the career of the rookie probation officer who narrates events. The young girl who is going off the rails in *My Teenage Daughter* (1956) is not the focus of the narrative, which is more concerned with punishing her single mother. The social problem film blends entertainment with factual information, thus assuring the audience of the film's authority in dealing with such taboo subjects. One of the best examples of this is the opening to *Passport to Shame* (1959). Inspector Fabian, whose commentary was more usually found at the end of each episode of BBC TV's *Fabian of the Yard* (1954–6), sombrely explains that the film is based on the shocking facts of the white slave trade which need to be known so that potential victims can be protected. The title sequence, with its jaunty music and humorously choreographed street scene of everyday criminal activity, belies his account of why it should be watched. Respect for those involved with law enforcement agencies became the preferred route for these films to comment upon contemporary public debates about crime. More police on the beat is proposed as the solution to the growth in armed robberies in *The Blue Lamp* (1950). The film opens by dramatising these headlines. Relph and Dearden are often quoted in their press releases as taking stories from the news and *Sapphire* (1959), which examines race relations as a social problem, is set against the background of the anti-immigrant Notting Hill riots of the previous year. *Sapphire* also offers a clear example of how this cycle of films concludes its potentially contentious narratives about crime and criminal sub-culture. Hill is concerned with how each film displaces the social and political dimensions of crime by private or personal dramas. In *Sapphire*, racial intolerance is replaced by female jealousy as the real motive for a murder; the illogical madness is located within the family and the issue of race can be solved by tolerant handshakes between the male protagonists. Similarly, *My Teenage Daughter* and *Cosh Boy* (1952) see reigns of terror carried out by the young resolved by the second marriage of the single mother at the centre of each plot.

Social realist films are important to British crime fiction because they have a direct influence on the way crime was represented in television drama. At the end of the 1950s, the British crime film had adopted northern locations to underscore its bid for greater realism and started to explore the underworld as something more than a transitory location for respectable fears. British film critics see a distinction between films which focused on the professional criminal and on the juvenile delinquent in the late 1950s and early 1960s. They identify a post-war 'spiv' cycle of films, concentrating on particular crimes such as armed robbery and racketeering, that have a different trajectory to the social problem film. Immediately post-war, films such as *Dancing with Crime* (1947) and *They Made Me a Fugitive* (1947) subjected ex-servicemen to the temptations of black marketeering. These films predominantly used crime to explore changing gender relationships culminating in a specific character type: the British working-class tough guy. This was a role perfected by Stanley Baker in a series of crime films starting with *Hell Drivers* (1957) which reconfigured US conventions from *film noir* and the Western to realise a particularly British response to crime and surveillance in a welfare state. *Hell is a City* (1960) cast Baker as a northern police inspector rather than an ex-convict, but the character's attitude and demeanour were the same.

The difference between the juvenile delinquent of the social problem film and the professional criminal is that the former might be absorbed back into the community. Prison in British films such as *The Criminal* (1960), which also cast Baker, was not a location for rehabilitation but a pause in a cycle of recidivism which emphasised the continuity of the criminal career.[23] The early 1960s was a prolific period for British crime films and as well as gender, class becomes a significant issue. *Offbeat* (1961) amongst others conveys a sense of transition and a new order which is morally uncertain.[24] Crime is shown as being organised into everyday business. To mirror this shift, the criminal milieu ceases to be Soho and the poverty-stricken East End and encompasses the decadent society of Mayfair and Chelsea. This is clearly evident in Leigh Vance's trilogy of films: *The Shakedown* (1960) and *Piccadilly Third Stop* (1960) associate crime with moral dissolution and upper-class decadence while *The Frightened City* (1961) locates it visually and narratively in British racketeering. Entertainment and conspicuous consumption rather than the seedy underworld become part of the crime thriller, but this is short lived and after the mid-sixties the crime caper replaces the hard hitting crime thriller. The model here was *The Lavender Hill Mob* (1951), one of the best-loved Ealing comedies, which concentrates on the perfect commission of a robbery. It was still being emulated in films such as *Law and Disorder* (1958) right through to *The Italian Job* (1969), all of which displace any sense of corruption or immorality through adventure and humour. This meant that the ruthless, uncontrolled nature of the return of the professional criminal-turned-investigator in *Get Carter* (1971) was shocking as, in the cinema at least, the genre had lost its dramatic momentum.

By the mid 1950s, cinemas had began to lose audiences on both sides of the Atlantic. The reason for this was a combination of new leisure patterns including television and – in Britain – new locations for housing which broke up the established habits of weekly local cinema going. In Britain the immediacy and innovation of television made it seem to have greater realism in contrast to the dated post-war conventions and restrictions on what could be portrayed on film. The launch of Independent Television in 1955 also brought across more US series. Crime on television in Britain was directly related to the social problem films. *Fabian of the Yard* (1954–6), the first BBC police series, was based on the life of a real Detective Inspector who would comment on the personal experiences being dramatised, but the attraction of the programme lay in forensic detective work and the activities of London's Flying Squad. The series was re-edited for cinema release, and when the BBC looked for something to replace it they resurrected George Dixon from *The Blue Lamp* (1950). This idealised character became the centre of a long-running series, *Dixon of Dock Green* (1955–76), which emphasised policing in the community.

Crime was a useful framework for building up the half-hour series episode through programmes such as *Murder Bag* (1957–9), which became *Crime Sheet* (1959) after its protagonist's promotion and finally carried through to *No Hiding Place* (1959–67). The formula of an indefatigable detective who could address a very broad range of crime became popular because it was generally perceived to be authentic. An earlier series, *Case Histories of Scotland Yard* (1955), established this appreciation of true crime representations because each episode re-enacted actual crimes. In contrast the American series on British screens concentrated on a more explosive and dramatic criminal atmosphere. This was apparent in one of the earliest US shows, *I'm the Law* (1954–5), which was narrated by George Raft, a well-known gangster actor from the 1930s film cycle who now played a lieutenant in the contemporary New York police department. *Dragnet* (1955–68) also emphasised action and drama by adopting a documentary style and announcing each episode with the statement 'Ladies and Gentlemen. The story you are about to see is true. Only the names have been changed to protect the innocent.' The action and car chases of *Highway Patrol* (1956–62) and its successors became a narrative format that would be emulated as far as possible by British television in the late 1960s and 1970s. However, the shift from the avuncular atmosphere of *Dixon of Dock Green* was made by pursuing further topics from the social problem films and by using documentary style, in programmes such as *Prison Officer* (1959–62).

The main format for the British crime show continued to be police drama, as in another long-running BBC series, *Z Cars* (1962–78). The programme was set in the north of England and aspired to realism both in the new types of crime it represented and the personal problems experienced by the police in their private and professional lives. Richard Sparks argues that the change in narrative style and emphasis in this show and its spin-offs is related to the perception that the police are now 'motorised, relatively distant, increasingly reliant on technology, marked by the development of specialist squads . . . with police-public encounters often overtly antagonistic'.[25] The superior officer Charlie Barlow's aggressive attitude and temperament generated enough interest to remove him and his partner to a programme of their own, *Softly Softly* (1966–76), which ran parallel to the original series. However, British television was also preoccupied with the traditional and unambiguously benign power of the detective. The BBC made a series of *Sherlock Holmes* tales between 1965–8, another series – *Detective* (1964) – based its episodes on classic detective literature, and programmes were also made which investigated crime in set historical periods. Unsurprisingly, it took some time before ITV would import *The Untouchables* (1966–9) which was strikingly more violent in its depiction of Prohibition Chicago. Uncomfortably for British visualisations of them, criminality and policing formed part of the way US television began to build up the glamorous side of crime, through *77 Sunset Strip* (1959–64), located in Hollywood, the courtroom drama of *Perry Mason* (1961–7) created by Erle Stanley Gardner, and *The FBI* (1965–75). *The Naked City* (1959–64) portrayed an exciting urban setting, whereas programmes such as *Mannix* (1971) were more concerned with the new technology of detection and the connection between crime drama and the spy series of the 1960s and 1970s.

Britain met this challenge by also turning to international themes, and the scale of these investigations began to foster a sense of police work as covert rather than high profile. *Ghost Squad* (1961–4), featuring Scotland Yard's International Investigation Department, confirmed this trend, making a connection with Cold War spy fiction. International espionage becomes associated with a glamorous and pleasure-seeking consumer lifestyle through television 'pop series' such as *The Avengers* (1961–9), which required their protagonists to thwart fantastic crimes. The action-oriented police series of the later 1960s and 1970s retained the colourful detective and police mavericks of the pop series, but the types of crime they investigated raised consistent issues of racial integration, the complexities of modern urban living, youth revolt and gender politics.[26] Though ranging from conservative – *Ironside* (1967–75), *Hawaii Five-O* (1968–80) – to liberal – *The Mod-Squad* (1968–73), *Starsky and Hutch* (1975–9) – these programmes shared 'a common theme of tough cops who worked within the system yet were individualistic and unorthodox in their fight against crime and disorder'.[27] Sparks sees these 'Cop Shows' as having a close relationship to Clint Eastwood's film *Dirty Harry* (1971) and its sequels, where only a cynical tough cop using extra-legal methods and force was able to bring criminals to justice.[28] The result on television was that narratives were given tight closure and an interest in moving crime from a mystery premise to one of adventure and male camaraderie. Francis Ford Coppola's adaptation of Mario Puzo's novel *The Godfather* (1972) and its sequels also helped to shape the types of criminal activity that television sought to address.

Whilst retaining the maverick detective who might have to operate outside the law, the more reassuring *Cannon* (1972–8), *McCloud* (1972–6), *McMillan and Wife* (1972) and *Columbo* (1972–9) were all popular series which started in the same year. *Columbo*, in particular, returned US crime series to the classical detective formula which would also be prominent in the successful updating of Miss Marple as a feisty New England widow in *Murder She Wrote* (1985–97). Though action was still important in American crime series, a particular socially concerned character type starts to emerge with Jack Lord in *Hawaii Five-o* (1970–82) and the medical examiner *Quincy* (1977–85), who have to deal with new technologies, international crime and civil rights. *Kojak* (1974–8) deals good-heartedly with similar problems in a more flamboyant version of urban crime. *Shaft* (1974–6), based on the popular film trilogy, begins to concentrate on a relationship whereby ordinary people need to be protected both from organised crime and the political manoeuvring of police resources: an imperative which is noticeably present in one of the most successful programmes of the decade, *Starsky and Hutch* (1975–9).

In Britain, at a seemingly slower pace, Nicolas Freeling's detective *Van Der Valk* (1972–3) continued a national fascination with the international detective which offered a legitimate means of examining crime amongst the better classes. However, a new version of London and criminal economy was being established in *Hazell* (1978–80) and *The Sweeney* (1975–8), with the latter becoming the dominant representation of crime fighting on British television. In keeping with the US shows of this decade, *The Sweeney* was all action with violence, insubordination and dedication to crime fighting sustained by banter between the two main protagonists, Detective Inspector Jack Regan and Detective Sergeant George Carter. This sense of a contemporary underworld was also captured in the six part drama series *Out* (1978), where a released bank robber moved through the intersections of criminal and respectable London looking for revenge.

In the US, the change of style between the 1970s and the 1980s is best exemplified by *The Rockford Files* (1975–82) and *Magnum PI* (1981–7). James Rockford was the epitome of the 1970s detective, investigating unsolved cases where the police had closed the books or were themselves complicit. In the last series Rockford was given a more successful rival. Lance White lacked the dogged determination and interest in social justice which defined Rockford and instead solved cases with ease and luck, flaunting his much more affluent lifestyle in the process. This character, played by Tom Selleck, evolved into the hero of *Magnum PI,* which was an extremely popular show and characteristic of 1980s television. Many 1980s programmes adopted a strong lone male hero who represented conservative law-and-order values. Douglas Kellner terms this 'macho-interventionism' and sees its fullest use in association with the screen realisation of very high tech weaponry in the many adventure formats which tackle crime and injustice.[29] This can be seen in several action adventure formats of the period such as *The A-Team* (1983–8) and *Knight Rider* (1982–6), but more explicitly in films, such as *Top Gun* (1986) or *Die Hard* (1988), and the way in which *Blade Runner* (1982) adapts *film noir* conventions into 'tech noir', validating a cinematic trend to visualise the future and its crime fighters as a series of dramatic special effects.[30]

The period of the maverick male detective also saw the emergence of popular female protagonists in *Police Woman* (1975–9) and *Charlie's Angels* (1977–82). In Britain, this trend is explored through *Juliet Bravo* (1980–5), *The Gentle Touch* (1980–4) and Lynda La Plante's series *Widows* (1983), the latter dealing with female criminals rather than law enforcers. In the US, series such as *Cagney and Lacy* (1982–8) were action-packed and are related to the other main trend of the 1980s, the glamorous couple or milieu found in *Moonlighting* (1986–9) and *Miami Vice* (1985–90). The personal as well as professional relations which dominated these narratives prepared the way for such programmes as *NYPD Blue* (1994) and *LA Law* (1987–92), where policing and crime become a site for anxieties about new work practices and industrial relations. In Britain the development of the soap operatic realism of *The Bill* (1994) also responded to these concerns making it one of the most popular shows on television. These programmes connect with the medical dramas of the 1980s and 1990s, e.g. *St Elsewhere* (1983–9) and *Casualty* (1986–), which also addressed crime in relation to professional practice and formed a complete contrast with the action adventure of the 1970s. Once again Britain returned to the classical crime formula with *The Agatha Christie Hour* (1982), *Miss Marple* (1984–92), *The Adventures of Sherlock Holmes* (1984–5), a new Victorian detective, *Cribb* (1980–1), and major investment in the high production values of *Agatha Christie's Poirot* (1989–97).[31] Televised versions of inter-war mystery and detective writers rose to prominence: Margery Allingham's *Campion* (1989–90), *A Dorothy Sayers Mystery* (1987) and Gladys Mitchell's *Mrs Bradley Mysteries* (1991) were broadcast with much attention to period detail and a nostalgic version of Englishness in keeping with many other forms of entertainment produced at this time. *Bergerac* (1981–91), *Taggart* (1983–) and – predominantly – *Inspector Morse* (1987–2000) associated crime with a specific landscape which needed to be husbanded as well as policed.

On British television the broad-based popularity of *Inspector Morse* made it the dominant articulation of the detective story. It blurred the boundaries between high and low culture through its bid to develop beyond Colin Dexter's novels into an extended televisual narrative with its own identity, and production values which drew it accolades as quality drama. *The Ruth Rendell Mysteries* (1987) and *P. D. James* (1983–5) also marked a shift in narrative emphasis to contemporary print fiction bestsellers and mystery rather than action as a means of negotiating crime. *Inspector Morse* carefully follows the development of the detective's troubled character and his response to the crimes that he encounters which are located in the excesses of yuppie lifestyle. The success of this programme prompted commentary in other series on the tension between the high-tech police world of computers and forensics and its antagonistic bureaucratic working conditions. A series of detective formats contrasted the styles of older investigators with their younger apprentices who are more familiar with political correctness and new technologies. *Wycliffe* (1997–8), *A Touch of Frost* (1992–), *Midsommer Murders* (1997–), *Dalziel and Pascoe* (1992–), *Hetty Wainthrop* (1996–8) and *Heartbeat* (1992–) all reinstated intuitive old-school detection and were based on popular detective novels that had specific scenic locations.

In the US, a small cycle of films featuring violent crime at the beginning of the 1990s was highly influential. Quentin Tarantino's *Reservoir Dogs* (1991) and *Pulp Fiction* (1994) re-engage with earlier cinematic stylisations of crime and the underworld. While violence had become an increasingly important element in action adventure movies, a new set of gangster films such as *Goodfellas* (1990), *Boyz N the Hood* (1991) and *New Jack City* (1991) strove for realism in depicting inner city life. These films and others narrating the actions of real-life serial killers, which fascinated the popular imagination during this decade, forge a close connection between the crime and horror genres.

The 1990s also saw a distinct group of British television programmes which constructed a world of uncontainable violent crime, often encouraged by internal police corruption. Interest is focused on small groups with highly specialised skills or responsibilities: *Between the Lines* (1992) follows the Complaints Investigation Bureau within the police force, *Cracker* (1993–6) has a police psychologist unravelling complicated crimes and *Touching Evil* (1997) is based on the Organised and Serial Crime Unit. American films such as *The Silence of the Lambs* (1990) and *Seven* (1995) are examples of tense thrillers following careful forensic investigations but more interested in the metaphysical and emotional dimensions of fictional detection. On British television, *Prime Suspect* (1991–6) develops this approach with a series of dramas, each following a single case and the factors determining its outcome.

The American series *Murder One* (1996–9) was able to expand this focus on the detail of a single case by basing the narrative in a law firm and charting the involvement of many different characters and agencies in policework, detection and trial proceedings.

Screen crime has a close relationship with print fiction and has boosted book sales as well as turning detectives into cultural icons. However, crime on film and television has always been subject to censorship and ratings in a more immediate way than other media. The transitions in film and television can generally be traced to these determinants and the way that crime narratives make changing alliances with different genres of popular fiction. Screen crime has had to negotiate specific areas of public concern, especially over the treatment of violence, suitable representations of authority and the relationship between fiction and true crime, in the face of an unshakeable belief that audiences are more susceptible to film and television portrayals of crime than to written ones. The depiction of crime in film and on television has provided a major focus for popular critical debate. It has also registered cultural mood and changing values associated particularly with class, race and gender. In order to accommodate these ideas and interests screen crime has needed to be extremely flexible, moving swiftly between mystery or adventure archetypes and the moral or intellectual concerns of genres outside the strictly detective formula.

## NOTES

1 André Gaudereault (1992), 'Detours in Film Narrative: The Development of Cross-Cutting', in Thomas Elsaesser (ed.) *Early Cinema: Space Frame Narrative* (London: BFI, 1997), p. 137.
2 Charles Musser, *Before the Nickelodeon: Edwin S. Porter and the Edison Manufacturing Company* (Berkeley and London: University of California Press, 1991), p. 257.
3 Charles Musser, 'The Travel Genre in 1903–1904: Moving Towards Fictional Narrative', in Elsaesser (ed.) *Early Cinema*, p. 130.
4 Christopher Redmond, *A Sherlock Holmes Handbook* (Toronto: Simon and Pierre, 1993).
5 Nicolas Pronay and Jeremy Croft 'British Film Censorship and Propaganda Policy During the Second World War', in J. Curran and V. Porter (eds), *British Cinema History* (London: Weidenfeld and Nicolson, 1983), p. 151.
6 Kevin Brownlow, *Behind the Mask of Innocence: Films of Social Conscience in the Silent Era* (Berkeley and London: University of California Press, 1990), p.13.
7 *Ibid.*, p.15
8 *Ibid.*, p. 184.
9 *Ibid.*, p. 189.
10 *Ibid.*, p. 160.
11 Andrew Bergman, *We're in the Money* (London: Harper and Row, 1971), p. xxi.

12 *Ibid.*, p. 7.
13 Nick Roddick, *A New Deal in Entertainment* (London: BFI, 1983), p. 7.
14 Bergman, *We're in the Money*, p. 77.
15 *Ibid.*, p. 6.
16 Roddick, *A New Deal in Entertainment*, p. 77.
17 Bergman, *We're in the Money*, p. 18.
18 *Ibid.*, p. 18.
19 Nino Frank 'Un nouveau genre policier: l'aventure criminelle', *L'Ecran Français*, August 1946.
20 There is no room to do justice to Hitchcock here, but see William Rothman's *Hitchcock: The Murderous Gaze* (Princeton NJ: Princeton University Press, 1982) for an in-depth analysis of his style and cinematography.
21 F. Krutnik, *In a Lonely Street* (London: Routledge, 1991), p. 46.
22 John Hill, 'The British "Social Problem" film – *Violent Playground* and *Sapphire*', *Screen* vol. 26, no. 1 (Jan–Feb 1985), pp. 34–48.
23 Steve Chibnall, 'Ordinary people: "New Wave" realism and the British crime film 1959–1963', in Steve Chibnall and Robert Murphy, eds., *British Crime Cinema* (London: Routledge, 1999).
24 *Ibid.*, p. 98.
25 Richard Sparks, '*Inspector Morse*: "The Last Enemy" (Peter Buckman)', in George W. Brandt, ed., *British Television Drama in the 1980s* (Cambridge University Press, 1993), p. 88.
26 David Buxton, *From The Avengers to Miami Vice* (Manchester University Press, 1990).
27 Bill Osgerby and Anna Gough-Yates, eds., *Action TV: Tough Guys, Smooth Operators and Foxy Chicks* (London: Routledge, 2001), p. 3.
28 Sparks, '*Inspector Morse*', p. 89.
29 D. Kellner, *Television and the Crisis of Democracy* (Boulder, Colorado: Westview Press, 1990), p. 60.
30 For a further discussion see Nickianne Moody, ' "A Lone Crusader in the dangerous world": heroics of science and technology in *Knight Rider*', in Osgerby and Gough-Yates, *Action TV*, pp. 69–80.
31 Jeremy Brett starred as Holmes in *The Return of Sherlock Holmes* (1986–8), *The Casebook of Sherlock Holmes* (1991) and *The Memoirs of Sherlock Holmes* (1994).

# 14

LAURA MARCUS

# Detection and literary fiction

Detective fiction has played and continues to play a complex and curious role in relation to the broader field of literature. On the one hand, detective fiction, like other genre fictions, is seen as a popular and lesser subset of high or 'proper' literature. On the other, the literature of detection, with its complex double narrative in which an absent story, that of a crime, is gradually reconstructed in the second story (the investigation), its uses of suspense, and its power to give aesthetic shape to the most brute of matter, has been seen as paradigmatic of literary narrative itself. Tzvetan Todorov's 'The Typology of Detective Fiction', which remains one of the most significant contributions to the field, sought to uphold the distinction between 'genre fiction' and 'literature' (as a question of structure rather than of value).[1] However, his identification of the two orders of story, inquest and crime, as equivalents to the Russian formalist distinction between *sjuzet* and *fabula* (often translated as 'discourse' and 'story' respectively), makes the detective story, as Peter Brooks writes, 'the narrative of narratives', its classical structure a laying-bare of the structure of all narrative in that it dramatises the role of *sjuzet* and *fabula* and the nature of their relation.[2] More recently, critics such as Peter Hühn and S. E. Sweeney have drawn attention to the self-reflexivity of detective narratives, defined as metaliterary stories which, dedicated to their own constructive principles, and openly displaying the similarities between the detection and the reading processes, become representative of literature in general.[3]

As Heta Pyrhönen writes, detective fiction 'serves as a kind of laboratory for testing various critical hypotheses and methodologies', and whereas structuralist critics of the 1960s turned to the genre to prove theories of 'closed' literary forms, their analyses in fact 'unwittingly opened it for a plethora of analytical readings that contradict their claim'.[4] Detective fiction has been central to psychoanalytic, hermeneutic, structuralist, semiotic, and poststructuralist narrative theories, and has been deployed both to secure and to trouble literary borders and boundaries, including the distinction between high and low literature and the divide between modernist and post-modernist fiction.

Whereas a number of critics in the early to mid-twentieth century set up a stark contrast between modernism and detective fiction (as I discuss later), the correlation made by a number of recent critics between 'modernism' and 'epistemology' (a concern with questions of knowledge) leads to a connection being drawn between modernist literature and the detective genre. Postmodernist literature, and postmodernist detective or 'anti-detective' fiction in particular, are then placed on the side of a 'negative hermeneutics' (in which the quest for knowledge is doomed to failure) and/or the realms of 'ontology', in which the focus is not on the problematics of knowledge (as in the epistemological field) but on world-making: in the words of the heroine of Thomas Pynchon's The Crying of Lot 49 (1966), Oedipa Maas, 'Shall I project a world?'.[5] Such divisions and correlations need to be approached with some caution; the category of the epistemological quest, which Brian McHale, for example, makes a defining aspect of modernist fiction, is a very general one, not necessarily linked to the epistemological forms and processes of detective fiction. For some modernist writers, such as Henry James, secrecy and detection are narrative motors; the same could not be said of Virginia Woolf or D. H. Lawrence. Neither 'modernism' nor 'postmodernism' are fully stable categories, and the relations between genre fictions and literature more broadly need to be understood in a nexus of interlocking, competing and shifting relations.

The literary and narrative issues raised by the detective genre are also incomplete without an understanding of social and historical contexts. The detective paradigm, it has been argued, shaped nineteenth-century fiction, with writers such as Charlotte Brontë, Dickens and Balzac structuring their narratives around secrets and their disclosure or, in the case of Balzac in particular, around the significance of small details. The centrality of detective fiction to the nineteenth century is seen as both aesthetic and ideological, as it mediates a culture in which crime and punishment are both profoundly internalised in the subjective sphere and externalised in ever more elaborate forms of discipline and surveillance, and in new legal institutions and judicial procedures, in particular the formation of the detective police, the rise of forensic science, and the development of trial by evidence. Although the turn to mythic and pre-modern texts as foundations for the detective genre, Oedipus Rex paramount among them, has been central to some of the most important accounts of the detective genre, there are compelling arguments for situating the emergence of detective fiction in the modernity of the early to mid-nineteenth century.

'The original social content of the detective story was the obliteration of the individual's traces in the big-city crowd', Walter Benjamin wrote in his study of Charles Baudelaire.[6] He explores the centrality of this motif in Edgar Allan Poe's 'The Mystery of Marie Rogêt' (1842–3) and in 'The Man of the Crowd', (1840) which, in his account of the significance of photography both for criminology and for the emergence of detective fiction, Benjamin describes as 'something like the X-ray picture of a detective story':

> In it, the drapery represented by crime has disappeared. The mere armature has remained: the pursuer, the crowd, and an unknown man who arranges his walk through London in such a way that he always remains in the middle of the crowd. This unknown man is the *flâneur*.[7]

These preoccupations were also explored in one of the first critical accounts of detective fiction, G. K. Chesterton's 'A Defence of Detective Stories', published in 1902. Chesterton's 'defence' rests on the claim that the detective story 'is the earliest and only form of popular literature in which is expressed some sense of the poetry of modern life':

> Of this realization of a great city itself as something wild and obvious the detective story is certainly the *Iliad*. No one can have failed to notice that in these stories the hero or the investigator crosses London with something of the loneliness and liberty of a prince in a tale of elfland, that in the course of that incalculable journey the casual omnibus assumes the primal colours of a fairy ship. The lights of the city begin to glow like innumerable goblin eyes, since they are the guardians of some secret, however crude, which the writer knows and the reader does not. Every twist of the road is like a finger pointing to it; every fantastic skyline of chimney-pots seems wildly and derisively signalling the meaning of the mystery . . . there is no stone in the street and no brick in the wall that is not actually a deliberate symbol – a message from some man, as much as if it were a telegram or a post-card. Anything which tends, even under the fantastic form of the minutiae of Sherlock Holmes, to assert this romance of detail in civilization, to assert this unfathomably human character in flints and tiles, is a good thing.[8]

Where Benjamin, however, blurs the distinction between pursuer and pursued, detective and criminal (a blurring which 'postmodernist' detective fiction will exploit to the limit), Chesterton places them on either side of the divide between civilisation and barbarism. The criminals, he asserts, are 'the children of chaos', while the detective 'is the original and poetic figure . . . The romance of the police force is thus the whole romance of man'.[9] Chesterton's image of the detective as knight-errant was echoed by Raymond Chandler some forty years later – 'down these mean streets a man must go who is not himself mean, who is neither tarnished nor afraid'[10] – but his representation of the city as the arena of signs and secrets reverberates even more powerfully in later twentieth-century fiction, and in particular in postmodern novels.

The concept of an urban hieroglyphics is central to writers such as Thomas Pynchon, Peter Ackroyd, Iain Sinclair and Paul Auster; they create fictional worlds in which writing and walking, interpretation and pursuit, are intertwined or identical activities. The heroine of Pynchon's *The Crying of Lot 49*, Oedipa Maas, learns that she has been named as an executor for a Californian property mogul, Pierce Inverarity. In exploring his estate, she seems to uncover the existence of an underground communications network, though neither she nor the reader ever learns conclusively if the organisation is real, manufactured as a hoax, or an hallucination: 'Behind the hieroglyphic streets there would be either a transcendent meaning, or only the earth'.[11] A number of the novels of Ackroyd and Sinclair could be defined as 'urban gothic', opening up hidden spaces within the city, and/or uncovering patterns which are both spatial and temporal, palimpsestic layerings of past events; often violent crimes which, leaving their mark on both place and history, are at one and the same time repetitions and repressions.[12]

Chesterton's striking account of detective fiction as a poetry of the city inscribed in urban hieroglyphics opens up the genre in two directions: towards an order in which reason and law prevail and, in an opposing movement, towards enigma and the fantastical. Many critics have sought to draw an absolute line between these elements, rather than acknowledging their possible coexistence. Thus 'classical' detective fiction, typified by the Sherlock Holmes stories, is represented as a 'closed' structure, in which every aspect of the narration leads towards the exposure of the means by which the crime was committed, the discovery of the criminal, and the re-establishing of order. 'Most popular mysteries', Geoffrey Hartman argued, 'are devoted to solving rather than examining a problem. Their reasonings put reason to sleep, abolish darkness by elucidation, and bury the corpse for good'.[13] 'The fantastic form of the minutiae of Sherlock Holmes', to which Chesterton points, tends to be passed over by those twentieth-century critics who have used detective fiction to divide up the literary field in strategic ways.

Marjorie Nicolson's 1929 article 'The Professor and the Detective' analysed the appeal of detective fiction to intellectuals as a reaction *against* literature, at least in its modern and modernist variants, and anticipated later formulations of the detective fiction–literary fiction relationship. Writing as an academic reader of detective stories, Nicolson defined the particular form of 'escape' offered by the genre: 'it is escape not from life, but from literature':

> We have revolted from an excessive subjectivity to welcome objectivity; from long-drawn-out dissections of emotion to straightforward appeal to intellect; from reiterated emphasis upon men and women as victims either of circumstances or of their glands to a suggestion that men and women may consciously plot and consciously plan; from the 'stream of consciousness' which threatens to engulf us in its Lethean monotony to analyses of purpose, controlled and directed by a thinking mind; from formlessness to form; from the sophomoric to the mature; most of all, from a smart and easy pessimism which interprets men and the universe in terms of unmoral purposelessness to a rebelief in a universe governed by cause and effect. All this we find in the detective story'.[14]

Nicolson thus opposed detective fiction to the literary fiction of her time. She defined the latter in ways which we would now associate with literary modernism, and more particularly literary impressionism, focusing on subjective narration and 'stream of consciousness' techniques, although her critique was in fact levelled against what she called 'contemporary realism'.

The terminology has shifted, but the view that detective fiction flourished in the early twentieth century as a reaction against modernist narrative has been taken up by more recent critics, and has had a particularly important impact on theories of detective narrative and *post*modernism. Michael Holquist, in his influential article 'Whodunit and Other Questions: Metaphysical Detective Stories in Post-War Fiction' (1971), echoed a number of Nicolson's assertions, arguing that detective stories are an 'escape from *literature* itself' and that they represent a demand for reason during a period in which 'the upper reaches of literature were dramatizing the limits of reason by experimenting with such irrational modes as myth and the sub-conscious'.[15] While high literature represented a world threatening to reason, detective fiction reassures through its rationalism: 'The same people who spent their days with Joyce were reading Agatha Christie at night'. The opposition structuring modernism, as Holquist defines it, is 'between the high art of the novel with its bias towards myth and depth psychology and the popular art of the detective story with its flatness of character and setting'.[16]

In the period after World War Two, Holquist argues, an emergent postmodernism, 'militantly *anti-psychological* and radically *anti*-mythical', defines itself against the modernism that preceded it by exploiting 'what had already become the polar opposite of that tradition in its own time'.[17] That is, postmodernism exploits the anti-literary (literature equating here with modernism) aspects of detective fiction for its own radical turn against the literary tradition and the concept of 'literature':

> What myth was to experimental fiction before World War II, detective fiction is to avant-garde prose after World War II. The possibilities for symbolic action and depth psychology which Homer provides for James Joyce are replaced in the later period by the ambiguous events, the psychologically flat and therefore mysterious world which Holmes and Poirot make available to Robbe-Grillet and Borges.[18]

Postmodernism does not, of course, merely return to pre-war detective fiction, but 'exploits detective stories by expanding and changing certain possibilities in them, just as modernism had *modified* the potentialities of myth'. For Alain Robbe-Grillet, for example, the *nouveau roman* is an inverted detective story. Writers such as Robbe-Grillet and Borges, Holquist writes, 'use as a foil the assumption of detective fiction that the mind can solve all; by twisting the details just the opposite becomes the case'. Postmodernist writing, and the metaphysical detective story in particular, give us not familiarity but strangeness, 'a strangeness which more often than not is the result of jumbling the well known patterns of classical detective stories'.[19]

Holquist's is in many ways a helpful model, though his account of modernism is a limited one, reliant on partial accounts of high modernist texts, such as T. S. Eliot's reading of Joyce's 'mythic method' in *Ulysses*. It overlooks the appeal of detective fiction to a number of 'high modernists', most notably Gertrude Stein, who were seeking to escape rather than to explore 'depth psychology'. 'I never was interested in cross word puzzles or any kind of puzzles but I do like detective stories', Stein wrote in *Everybody's Autobiography*. 'I never try to guess who has done the crime and if I did I would be sure to guess wrong but I like somebody being dead and how it moves along'.[20] In 'What are Masterpieces and Why Are There So Few of Them', she discussed:

> The detective story which is you might say the only really modern novel form that has come in to existence gets rid of human nature by having the man dead to begin with the hero is dead to begin with and so you have so to speak got rid of the event before the book begins.[21]

The significance of the murder in detective narrative, in this account, is that it kills off both character and event, creating a radically altered literary space. Stein later qualified this view, acknowledging that the detective becomes the hero. She also came up against a limit when she herself wrote a detective novel, *Blood on the Dining-room Floor* (1948), based on two mysterious deaths in Bilignin, the French village in which she was living in the early 1930s. As she wrote later, the novel was not altogether successful: 'on the whole a detective story has to have if it has not a detective it has to have an ending and my detective story did not have any . . . I was sorry about it because it came so near to being a detective story and it did have a good title.'[22] Nonetheless, she retained a sense of the radical narrative possibilities of detective fiction, intertwined with her foremost preoccupation, the question of identity and its displacement:

> So if this Everybody's Autobiography is to be the Autobiography of every one it is not to be of any connection between any one and any one because now there is none. That is what makes detective stories such good reading, the man being dead he is not really in connection with anyone. If he is it is another kind of a story and not a detective story.[23]

If Michael Holquist's article defines modernism too narrowly, it also gives too fixed and rigid an account of 'classical' detective narrative, rather than exploring the ways in which earlier detective fiction can also be opened up to 'strangeness' rather than 'familiarity'. The same could be said of a number of critics who have used detective fiction to point up the boundaries between realist and experimental fiction, or between modernism and postmodernism. William Spanos, in his essay 'The Detective and the Boundary', equated an existential and a postmodern imagination, in his differentiation between 'an early or symbolist modernism and a later "postmodernism"'. The existential or postmodernist imagination is opposed to 'the rational or rather the positivistic structure of consciousness that views spatial and temporal phenomena in the world as "problems" to be "solved", *domesticating* "the threatening realm of Nothingness"'.[24]

The reaction against this rationalist universe and its literary products, Spanos argues, arises with the 'postmodern literary imagination', whose 'paradigmatic archetype . . . is the antidetective story (and its antipsychoanalytic analogue), the formal purpose of which is to evoke the impulse to "detect" and/or to psychoanalyse in order to violently frustate it by refusing to solve the crime (or to find the cause of the neurosis)'. Works in this category include Kafka's *The Trial* (1925), Graham Greene's *Brighton Rock* (1938), Robbe-Grillet's *The Erasers* (1953) and Natalie Sarraute's *Portrait of a Man Unknown* (1948). This last text, Spanos notes, was described by Sartre as an 'anti-novel that reads like a detective story', and as 'a parody on the novel of "quest" into which the author has introduced a sort of impassioned detective [who] doesn't find anything . . . and gives up the investigation as a result of a metamorphosis; just as though Agatha Christie's detective, on the verge of unmasking the villain, had himself suddenly turned criminal'.[25]

Stefano Tani followed Spanos in arguing that 'existentalism's stress on the limits of human reason and man's necessary acceptance of the inherent absurdity of his life had a crucial influence on the recent inversion of the detective's role in serious fiction'. He argues that:

> A notable aspect of contemporary fiction is the increasing importance acquired by the detective as a literary figure . . . The detective novel, a reassuring "low" genre which is supposed to please the expectations of the reader, becomes the ideal medium of postmodernism in its inverted form, the anti-detective novel, which frustrates the expectations of the reader, transforms a mass-media genre into a sophisticated expression of *avant-garde* sensibility, and substitutes for the detective as central and ordering character the decentering and chaotic admission of mystery, of non-solution.[26]

While on the one hand Tani starkly opposes the traditional detective novel and the anti-detective novel, on the other he suggests that the two forms exist in a symbiotic relationship, the conservative (or, in Roland Barthes's term, 'readerly') form of the one making it the perfect vehicle for subversion by the other. Thus, 'paradoxically, contemporary literary fiction is the result of the wreckage and decentralization of the "low" detective novel's code. Largely, any good contemporary fiction is basically an anti-detective fiction, the ultimate "grinding" (inversion or even "pulverization") of the Poesque rules.'[27]

The arguments of Holquist (1971), Spanos (1972) and Tani (1982) were, as Heta Pyrhönen notes, attempts to elevate the postmodern detective novel 'as a new instance of avant-garde expression' at a time when postmodern discursive strategies were more in need of legitimation than they are at present. It is now possible to see 'the boundary between the postmodern metaphysical detective story and its mainstream cousin as much more volatile, on account of the shared legacy and the many precursors of postmodern tendencies within "straight" detective fiction'.[28]

We can identify a relatively coherent category of twentieth-century texts, gaining momentum in the post-war period, which simultaneously deploy and subvert traditional detective-story conventions, and, as Patricia Merivale and S. E. Sweeney argue, 'apply the detective process to [the detective] genre's own assumptions about detection'.[29] Such writings, marked by their intertextuality, often look back to precursors such as Poe, Conan Doyle and Chesterton, while also establishing relations between one another, as in the case of Borges, Robbe-Grillet, Pynchon, Eco and Auster. At the same time, we can qualify the concept of a radical break postulated by Holquist, Spanos and Tani, and suggest firstly, that there is a relationship of reciprocity between popular and 'metaphysical' detective stories, and secondly, that earlier writers such as Poe and Conan Doyle deployed not only many of the tropes but also the strategies of self-reflexivity which we now identify with post-modernist narrative.

Jorge Luis Borges identified both conventionality and complexity in his essays on G. K. Chesterton, whom he names, along with writers such as Robert Louis Stevenson, as a crucial influence on his own writing practices. Borges seems to echo, in a short review essay entitled 'On The Origins of the Detective Novel', the views expressed by Nicolson and Holquist:

> Oscar Wilde has observed that [very prescriptive verse forms such as] rondeaus and triolets prevent literature from being at the mercy of genius. At this point one could observe the same of detective fiction. Whether mediocre or awful, the detective story is never without a beginning, a plot and a denouement. The literature of our time is exhausted by interjections and opinions, incoherences and confidences; the detective story represents order and the obligation to invent.[30]

Nonetheless, the appeal of Chesterton to Borges – Borges at one point referred to Chesterton as 'my master'[31] – would not seem to lie in his rationalism. 'Chesterton and the Labyrinths of the Detective Narrative' is a telling title in the context of Borges's labyrinthine imaginings, while in the essay 'Modes of G. K. Chesterton' Borges described Chesterton as 'an incomparable inventor of fantastic stories'. 'Unfortunately', Borges continued, 'he sought to extract from them a moral, thus reducing them to mere parables. Fortunately, he never really succeeded in doing so.'[32] Chesterton's exceptional qualities, for Borges, lie both in his skill as a writer and in his ability to bridge two seemingly incompatible generic forms:

> Edgar Allan Poe wrote stories of pure, fantastic horror or of pure *bizarrerie*; Poe was the inventor of the detective story. This is no less certain than the fact that he never combined the two genres . . . Chesterton, in the diverse narrations that constitute the five-part saga of Father Brown and those of the poet Gabriel Gale and those of the "Man Who Knew Too Much," executes, always, that tour de force. He presents a mystery, proposes a supernatural explanation and then replaces it, losing nothing, with one from this world. . . . In [one of Chesterton's detective stories] there is a legend at the beginning: a blasphemous king raises with Satanic help a topless tower. God fulminates against the tower and makes it a bottomless pit, into which the king's soul is forever falling. This divine inversion somehow prefigures the silent rotation of a library, with two small cups, one with poisoned coffee, which kills the man who had intended it for his guest.[33]

The first part of this passage echoes Howard Haycraft's account of Chesterton in *Murder for Pleasure*: 'A few of the individual [Father Brown] stories are undeniably brilliant, whether judged as detective tales or as that problematical thing called Art. Chesterton is at his best when he states a problem in apparently supernatural terms and then resolves it by philosophical paradox.' Haycraft argued that Chesterton 'brought new blood to the genre; gave it a needed and distinctly more "literary" turn that was to have far-reaching effect. Most crucially, perhaps, he suggested that 'Chesterton's chief contribution to the genre [was] that he perfected the *metaphysical* detective story'.[34] He is referring here to the philosophical (shading into theological) dimensions of Chesterton's detective fiction, but his coinage – the 'metaphysical' detective story – has been taken up substantially in postmodernist reformulations and reworkings of detective narrative. In Merivale and Sweeney's definition: 'A metaphysical detective story is a text that parodies or subverts traditional detective story conventions – such as narrative closure and the detective's role as surrogate reader – with the intention, or at least the effect, of asking questions about mysteries of being and knowing which transcend the mere machinations of the mystery plot.'[35]

Many of Borges's short stories inscribe the topoi and tropes which become central to postmodernist detective fiction – the labyrinth and the library, the book within a book, mirrors and doubles – and exploit the puzzle elements of the detective story genre, and the potential for both reading and misreading the nature of plot and pattern. Detective fiction, Gene Bell-Vilada notes, 'had a special appeal to Borges because of its minimal psychology and peculiar narrative mechanics. The actions in a detective story are dictated not by personality traits but by a strict set of possibilities inherent in a situation.'[36]

In Borges's short story 'Death and the Compass' (1942; in part a rewriting of Chesterton's story 'The Wrong Shape' (1911), which revolves around a manuscript and a quotation), detective Erik Lönnrot, who 'believed himself a pure reasoner, an Auguste Dupin, [though] there was something of the adventurer in him, and even a little of the gambler', is involved in the detection of a sequence of murders.[37] Borges opens up a gap between the detection of the murderer and the divination of 'the secret morphology behind the fiendish series'. Lönnrot's colleague Inspector Treviranus looks to an explanation of the first murder as the product of chance – 'We needn't lose any time here looking for three-legged cats' – hypothesising that a robber broke into the wrong room in a hotel and killed the man whom he had disturbed. Lönnrot finds this explanation 'possible but not interesting', and looks for 'a purely rabbinical explanation' for the murder of Yarmolinsky, a delegate at the Third Talmudic Congress. Examining the dead man's books rather than his corpse – a significant move in the obsessively textual world of the 'metaphysical' detective story – Lönnrot carries off the tomes, which include 'a monograph (in German) on the Tetragrammaton; another, on the divine nomenclature of the Pentateuch': 'Indifferent to the police investigation, he dedicated himself to studying them'. [38] He locates connections between a note found at the scene of the crime – 'the first letter of the Name has been uttered' – and the teachings of the Cabalistic texts, which revolve around the name or names of God.

After a third murder is committed, Lönnrot receives a note informing him that the sequence is complete; the triad of the murders is perfectly finished in its equivalence to a temporal sequence (the murders are committed on the third of the month) and a spatial one (the locations of the murder form 'the perfect vertices of a mystic equilateral triangle'). Lönnrot's researches, however, lead him to read the note as a bluff, and he travels to a lonely villa in search of the solution to the murders, believing that Yarmolinsky was killed by Hasidic Jews searching for the secret Name of God. In the house, interior spaces are doubled or multiplied in mirrors, and a spiral staircase leads him to Red Sharlach, his sworn enemy, who reveals that he has entrapped Lönnrot (the 'rot' or 'red' of whose name is an echo or mirroring of Sharlach's own, as Red Sharlach translates into Red Scarlet, the doubly red or, perhaps, 'read') by weaving a labyrinth around him: 'I have woven it and it is firm: the ingredients are a dead heresiologist, a compass, an eighteenth-century sect, a Greek word, a dagger, the diamonds of a paint shop.'[39]

All these signs indicate quadruples rather than triads ('the Tetragrammaton – the name of God, JHVC – is made up of *four* letters'). Sharlach's web has led Lönnrot to look beyond the triangle of the three murders, and he now occupies the fourth corner, the missing point, in which he, the detective, will be killed by Sharlach's bullet.[40] Lönnrot has followed the path or map laid down for him to, in Sharlach's words, 'the point which would form a perfect rhomb, the point which fixes in advance where a punctual death awaits you'.[41] Yet, as Borges wrote in a note to the tale: 'The killer and the slain, whose minds work in the same way, may be the same man. Lönnrot is not an unbelievable fool walking into his own death trap but, in a symbolic way, a man committing suicide.'[42]

Alain Robbe-Grillet's first published novel, *The Erasers* (*Les Gommes)* (1953), also plays with the concept of the mirrored selves of detective and criminal, working towards a dénouement in which the special investigator, Wallas, becomes the killer of Daniel Dupont, whose apparent murder he is investigating. Dupont has in fact only been injured; he returns to his home, to encounter Wallas, who, waiting for the man or men whom he believes responsible for Dupont's murder, shoots him dead. This variant on the Oedipus narrative, which shifts the 'crime' from past to future, is accompanied by numerous references to the Oedipus myth, including a picture of

Thebes in a shop-window and a statuette of a child leading a blind man, ambiguous father-son relationships, and the riddles, reinscriptions of that of the Sphinx, which are posed by a drunk in a bar: 'What animal is parricide in the morning, incestuous at noon, and blind at night?'[43] Yet the Oedipal narrative does not operate as an ordering or explanatory principle in the text and, it could be argued, 'man' in Robbe-Grillet's fictional universe is not the answer to the riddle. For the novelists associated with the *nouveau roman*, and Robbe-Grillet in particular, the appeal of detective fiction as a genre lay substantially in its devaluation, even evacuation, of psychological and social 'character'.

As in G. K. Chesterton's account of detective fiction, walking the city and reading its signs and inscriptions appear to be at the heart of *The Erasers*:

> Wallas likes walking. In the cold, early winter air he likes walking straight ahead through this unknown city. [. . .] It is of his own free will that he is walking towards an inevitable and perfect future. In the past, he has too frequently let himself be caught in the circles of doubt and impotence, now he is walking; he has recovered his continuity here.[44]

The city thus seems to endow Wallas with both the loneliness (he is 'the only pedestrian') and the liberty described by Chesterton. Wallas's assumption of free will is, however, illusory, and the continuity and rationality to which he believes he has acceded are belied by the circularity of the plot in which he is thoroughly caught. Signs, clues and characters remain opaque, and the narrative disrupts chronology, repeatedly reverting to events that subsequently turn out to be imaginings or speculations. Details – including the 'stock' elements of detective fiction, such as fingerprints, footprints, and an unfinished sentence in a manuscript – are displaced as 'clues' as they become subjected to a narrative attention which seeks to re-establish the 'thingness' of the physical world and to cleanse it of meanings imposed through metaphors and anthropomorphism. The 'erasers' of the title are linked to the ways in which Robbe-Grillet, as Raylene Ramsay notes, frequently puts 'homage' (the homage to generic and literary models) in relation to 'gommage' (erasure); '*Homage* thus both designates an influence and constitutes a sign of its own imminent work of deconstruction.'[45]

Umberto Eco's *The Name of the Rose* (1980) owes much to Borges's fictions, and in particular 'Death and the Compass', deploying, as Joel Black notes, the central motif of a cryptic message which a detective 'attempts to decipher in order to gain access to a priceless secret, in pursuit of which others have already perished'.[46] The detective figure in Eco's novel, William of Baskerville (whose name proclaims a connection with both the empiricist Medieval philosopher William of Ockham and the Holmes of Conan

Doyle's *The Hound of the Baskervilles*), accompanied by his young protégé Adso, is investigating the murder of Venantius, a monk murdered in 1327 because he has located a valuable book hidden in the library of the monastery. Venantius had recorded the book's location in an encrypted message, which William must decipher in order both to solve the mystery of the murder – one of a series of murders in the monastery – and to find the hidden text. The detective's task is thus one of decipherment, and delay is the product of misreading and misinterpretation.

The encrypting of texts is also echoed in the space to which William is finally led – the library as labyrinth – while the letter literally kills, as the murderer, Jorge of Burgos, poisons the pages on which the secret book is written, thus destroying those who attempt to read it. The name of the murderer, and the attribute of blindness, with its distant Oedipal echo, is very close to the name and the identity of Jorge Borges. As Eco wrote in his 'Postscript' to the novel: 'I wanted a blind man who guarded a library (it seemed a good narrative idea to me), and library plus blind man can only equal Borges, also because debts must be paid'.[47] The concept of literary debt would in this instance seem an ambiguous one, with at least some kinship to the contiguity between 'homage' and 'gommage' central to Robbe-Grillet's literary universe.

The 'Postscript' gives a detailed account of the novel's conception, its 'intertextuality' (it is a novel almost entirely made up of other texts) and 'enunciative duplicity' (the narration of the young and the old Adso), Eco's imaginary constructions of his 'ideal reader', and his choice of generic models: 'since I wanted you to feel as pleasurable the one thing that frightens us – namely, the metaphysical shudder – I had only to choose (from among the model plots) the most metaphysical and philosophical: the detective novel'.[48] Yet, as Eco notes, 'this is a mystery in which very little is discovered and the detective is defeated'.

Brian McHale has argued, in *Constructing Postmodernism*, that William of Baskerville conspicuously fails as a detective, a failure that 'undermines the basic assumption of the detective story from Poe's Dupin through Sherlock Holmes to Hercule Poirot and Miss Marple and beyond, namely, the assumption of the adequacy of reason itself, of ratiocination'.[49] William stumbles upon the truth rather than arriving at it through a successful chain of deductions:

> "There was no plot," William said, "and I discovered it by mistake . . . I have never doubted the truth of signs, Adso; they are the only things man has with which to orient himself in the world. What I did not understand was the relation among signs . . . I behaved stubbornly, pursuing a semblance of order, when I should have known well that there is no order in the universe."[50]

McHale uses *The Name of the Rose* as a way of conceptualising the nature of the divide between modernist and postmodernist fiction. 'A modernist novel', he argues (in my view reductively), 'looks like a detective story. Classic detective fiction is the epistemological genre *par excellence*.'[51] Modernist fictions, from Henry James to 'the late-modernist epistemological quests of Joseph McElroy', 'revolve round problems of the accessibility and circulation of knowledge, the individual mind's grappling with an elusive or occluded reality'. Eco's novel would seem to be part of this grouping, and to dramatise an epistemological quest, but in its construction of a detective who fails it properly belongs with the genre of the 'anti-detective novel', and with those fictions which 'by deliberately crippling the detective story's epistemological structure, . . . in effect evacuate the detective story of its epistemological thematics'. 'What rushes in', McHale asks rhetorically, 'when the anti-detective story empties the detective model of its epistemological structure and thematics? What else but ontological structure and thematics: postmodernist poetics.'[52]

McHale locates the 'postmodernism' of *The Name of the Rose* in its metafictionality and 'its relative ontological "weakness" *vis-à-vis* its own author, whose presence it reveals "behind" it'; in its strategies for destabilising the projected world of the novel itself, including deliberate historical anachronism; in its characteristically postmodernist themes of labyrinthine and disorientating space and of displaced apocalypse, in which a parallel is drawn between the destruction of a book, figurative (through the exposure of its fictionality) or literal, and the destruction of a world. Finally he argues, however, that the novel cannot be located as either modernist or postmodernist, and that 'it calls into question the entire opposition of modernist post-modernist'.[53] It is an 'amphibious' text which serves to trouble the literary-critical tendency to reify categories which can never be anything but 'literary-historical discursive constructs'.[54] This argument has some relation to Teresa de Lauretis's more cynical claim that 'in *The Name of the Rose* Eco wants to "have his carcase" – he wants a mystery both with and without solution, a text both open and closed, an epistemology with and without truth'.[55]

Paul Auster's *The New York Trilogy* (*City of Glass*, *Ghosts*, *The Locked Room*) also deploys and subverts the conventions of detective fiction, and in particular the private eye novel, in its explorations of identity, authorship and narrative. In all three parts of the trilogy, the central figures (only one of whom, that of *The Locked Room*, is a first-person narrator) are called into service as detectives in ways familiar from the fiction of Raymond Chandler or Dashiell Hammett: a phone call, a visit from a mysterious stranger, a letter. Yet from the very start the interpellations do not establish and secure the identity of the private eye, but render it uncertain, and even mistaken, as in the opening lines of *City of Glass*: 'It was a wrong number that started it, the telephone ringing three times in the dead of night, and the voice on the other end asking for someone he was not.'[56] Daniel Quinn, the recipient of the phone call, is a writer of mystery novels under the name of William Wilson (the name of one of Poe's characters) and his private eye narrator is one Max Work; the voice at the other end of the phone asks to speak to Paul Auster of the Auster Detective Agency. As the phone calls repeat themselves, Quinn decides to take on the identity of Auster the private eye and the case that is presented to him; that of finding and following Peter Stillman, recently released from prison after a long sentence imposed for his cruelty to his son, and thus preventing him from returning to do further harm. Quinn becomes the client of Virginia Stillman, wife of Peter Stillman's son, also called Peter (as was Quinn's dead son), irrevocably damaged by his father's treatment of him. As a very young child he had been locked in a dark room, and denied all access to human contact and the outside world, as his father sought to prove his theories about an 'original' language. The question of naming, and of a 'natural' relationship between words and things, recurs throughout the *Trilogy*.

Quinn abandons all other activities in order to follow Peter Stillman senior, tracking the old man in an echo of the pursuit enacted in Poe's 'The Man of the Crowd' (1840). As Quinn shadows Stillman through the streets of New York, recording his observations in a red notebook, he finds that the monotony of the pursuit is alleviated by the activity of writing:

> Not only did he take note of Stillman's gestures, describe each object he selected or rejected for his bag, and keep an accurate timetable of all events, but he also set down with care an exact itinerary of Stillman's divagations, noting each street he followed, each turn he made, and each pause that occurred. In addition to keeping him busy, the red notebook slowed Quinn's pace. There was no danger now of overtaking Stillman. The problem, rather, was to keep up with him, to make sure he did not vanish. For walking and writing were not easily compatible activities. If for the past five years Quinn had spent his days doing the one and the other, now he was trying to do them both at the same time.[57]

While at one level 'walking and writing may not be easily compatible activities', at another they become inseparable in Auster's depiction of *Wandersmänner*; walkers, in Michel de Certeau's words, 'whose bodies follow the thicks and thins of an urban "text" they write without reading'.[58] Quinn seeks to locate meaning in Stillman's perambulations, mapping the old man's wanderings and finding in them shapes equivalent to alphabetical letters: 'He wanted there to be a sense to them, no matter how obscure'.[59]

Like the Oedipa Maas of Pynchon's *The Crying of Lot 49*, Quinn finds himself at, in Peter Middleton and Tim Woods's phrase, 'a hermeneutic impasse'.[60] Opting for meaning rather than arbitrariness, he finds that the movement of Stillman's steps, when transcribed as diagrams, makes the shape of the letters OWEROFBAB, which Quinn completes as THE TOWER OF BABEL, conjuring up the Biblical narrative of the fall into linguistic multiplicity which underlies Stillman's belief in a single 'natural' language of humanity. Quinn invokes Poe's *The Narrative of A. Gordon Pym* (1838) here, with its closing discovery of 'the strange hieroglyphs on the inner wall of the chasm – letters inscribed into the earth itself, as though they were trying to say something that could no longer be understood'.[61] He qualifies this association immediately; the pictures/letters exist 'not in the streets where they had been drawn, but in Quinn's red notebook'. They exist, that is, in writing, not in nature.

The invocation of Poe in connection with a hieroglyphic language is, however, one of a network of references throughout the *Trilogy* to American writers for whom 'hieroglyphics' have been central: Emerson, Thoreau, Melville, Hawthorne and Whitman. It seems probable that Auster was drawing upon John T. Irwin's *American Hieroglyphics,* a study of nineteenth-century American writers' relationships to the recent decipherment of Egyptian hieroglyphics, which links 'the image of the hieroglyphics to the larger reciprocal question of the origin and limits of symbolization and the symbolization of origins and ends'.[62] In *Ghosts*, the detective-figure Blue, set to watch Black, starts, with difficulty, to read Thoreau's *Walden*, which he sees, through his binoculars, Black reading at his desk: 'What he does not know is that were he to find the patience to read the book in the spirit in which it asks to be read, his entire life would begin to change, and little by little he would come to a full understanding of his situation – that is to say, of Black, of White, of the case, of everything that concerns him.'[63] Black abandons Thoreau's book, but retains something from the text that clarifies his situation as the watcher watched. In *Walden,* 'we are not where we are, he finds, but in a false position. Through an infirmity of our natures, we suppose a case, and put ourselves into it, and hence are in two cases at the same time, and it is doubly difficult to get out.'[64]

This doubleness, or duplicity, is echoed in the dual possibilities presented to Auster's detective figures; the narrative in which plot elements cohere and have meaning, and that ruled by chance and contingency in which the creation of a coherent story is a consolatory fiction. It also bears on the situation of authorship itself, and, to quote Irwin, 'with the notion of the writer's corpus as an inscribed shadow self, a hieroglyphic double'.[65] In *City of Glass*, Quinn decides to contact 'Paul Auster'; he finds not a detective but a writer, whose description we recognise as that of the 'real' Paul Auster whose novel we are reading. The Paul Auster inside the novel is writing an essay on *Don Quixote* (whose initials are shared by Daniel Quinn), the 'first' novel, and in particular on its authorship: 'the book inside the book Cervantes wrote, the one he imagined he was writing'.[66] Like *Don Quixote*, *New York Trilogy* is a vertiginous structure of embedded stories, found texts and fictional disguises: the plot of *City of Glass* is, as Stephen Bernstein notes, 'significantly motivated by several references to Cervantes' novel of quests gone mad'.[67] Auster's novel also alludes to Borges's story, 'Pierre Menard, Author of the *Quixote*' (1941), in which the retranscription of *Don Quixote* becomes its recreation.

Auster's *Trilogy* has achieved both considerable popular success and attracted very extensive critical and theoretical attention. This seems largely due to the fact that it operates simultaneously, and in highly successful ways, as both a detective and as an 'anti-detective' novel, drawing upon the conventions of Hammett and Chandler as well as Kafka and Beckett. It deploys a whole repertoire of 'classical' detective devices and locations, such as the 'locked room', as the conditions of an existential predicament. Like Pynchon's *The Crying of Lot 49*, it 'hesitates' between models of excess and of exhaustion, of too much meaning or too little. Moreover, while contemporary novelists continue to use the figure of the detective in complex and challenging ways – Kazuo Ishiguro's *When We Were Orphans* (2000) is a particularly teasing example – Auster's *Trilogy* could be seen not only as transgressing and travestying the norms of traditional detective and private eye fictions but as both a culmination and an evacuation of the forms and norms of the 'metaphysical' detective novel. In other words, the 'metaphysical' or 'anti-detective' novel has become not only the text which subverts but one which can now itself be subverted. It remains to be seen whether this openness to subversion signals the end of the line or, as I suspect, the means of its renewal.

Critics and commentators of the 1920 and 1930s argued that the 'literary' dimension of detective fiction is partly secured by the genre's status as the popular reading matter most beloved of intellectuals. Dorothy Sayers quoted Philip Guedalla's claim that 'the detective-story is the normal recreation of noble minds', adding that 'it is remarkable how strong is the fascination of the higher type of detective-story for the intellectual-minded, among writers as well as readers'.[68] Sayers, Marjorie Nicolson, Q. D. Leavis and others saw strong connections between detective fiction and games such as bridge, chess and crossword puzzles, arguing that the pleasures of the detective novel were, for the modern reader, almost entirely 'ratiocinative'. The concept of 'fair play' in the construction of detective narratives suggested an ethical dimension, but was rather more important as a way of emphasising the ludic aspects of the genre, central to the theories of writers on detective fiction such as Roger Caillois, whose work has had a significant influence on postmodern theory. Caillois was fascinated by the role of games and play in culture and, as Jorge Luis Borges noted in his review of Caillois's *Le Roman policier*, analysed the role of detective fiction as 'rational game, lucid game'.[69] More generally, detective fiction, as Dennis Porter has argued, constructs an 'ambience of play' in the form of the 'surprise of crime', which emerges in, for example, the use of the most unlikely suspect and the most improbable detective figure, the classic example of whom is Agatha Christie's Miss Marple.[70]

Detective fiction was of central interest to the Oulipo, (*Ouvroir de Literature Potentielle*), founded by the experimental writers Raymond Queneau and François Le Lionnais in 1960 to explore the ways in which abstract restrictions could be combined with imaginative writing (as in George Perec's novel *La Disparition* (1969), written without the letter *e*). In 1973, Le Lionnais inaugurated the Oulipopo (*Ouvroir de Litterature Policière Potentielle*); its first projects were analyses 'dissecting many known or possible combinations concerning situation and character in the mystery story' (Analytic Oulipopo), proceeding to ways 'to discover, distinguish, or invent procedures or constraints that could serve as "aids to imagination" of writers of detective stories' (Synthetic Oulipopo).[71] Oulipopian experiments included 'Haikuisation' – 'A version of the Oulipian procedure whereby the first and last sentences or phrases of a detective novel are alone retained, these being traditionally the most significant in works of this genre' – and the writing of a detective novel in which the reader is guilty. The Oulipopo group were fascinated by the construction of rules for composing detective fiction, particularly those of S. S. Van Dine and Ronald Knox, turning these early twentieth-century attempts to define the conventions and limits of the detective genre into literary games that combined surrealism and structuralism. George Perec's final novel *53 Days* (2000), unfinished at his death and completed from his notes by Oulipians Harry Matthews and Jacques Roubaud, is a 'literary thriller' which inscribes, among other texts, Stendhal's *The Charterhouse of Parma* (the 53 days of Perec's title refers to the time taken by Stendhal to dictate his novel), Agatha Christie's *And Then There Were None* (1939) in which, in Perec's words, 'nine unconvicted culprits are executed . . . by a judge who makes it seem as if he is the tenth (but not the last) victim', and a short story by the crime writer Maurice

Leblanc entitled 'Swan-Neck Edith' (1913). In *53 Days*, Jacques Roubaud wrote:

> Life appears as a puzzle endlessly destroying its own solutions. The multiplicity of the explanations of a death, of a murder, forms an allegory of a life that does not know its own end.[72]

In less experimentalist contexts, academia has been a favoured site for detective fiction, most famously, perhaps, in Dorothy L. Sayers's use of an Oxford women's college in *Gaudy Night*, and pursued in detective novels by 'Amanda Cross', the pseudonym of Carolyn Heilbrun, an English literature professor at Columbia University. The academic arena offers not only the advantages of a (relatively) closed community, but brings to the fore the concept of literary scholarship as a form of detective work. Michael Innes's *Hamlet, Revenge* takes several chapters to produce a corpse, carefully setting the scene in the country house in which the murder will take place, and taking the narrative time to 'rehearse' the amateur production of *Hamlet* which is the occasion for the gathering together of the novel's protagonists. The murder of the elder statesman playing the part of Polonius creates its own play on 'the play within a play' central to *Hamlet*, while the play's director, Gott, is, like his creator ('Michael Innes' is the pseudonym of novelist and critic J. I. M. Stewart) both an Oxford English don and a writer of detective novels. Such self-referentiality is characteristic of academic writers of detective fiction who are both consciously crossing over literary borders (the high and the popular) and at the same time intent on showing that detective fiction can claim literary status.

Numerous twentieth-century novelists have explored the relationship, noted by early twentieth-century critics, between biography and detective work. Fictions such as Vladimir Nabokov's *The Real Life of Sebastian Knight* (1941), Penelope Lively's *According to Mark* (1984), Carol Shields's *Mary Swann* (1990) and A. S. Byatt's *Possession* (1990) portray a biographer tracking his or her subject across the territory, following (in) his or her footsteps, and often losing the trail. Biographical knowledge, the knowledge of the other, is rendered uncertain and incomplete. The elements which become more or less explicit are, first, the biographer's identification with or desire for the subject whom he or she pursues, and, second, the nature of the 'evidence' and the means of its gathering.

A. S. Byatt's *Possession* uses the suspense devices of the detective novel to explore the ways in which the feminist 'recovery' of forgotten women writers becomes a form of literary detection. In the service of scholarship, two young academics, Roland Michell and Maud Bailey, pursue the manuscripts of, respectively, Victorian poets Randolph Henry Ash and Christabel LaMotte, and find through their researches the story of a passionate and illicit love affair between the two. In Carol Shields's novel, the quarry is not the murderer of the woman poet Mary Swann; her farmer-husband confesses immediately to her violent murder, and her fragmented body-parts do not come under any forensic gaze. The novel instead explores the fate of other kinds of fragments: of her life, her poetry and her literary 'remains'. Quartering her own novel, Shields gives the narration over to, in sequence, Sarah Maloney, a feminist scholar fascinated by Swann's 'naïve' poetry; Morton Jimroy, Swann's biographer; Rose Hindmarsh, the librarian in the small Canadian town near to the Swanns' farm, and Frederic Cruzzi, the retired newspaper editor to whom Mary Swann brought a paper-bag full of her poems hours before her murder. All four meet at a conference on Mary Swann's work which is both the summation of the novel and its undoing, as the intimacy of first-person narratives gives way to 'postmodern' self-consciousness.

As we have seen, the work of writers such as Pynchon, Eco and Auster testifies to the continuing impact of the detective paradigm on contemporary literature, and to the detective genre's openness to subversion and renewal, 'homage' and 'gommage'. Novels such as Byatt's *Possession* and Shields's *Mary Swann* add a further dimension, in their articulation of the complex relationship between biographical fiction and detective fiction, and its implications for our notions of selfhood and for the subjective authority both claimed and renounced by the narrative voices of our time.

## NOTES

1 Tzvetan Todorov, 'The Typology of Detective Fiction', *The Poetics of Prose*, trans. Richard Howard (Ithaca, NY: Cornell University Press), pp. 42–52.
2 Peter Brooks, *Reading for the Plot: Design and Intention in Narrative* (Oxford: Oxford University Press, 1984), p. 25.
3 Peter Hühn, 'The Detective as Reader: Narrativity and Reading Concepts in Detective Fiction', *Modern Fiction Studies* 33, 3 (1987): 451–66: S. E. Sweeney, 'Locked Rooms: Detective Fiction, Narrative Theory, and Self-Reflexivity', in *The Cunning Craft: Original Essays on Detective Fiction and Contemporary Literary Theory*, eds. Ronald G. Walker and June M. Frazer (Macomb: Western Illinois University Press, 1990), pp. 1–14.
4 Heta Pyrhönen, *Murder from an Academic Angle: An Introduction to the Study of the Detective Narrative* (Columbia, SC: Camden House, 1994), p. 6.
5 Thomas Pynchon, *The Crying of Lot 49* (London: Picador, 1979), p. 60.
6 Walter Benjamin, *Charles Baudelaire: a Lyric Poet in the Era of High Capitalism*, trans. Harry Zohn (London: Verso, 1983), p. 48.
7 *Ibid.*
8 G. K. Chesterton, 'A Defence of Detective Stories' (1902), reprinted in Howard Haycraft (ed.), *The Art of the Mystery Story* (New York: Carroll & Graf, 1983), p. 4.

9  *Ibid.*, p. 6.

10  Raymond Chandler, 'The Simple Art of Murder' (1944), reprinted in Haycraft (ed.), *The Art of the Mystery Story*, p. 237.

11  Pynchon, *The Crying of Lot 49*, p. 125.

12  See, for example, Peter Ackroyd, *Hawksmoor* (London: Abacus, 1985); Iain Sinclair, *White Chappell Scarlet Tracings* (London: Granta Books, 1988).

13  Geoffrey H. Hartman, 'Literature High and Low: The Case of the Mystery Story', *The Fate of Reading and Other Essays* (Chicago: University of Chicago Press, 1975), p. 212.

14  Marjorie Nicolson, 'The Professor and the Detective' (1929), in Haycraft (ed.), *The Art of the Mystery Story*, p. 485.

15  Michael Holquist, 'Whodunit and Other Questions: Metaphysical Detective Stories in Post-War Fiction', *New Literary History*, Vol 3, No. 1. Autumn 1971, p. 147.

16  *Ibid.*

17  *Ibid.*, p. 148.

18  *Ibid.*

19  *Ibid.*, p. 155.

20  Gertrude Stein, *Everybody's Autobiography* (London: Heinemann, 1938), p. x.

21  Stein, 'What are Masterpieces and Why are There So Few of Them', reprinted in *Gertrude Stein: Look at Me Know and Here I Am: Writings and Lectures 1911–1945* ed. Patricia Meyerowitz (London: Peter Owen, 1967), p. 149.

22  Stein, 'Why I Like Detective Stories' (1937), in *How Writing is Written*, Vol. 2 of *The Previously Uncollected Writings of Gertrude Stein* ed. Robert Bartlett House (Santa Barbara, Cal: Black Sparrow Press, 1977), p. 148.

23  Stein, *Everybody's Autobiography*, p. 80.

24  William Spanos, 'The Detective and the Boundary', in Paul A.Bove (ed.), *Early Postmodernism: Foundational Essays* (Durham, NC: Duke University Press, 1995), p. 20.

25  *Ibid.*, p. 25.

26  Stefano Tani, 'The Dismemberment of the Detective', *Diogenes*, No, 120, Winter 1980, p. 24.

27  *Ibid.*, p. 41.

28  Pyrhönen, *Murder from an Academic Angle*, pp. 44–5.

29  Patricia Merivale and Susan Elizabeth Sweeney (eds.), *Detecting Texts: the Metaphysical Detective Story from Poe to Postmodernism* (Philadelphia: University of Pennsylvania Press, 1999), p. 3.

30  Jorge Luis Borges, 'On the Origins of the Detective Novel', in Emir Rodriguez Monegal and Alastair Reid (eds.), *Borges: A Reader* (New York: Dutton, p. 1981), p. 148.

31  Quoted by Gene H. Bell-Vilada, *Borges and his Fiction* (Austin: University of Texas Press, 1999), p. 32.

32  Borges, 'Modes of G. K. Chesterton', in *Borges: A Reader*, p. 89.

33  *Ibid.*, pp. 89–90.

34  Howard Haycraft, *Murder for Pleasure: The Life and Times of the Detective Story* (1942; New York: Biblio and Tannen, 1974), p. 76.

35  Merivale and Sweeney, *Detecting Texts*, p. 1.

36  Bell-Vilada, *Borges and his Fiction*, p. 35.

37 Borges, 'Death and the Compass', in *Labyrinths* (Harmondsworth: Penguin, 1970), p. 106.

38 *Ibid.*, p. 108.

39 *Ibid.*, p. 115.

40 As John T. Irwin notes, Borges reworks the numerical/geometrical structure of Poe's 'The Purloined Letter', while the play between the three-fold and the four-fold is echoed in the debate between Lacan and Derrida in their readings of Poe's text. See John T. Irwin, 'Mysteries We Reread, Mysteries of Rereading: Poe, Borges, and the Analytic Detective Story', in Merivale and Sweeney (eds.), *Detecting Texts*, pp. 27–54. For the essays by Lacan and Derrida, see John P. Muller and William J. Richardson (eds.), *The Purloined Poe: Lacan, Derrida, and Psychoanalytic Reading* (Baltimore: Johns Hopkins University Press, 1988).

41 Borges, 'Death and the Campass', p. 117.

42 Borges, 'Commentaries', in *The Aleph and Other Stories, 1933–1969*, trans. Norman Thomas di Giovanni (New York: Dutton, 1978), p. 269.

43 Alain Robbe-Grillet, *The Erasers*, trans. Richard Howard (London: John Calder, 1987), p. 192.

44 *Ibid.*, pp. 36–7.

45 Raylene Ramsay, 'Postmodernism and the Monstrous Criminal in Robbe-Grillet's Investigative Cell', in Merivale and Sweeney (eds.), *Detecting Texts*, p. 213.

46 Joel Black, '(De)feats of Detection: The Spurious Key Text from Poe to Eco', in Merivale and Sweeney (eds.), *Detecting Texts*, p. 84.

47 Umberto Eco, Postscript to *The Name of the Rose*, trans. William Weaver (New York: Harcourt Brace Jovanovich, 1984), p. 28.

48 *Ibid.*, p. 53.

49 Brian McHale, *Constructing Postmodernism* (New York: Routledge, 1992), p. 15.

50 Umberto Eco, *The Name of the Rose*, trans. William Weaver (London: Picador, 1984), pp. 491–2.

51 McHale, *Constructing Postmodernism*, p. 147.

52 *Ibid.*, p. 151.

53 *Ibid.*, p. 163.

54 *Ibid.*, p. 164.

55 Teresa de Lauretis, *Technologies of Gender: Essays on Theory, Film and Fiction* (Bloomington: Indiana University Press, 1984), p. 60.

56 Paul Auster, *The New York Trilogy* (London: Faber, 1987), p. 3.

57 *Ibid.*, p. 62.

58 Michel de Certeau, 'Walking in the City', in *The Practice of Everyday Life*, trans. Steven Rendall (Berkeley and Los Angeles: University of California Press, 1984), p. 93. See also Mireille Rosello, 'The Screener's Maps: Michel de Certeau's "Wandersmänner" and Paul Auster's Hypertextual Detective', in *Hyper/Text/ Theory*, ed. George P. Landow (Baltimore: Johns Hopkins University Press, 1994), pp. 121–58.

59 Auster, *The New York Trilogy*, p. 69.

60 Peter Middleton and Tim Woods, *Literatures of Memory* (Manchester: Manchester University Press, 2000), p. 296.

61 Auster, *The New York Trilogy*, pp. 70–1.

62 John T. Irwin, *American Hieroglyphics* (New Haven, CT: Yale University Press, 1980), p. xi.

63 Auster, *The New York Trilogy*, p. 163.

64 *Ibid.*, p. 168.

65 Irwin, *American Hieroglyphics*, p. xi.

66 Auster, *The New York Trilogy*, p. 97.

67 Stephen Bernstein, '"The Question Is the Story Itself": Postmodernism and Intertextuality in Auster's *New York Trilogy*', in Merivale and Sweeney (eds.), *Detecting Texts*, p. 139.

68 Dorothy L. Sayers (ed.), *Great Short Stories of Detection, Mystery and Horror*, Part 1, *Detection and Mystery* (London: Gollancz, 1928), p. 44.

69 Borges, 'On the Origins of the Detective Story', in *Borges: a Reader*, p. 148.

70 Dennis Porter, 'The Language of Detection', in Tony Bennett (ed.), *Popular Fiction: Technology, Ideology, Production, Reading* (London: Routledge, 1990), pp. 81–93.

71 See *Oulipo Compendium*, compiled by Harry Mathews and Alastair Brotchie (London: Atlas Press, 1998), pp. 251–271.

72 Quoted David Bellos, *George Perec: A Life in Words* (Boston: David R. Godine, 1993), p. 704.

# GUIDE TO READING

## General

Barzun, Jacques, *The Delights of Detection* (New York: Criterion, 1961)

Binyon, T. J., *'Murder Will Out': The Detective in Fiction* (Oxford: Oxford University Press, 1990)

Cawelti, John G., *Adventure, Mystery and Romance: Formula Stories as Art and Popular Culture* (Chicago: Chicago University Press, 1976)

Cohen, Michael, *Murder Most Fair: The Appeal of Mystery Fiction* (Cranbury, NJ: Associated University Presses, 2000)

Grossvogel, David I., *Mystery and its Fictions: From Oedipus to Agatha Christie* (Baltimore: Johns Hopkins University Press, 1979)

Haycraft, Howard, *Murder for Pleasure: The Life and Times of the Detective Story* (1942; New York: Biblio and Tannen, 1974)

ed., *The Art of the Mystery Story: A Collection of Critical Essays*, 2nd edn (1946; New York: Carroll and Graf, 1983)

Herbert, Rosemary, ed., *The Oxford Companion to Crime and Mystery* (New York: Oxford University Press, 1999)

Keating, H. R. F., ed., *Whodunit? A Guide to Crime, Suspense and Spy Fiction* (London: Windward, 1982)

Knight, Stephen, *Form and Ideology in Crime Fiction* (London: Macmillan, 1980)

Mandel, Ernest, *Delightful Murder: A Social History of the Crime Story* (London: Pluto, 1984)

Most, Glenn W., and William W. Stowe, eds., *The Poetics of Murder* (New York: Harcourt Brace Jovanovich, 1983)

Ousby, Ian, *Bloodhounds of Heaven: The Detective in English Fiction from Godwin to Doyle* (Cambridge, MA: Harvard University Press, 1976).

Palmer, Jerry, *Thrillers: Genesis and Structure of a Popular Genre* (London: Arnold, 1978)

Pederson, Jay P., ed., *The St James' Guide to Crime and Mystery Writers* (Chicago: St James's Press, 1991)

Porter, Dennis, *The Pursuit of Crime: Art and Ideology in Detective Fiction* (New Haven, CT: Yale University Press, 1981)

Priestman, Martin, *Detective Fiction and Literature: The Figure on the Carpet* (Basingstoke: Macmillan, 1990)

*Crime Fiction from Poe to the Present* (Plymouth: Northcote House, 1998)

Pyrhönen, Heta, *Murder from an Academic Angle: An Introduction to the Study of the Detective Narrative* (Columbia, SC: Camden House, 1994)

Stewart, R. F., *And Always a Detective: Chapters on the History of Detective Fiction* (Newton Abbot: David and Charles, 1980)

Symons, Julian, *Bloody Murder: From the Detective Story to the Crime Novel: A History*, 2nd edn (Harmondsworth: Penguin, 1985)

Todorov, Tzvetan, *The Poetics of Prose*, trans. R. Howard (Oxford: Blackwell, 1977)

Winks, Robin W., ed., *Detective Fiction: A Collection of Critical Essays* (Englewood Cliffs, NJ: Prentice-Hall, 1980)

Winks, Robin W., and Maureen Corrigan, eds., *Mystery and Suspense Writers: The Literature of Crime, Detection, and Espionage* (New York: Scribner's, 1998)

## Eighteenth-century crime writing

Bell, Ian A., *Literature and Crime in Augustan England* (London: Routledge, 1991)

Beattie, J. M., *Crime and the Courts in England 1660–1800* (Oxford: Clarendon, 1986)

Foucault, Michel, *Discipline and Punish: The Birth of the Prison*, trans. A. Sheridan (London: Allen Lane, 1977)

Hay, Douglas, *et al.*, eds., *Albion's Fatal Tree: Crime and Society in Eighteenth-Century England* (London: Allen Lane, 1976)

Howson, Gerald, *It Takes a Thief: The Life and Times of Jonathan Wild* (London: Cresset Library, 1987)

Radzinowicz, Sir Leon, *A History of English Criminal Law and its Administration from 1750: Vol. 1, The Movement for Reform* (London: Stevens & Sons, 1948)

Richetti, John J., *Popular Fiction Before Richardson: Narrative Patterns, 1700–1739* (Oxford: Clarendon, 1969)

## The Newgate novel and sensation fiction

Altick, Richard D., *Victorian Studies in Scarlet: Murders and Manners in the Age of Victoria* (London: Dent, 1972)

Brantlinger, Patrick, *The Spirit of Reform: British Literature and Politics, 1832–67* (Cambridge, MA: Harvard University Press, 1977)

Cvetkovich, Ann, *Mixed Feelings: Feminism, Mass Culture and Victorian Sensationalism* (New Brunswick, NJ: Rutgers University Press, 1992)

Engel, Elliot, and Margaret F. King, *The Victorian Novel Before Victoria: British Fiction during the Reign of William IV, 1830–37* (New York: St Martin's Press, 1984)

Hollingsworth, Keith, *The Newgate Novel, 1830–1847: Bulwer, Ainsworth, Dickens and Thackeray* (Detroit: Wayne State University Press, 1963)

Hughes, Winifred, *The Maniac in the Cellar: Sensation Novels of the 1860s* (Princeton University Press, 1980)

Kalikoff, Beth, *Murder and Moral Decay in Victorian Popular Literature* (Ann Arbor: UMI Research Press, 1987)

Leps, Marie-Christine, *Apprehending the Criminal: The Production of Deviance in Nineteenth-Century Discourse* (Durham, NC: Duke University Press, 1992)

Miller, D. A., *The Novel and the Police* (Berkeley: University of California Press, 1988)

Pykett, Lyn, *The Sensation Novel from 'The Woman in White' to 'The Moonstone'* (Plymouth: Northcote House, 1994)

### The short story from Poe to Chesterton

Allen, Walter, *The Short Story in English* (Oxford: Clarendon Press, 1981)

Bloom, Clive, et al., eds., *Nineteenth-Century Suspense: From Poe to Conan Doyle* (Basingstoke: Macmillan, 1988)

Greene, Hugh, ed., *The Rivals of Sherlock Holmes: Early Detective Stories* (Harmondsworth: Penguin, 1971)

*Further Rivals of Sherlock Holmes* (Harmondsworth: Penguin, 1976)

*More Rivals of Sherlock Holmes* (Harmondsworth: Penguin, 1973)

Kayman, Martin A., *From Bow Street to Baker Street: Mystery, Detection and Narrative* (Basingstoke: Macmillan, 1992)

Queen, Ellery, *Queen's Quorum: A History of the Detective-Crime Short Story as Revealed by the 106 Most Important Books Published in This Field since 1845* (Boston: Little, Brown & Co., 1951)

Reed, David, *The Popular Magazine in Britain and the United States 1880–1960* (London: The British Library, 1997)

Slung, Michele B., ed., *Crime on Her Mind: Fifteen Stories of Female Sleuths from the Victorian Era to the Forties* (London: Michael Joseph, 1975)

### French crime fiction

Fondanèché, Daniel, *Le Roman Policier, thèmes et études* (Paris: Ellipses, 2000)

Hale, T. J., ed., *Great French Detective Stories* (London: The Bodley Head, 1983)

Bonniot, Roger, *Emile Gaboriau ou la Naissance du Roman Policier* (Paris: Editions J. Vrin, 1985)

Benjamin, Walter, *Charles Baudelaire; A Lyric Poet in the Era of High Capitalism*, trans. *Harry Zohn* (London: Verso, 1973)

Lacassin, Francis, *Mythologie du Roman Policier* (Paris: Union Général d'Editions, 1974)

Marnham, Patrick, *The Man who wasn't Maigret, A Portrait of Georges Simenon* (London: Penguin, 1992)

Messac, Régis, *Le Detective-Novel et l'Influence de la Pensée Scientifique* (Paris: Slatkine Reprints, 1975)

Perry, Sheila, and Marie Cross, eds., *Voices of France; Social, Political and Cultural Identity* (London: Pinter, 1997)

Rhodes, Henry T. F., *Alphonse Bertillon, Father of Scientific Detection* (London: George G. Harrap & Co., 1956)

Stead, Philip John, *Vidocq, a Biography* (London: Staples Press, 1953)
*The Police of France* (London: Macmillan, 1983)


## The golden age

Barnard, Robert, *A Talent to Deceive: An Appreciation of Agatha Christie* (London: Collins, 1980)

Christie, Agatha, *An Autobiography* (London: Collins, 1977)

Hitchman, Janet, *Such a Strange Lady: An Introduction to Dorothy L. Sayers* (London: New English Library, 1975)

Joshi, S. T., *John Dickson Carr: A Critical Study* (Bowling Green, OH: Popular Press, 1990)

Light, Alison, *Forever England: Femininity, Literature and Conservatism between the Wars* (London: Routledge, 1991)

Mann, Jessica, *Deadlier than the Male: An Investigation into Feminine Crime Writing* (Newton Abbot: David and Charles, 1981)

Panek, LeRoy L., *Watteau's Shepherds: The Detective Novel in Britain 1914–1940* (Bowling Green, OH: Popular Press, 1979)

Routley, Erik, *The Puritan Pleasures of the Detective Story* (London: Gollancz, 1972)

Shaw, Marion, and Sabine Vanacker, *Reflecting on Miss Marple* (London: Routledge, 1991)

Turnbull, Malcolm J., *Elusion Aforethought: The Life and Writing of Anthony Berkeley Cox* (Bowling Green, OH: Popular Press, 1996)

Tuska, Jon, *Philo Vance: the Life and Times of S. S. Van Dine* (Bowling Green, OH: Popular Press, 1971)

Watson, Colin, *Snobbery with Violence: English Crime Stories and Their Audience* (London: Eyre and Spottiswoode, 1971)

Wells, Carolyn, *The Technique of the Mystery Story* (Springfield: The Home Correspondence School, 1913)


## The private eye

Bruccoli, Mathew, *Ross Macdonald* (San Diego: Harcourt Brace Jovanovich, 1984)

Geherin, David, *The American Private Eye: The Image in Fiction* (New York: F. Ungar, 1985)

Gross, Miriam, ed., *The World of Raymond Chandler* (New York: A & W, 1978)

Hart, James D., *The Popular Book: A History of America's Literary Taste* (Berkeley: University of California Press, 1950)

Johnson, Diane, *The Life of Dashiell Hammett* (New York: Random House, 1983)

MacShane, Frank, *The Life of Raymond Chandler* (London: Jonathan Cape, 1976)
ed., *The Notebooks of Raymond Chandler* (London: Weidenfeld and Nicolson, 1976)

Nelson, James, ed., *The Simple Art of Murder* (New York: Norton, 1968)

Nolan, William F., *Dashiell Hammett: A Casebook* (Santa Barbara: McNally and Loftin, 1969)
*Hammett: A Life at the Edge* (New York: Congdon and Weed, 1983)

Schopen, Bernard, *Ross Macdonald* (Boston: Twayne, 1990)

## Spy fiction

Amis, Kingsley, *The James Bond Dossier* (London: Jonathan Cape, 1965)

Barley, Tony, *Taking Sides: The Fiction of John Le Carré* (Milton Keynes: Open University Press, 1986)

Bennett, Tony, and Janet Woollacott, *Bond and Beyond: The Political Career of a Popular Hero* (Basingstoke: Macmillan, 1987)

Bloom, Clive, ed., *Spy Thrillers: From Buchan to Le Carré* (Basingstoke: Macmillan, 1990)

Bloom, Harold, ed., *John le Carré: Modern Critical Views* (New York: Chelsea House, 1987)

Cawelti, John G., and Bruce A. Rosenberg, *The Spy Story* (Chicago: University of Chicago Press, 1987)

Denning, Michael, *Cover Stories: Narrative and Ideology in the British Spy Thriller* (London and New York: Routledge & Kegan Paul, 1987)

Eco, Umberto, and Oreste Del Buono, eds., *The Bond Affair* (London: Macmillan, 1966)

Merry, Bruce, *Anatomy of the Spy Thriller* (Dublin: Gill and Macmillan, 1977)

Panek, LeRoy L., *The Special Branch: The British Spy Novel, 1890–1980* (Bowling Green, OH: Popular Press, 1981)

Stafford, David, *The Silent Game: The Real World of Imaginary Spies*, rev. edn (Athens: University of Georgia Press, 1991)

## The thriller

Bloom, Clive, ed., *Twentieth-Century Suspense: The Thriller Comes of Age* (Basingstoke: Macmillan, 1990)

Butler, William V., *The Durable Desperadoes* (London: Macmillan, 1973)

Copjec, Joan, ed., *Shades of Noir: A Reader* (London: Verso, 1993)

Denning, Michael, *Mechanic Accents: Dime Novels and Working-Class Culture in America* (London: Verso, 1987)

Harper, Ralph, *The World of the Thriller* (Cleveland: Case Western Reserve University Press, 1969)

Haut, Woody, *Pulp Culture: Hardboiled Fiction and the Cold War* (London: Serpent's Tail, 1995)

  *Neon Noir: Contemporary American Crime Fiction* (London: Serpent's Tail, 1999)

Hilfer, Tony, *The Crime Novel: A Deviant Genre* (Austin: University of Texas Press, 1990)

Holland, Steve, *The Mushroom Jungle: A History of Postwar Paperback Publishing* (Westbury: Zeon Books, 1993)

Messent, Peter, ed., *Criminal Proceedings: The Contemporary American Crime Novel* (London: Pluto Press, 1997)

Webster, Duncan, *Looka Yonder! The Imaginary America of Populist Culture* (London: Comedia, 1988)

Williams, John, *Into the Badlands: Travels through Urban America* (London: Paladin, 1991)

## Post-war American police fiction

Cobley, Paul, *The American Thriller: Generic Innovation and Social Change in the 1970s* (Basingstoke: Palgrave, 2000)

Dove, George N., *The Police Procedural* (Bowling Green, OH: Popular Press, 1982)

Dove, George N., and Earl F. Bargainnier, eds., *Cops and Constables: American and British Fictional Policemen* (Bowling Green, OH: Popular Press, 1986)

Winston, Robert P., and Nancy C. Mellerski, *The Public Eye: Ideology and the Police Procedural* (Basingstoke: Macmillan, 1992)

## Post-war British crime fiction

Benstock, Bernard, and Thomas F. Staley, *British Mystery and Thriller Writers since 1940*, 1st series (Detroit: Gale, 1989)

Duncan, Paul, ed., *The Third Degree: Crime Writers in Conversation* (Harpenden, Herts.: No Exit, 1997)

Freeling, Nicolas, *Criminal Conversations: Errant Essays on Perpetrators of Literary Licence* (Boston, MA: David R. Godine, 1994)

Herbert, Rosemary, ed., *The Fatal Art of Entertainment* (New York: G. K. Hall & Co., 1994)

James, P. D., *Time to be in Earnest: A Fragment of Autobiography* (London: Faber & Faber, 1999)

Keating, H. R. F., ed., *Crime Writers: Reflections on Crime Fiction* (London: BBC, 1978)

Rowland, Susan, *From Agatha Christie to Ruth Rendell: British Women Writers in Detective and Crime Fiction* (Basingstoke: Palgrave, 2001)

Siebenheller, Norma, *P. D. James* (New York: Frederick Ungar, 1981)

Tamaya, Meera, *H. R. F. Keating: Post-Colonial Detection. A Critical Study* (Bowling Green, OH: Popular Press, 1993)

## Women detectives

Craig, Patricia, and Mary Cadogan, *The Lady Investigates: Women Detectives and Spies in Fiction* (London: Gollancz, 1981)

Irons, Glenwood, ed., *Feminism in Women's Detective Fiction* (Toronto: University of Toronto Press, 1995)

Klein, Kathleen Gregory, *The Woman Detective: Gender and Genre* (Urbana: University of Illinois Press, 1988)

McDermid, Val, *A Suitable Job for a Woman: Inside the World of Women Private Eyes* (London: Harper Collins, 1995)

Munt, Sally R., *Murder by the Book? Feminism and the Crime Novel* (New York: Routledge, 1994)

Newton, Judith, and Deborah Rosenfelt, eds., *Feminist Criticism and Social Change* (New York: Methuen, 1985)

Reddy, Maureen T., *Sisters in Crime: Feminism and the Crime Novel* (New York: Continuum, 1988)

## Black American crime fiction

Collins, Jim, *Uncommon Cultures: Popular Culture and Post-modernism* (London and New York: Routledge, 1989)

McCracken, Scott, *Pulp: Reading Popular Fiction* (Manchester and New York: Manchester University Press, 1996)

Pepper, Andrew, *The Contemporary American Crime Novel: Race, Ethnicity, Gender, Class* (Edinburgh: Edinburgh University Press, 2000)

Reddy, Maureen T., *Traces, Codes, and Clues: Reading Race in Crime Fiction* (New Burnswick, NJ: Rutgers University Press, 2003)

Soitos, Stephen, *The Blues Detective: A Study of African-American Detective Fiction* (Amherst, MT: University of Massachusetts Press, 1996)

Willett, Ralph, *The Naked City: Urban Crime Fiction in the USA* (Manchester and New York: Manchester University Press, 1996)

## Crime in film and on TV

Bergman, Andrew, *We're in the Money* (London: Harper and Row, 1971)

Brandt, George W. ed., *British Television Drama in the 1980s* (Cambridge: Cambridge University Press, 1993)

Brownlow, Kevin, *Behind the Mask of Innocence: Films of Social Conscience in the Silent Era* (Berkeley and London: University of California Press, 1990)

Buxton, David, *From The Avengers to Miami Vice* (Manchester University Press, 1990)

Chibnall, Steve, and Robert Murphy, eds., *British Crime Cinema* (London: Routledge, 1990)

D'Acci, Julie, *Defining Women: Television and the Case of Cagney and Lacey* (Chapel Hill, NC: University of North Carolina Press, 1994)

Hill, John, *Sex, Class and Realism* (London: BFI, 1986)

Krutnik, Frank, *In a Lonely Street* (London: Routledge, 1991)

Lewis, Jon, ed., *The New American Cinema* (London: Duke University Press, 1998)

Murphy, Robert, *Sixties British Cinema* (London: BFI, 1992)

Musser, Charles, *Before the Nickelodeon: Edwin S. Porter and the Edison Manufacturing Company* (Berkeley and London: University of California Press, 1991)

Naremore, James, *More Than Night: Film Noir in its contexts* (Berkeley: University of California Press, 1998)

Osgerby, Bill, and Anna Gough-Yates, eds., *Action TV: Tough Guys, Smooth Operators and Foxy Chicks* (London: Routledge, 2001)

Roddick, Nick, *A New Deal in Entertainment* (London: BFI, 1983)

Sparks, Richard, *Television and the Drama of Crime* (Milton Keynes: Open University Press, 1992)

## Detection and literary fiction

Barone, Dennis, ed., *Beyond the Red Notebook: Essays on Paul Auster* (Philadelphia: University of Pennsylvania Press, 1995).

Inge, Thomas M., ed., *Naming the Rose: Essays on Eco's The Name of the Rose* (Jackson: University of Mississippi Press, 1988)

Irwin, John T., *The Mystery to a Solution: Poe, Borges, and the Analytic Detective Story* (Baltimore: Johns Hopkins University Press, 1994)

McHale, Brian, *Constructing Postmodernism* (New York: Routledge, 1992)

Merivale, Patricia, and Susan Elizabeth Sweeney, eds., *Detecting Texts: the Metaphysical Detective Story from Poe to Postmodernism* (Philadelphia: University of Pennsylvania Press, 1999)

Muller, John P., and William J. Richardson, eds., *The Purloined Poe: Lacan, Derrida, and Psychoanalytic Reading* (Baltimore: John Hopkins University Press, 1998)

Tani, Stefano, *The Doomed Detective: The Contribution of the Detective Novel to Postmodern Italian and American Fiction* (Carbondale: Southern Illinois University Press, 1984)

Walker, Ronald G., and June M. Frazer, eds., *The Cunning Craft: Original Essays on Detective Fiction and Contemporary Literature* (Macomb: Western Illinois University Press, 1990)

# INDEX

# CAMBRIDGE COMPANIONS TO LITERATURE